Passions for Nature

Passions for Nature

Nineteenth-Century America's

Aesthetics of Alienation

ROCHELLE L. JOHNSON

The University of Georgia Press

Athens & London

© 2009 by the University of Georgia Press
Athens, Georgia 30602
www.ugapress.org
Set in 11/14 Adobe Garamond by BookComp, Inc.
Printed and bound by Thomson-Shore
The paper in this book meets the guidelines for
permanence and durability of the Committee on
Production Guidelines for Book Longevity of the
Council on Library Resources.

Printed in the United States of America
13 12 11 10 09   C   5 4 3 2 1
13 12 11 10 09   P   5 4 3 2 1

Library of Congress Cataloging-in-Publication Data
Johnson, Rochelle.
    Passions for nature : nineteenth-century America's
aesthetics of alienation / Rochelle L. Johnson.
        p. cm.
    Includes bibliographical references and index.
    ISBN-13: 978-0-8203-3289-5 (alk. paper)
    ISBN-10: 0-8203-3289-5 (alk. paper)
    ISBN-13: 978-0-8203-3290-1 (pbk. : alk. paper)
    ISBN-10: 0-8203-3290-9 (pbk. : alk. paper)
    1. Natural history—Philosophy—United States—19th century.
2. Natural history—History—United States—19th century.
3. Philosophy of nature—United States—19th century.
4. Nature (Aesthetics)—History—United States—19th century. I. Title.
    QH14.3.J64 2009
    508.01—dc22   2008037787

British Library Cataloging-in-Publication Data available

for my daughter, while I waited

and for Don,
who waited with me

There is plenty of genial love of nature, but not so much of Nature herself.
HENRY DAVID THOREAU, "Walking"

CONTENTS

ILLUSTRATIONS

FIGURES

PLATES

PREFACE

ON A RAINY July afternoon in Juneau, Alaska, in 2005, at the Bread Loaf School of English, I found myself part of an engaging conversation. My students and I were talking about the implications of the ways in which different writers express their deep appreciation for the natural world. We had read some of Ralph Waldo Emerson's work for this day's meeting, but our course materials had taken us back through history to early discoverers' accounts of the marvels of the North American landscape; in future class sessions, they would bring us forward to our own time, and to Barry Lopez's recent proposal that contemporary Americans need to "rediscover" the North American continent. Lopez suggests that most of us know little about the physical environment that comprises our world, our surroundings, what Wendell Berry has called this "good land." On that particularly wet July afternoon, my students and I found ourselves wading through deep issues: the complexities of expressing appreciation for nature through creative work; the limitations of language to represent natural phenomena; and the human desire to understand the material world in spite of our ultimate inability to do so. At one point in our discussion, I voiced a thought, one that remained vague and undeveloped in my own mind—a dangerous thing for a teacher to do, to be sure, but I thought it might offer us a way forward in our discussions. Some expressions of passion for nature that we find throughout American history, I suggested, themselves seem based in metaphor, and they seem to have an alienating effect. I tried to clarify my idea: by suggesting a meaning for nature through metaphor, some creative works inadvertently alienate readers or viewers from the very subject of their creators' affections—the natural world. One particularly inquisitive student asked me to explain further. I tried. Still unsure, but fascinated and admirably persistent, she asked me to try again, to please tell her more. While my response that day was necessarily abbreviated and, probably, inadequate, *Passions for Nature* is my full reply—slow in coming, to be sure, but much more complete than either time or circumstance allowed me that afternoon.

My answer to my student's question grows out of my previous work on a relatively little known nineteenth-century writer and environmental thinker: Susan Fenimore Cooper. Although many of Cooper's works are now available to readers, we still need to understand more fully her efforts to turn the attention of Americans toward the natural world. Her writings strike me and my students as noteworthy, but also as a bit strange or unfamiliar. Having spent much time with Cooper's works, I now wanted to grasp why, when they struck me and my students as unusual, Cooper's contemporaries saw her work as so significant in terms of her representations of her encounters with her world. What had we lost sight of, as readers, and what might we be missing as we tried to understand her work?

I realized that answering these questions would involve exploring—for myself, my students, and general, interested readers—the relationship between nineteenth-century celebrations of the natural world and our own understandings of that world. I would also need to delve into what Kenneth John Myers has described as "the historical process by which culturally produced assumptions and expectations determine individual environmental experiences."[1] More specifically, I would need to know the ways in which particular creative expressions of passion for nature determine "culturally produced assumptions," and how those assumptions might then inform individual relationships to the natural world. Cooper's works led me to some of her era's most influential expressions of passion for nature: the art of the Hudson River School painters, for example, and the craze for landscape design popularized by Andrew Jackson Downing. Investigations of these cultural forms would take me to the dense topic of metaphor, and to three metaphors in particular. In essence, I pursued the relationship between art forms and landscape, and between expression and understanding of the material world. While Cooper started me on my way, her contemporaries came to occupy much of my research and many of my days in the archives of libraries.

In sum, my studies taught me this: the widespread passion for nature that gripped mid-nineteenth-century America can help us clarify our contemporary relationship with the physical world. This is especially the case because of the distinctly *different* passions for nature voiced in nineteenth-century art, literature, natural history, and popular culture. Particularly those creative works that are most foreign to us and that seem most distinct from our contemporary forms of environmental appreciation have much to teach us.

I am fortunate to work, as a teacher and researcher, at the crossroads of literary studies and the environmental humanities, and this book reflects my interdisciplinary leanings. Its subjects range from landscape painting to philosophy, and from natural history to theories of landscape design. It also reflects the influence of a range of compelling theoretical paradigms. Especially relevant to my topic here are those paradigms treating the relationship between dominant American culture, popular consciousness, canonized texts and works of art, and the "reality" of the physical environment. Although I may not cite them frequently in the following pages, my work owes great debt to the following thinkers, who themselves represent a wide range of specializations: Wendell Berry, Michael P. Branch, William Cronon, Jacques Derrida, John Elder, Michel Foucault, Dominick LaCapra, Barry Lopez, Mary Oliver, and, in more distant ways, Virginia Woolf. I am also indebted to Jennifer Price's smart book, *Flight Maps*, which develops the point that, through our habits of living, we make and participate in a story about who we are in relation to nature; we both create a cultural identity and help shape environmental history.

A necessary note on terminology: throughout this book, I use the terms *nature, natural world, physical environment, nonhuman world*, and *landscape* to refer to the organic and material environment in which humans live. While the natural world certainly includes Homo sapiens, I use the above terms in an attempt to invoke a distinction between humans and the other-than-human world. I do so in order to bring attention to the fact that human beings have a powerful relationship to their physical environments even while we are a part of them. In many ways, we influence the environment of which we are a part. I also employ the term *landscape*, which, according to the *Oxford English Dictionary*, has traditionally meant "a picture representing natural inland scenery," or "a view or prospect of natural inland scenery, such as can be taken in at a glance from one point of view." In the vernacular, the term commonly refers to shaped land—that is, land that bears the physical imprint of humankind. Although I occasionally use the term "landscape" in this way, I more frequently use it while assuming a slightly different meaning—one common to the study of ecology, where "landscape" refers to a "heterogeneous area composed of a cluster of interacting ecosystems that are repeated in a similar manner throughout."[2] Finally, the terms *America, American*, and *Americans* appear in reference to the United States of America, its cultural productions, and its peoples. In using these terms, I do not mean to perpetuate or participate in the privileging of the United States of America over the other nations comprising the Americas. Rather, I use those terms as "convenient shorthand," to borrow Angela Miller's phrase, for alternative phrasings often are quite clumsy.[3]

Although I now live in southwestern Idaho, I spent my childhood and college years in the northeastern part of the United States, and, in a sense, this project took me back home. In that region during the nineteenth century, nature seemed to be at the center of everything. Certain individuals meticulously painted grand scenes from American nature on large canvases for display, others designed the areas around their homes so as to feature certain natural details in as beautiful a way as possible, and others still—a group in Concord, Massachusetts, especially—saw nature as a fruitful means to expand the potential of humanity. Nature seemed at the center of attention. Today, however, our culture seems distant from nature: indeed, we hear daily of the threats of global climate change, decreasing supplies of water across the planet, and the enormous changes being wrought on local ecosystems by invasive species. While America of the nineteenth century seemed devoted to the physical world, the America of today seems frighteningly unaware of the realities of that world, even amid scientific cries of alarm, calls for a more humble environmental ethic, and widespread public concern for changes in our daily environmental practice. Given these conflicts and complexities, the American relationship to nature strikes me as deeply paradoxical. Teasing out the paradoxes inherent in American passions for nature is crucial to clarifying just how we got where we are today. This book is my small contribution to the large project of understanding how we have come to be a nation that simultaneously has celebrated the natural world so passionately and grown so distant from it.

ACKNOWLEDGMENTS

WORKING ON THIS project has been an immense privilege. I have had the assistance of many of my colleagues in the environmental humanities and American literature, and while I risk leaving out the names of some who have influenced my thinking, provided me with insights, and deepened my relationship to the materials about which I write, I want to acknowledge and thank publicly those whose names come readily to mind. For enriching conversations, both in person and over the various wires that run through our lives, I thank Karla Armbruster, Alan Axelrad, Wes Berry, Sue Ellen Campbell, Jerry Dollar, John Elder, Ann Fisher-Wirth, Wayne Franklin, Cheryll Glotfelty, Tom Hallock, Annie Ingram, Lauren LaFauci, Mark Long, Rick Magee, Hugh MacDougall, T. S. McMillan, Daniel Patterson, Dan Peck, Michael Pikus, Jessie Ravage, Kent Ryden, Scott Slovic, Rachel Stein, John Tallmadge, Allison Wallace, and Jim Warren. Many of these fine people are my colleagues in the Association for the Study of Literature and Environment (ASLE), an organization that I consider my professional home. Additional and special thanks go to my colleagues in the Thoreau Society, and especially to Bob Hudspeth, for his early and continuous encouragement as I journey in the environmental humanities.

For opening their home to me and sharing precious family papers and memorabilia, I owe profound thanks to Henry and Rebecca Weil. Thanks also to Michael P. Branch, whose friendship and gracious, wise counsel has provided me with much appreciated mentoring at various stages in my career; to Jonathan Cobb, whose kind direction on this project felt like a blessing from the skies; and to Kathryn DeZur, Tina Gianquitto, Ian Marshall, and Rob Stacy, who generously read early versions of the manuscript and provided essential feedback that shaped my work at a formative stage. I am also grateful to Nancy Grayson for her early interest in this project, to Jon Davies and Douglas Clayton for their careful editing and gracious guidance, and to the many invisible hands at the University of Georgia Press who contributed to the book's completion. My greatest professional debts are to Dan Philippon and Laura Dassow Walls, whose meticulous feedback and smart questions challenged me both to clarify my thinking and to tighten my claims. This book is better for their wisdom. Of course, any errors are my own.

I am also grateful to the Idaho Humanities Council, a state-based program of the National Endowment for the Humanities, which provided me with research funds in support of this project. Of course, any views, findings, conclusions, or recommendations expressed in this book do not necessarily represent those of the Idaho Humanities Council or the National Endowment for the Humanities.

The students, faculty, and staff of the College of Idaho also have provided me with several types of support, including the sabbatical during which this work began and funds for research travel expenses. My colleagues in English and Environmental Studies shouldered some additional administrative burdens during my absence, for which I am grateful. Special thanks to my colleagues in the Environmental Studies Suite: Chris Walser, Jim Angresano, and Scott Knickerbocker. For illuminating discussions of art history, thanks to Karen Brown and Garth Claassen. For early secretarial assistance, I thank Rhonda Prudhomme, and for her ongoing support in various ways, JoAnn Bellon. For assistance with obtaining even the most obscure interlibrary loan sources and getting them to Idaho, I thank Kathryn Jepko and Christine Schutz—librarians extraordinaire.

Special collections librarians at other institutions also assisted my efforts; thanks to the capable and helpful staffs at the Rare Book, Manuscript, and Special Collections Library at Duke University; the Houghton Library at Harvard University; the New York Public Library; the New York State Historical Association Research Library in Cooperstown, New York; and the Beinecke Rare Book and Manuscript Library at Yale University. I am grateful to these libraries for kindly permitting me to quote from materials in their holdings and reproduce images from their archives. The following museums also provided images included here: the Fenimore Art Museum; the New-York Historical Society; the Metropolitan Museum of Art; and the Museum of Fine Arts, Boston.

Some of the ideas that I present here appeared in much earlier forms as articles or book chapters, and I am grateful to the following publications for the opportunity to develop my earlier work: *ILS: Interdisciplinary Literary Stud-*

ies; *ISLE: Interdisciplinary Studies in Literature and Environment*; *James Fenimore Cooper: His Country and His Art* (Papers from the 1999 James Fenimore Cooper Seminar); and *Thoreau's Sense of Place: Essays in Environmental Writing*, edited by Richard J. Schneider (Ames: University of Iowa Press, 2000).

Many of my current and former students both at the College of Idaho and at the Bread Loaf School of English have given me occasion to articulate the thoughts that form the subjects of this book, and I fear that I cannot thank all of them. I do, however, want to mention several who continue to remind me through their example of the importance of living deliberately: Latisha Bowman, Brad Brooks, Lindsay Brown, Amanda Mae Peacher, and Cristina Watson. I owe particular thanks to Taylor Horner, to whom I refer in my preface; her insightful questions helped provide me an entry point to this study.

Friendships feed the soul, and mine has been fed heartily. Whether we were walking, gardening, camping, making music, or sharing a meal, many gracious friends have provided me with much support during my work on this project: deep thanks to Karen Brown and Garth Claassen; Robin Cruz and Michael and Paul Roach; Megan Dixon and Scott Knickerbocker; Brenda and Stephen Fisher; Mary Forsythe; Tim Otter and Lynn Kammermeyer; Sue Schaper; and Kathy Seibold. And while I know that my mind is supposed to be clear during my yoga practice, often my ideas became most clear then, and I am grateful to my supportive classmates for creating that centering space with me.

Finally, I want to thank my family members both near and far for their unfailing support of me and my work, which all too often interrupts time that I might otherwise spend with them. My deepest thanks go to those who, it seems, root me to this earth: my mother and stepfather, Priscilla Webster-Williams and Earl Huband, both poets whose grace and love remind me daily of the richness and rewards of a life devoted to words; and my father and stepmother, Alden Johnson and Ginny Johnson, whose admirable commitments to service and humanity inspire my humble efforts to give something to my community. I am also extremely indebted to the loving, faithful support provided to me by Rebecca Johnson McClay (Sister Butterfly) and Jacqueline Johnson: you two are the foundation of my days. Thanks, too, to other members of my family who have indulged and encouraged my quirky working life: Leo Contreras, Don Heppenstall, Marina Heppenstall, Nick Heppenstall, Doug Gilson, Kerstin Lindgren, Peter Lindgren, Emily Mansfield, Helen Mansfield, Marge Mansfield, Justin McClay, Ryan McClay, and Kerstin Palm. To Anna, Ethan, and Don Mansfield, I owe perhaps the largest debt of gratitude for the daily joys of family, the most complex and beautiful passions of all. My deepest thanks go to Don—clarity and center.

Passions for Nature

We must dispel the great fallacy of the modern age that
human society no longer requires varied and satisfying
connections with the nonhuman world.

STEPHEN KELLERT, *The Value of Life*

INTRODUCTION

Nature and Aesthetics in Nineteenth-Century America

ON SEPTEMBER 4, 1848, a woman wandered out of her small, rural village, which was nestled at the foot of a lake in the rolling hills of New York State. She walked along crude roads and then through nearby meadows that lay at the base of cleared hillsides. Entering a patch of remaining woods, she noticed something peculiar. Later she would record in her journal what she had seen: many of the leaves on maple trees bore "brilliant crimson patches." These ruddy areas on the leaves presented something of a mystery.

What were they? They could not be the first signs of autumn's changing colors; no, it was too early for that. Perhaps the crimson patches were outgrowths—or "excrescences"—caused by insects depositing their eggs into the leaf, a phenomenon that the woman had learned of through her reading. However, she dismisses this idea, for the explanation just does not fit. In her journal she explains her reasoning: if the crimson patches were insect eggs, they would be covered by the casing of the leaf itself, given that an insect laying eggs pierces the leaf in order to insert the eggs within the leaf's protective covering. Unlike egg casings, these curious crimson patches were on top of the leaf: they "rise above [the leaf], and are quite distinct from it."

After rejecting the possibility that the patches are excrescences, the woman suggests in her journal an altogether different explanation for the phenomenon. The marks, she decides, are "a tiny parasitic vegetable, of the fungus tribe." The fungi grow on the leaf, rather than in it, resulting in these "brilliant crimson patches"—the curious marks of color that had caught her attentive eye. With this explanation, the woman solves satisfactorily the botanical mystery that she encountered on this day's walk through the byways and woods near her home.[1]

This mystery of the crimson patches was recorded by Susan Fenimore Cooper (1813–1894) and later published as part of her literary daybook, *Rural Hours* (1850). Cooper published in several genres during her life, but she was best known for this 1850 book. The book is part journal, part village sketch, and part regional history. Indeed, *Rural Hours* remains difficult to categorize because it engages with so many aspects of the mid-nineteenth-century culture from which it emerges: the book conveys an ardent nationalism, an interest in domesticity, a fascination with the need for moral improvement in American society, a familiarity with aesthetic movements of the period, and a strong Protestantism, all of which pervaded Cooper's era and frame her personal encounters with her world. Above all, however, *Rural Hours* displays Cooper's deep passion for natural phenomena. Whether distinguishing fungi from egg casings or identifying the birds frequenting her village environs, Cooper conveys her extensive knowledge of biota and her careful observations of seasonal changes. Through this clear expression of devotion to the physical environment, *Rural Hours* illustrates a key feature of this period in the literature and history of the United States: the nineteenth century was an age of passion for nature.

Passions for Nature explores mid-nineteenth-century American celebrations of the natural world and suggests that we find there some roots of our twenty-first-century ecological crisis. Specifically, the book investigates two distinct types of passion for nature in the middle of the nineteenth century, from approximately 1836 to 1862. The first type of passion for nature is evident in three of the most memorable cultural achievements of this period: the landscape painting of Thomas Cole, the landscape design movement of Andrew Jackson Downing, and the transcendental philosophy of Ralph Waldo Emerson. We continue to celebrate these creative achievements today as we look to America's dawning environmental consciousness, because—at least on the surface—they led people to a deeper appreciation for nature. I argue, however, that each of these three expressions of passion for nature represents the natural world as a metaphor for a specific aspect of American experience, creating an aesthetic that renders nature's meaning abstract by positing it as a feature of humanity. For landscape painting, nature serves as a metaphor for American progress; for landscape design theories, nature serves as a metaphor for refinement; and for Emersonian philosophy, nature serves as a metaphor for human reason.

Against these passions for nature based in metaphor there also developed in these years a second type of passion for nature, a counteraesthetics. This second type of passion for nature was less prevalent in popular culture, challenged the more common aesthetics mentioned above, and is less remembered today. I focus on two writer-naturalists—Susan Fenimore Cooper and Henry David Thoreau—who struggled to overcome metaphors for nature by creating this counteraesthetics, which assumed that the value of nature resided in its physicality, rather than in metaphors for human experience. Cooper and Thoreau suggested that there were dangers accompanying their contemporaries' approaches to nature: they felt that the passions for nature based in metaphor threatened American cultural identity, the physical landscape, and the relationships that individuals might develop with the natural world. Furthermore, they believed that passion based in metaphor threatened to alienate the American people from the physical landscapes that the nation enthusiastically embraced. While the nineteenth century may have been an age of passion for nature, this passion was complicated and paradoxical. Analyzing the aesthetic assumptions of these two different perspectives clarifies American cultural understandings of the natural world.

Before we turn to these two conflicting passions for nature, it is useful to consider the relationship between Americans of this period and the natural world. When we think of passion for nature in the nineteenth century, we typically think of Thoreau's devotion to it, which he so powerfully articulated in *Walden* (1854), a text that remains (in Frank Stewart's phrase) "the model for [nature writers'] form of literary expression." Indeed, Thoreau's *Walden* stands as one of America's most memorable celebrations of the benefits of a life lived close to nature. Thoreau's sojourn to Walden Pond is well documented—and even idealized—throughout our history, and as scholars have demonstrated, the Thoreauvian pastoral retreat dominates popular visions of the ultimate connection to nature. As Lawrence Buell notes, "Thoreau has become the closest approximation to a folk hero that American literary history has ever seen." No pre-twentieth-century American better exemplifies a passionate relation to nature in the popular imagination than the narrator of *Walden*, who was introduced to many of us as the iconoclast who fled his bustling village to dwell for two years on the shores of Walden Pond, communing with nature in order to improve himself. This idealized relationship to nature emerges in school books, environmental rhetoric, and even advertising campaigns. *Walden* epitomizes a romanticized communion with nature, the foundation of which is so ingrained in our culture that we have difficulty recognizing it. In a sense, we tell ourselves a story about the ideal relationship to nature, and the Thoreau of *Walden* is our central character. But this cultural narrative about who we are in relation to nature omits important issues and key figures and rests largely on an incomplete understanding. Many nineteenth-century Americans held an ardent enthusiasm for the natural world and its phenomena. Uncovering the varieties of their enthusiasm shakes up the typical story of nineteenth-century American passion for nature and draws our attention to some inconsistencies in our familiar story of the ideal relationship to nature.[2]

Today we often identify devotion to nature with intense and adventurous outdoor activities, fleece jackets, and contributions to the Sierra Club. But understanding the roots of America's relationship to nature demands that we conceptualize passion for nature more broadly. During the early to mid-1800s, a few Americans, like Cooper, set out to learn the natural history of their surroundings, while others celebrated the physical world through art and literature. Some became landscape designers who popularized their visions of how to shape the natural features surrounding a home; others expressed their delight for nature by putting into practice the visions of those landscape designers. Still others undertook ambitious journeys through the landscape with the goals of discovering its mysteries and charting the continent. Explorations happened on both public and private scales: the government funded large expeditions to map the nation's terrains, such as those undertaken by Lewis and Clark, Zebulon Pike, and John Powell; and individual citizens headed west as well, beginning the daunting work of "settling" the continent. On the eastern seaboard, home to the nation's population centers, people also explored American nature. They did so by canoe, by carriage, and by foot in backyards and byways. Whether recording modest investigations of crimson patches on maple leaves, amassing collections of bird specimens, learning the language of flowers, compiling lists of botanical species, or completing arduous expeditions, many Americans of the nineteenth century undertook considerable efforts to gain knowledge about the physical environment. In fact, natural history—the formal study of species and natural phenomena—was never so popular as in the early decades of the nineteenth century, as scholars such as Sally Kohlstedt and Margaret Welch have demonstrated. Americans of the first half of the nineteenth century could have encountered discussions of natural history subjects in "parlors, primers, and public schooling," to borrow Kohlstedt's phrase, as well as in children's books, public lectures, popular magazines, museums, and textbooks. While men were particularly welcome in these discussions, women also played significant roles as the educators of young children and, less often, as important contributors to the production of natural history. As Welch demonstrates, the general language, subjects, and images of natural history permeated popular culture.[3]

This widespread attention to nature was likely due in part to the fact that in the first half of the century most Americans lived in rural areas. In 1800 94 percent of the population lived in what the U.S. Census Bureau considers "rural" areas, which are defined as those with fewer than 2500 inhabitants. The first half of the century saw great changes in the distribution of the American population, and these changes may have had some bearing on the American relation to nature. By 1860 that 94 percent of the population that had lived in rural areas in 1800 had fallen to 80 percent. This trend toward urban living would continue throughout the century: by 1900, just 60 percent of the population would live in locations with fewer than 2500 inhabitants. Still, well into the second half of the nineteenth century, the majority of Americans were farmers. In his study of American space in the middle of the nineteenth century, John Brinckerhoff Jackson notes that as late as 1870 "more Americans were engaged in agriculture than in any other occupation, except in industrialized New England and the Middle Atlantic States, and in California and Nevada where mining was favored." Certainly many American farmers held more than a loose familiarity with the natural world. As some scholars have demonstrated about specific segments of the population who worked the land, a certain number of agricultural workers had relationships to the natural world that were highly mediated by specific cultural conditions: African Americans, for example, worked the land in a state of bondage and often under severe duress. Nonetheless, many individuals who worked closely with the land learned its seasons and cycles, grew to understand its flora and fauna, and observed its subtle changes over time.[4]

Yet, these barometers of nature appreciation mask greater complexities. For example, in spite of the vast number of rural dwellers throughout the century, the number of urban areas rose dramatically. Whereas in 1800 there were only thirty-three places where more than 2500 people lived, by 1860, 392 locations claimed this "urban" designation. And whereas in 1800 just slightly more than three hundred thousand people lived in those thirty-three urban areas, by 1860 over six million people found their homes in those denser population centers. Jackson notes that what constituted "urban" in the minds of many Americans also likely changed throughout the century as these urban centers grew in size: if we consider "large" cities as those having between 250,000 and 500,000 inhabitants, in 1850 there was only one (New York), but by 1870 there were five (New York, Philadelphia, Brooklyn [then distinct from New

York], St. Louis, and Chicago). Many people were moving to urban areas, and those areas were, of course, growing. In the Northeast, where most of the individuals whom I discuss lived, population density was highest. Significantly, this urban growth occurred in spite of the westward migration that also happened throughout the century. Whereas the U.S. Census Bureau calculates that the mean center of the country's population was in Howard County, Maryland in 1800, it migrated—with many of its citizens—to Pike County, Ohio, in the course of just sixty years. Part of what we find throughout the century, then, is an increasing number of people living in well populated, urban areas—an effect that could result in relatively fewer people having a very deep knowledge of the natural world.[5]

Another example of the complexity of nature appreciation in this era concerns natural history, the formal practice of which occupied relatively few individuals, even if many people were generally drawn to it. Welch reveals that the explosion of print culture in antebellum America brought the language and images of natural history "to a large audience" consisting primarily of the literate middle and upper classes, but it often did so though a variety of media that bore little relation to the actual practice of natural history study—getting out into the physical environment to examine biota, landscapes, and other natural phenomena. Natural history discourse and drawings surface in keepsakes, paintings, and biblical histories, for example, forms noticeably removed from the natural world. While these media reached large audiences, they also provided a means for the dissemination of natural history that minimized one goal of formal natural history study: a practiced physical engagement with nature. Thus, while the discourse of natural history may have been popular, actual studies in natural history remained the province of a just a few. Most Americans were not "actively seeking out, collecting, and classifying birds, snails, or wildflowers." Rather, they brought their visions of idealized encounters with nature, gleaned from second- or third-hand representations of natural history sources, to bear on their understandings of the physical world, whether those gleanings occurred in popular magazines, books, or parlors.[6]

As a final example of the complexities of nature appreciation in nineteenth-century America, we might consider the relationship that farmers had with the land. By the first decades of the nineteenth century, many American farmers in the Northeast were working lands that were depleted, and they went to admirable lengths to adapt to their environmental conditions. These adaptations involved learning much about the natural world that sustained them. Indeed, as Richard Judd remarks in his analyses of agricultural populations in northern New England, "The study of nature had immense appeal," as knowledge could improve yield and, therefore, finances. Judd argues, however, that this appeal was multifaceted: it was simultaneously rooted in both ideals that would spur the conservation movements of the late nineteenth century and in moral assumptions that rendered even the typical northern farmer's relation to nature "radical[ly] anthropocentri[c]" and "supremely imperialistic." When such farmers studied nature, they did so in order to increase profits and shape the landscape to better meet their goals: they took "an aggressive approach to reshaping nature to serve human needs," imposing a "perfectionist vision of the balance of cultural and natural features in the evolving landscape."[7]

In the first half of the nineteenth century, then, we might say—to quote Welch—that "the bulk of the population" was "highly receptive to 'Nature' and the natural world." The *idea* of nature appealed to them. What this appeal meant in practical terms, however, is not so obvious. Most of us in the twenty-first century—when experts warn us of the dangers of "nature-deficit disorder" and of the intellectual deprivations facing generations of children who have had little experience in nonurban environments—could still be described as "receptive to nature." Yet, most of us also know only a few individuals who make it a point to be truly familiar with their local habitats—to know the names of the local birds or plants, for example, or to watch for patterns in fungi or stars. Most of us would likely venture to say, in fact, that the majority of Americans may be receptive to nature but that they do not have a close knowledge of their physical environment. The same can be said of mid-nineteenth-century America. As Welch explains, "there were (and continue to be) two groups consistent in U.S. history": those dedicated to natural history study and to acquiring accurate knowledge of the physical world, and those "who could not and would not." The vast majority of nineteenth-century Americans fit this second category. Perhaps this superficial quality of many Americans' relation to nature is what led Thoreau to say, "There is plenty of genial love of nature, but not so much of Nature herself." Many Americans may have had a "genial" love for nature, but such a passion was merely cordial and superficial, rather than devoted and deep. *Most* Americans were citizens of a "new" land about which they knew remarkably little. A generalized passion for American nature may have been intense and widespread, but actual attention to the "real" physical world was relatively uncommon, and this was increasingly so throughout the century, as the developing "sciences" became the purview of professionals and experts. Here is the paradox of nature appreciation in this era: passion for nature was widespread, but knowledge of the actual physical environment was limited.[8]

This paradox provides a useful context for understanding an observation that Alexis de Tocqueville made upon his visit to the United States in 1830–1831:

> Europe is much occupied with the wilderness of America, but the Americans themselves scarcely think of it. The marvels of inanimate nature find them insensible, and they so to speak perceive the admirable forests that surround them only at the moment at which they fall by their strokes. Their eyes are filled with another spectacle. The American people sees itself advance across this wilderness, draining swamps, straightening rivers, peopling the solitude, and subduing nature. This magnificent image of themselves is not offered only now and then to the imagination of the Americas; one can say that it follows each of them in the least of his actions as in his principal ones, and that it is always there, dangling before his intellect.[9]

Despite their professed celebrations of the natural world, many Americans were attending more devotedly to potential economic gains through modifications of that world. As their nation grew, they paid little mind to what we would now call the ecological integrity of unique landscapes. Their "magnificent image of themselves"—the national identity in relation to nature that de Tocqueville saw Americans developing—depended on both damaging the continent and commodifying the natural world: trees became most valuable only as they fell. Their attention to nature functioned, then, as a complex inattention to the fate of the material world. Again, this was the paradox of American passion for nature.

The first half of the nineteenth century may have been an age of nature celebration, but it was also—and increasingly—an age in which the nation sought to establish its political and cultural independence through both aggressive expansion and artistic expression. This cultural tension resulted in creative works—or "cultural productions"—that would manifest this paradox. As de Tocqueville recognized, fervor for nature informed America's intellectual imagination, which was not the province merely of "scientists." Among the nonscientific celebrations of nature were the works of perhaps the most famous American artist of the period, Thomas Cole, whose landscape paintings helped establish the Hudson River School; the publications of Andrew Jackson Downing, whose theories about tasteful landscape design led the landscape design movement in the Northeast; and the celebrated treatises of Ralph Waldo Emerson, whose philosophical understanding of nature would propel American transcendentalism. Each of these figures is the subject of a chapter in this book. The pages here also refer briefly to the works of several others: to the novels of James Fenimore Cooper, for instance, and to the poetry of William Cullen Bryant, as well as to the influential ideas of Archibald Alison, a Scottish philosopher. Significantly, most of these individuals were privileged, educated, Caucasian men from the northeastern United States,[10] and their creative works would reach more audiences in the mid-nineteenth century—if not literally, then through reputation—than would Thoreau's *Walden*. Each of their celebrations of nature represents the natural world while giving scant attention to its physicality, suggests certain ways of living in relation to the land, and asserts a different sort of passion. The assumptions and beliefs that framed these model relations warrant our study, for they established an American tradition in which passion for nature can have little relation to nature itself.

Part of what we discover through examining these nineteenth-century cultural productions are the aesthetic origins of what C. P. Snow called in the mid-twentieth century "the two cultures," by which he meant to indicate the schism between scientific and humanistic ways of understanding the world. Snow identified this schism in Western culture as rooted especially in the scientific revolution of the early twentieth century, when there began to be an increasing division in society between the professional sciences, which are based on a mechanistic approach to understanding life, and "the rest of the intellectual world" (or "the non-scientists"), whose approach to understanding life emphasizes values, aesthetics, and emotion. Snow's central claim is that with the professionalization of science, scientists became less educated about humanistic concerns, and nonscientists became increasingly ignorant about the natural world and scientific processes, "[a]s though the exploration of the natural order was of no interest either in its own value or its consequences." In other words, the disciplinization and professionalization of the sciences resulted in scientists neglecting knowledge concerning aesthetics, values, and imagination; conversely, in literary and humanities circles, study of the natural world became uncommon, "as though the natural order didn't exist." Snow argues that this split in ways of knowing remains with us and, finally, that our inability to blend scientific and humanistic ways of knowing limits our culture tremendously.[11]

However, this debilitating schism in our culture between scientific knowledge and humanistic concerns also developed by means of aesthetic pursuits that have become subsumed by the humanities themselves. Whereas Snow looks to the professionalization of science as a root cause of our culture's separation of humanistic values from knowledge of the natural world, I turn attention to the ways in which the separation was brought about by cultural productions that are based squarely *in* humanistic values. Through an examination of landscape painting, landscape design, and Emersonian philosophy, we see how aesthetics became divorced from literal attention to the material world. These artistic pursuits gave little notice to the realities of the physical realm, fostering a paradoxical aesthetics—one that has the effect of alienating people from the very object of the aesthetic pursuit: the material world. These are cultural productions that abstract the natural world even as they seem most dedicated to representing it, thereby cultivating an American aesthetics of alienation.

This perspective on the nineteenth century enables us to realize that our cultural distance from the natural world predates the scientific revolution upon which Snow focuses his attention and, furthermore, has its roots in humanistic endeavors. In nineteenth-century landscape painting, landscape design theory, and Emersonian transcendental philosophy, we find the foundations of the modern American disconnection between the material world and the world of humanistic concern: aesthetics and ethics. Most intriguing is the fact that we find this disconnection being born in works that, on the surface, purport to express profound passion for the material world. These are artistic forms devoted to nature. Ironically, some of America's cultural productions most devoted to expressing love for the natural world had the effect of distancing—or obscuring—that world.

But the story of nineteenth-century America's aesthetics of nature does not end here. In addition to the paradoxical expressions of passion for nature that we find in landscape painting, landscape design theory, and Emersonian transcendental philosophy, there was another form of environmental devotion. This form was not widely remembered by the twentieth century—to say nothing of the twenty-first. This is a passion for nature quite distinct from the passion expressed by those figures and art forms mentioned above, because it recognized the paradox inherent in these better known passions for nature, and it concerned itself with forging an aesthetics that might connect the human imagination with the material world. We might call this second, lesser known counterpassion for nature *the aesthetic pursuit of nature's physicality.*

We find this lesser known form of attending to nature in the writings of Susan Fenimore Cooper and Henry David Thoreau, though not particularly in the pages of *Walden*. Rather, Thoreau's private journal writings and his ambitious natural history projects offer us new insights into both his evolving understanding of nature and the range of passions for nature in his era. When seen in light of this lesser known passion embraced by Cooper and the Thoreau of the journals and later natural history projects, *Walden*, previously seen as a startling contribution to American environmentalism, seems less revolutionary, since it seems to endorse the paradoxical passion for nature that we find in Cole, Downing, and Emerson, whose aesthetics divorce nature from its materiality. In his journals and later natural history projects, however, we find Thoreau engaged in a different sort of work. Ultimately, the passion of Cooper and this other Thoreau is a passion for nature's physicality. In pursuing this counterpassion for nature, both writers struggle with complex issues: how to approach nature on its own terms; how to diminish the tendency to render the natural world into a metaphor for human experience; and how we might discover nature's "truth" through its materiality.

In our time, any reference to nature's "truth" warrants qualification. The very question of whether nature has any truth—or meaning—aside from those truths or meanings that human beings ascribe to it has motivated many contemporary environmental writers, literary critics, historians, and philosophers. Most adherents of poststructuralist thought argue that nature's meaning is culturally constructed—that our understandings of the physical environment are the products of ideology. Proponents of this view suggest that we can not understand nature beyond our cultural and ideological blinders because all we have are these blinders: cultural forms such as language must mediate our sense of reality. Nature cannot have any "truth," "meaning," or "inherent value," according to this line of thought, because all truth, meaning, and value must be mediated by the human mind and, therefore, by culture. Other theorists argue, however, that an emphasis on the cultural constructedness of environmental understanding aggrandizes humanity at the expense of the physical world, which they presume has integrity and authenticity, regardless of whether humans can know it. In the words of Onno Oerlemans, the risk of what has been called the "ecopoststructuralist" position is "ultimately erasing the materiality of nature through a kind of ontopomorphism in which human subjectivity and discourse become the sole reality." Scholars such as Oerlemans insist that there is a there there, to borrow a phrase from Gertrude Stein.[12]

One can complicate the questions of nature's truth further by recalling that human beings are, after all, themselves part of nature and that our discourse is, so to speak, merely one aspect of the natural world. Therefore, it may seem odd even to suggest that human beings have a relationship with the natural world; after all, we are most certainly a part and product of that world—and hardly separate from it. Nonetheless, as many historians and theorists have shown, Americans have, for the most part, believed at some deep level in this odd paradox: we tend to think of ourselves as separate from the natural environments in which we live. William Cronon offers a helpful discussion of this paradox: he remarks that Americans have operated throughout most of recent history under the "premise that nature, to be natural, must also be pristine—remote from humanity and untouched by our common past." He further argues that by conceptualizing "nature" as a place untouched by human presence, we perpetuate the dualism between human culture and nature, limiting our chances of both recognizing humanity as part of nature and improving the condition of the planet.[13]

My interests here lie squarely in the notion that, as Ursula Heise puts it, "the authenticity of natural encounters is itself culturally shaped," and the following chapters attempt to trace how this shaping has occurred. As Daniel Philippon suggests, there is value in "tracing a history of 'nature' as an object of discursive practices" and in exploring "specific attempts to circumscribe a nature unable to be *fully* captured in discourse." In doing so, we uncover the richness of our cultural history, the various understandings of nature over time, and the implications of aesthetic renderings of the physical environment. We also gain insight into the fact that the relationship between phenomena, language, and aesthetics was seen by some mid-nineteenth-century Americans as central to the health of America's relationship to its physical environment; they struggled to understand the "otherness" of that which cannot "be fully captured." Tracing these aesthetic representations of nature demands that we recognize that some nineteenth-century Americans believed that nature's meaning is inherent, somehow, in nature's materiality itself— that nature has an authenticity and integrity, a "truth" beyond humanity's constructions of it.[14]

If we consider for a moment the state of natural history in the nineteenth century, we can better understand the impetus to a quest for nature's truth in that period. Increasingly, natural history changed from being an enterprise that *assumed* nature's truth to one that *pursued* a truth. This change occurred because natural history slowly became divorced from pursuits of morality. Natural history had long been considered one of the most moral endeavors; in fact, originally it was a religious pursuit, a point clearly demonstrated by its close relation to natural theology. The natural historian was a theologian of sorts—one who studied God through the works of His creation. However, during the late eighteenth century and into the nineteenth century, nature's assumed meaning—that the truth of God is made manifest in the creation— became increasingly open to question. Natural historians pursued an alternate truth for nature, one different from the truth that had been assumed by natural theologians, who saw Christianity as the source of all truth.

This separation of natural history from natural theology was a long and complicated process, but for our purposes, we need only draw a basic outline.[15] For centuries, the peoples of European cultures had studied nature as a means to praising God. Nature, they believed, was God's truth as it was visible in the earthly realm. But as scholars of the history of science have shown, the direct connection between God's creation and the physical environment began to undergo scrutiny as natural historians discovered truths that challenged the static vision of life upon which this older assumption rested. They discovered startling information about the age of the earth, the changes brought about by geological processes over long periods of time, and the diversity of life forms throughout the ages. While these issues would receive their most memorable attention in the work of Charles Darwin, who would publish *The Origin of Species* in 1859, they were circulating in scientific and public discourse well before his landmark publication. While no one would have articulated it in quite this way, nature's truth—or meaning—was increasingly up for question.

Given these changing notions concerning the meaning of nature, the pursuit of natural history became, throughout the nineteenth century, the pursuit of natural phenomena in need of an organizing principle. In other words, natural historians sought a framework other than "God" through which to organize their many observations of natural phenomena. Some people thus sought another truth for nature. Given the enormity of this change, it is not surprising that, during this time period, anxiety about nature's meaning surfaces in art, philosophy, and literature. In aesthetic forms as diverse as landscape painting, the landscape design movement, transcendental philosophy, and literature, we find attempts at asserting new meanings for nature. "Nature" came to mean something other than the material, nonhuman realm. Rather than representing nature as the physical environment itself—as individual species and seasonal cycles, for example—the word *nature* took on different meanings. That is, the various passions for nature embodied in landscape painting, landscape design theory, and transcendental philosophy assumed various understandings of nature's truth.

Cooper's and, eventually, Thoreau's pursuits of natural history provided them with what they considered satisfying alternatives to nature's truth as it was conveyed in landscape painting, landscape design theory, and transcendental philosophy. As Stephen Kellert claims, we especially need "varied and satisfying connections with the nonhuman world" now, in this age of increasing environmental degradation stemming from our increasing distance from an understanding of nature itself. Yet this counterpassion for nature—the one for nature's materiality that was shared by Cooper and the Thoreau of his journals and later natural history projects—is not well reflected in the typical story of the American relationship to nature. That story, as it is conveyed in textbooks and the media, is much more likely to include discussions of Thoreau's *Walden* and the works of Cole, Downing, and Emerson than it is Cooper's works or the journals and late natural history projects of Thoreau. It is useful to ask why we remember some of these figures and their works more than others.[16]

First, we remember certain figures because of their success in their time. Both during their lives and since their deaths, they have been well-known— even "popular"—figures. This is not to suggest that a majority of the population encountered their works directly in the nineteenth century; certainly they were most familiar to the literate, educated, middle and upper classes. However, as Lawrence Levine has established about early nineteenth-century America, "shared public culture was less hierarchically organized, less fragmented" than we know it to be today; there was more "shared culture," more commonality in terms of popular culture and the circulation of ideas. To say that the works of Cole, Downing, and Emerson were "popular" in their time, then, is to say that they were among "those creations of expressive culture that actually had a large audience"—whether through direct encounters with the creations themselves or through encounters with other media propagating the basic ideas, aesthetic assumptions, and ideological values of these works. There is a clear parallel to Welch's argument about natural history: that even though only a small minority of Americans practiced natural history, many additional thousands were familiar with the general interests, language, and images of that particular pursuit. In this sense, these passions for nature could be both "popular and elite," to borrow Levine's phase—that is, both commonly recognized in the society by literate, middle- and upper-class individuals, and truly studied by only a few. As T. J. Jackson Lears explains, "The ideas, values, and experiences of dominant groups [are] validated in public discourse." Because these men—Cole, Downing, and Emerson—held prominent positions in society, and because their work met with much acclaim, their ideas and aesthetics would have circulated widely.[17]

Second, we remember these figures because they have entered into the canons of literature, art, landscape design, philosophy, and even environmental history. The particular reasons for our canonization of these figures have not received much critical attention. Of literary canons, Lawrence Buell explains, "Little has been written about the phenomenon of canonical investment itself: that is, the rituals of remembrance through which those regarded for whatever reason as literary heroes become enshrined." Much the same could be said for environmental-historical canons, although scholars have made helpful contributions to our understandings of the reception of these particular men. As Buell notes, we do recognize that "canons are culture-specific instruments of promotion and exclusion," and that they are forceful agents in a society. We might think of artistic cultural productions—whether literature, landscape art, landscape design theories, or philosophical treatises—as Jane Tompkins does: "powerful examples of the way a culture thinks about itself." And we might think of the canonization of certain figures as our collective endorsement of how our culture should think about itself. Our celebration of certain figures—both at the time of their productivity and later—could be said to indicate both who we want to be and who we feel we are. Canons therefore reflect the periods of their durations, "embrac[ing]," as Tompkins puts it, "what is most widely shared" and "affect[ing] the way people understand their lives and hence [becoming] responsible for defining historical conditions." This is the power of canonization: in the words of T. J. Jackson Lears, the process both reflects and establishes public discourse, making "some forms of experience readily available to consciousness while ignoring or suppressing others." In exploring voices outside of the canon, then, we no less than uncover alternate possible cultural identities.[18]

Given the mechanisms of canon formation, we can easily understand why the American story of nature has, until fairly recently, overlooked the works of Susan Fenimore Cooper and the private writings of Thoreau. Furthermore, regarding Thoreau's private writings, they remained inaccessible to all but the most devoted scholars of his life's works. This alone explains their absence from popular understandings of the period. But how did we manage to forget Susan Fenimore Cooper completely? *Rural Hours* reached relatively large audiences: it appeared in five editions in the five years following its initial publication. (In contrast, *Walden* saw only one edition before Thoreau's death in 1862, but eventually overcame this lukewarm reception to become an icon of America's story of nature.) Even in the decades following those first five editions of *Rural Hours*, Cooper's book saw additional printings. She also continued to publish books and articles devoted to nature's details throughout her century. Her efforts remain important today because she was one of the first Americans who publicly recognized the environmental and national importance of localized environments, and because she was an early voice on behalf of native species lost due to Anglo-European settlement—a phenomenon that we now call "ecological imperialism." In addition, she pointed out that the alarming loss of species and habitats that accompanied America's development resulted in a startling diminishment of human experience—a diminishment that recent environmental thinkers call "the extinction of experience." Significantly, Cooper's published attention to these issues predated Henry David Thoreau's, making her one of early America's most forward-thinking environmental advocates.

Why have her works been neglected, until recently, by almost all of us?[19] Undoubtedly, there are many reasons for this omission. For starters, we simply cannot keep every book alive from century to century. Also, until recently we have not been very effective at making female writers into canonical ones. While scholars continue to recover the work of women writers, asserting their value has been a challenge. In addition, Cooper writes about a relatively small area of the country, so some readers may assume her project is provincial—although Thoreau, of course, also wrote about a limited area in *Walden*. In general, our exclusion of Cooper from cultural memory probably has something to do with the story that we tell ourselves about who we are in relation to nature. If we assume that Thoreau's *Walden* fits that story—and a century of literary scholarship and popular demand for his book suggests that we can—then we might learn something by briefly comparing her book to his. Like Thoreau, Cooper writes an account of two years of life in a specific place with a particular focus on nature, and, like him, she condenses that two years' worth of experience into one. Like him, she even lives by a body of water. But here similarities largely cease.[20]

Cooper's passion for nature does not fit very well with the story of nature represented by *Walden*. We can gain insight into why this is the case through the words of Marjorie Hope Nicholson, who states, "we see in Nature what we have been taught to look for, we feel what we have been prepared to feel." In other words, certain ways of relating to nature are comfortable and familiar to us, and others are not. James Kirwan puts the matter in a slightly different way: "[J]ust as there are forms of art that become dated there are forms of nature that do the same." Our sense of nature's meaning, that is, reflects who we are as a people at a given point in time. Perhaps, then, Cooper's sense of nature's meaning feels dated.[21]

Cooper's love for nature was not completely unique in her era. In his journals and private writings, Thoreau would explore a similar passion for the physical environment. The understandings of nature that both Cooper and Thoreau eventually reached are fairly foreign to our popular culture. Because of their unfamiliarity and the force of their visions of nature, I believe that we should reconsider them now, for (in the words of Scott Russell Sanders) "[w]e learn by coming up against what we do not already know." We do not know well Cooper's and the private Thoreau's ways of loving the natural world.[22] As many environmental philosophers, activists, and scientists recognize, we need an alternative story for nature. America's dominant current environmental approach may be characterized as blindly perpetuating a profound, even diseased, disconnection between, on the one hand, ecological understandings of natural phenomena and processes, and, on the other, our cultural values and habits of living—a disconnection that continues to result in significant environmental degradation. By looking back at the first half of the nineteenth century, we can find the roots of our current disconnection from nature, as well as a path to a different sort of relation to nature.

Passions for Nature demonstrates that part of the American alienation from nature occurred by means of a tool that is common to us all: *metaphor*. In the pages that follow, I examine three metaphors for nature that became important in this period: 1) nature as national progress; 2) nature as the refinement of the American people; and 3) nature as human reason. Over time, these metaphors for nature came to replace nature itself. The fact that the metaphors provided a mere association (by which people compared nature to something else) was lost sight of, and nature came to *mean* that something else. As George Lakoff and Mark Johnson suggest in their groundbreaking study of metaphor, this confusion sometimes occurs through metaphor: as "we start to comprehend our experience in terms of a metaphor," the metaphor begins to create "a new reality," which "becomes a deeper reality when we begin to act in terms of it." This was the case with the aesthetics of landscape painting, landscape design theories, and Emersonian philosophy, which employed metaphors for nature as, respectively, national progress, refinement, and human reason. In rhetorical terms, the "vehicle" in each of these metaphors replaced the "tenor." That is, the image or concept associated with the physical world—in this case, "progress," "refinement," or "reason"—replaced the thing being represented (in this case, the physical world itself). When we explore the metaphors for nature that form the aesthetics that I examine here, we discover the potential of metaphor to alienate us from nature.[23]

This not a critique of metaphor per se. I do not mean to suggest that metaphor is inherently bad, or that we should—or even can—seek to understand nature without metaphor. In fact, most theorists of metaphor would argue the impossibility of doing so. Indeed, metaphor may be the best way for us to address environmental problems at the current time. According to Lakoff and Johnson, "Much of cultural change arises from the introduction of new metaphorical concepts and the loss of old ones," and new metaphors for nature provide new opportunities for addressing both contemporary alienation from nature and environmental problems. (Consider the recent metaphors of the *earth as home*, for example, and of individuals as citizens of a *global community*, both of which have spurred helpful change.) However, precisely because "metaphor plays a very significant role in determining what is real for us," we need to interrogate the bases of our metaphors as a means of interrogating our own notions of reality. Metaphors, we are reminded, "can be self-fulfilling prophecies." As environmental historian William Cronon suggests, interrogating such linguistic prophecies is essential to understanding our place in the world: "[O]ur language and our culture give us the vocabulary through which we experience the world around us. The nature inside our heads is as important to understand as the nature that surrounds us, for the one is constantly shaping and filtering the way we perceive the other. Unless we are willing to perform the hard work of exploring and analyzing our own cultural assumptions . . . we run the grave risk of misunderstanding not only ourselves but the rest of nature besides." Nonetheless, as a society we are not accustomed to discussing these levels of meaning. Yet these metaphors for nature in the past have become reality now, and we should investigate the ways in which those metaphors were constructed in the first place.[24]

The metaphorical conceptions that I explore here assume different meanings for nature, but they hold in common the promise to lead to nature's truth. What an exploration of the literary and cultural expressions of nature in this period reveals, therefore, is that many people believed that they understood nature's truth in this era, yet their notions of truth were grounded in metaphorical conceptions of the physical environment, each of which had something to do with humanity. "Nature" came to mean something about humanity—about national progress, reason, or refinement. The "truth" of nature was therefore inevitably more about humanity than about nature itself. People told a story on behalf of nature, in the sense that their conception of nature's truth depended on a fiction—or on an abstract understanding of the physical environment.

Understanding these various passions for nature requires detailed examinations of works of art, statements of philosophy, and literary texts. Many of the assumptions, beliefs, and values that inform these works become the basis not only of America's relationship to nature but also, of course, of our culture. For our culture assumes a particular understanding of the natural world, a particular sense of its truth. In exploring the contemporary beliefs and values that informed various nineteenth-century passions for nature and the different understandings of its truth, we are dissecting the ways in which culture—and, to some degree, nature—is made. What we find again and again in these creative works is that culture makes nature in its own image—assuming for it "truths" that are merely passing cultural preoccupations. While contemporary theorists have argued that this is always the case (humans understand nature only through the lens of culture), these nineteenth-century cultural productions allow us to see this cultural construction of nature at work. Furthermore, by uncovering the mechanisms of the aesthetics through which we translate the material realm into the ideological one, we uncover how nineteenth-century encounters with the natural world became encounters with humanity.

Fascinatingly, in addition to noting the seeming abandon with which Americans destroyed their forests, Alexis de Tocqueville also remarked directly upon this nineteenth-century American tendency to see nature in terms of humanity. He wrote in *Democracy in America*, "I am convinced that in the long term democracy turns the imagination away from all that is external to man to fix it only on man," suggesting that this fixation on humanity especially applied to encounters with the physical world: "Democratic peoples can amuse themselves well for a moment in considering nature; but they only become really animated at the sight of themselves." Even in the nineteenth century, observers of America's relation to nature noted the nation's inattention to its physical setting.[25]

Susan Fenimore Cooper's works provide a fine lens through which to view the fascination that de Tocqueville claimed Americans found in themselves. Cooper's works are valuable because they simultaneously illuminate her contemporaries' metaphoric passions for nature and point to a largely forgotten way of expressing love for the nonhuman environment, one that is not primarily metaphoric. What we realize through her works is that, whereas Cooper told repeatedly a story of the natural world that emphasized the value of specific species, indigenous life forms, and knowledge of natural history, most of her contemporaries created a story in which the natural world served as a metaphor for some aspect of their humanity (for progress, refinement, or reason). Amid the potent tradition of understanding nature through metaphor, Cooper tries to find nature's meaning in nature itself.

Chapter 1 explores Cooper's own passion for nature, particularly as she expresses it through her seminal book of 1850, *Rural Hours*. In pursuing what she called "the track of truth" in representing the material world, Cooper's works suggest three necessary components to understanding nature's meaning: the practice of a revised type of natural history, the skill of observation, and the assumption of humility.[26] Cooper's vision of natural history involved a revision to its conventional, theological practice. For Cooper, nature's "truth" is not the truth of God alone; she seeks rather to locate nature's truth in a broader context—that of its own history, variety, and mystery. Her writings suggest that an individual cannot have an accurate sense of nature's meaning without a detailed knowledge of its forms, attention to specific biota, and feelings of awe at its simultaneous multiplicity and constancy.

To those of us familiar with twenty-first-century science's pursuit of knowledge of nature, Cooper's sustained attention to nature's details and variety may seem pedestrian. After all, understanding nature clearly means heeding its forms and details. This sense of nature's truth, however, was not widely shared in her day (just as while many of us today may say we value close knowledge of nature, few of us pursue that knowledge). Instead of investigating the cause of crimson patches on maple leaves, the majority of Cooper's contemporaries studied the literal physical world very little. Increasingly, this sort of detailed study became the province of professional scientists.[27] For most members of the general public—even the well-educated—passions for nature were rooted in certain metaphors that permeated mid-nineteenth-century American culture. Each of the following three chapters establishes the philosophical assumptions and core ideas of a major figure (Thomas Cole, Andrew Jackson Downing, and Ralph Waldo Emerson) in order to explain how metaphor came to structure his aesthetic approach to nature.

Chapter 2 discusses the metaphor of nature as national progress through the work of the Hudson River School landscape painters, and of Thomas Cole in particular. As the most famous painter of American landscapes of the early nineteenth century, Cole's metaphorical vision of nature as progress reached thousands upon thousands of viewers. Central to Cole's vision was a faith in the progress of the nation. While he would question the nation's progress in several of his works, his paintings were received as a strong endorsement of the nation's course. While Cooper embraced aspects of this vision, she also saw its serious limitations, especially its tendency to obscure natural history.

Chapter 3 explores the prevalent nineteenth-century belief in the refining properties of nature. Andrew Jackson Downing's popular philosophy of landscape design best epitomizes America's large-scale quest for refinement through nature. Downing's popular landscape design movement suggested that nature's meaning was tied to the good taste of his fellow citizens. Crucial to Downing's philosophy are the writings of Archibald Alison, the Scottish thinker who had developed an elaborate theory of "taste" in the latter part of the eighteenth century. In Downing's work, American nature came to signify the good taste of its people, and nature served metaphorically as the site of "refinement." In several of her works, Cooper countered this vision by suggesting that America's pursuit of refinement elided close observation of nature and enabled a frightening abstraction of the natural world.

Chapter 4 exposes beliefs about the positive role that nature could play in counteracting the negative influences of cities. Ralph Waldo Emerson was a proponent of this view, and he urged Americans to understand nature as a path to the heights of human reason. By pursuing their own reason through nature, they might transcend the material realm—along with its corrosive influences—and live the life of pure reason. Viewing nature as a path to human reason prevented one from recognizing its complexity and variety—qualities of nature that led, in Cooper's vision, to humility. Emerson's passion for nature, which presented nature as a metaphor for "reason" and assumed for humans a tremendous amount of power, contrasted sharply with Cooper's, which insisted on humility in understanding nature.

Chapter 5 explains the formative power of the three metaphors considered in the preceding chapters in shaping nineteenth-century culture, the degree to which these metaphorical understandings of nature were based on abstraction, and the dangerous results of this basis for the American relationship to nature. It does so by turning to the work of Henry David Thoreau, and particularly to his private writings and later natural history projects, which clarify his lifelong struggle with metaphor and its role in expressing nature. Thoreau's private writings reveal him to be another figure who, like Cooper, hoped to find a way of loving nature that escaped the seemingly destructive powers of metaphor. In his journal writings, Thoreau's vision of nature was, much like Cooper's, informed by natural history, observation, and humility.

Amid a potent tradition of understanding nature through metaphor, Cooper and Thoreau worked diligently to find nature's meaning within the physicality of nature itself. It seems important that we recover this possibility for understanding nature's truth as residing in its physicality rather than in the meanings that humans ascribe to it through metaphor, because this unique passion for nature has been largely forgotten by us today, eclipsed by our popular culture's adherence to metaphorical visions. Although today we can find scientists and nature writers dedicated to understanding nature's physicality, a love for the material world like Cooper's and Thoreau's—one that is rooted in detailed knowledge of nature's ways, wonder, and humility—did not become a widespread and enduring feature of America's relationship to the physical world. Instead, the power of metaphor pervades our contemporary relationship to nature, often preventing us from recognizing crucial ways in which our lives participate in the degradation of the nonhuman world, even while we seem to revere it.

Ultimately, my hope is that this book will provide the sort of contribution to the environmental humanities envisioned by Scott Slovic when he called for "vigorous historical and cultural contextualization of our environmental ideas." Getting at the cultural roots of our environmental ideas requires looking closely at words, images, and the ideas behind both. We need to investigate assumptions, values, and ethics—those beliefs that form the basis of what Jennifer Price has called "entrenched American definitions of nature."[28] We need, in other words, to look closely at the cultural construction of nature through metaphor.

Mid-nineteenth-century America was a period in which we can witness this process: the metaphorical transposition of a material reality into the abstract realm of human affairs. In witnessing this process, we are watching part of the means by which our young country undertook the ideological work of distancing itself from its material reality. Given America's global influence, this process remains relevant to us all. In addition, we are witnessing the specifically American roots of our relationship to nature. This sort of passion for nature could not, of course, provide a sustainable future for the natural landscape of the nation. Nonetheless, amid our fears of what may become of the earth, our dominant culture continues to treat the natural world as an abstraction and not as the material reality that it remains: a concrete, physical realm demanding the sort of attention to particulars that Susan Fenimore Cooper gave to those crimson patches she discovered on maple leaves. Such attention to the details of natural phenomena have become in our time the province of only certain scientists and those dedicated few who are keeping alive the art of natural history.

It is to that passion for material nature that we now turn.

Mere facts & names & dates communicate more
than we suspect—

HENRY DAVID THOREAU, *The Journal*

CHAPTER ONE

Tracking Nature's Truth

Susan Fenimore Cooper

AS SUSAN FENIMORE COOPER indicated in her preface to *Rural Hours*, hers was meant to be a "simple" book. In the preface she wrote: "The following notes contain, in a journal form, the simple record of those little events which make up the course of the seasons in rural life." We can recognize this modest introduction as typical of a female author at the beginning of her career in the middle of the nineteenth century—a sort of modernized apologia. However, Cooper's self-effacing characterization anticipates the unassuming narrative presence that she will employ throughout her book. In most of the book's journal entries, she will merely record what she witnesses, with little attempt to suggest any larger implications for her observations. She only writes what she witnesses in the world around her, resulting in a style that is matter-of-fact and undemanding.[1]

While Cooper's "simple" project was praised by her contemporaries, the book's value can be difficult for modern readers to recognize. Today we tend to think of "simple" prose as superficial, trite, or unimportant. But the mid-nineteenth-century reviewers of Cooper's book did not use the word in this way. Rather, "simple" meant to them "undesigning," "straightforward," "devoid of ostentation," "free from elaboration or artificiality," and "unaffected"—all meanings ascribed to "simple" in the *Oxford English Dictionary*. In its time, the simplicity of *Rural Hours* was one of its strengths. Given this fact, one of the twenty-first-century's challenges in uncovering Cooper's passion for nature is to make better sense of the simplicity of *Rural Hours*.

For help we might turn to the work of one mid-nineteenth-century re-

FIGURE I. Susan Fenimore Cooper, ca. 1840. Courtesy of the Cooper family.

viewer of Cooper's book who noticed and praised this simplicity. Shortly after the publication of *Rural Hours* in 1850, a reviewer for the popular *Harper's New Monthly Magazine* would commend what he characterizes as Cooper's "intellectual honesty and simplicity." A careful reading of his review reveals that what he means by these terms is that *Rural Hours* contains a prose lacking affectation and pomp. Her language is "honest" and "simple" in the sense that it merely records her experiences of nature and makes little attempt at metaphysics or philosophizing. For the most part, Cooper's book bears a prose style devoted to conveying only what she witnesses as the seasons change in her region of New York State. In her day, these qualities of "honesty" and "simplicity" were apparently rare, but according to this reviewer, they were clearly the qualities that gave Cooper's work its force.[2]

While it will be useful to examine contemporary reviews of *Rural Hours* at some length in order to understand the book's impact on its readers, for now let us consider *Rural Hours* itself. What we find is that *Rural Hours* presents a "simple record," but one through which we gain great insight into the complexity of mid-nineteenth-century America's passion for nature precisely because Cooper's prose is straightforward, devoid of ostentation, and unaffected. In part, we discover in *Rural Hours* a candid portrait of Cooper's place at a particular moment in time. Such a portrait from an era gone by—especially one with such devotion to natural phenomena—is rare. In addition, we notice her attempt to demonstrate a relationship with the nonhuman world based on direct encounters. Her book is valuable to us today not only as a portrait of a specific place but also as an endeavor to live a life in pursuit of what Cooper would call in *Rural Hours* the "real"—the phenomena and forms comprising the natural world. Cooper's work therefore had an educational purpose, in that she aimed at teaching readers about the joys of her particular passion for nature. Similarly, in our time the book can also be instructive: Cooper's work challenges modern-day readers to discern the importance of a "simple record" of the "real."[3]

We start to see the force of Cooper's project in the first paragraph of *Rural Hours*. Following the format that she will use throughout the volume, Cooper opens her first day's entry by noting the day and date, providing a quick description of the weather, and then launching into her topic, which, on any given day, may occupy her for a mere few lines or for several pages. In this first entry for March 4, she establishes herself as one who wants to escape the hearth for the field, even if she must do so in a carriage in frigid temperatures:

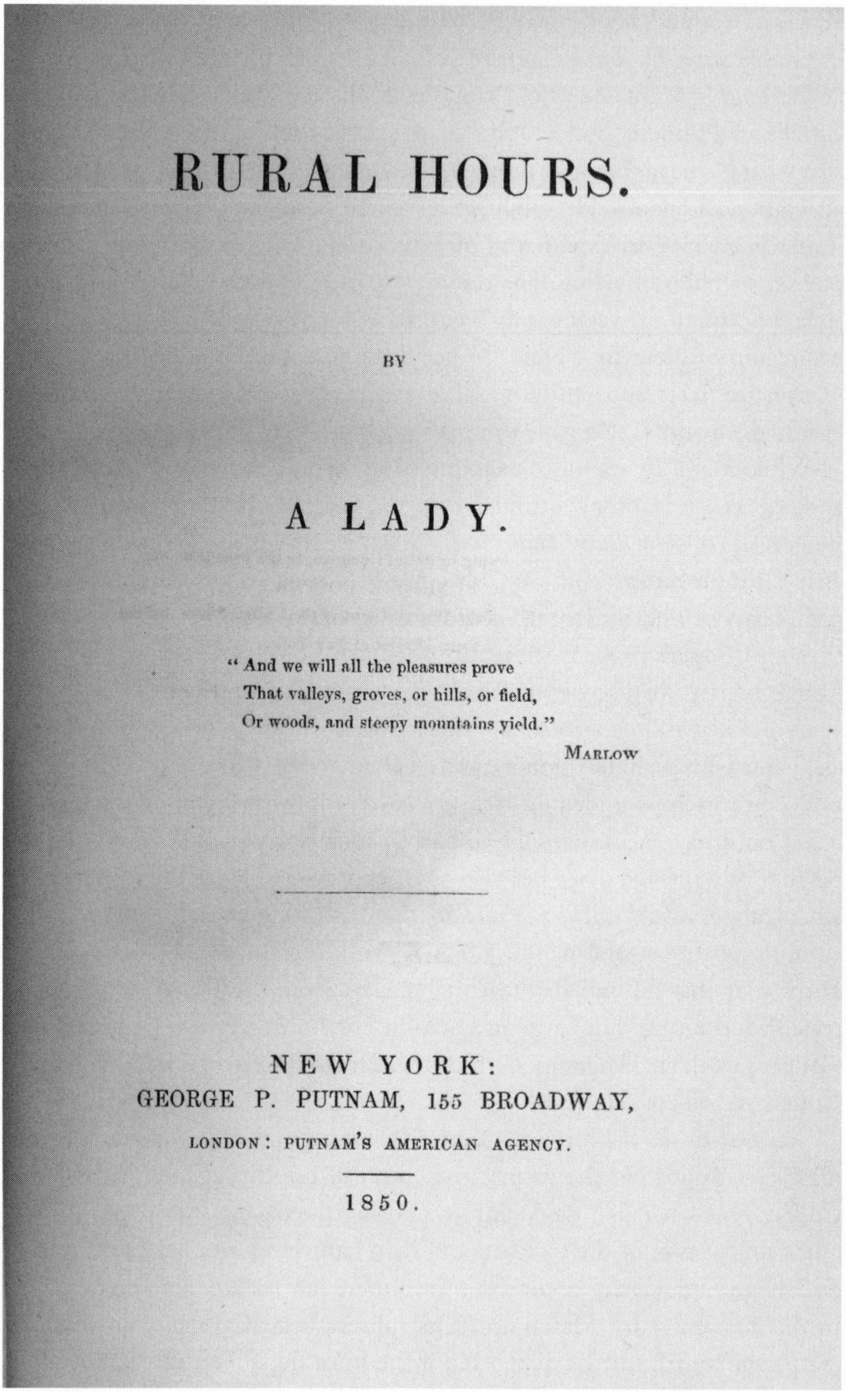

RURAL HOURS.

BY

A LADY.

" And we will all the pleasures prove
That valleys, groves, or hills, or field,
Or woods, and steepy mountains yield."

MARLOW

———

NEW YORK:
GEORGE P. PUTNAM, 155 BROADWAY,
LONDON: PUTNAM'S AMERICAN AGENCY.

———

1850.

FIGURE 2. Title page, *Rural Hours*, 1850.

Saturday, March 4th.—Everything about us looks thoroughly wintry still, and fresh snow lies on the ground to the depth of a foot. One quite enjoys the sleighing, however, as there was very little last month. Drove several miles down the valley this morning in the teeth of a sharp wind, and flurries of snow, but after facing the cold bravely, one brings home a sort of virtuous glow which is not to be picked up by cowering over the fireside; it is with this as with more important matters, the effort brings its own reward.

There the entry ends, with the suggestion that strength of character, "virtue," grows from such an escape from the hearthside—a topic upon which Thoreau would elaborate in the first chapter of *Walden*.[4]

With this first paragraph, Cooper sets the scene for her account of her life in a rural village, much of it spent in the out-of-doors. As she does here, throughout *Rural Hours* Cooper provides journal records of her experience of the natural phenomena that she witnesses in the Lake Otsego region of New York State, and, more specifically, in the environs of her small village, Cooperstown. The book contains no "narrative" in a traditional sense; just as nature has no narrative or formal structure, *Rural Hours* has no plot. The book is a record of days, structured only by dates and the four seasons. Frequently, her daily account is lengthier than this first one, and often her entries lead into discussions of the natural-historical contexts of her observations. While weather keeps Cooper indoors occasionally, even then her nearly daily records attend to topics relevant to her devotion to the natural world. Her fascinations with ornithology and botany dominate her observations, although readers leave her volume with a solid sense of her landscape and its natural rhythms, as well as of the lifestyles of its human inhabitants.

Throughout *Rural Hours*, Cooper's style is plain, unadorned, and straight-forward. The opening entry exhibits characteristics of her prose: she frequently uses precise phrases, peppered with measurements (e.g., "snow lies on the ground to the depth of a foot," "several miles") and adjectives ("fresh snow," "a sharp wind"), but devoid of much philosophizing. Occasionally she omits verbs ("Thunder shower about sunrise."), lending immediacy to her reports, and she typically avoids anthropomorphizing, preferring just to name what she sees: "Many crows were stirring; some passing over us with their heavy flight, while others were perched on the blasted hemlocks just within the verge of the wood." Many passages use adverbs sparingly, helping to make her language plain: "*Friday, 12th.*—Severely cold. Thermometer 17 below zero at sunrise. Clear, bright weather. White frost on the trees this morning; the sign of a thaw." While her style remains spare, her content varies widely; she records her experiences of her world.[5]

Cooper's style and content merge, however, to provide the "simplicity" that her contemporaries so admired in *Rural Hours*. Through this merging of style and content, Cooper's writings help us recognize what was at stake in mid-nineteenth-century discussions of the ideal human relationship to nature. What was at stake in a general sense was the role that the natural world occupied in the minds and lives of Americans. At issue especially was the meaning of nature in the United States—or how people would conceive of themselves in relation to the natural life forms around them. Throughout her book, Cooper attempts to persuade people toward one particular sense of nature's meaning in their lives—toward one "truth," as it were, for nature. She suggests that Americans should develop a passion for nature dependent on three essential elements: 1) a solid knowledge of natural history, 2) frequent and detailed observation of natural life forms, and 3) an approach to one's physical surroundings based in humility.

Close study of the development of these three themes in *Rural Hours* reveals that Cooper's book is nothing less than an attempt to model a specific understanding of the human relation to nature. That understanding depends on these three characteristics. Each of these elements of Cooper's passion for nature bears discussion in some detail, for through them Cooper distinguishes her particular passion for nature from that held by several of her more influential literary and artistic contemporaries. What we realize is that a passion for nature based on recognizing nature's history, practicing observation, and assuming humility provides Cooper with a means of illuminating the dangerous path her nation was pursuing in its connection with the natural world.

Most significantly, these three qualities become Cooper's means of demonstrating the force of "simplicity"—the power of recognizing nature's truth as lying in nature itself. *Rural Hours* is a testament to nature's truth residing in its material reality. The relationship, then, of the three main vehicles for Cooper's expression of her passion for nature—history, observation, and humility—is tangled but powerful. Together, they reveal the deep meaning that can result from quiet observation and a dedicated pursuit of natural history. They result in a prose form that seems bare, effortless, and even superficial, and in a passion for nature that assumes meaning merely by providing a thorough record of nature's details. Through simplicity, Cooper demonstrates, we can arrive at nature's truth.

As we will see in the chapters that follow, Cooper's was a unique attention to nature. When we examine her interests in relation to those of her contemporaries, we recognize the revisionary power of her work. Her suggestions regarding history, observation, and humility result in an expression of a distinct passion for nature: one largely bereft of metaphor. Through a close consideration of each of these three key elements of her passion, we gain insight into the foundations of Cooper's vision of the relationship between Americans and their beloved homeland. We also recognize the power of writing a "simple record" of nature. As Henry David Thoreau would one day discover, "Mere facts & names & dates [can] communicate more than we suspect." We discover as much through *Rural Hours*. There, Cooper recorded the facts, names, and dates that corresponded to her observations of nature. Through this record, she hoped to educate her readers about the value that she saw as inherent in the natural world.[6]

History

The various ways in which Cooper uses historical materials in *Rural Hours* reveals the importance of "history" to her passion for nature. There are several uses of history in the book, and they differ in function. For instance, Cooper records nature's own history, she incorporates the literary history of nature, and, finally, she describes losses experienced by the natural world throughout time—in particular, losses of species and earlier landscapes. This last use of history is one that we might call a historical record of a diminished place. Through these various uses of historical materials, *Rural Hours* pronounces the recent changes that have occurred in the natural environment and invites readers to consider the tragedy represented by these transformations.

Cooper's use of historical materials has the effect of expanding a conventional understanding of history itself. By including in her portrait of her region information about natural history, representations of nature in literature, and the history of the land itself, Cooper suggests that history, which usually focuses on people and a nation's progress, should also include details about natural phenomena. Cooper thus revises American history to include various forms of loss. As the country incurs losses to its native flora and fauna, the possibilities for what America might be are decreased, in the sense that one of the bases for its unique identity—the natural phenomena of the nation—is compromised. Cooper therefore sounds an early cry here for preservation—especially for the preservation of native species and forests—as integral to national identity.

Aside from expanding the standard notion of history to include the story of nature and suggesting that American identity depends on the preservation of its ecosystems, Cooper also suggests that both individuals and the nation suffer as landscapes are altered. Because most people are ignorant of natural history, they are not aware that the landscape of the present results from past alterations to the land, losses of species and habitats, and disrupted ecosystems. This lack of awareness means that Americans develop an elusive sense of their country—one based not on an accurate knowledge of natural phenomena but, instead, on a landscape whose appearance obscures its own history. For Cooper, such ignorance of natural history diminishes people's experience of the landscape, but it also diminishes the nation's physical presence, which serves as a significant aspect of its identity. In advocating a passion for nature that acknowledges the truths of nature's history, Cooper thereby alerts her contemporaries to the fact that aspects of America's potential and unique identity were disappearing before their very eyes.

By considering Cooper's many uses of historical materials throughout *Rural Hours*, we gain a sense of her passion for nature and her vision of America's ideal relationship with the natural world. First we will consider Cooper's attention to nature's own history. By recording a chronological record of events, Cooper emphasizes the fact that nature itself has a history, and that we witness this progressing history with every change of the seasons. We see this sense of history even in the opening pages of *Rural Hours*, which include basic records of the changes in cyclical, seasonal phenomena over the years and previous literary observations of natural phenomena. For example, in her second entry—that of Tuesday, March 7—Cooper begins with the usual statement about the weather ("Milder; thawing.") and then proceeds to her topic of the day, which is based on her activities in the outdoors. She writes, "Walking near the river this afternoon, we saw a party of wild ducks flying northward. . . . Three large waterfowl also passed along in the same direction; we believed them to be loons; they were in sight only for a moment, owing to the trees above us, but we heard a loud howling cry as they flew past like that of those birds." She notes, however, "It is early for loons," and indicates her fascination with the historical record of seasonal changes when she mentions that loons usually appear in her region "about the first of April." This aspect of history pervades *Rural Hours*: the book contains regular notes about when natural phenomena usually occur in a given season.[7]

Cooper also calls attention to seasonal changes by making references to birds as they return in the warming weather and to plants as they come on. In just the first ten pages of *Rural Hours*, she records the first sightings of a robin and of a phoebe, the emergence of skunk cabbage, her first notice of a caterpillar, and the return of song sparrows and bluebirds to the area. Later in the book, she notes when certain plant species die back and when birds leave for the winter: the chimney swallows, for example, depart the village close to September 5. Other cycles gain Cooper's attention as well: she remarks on the dates that the lake freezes over and when it thaws. Cooper's many brief references to seasonal occurrences help her evoke the vibrant, shifting, unique environment in which she lives, demonstrating that her sense of the past includes the story of recurring and cyclical events in the natural world. Readers thus come to recognize that the story of this place includes the history of nature itself: a *natural* history, if you will.[8]

Cooper also employs history in a second sense: by including the literary history of nature, which most often takes the form of discussions of previous written records of phenomena under discussion. Her daily entries are based, therefore, only in part on her own observations over the years; they also entail references to the written observations of others, whom she readily credits. (In this she is like her contemporary Thoreau, who would mention Cooper's March 7 entry from *Rural Hours* in his own journal writings on loons.) In her March 7 entry, after writing about the loons in question, Cooper proceeds to consider another underwater bird: the dipper. As she does so, she shares one of her sources with her readers: Charles Bonaparte's account of the dipper, which appears in his 1828 edition of *American Ornithology*. Throughout the book, she will incorporate the observations of prominent amateur naturalists, travel writers, and scientists, including John James Audubon, Georges Cuvier, and Charles Lyell. She will also include sources traditionally considered literary, such as writings by Chaucer, Shakespeare, and Wordsworth, among many others. Her references to literature demonstrate that Cooper appreciated the traditional metaphorical representations of nature found in literature, even if she chose to depart from this tradition in her own writing. By including references to other writers' works, Cooper's book provides a compendium of literary discussions on a given topic, thereby serving as a record of *literary* natural history.[9]

For example, on one spring day during which Cooper observes plants beginning to leaf, she quotes a brief passage from Chaucer in which he describes a similar phenomenon: "branches broad; laden with leaves newe,/ That springen out against the sunne's sheene,/ Some very red, and some a glad light greene." Not content to generalize, Cooper follows her reference to Chaucer by specifying the precise colors that she sees in the plants of her region. The "leaves of the June-berry are dark reddish brown," for instance, whereas "the small oak leaves, especially those of the younger trees, are the deepest crimson," and "the bracts of the moosewood are quite rosy." Cooper's reference to literature simultaneously serves as a means of emphasizing nature's continuing cycles throughout history and provides her the opportunity to share particular details about her specific surroundings.[10]

In this sense, history informs Cooper's book by providing her observations with a context—both physical, in terms of seasonal changes in the landscape, and literary, in terms of previous writings on a topic. This is certainly the case in Cooper's exhaustive discussion of literary treatments of autumn, which she offers as a means of demonstrating the tendency throughout human history to assume that autumn is a somber season—an interpretation that she will question based on her close observations. In this particular section, she quotes from dozens of literary writers. Readers recognize that natural phenomena do not exist in isolation but rather in a historical continuum of organic processes and representations in language.[11]

These first two uses of history help establish *Rural Hours* as, paradoxically, both very much a product of its particular place and very much a part of a larger, nearly global conversation about natural phenomena. When Cooper focuses on cycles in nature, such as when certain birds or plants reappear in her village each year, she establishes her book as an account of local history, relevant, it would appear, to only those readers whose locales have seasonal and annual cycles comparable to her own. But when she contextualizes her remarks within the larger body of work on any given subject—such as mentioning Bonaparte's writings on dippers—she de-emphasizes her own particular place a bit, deferring to the literary history of the topic at hand as it pertains to places beyond her region. For example, Bonaparte, as Cooper notes, "mentions having frequently watched [dippers] among the brooks of the Alps and Apennines"—not in New York State, or even in North America. While such faraway observation of the dipper may seem irrelevant to Cooper's account of her specific place, she regularly includes accounts based in distant locations—South America, Central America, Europe, and as far away as China.[12]

This pairing of narrowness and inclusivity, of provincialism and worldliness, helps point to one of Cooper's main goals in recording her natural year: to merge local natural history with the larger global-historical record. Cooper's methods suggest that the rhythms of what we would now call a bioregion should inform a more encompassing historical identity. In this sense, Cooper contributes to history as much as she invokes it. That is, she invokes history by placing her own observations in natural and literary contexts, and she contributes to it by adding her eyewitness accounts to that larger record.

It is here that we begin to recognize the educational dimensions of *Rural Hours*. As Cooper records her simple, daily entries, she broadens the historical record in order to alert readers to unique features of the American landscape. We gain the sense that Cooper is most concerned with broadening her readers' knowledge of the physical environment of the young nation. We see this especially through her repeated discussions of indigenous species. For example, as she concludes her entry on the American dipper for March 7, she notes, "The American bird differs slightly in some of its markings, from those of the Eastern continent." While this notation of a "slight" difference may seem tangential, we quickly realize that Cooper is engaged in educating Americans about the distinctive elements of their land. Especially by invoking other natural-historical writings on a subject for the sake of international comparison, Cooper can distinguish the unique natural-historical identity of her particular region.[13]

Because she refers to texts from all over the globe, Cooper ends up educating readers about the natural phenomena indigenous to different regions, but she also clearly does so in order to inform them of the astounding botanical and avian variety of the young American nation. Her aim is to teach her readers very specifically about their natural surroundings. For instance, on May 11, Cooper introduces readers to the varieties of honeysuckle common to her region. She begins the entry by mentioning a fly-honeysuckle that she saw "in full leaf" during her walk in the woods. She then notes several honeysuckle varieties that are native to her area:

> We have several varieties of the honeysuckle tribe in this State. The scar-
> let honeysuckle, so common in our gardens, is a native plant found near
> New York, and extending to the southward as far as Carolina. The fragrant
> woodbine, also cultivated, is found wild in many woods of this State; the
> yellow honeysuckle grows in the Catskill Mountains; a small variety with
> greenish yellow flowers, and the hairy honeysuckle with pale yellow blossoms
> and large leaves, are among our plants. There are also three varieties of the
> fly-honeysuckle, regular northern plants, one bearing red, another purple,
> another blue berries; the first is very common here, found in every wood;
> there is said to be a plant almost identical with this in Tartary.

This passage seems quite simple on the surface: it lists and describes several varieties of honeysuckle. But Cooper also includes information here on indigenous species, adding to the purpose of the paragraph. As she calls attention to plant distribution patterns of the honeysuckle, she notes both "native" and "cultivated" appearances of the plant varieties. Her description therefore serves the purpose of instructing her regional readers on which varieties they may see and which are native to their area.[14]

Part of her purpose is to illustrate the differences between American and Old World species. On March 30, for instance, she devotes a full paragraph to the distinctions between European and American robins—differences in physical appearance, behavior, habitat, nesting preferences, song, and migration time. Again, her attention to such distinctions informs readers about native species, but it does so while setting the new nation apart from its European parentage. On May 4, she emphasizes which of the swallow varieties are native to her land: the white-bellied swallow [tree swallow] is "peculiar to America"; the barn swallow "resembles, in many respects, the European chimney-swallow" but "is, in fact, a different variety—entirely American"; the "chimney-swallow is also wholly American"; and the "purple martin is another bird belonging to our Western World."[15]

Even in her first (March 7) entry, she makes this rhetorical move that will become a commonplace in her work, distinguishing American species from European ones. On May 9 Cooper takes an evening stroll by the bridge over the river, and there she sees several varieties of birds—"robins, sparrows, swallows, ruby crowns [kinglets], blue-birds, goldfinch, Phœbe-bird, chicadee, kingfisher," and a pair of "strangers," which Cooper identifies from books as yellow red-polls—"all varieties peculiar to America." In a similar move, Cooper notes that the golden-winged woodpecker (northern flicker), the wood-pewee, and the black-poll warbler that she encounters on June 2 "are all peculiar to our part of the world." In her attention to uniquely American species, Cooper slowly announces her nationalistic purpose. She wishes not merely to inventory species but also to build passion for them as integral parts of the nation's identity and nascent history.[16]

Efforts to build national pride were a commonplace in Cooper's day, and we can see her records of native species as part of the era's attempts to celebrate the young nation. As the daughter of James Fenimore Cooper, the author often described as the nation's first novelist of things distinctively American, Susan Cooper knew well her culture's desire to assert a specifically American identity by distinguishing its cultural heritage from that of Europe. The young nation used England's language, relied on European traditions, and largely adapted European art forms. Yet artists depicted distinctly American scenes in their paintings, and writers in nearly every genre tried to craft stories specific to the American experience. Throughout *Rural Hours*, Cooper participated in these efforts: she wrote a lengthy description of the process for making maple sugar (a phenomenon practiced widely only in North America), she explained her experience of the arrival of spring in the New World, and she included an essay-length correction of Old World literary depictions of autumn in hopes of adjusting misconceptions regarding the Northeast American experience of that season. Given this attention to American phenomena, we see that Cooper also wrote for European audiences—educating them, as well.[17]

However, Cooper's concern about disappearing species dominates her book, making it more than a mere celebration of the values of rural American life. Indeed, her attention to native species frequently has a mournful quality to it, and we can recognize this mournful quality as another aspect of her educational purpose. At a time when large numbers of the nation's literati were intent on defining a specifically American culture and identity through literature, one American author—Susan Fenimore Cooper—urged attention to the fate of disappearing species. Failing to notice them, she suggests, is tantamount to treason.

In her descriptions of indigenous plants being driven out by nonnative species, we recognize Cooper's belief that American natural history was crucial to the establishment of Americans' sense of themselves. On May 19 she visits an especially fertile stretch of land that borders a meadow and a wooded area (what ecologists today call an "ecotone"); what she witnesses there irks her: "The wild natives of the woods grow there willingly, while many strangers, brought originally from over the Ocean, steal gradually onward from the tilled fields and gardens, until at last they stand side by side upon the same bank, the European weed and the wild native flower." Lest we think that Cooper's imagery is intended to evoke some transatlantic camaraderie, she states, "These foreign intruders are a bold and hardy race, driving away the prettier natives." The image she depicts is one of confrontation: the nonnative species threaten the native ones. Later in the season, on June 19, she examines a similar conflict while describing varieties of grass. She distinguishes which grasses are native or foreign, again lamenting the ones that have become "troublesome weeds." But her most damning references to "troublesome plants" from "the Old World" occur in her writings of June 6. There we find that even the weeds of the fields are relevant to forming a national identity, because nonnative species threaten the integrity of American nature.

A very large proportion of the most common weeds in our fields and gardens, and about our buildings, are strangers to the soil. It will be easy to name a number of these:—such, for instance, as the dock and the burdock, found about every barn and out-building; the common plantains and mallows—regular path-weeds; the groundsel, purslane, pigweed, goose-foot, shepherd's-purse, and lamb's-quarters, so troublesome in gardens; the chickweed growing everywhere; the pimpernel, celandine, and knawel; the lady's thumb and May-weed; the common nettles and teazel; wild flax, stickseed, burweed, doorweed; all the mulleins; the most pestilent thistles, both the common sort and that which is erroneously called the Canada thistle; the sow thistles; the chess, corn-cockle, tares, bugloss, or blue-weed, and the pigeon-weed of the grain-fields; the darnel, yarrow, wild parsnip, ox-eye daisy, the wild garlick, the acrid buttercup, and the acrid St. John's wort of the meadows; the nightshades, Jerusalem artichoke, wild radish, wild mustard, or charlock, the poison hemlock, the henbane,—ay, even the very dandelion, a plant which we tread under at every turn.

At this point in her expansive treatment of weeds, Cooper offers a footnote, rare in her book, to the work of "Dr. [John] Torrey," whose *A Flora of the State of New-York* (1843) she had consulted as she composed her list. And then she goes on, naming additional culprits in her list of nonnative species. The American "fields" are now hardly American at all: instead, they serve as physical evidence of a European invasion.[18]

"Invasion" is a strong word, but Cooper clearly felt strongly about the issue of what we now call invasive species. With more care, the fields could be visual testaments to a new nation complete with its unique flora; but given the degree to which invasive species were overtaking indigenous ones, Cooper saw the fields as demonstrations of foreign power. She saw that many weeds overgrew native plants, which resulted in a literal eradication of an exceptional American physical environment. While today scientists recognize this severe threat of invasive species to ecosystems, in Cooper's day such discussions were rare. Nonetheless, we find lamentations over diminishing species throughout her book.[19]

Even in the first few pages of Cooper's *Rural Hours*, she laments the substantial decrease in the number of wild pigeons that fly over her area, mourns the felling of several local pines, and notes the dwindling numbers of partridge and quail in her valley: "When this valley was first peopled by the whites, quails were . . . found here in abundance, among the common game-birds of the region, but . . . one never hears of them, and it is said that they soon disappeared after the country had been cleared." She later mentions that the pinnated grouse is becoming rare in New York State, notes the regional disappearance of the wild turkey, and laments the increase in roadways and sidewalks, which was leading to the destruction of hemlock trees. Trees have a special place in her valuation of a landscape: she exclaims that even an area made into a "garden crowded with the richest crops" will be "wanting" without forests: "No perfection of tillage, no luxuriance of produce can make up to a country for the loss of its forests." America's natural losses were permanent and scarring.[20]

As a result of its attention to environmental change, we might say that *Rural Hours* becomes a form of environmental history. That is, *Rural Hours* functions as a means of preserving in words the landscape that Cooper saw as threatened. Given Cooper's references to increasing numbers of roads, and to development in general, we might see even her detailed accounting of natural facts as intended to help American readers recognize precisely where they were and what they might notice around them. Her book serves as a testimony to—and an accounting of—the natural phenomena of her specific place and time. Through it, she revises the dominant notion of American history as centered on the progress of human civilization and suggests instead that "nature's nation" should base its identity on the natural world, which would entail altering the popular forms of literary nationalism of her period by attending to specific details of the physical environment.[21]

Cooper's discussions of the degree to which the environment is suffering losses reveals her concern that, increasingly, Americans will know little about the natural phenomena native to their respective places. Her remarks of May 19 attest to this concern:

> It is frequently remarked by elderly persons familiar with the country, that our own wild flowers are very much less common than they were forty years since. Some varieties are diminishing rapidly. Flowers are described to us by those on whom we can place implicit reliance, which we search for, in vain, to-day. The strange pitcher-plant is said to have been much more common, and the moccasin-flower abounded formerly even within the present limits of the village. Both are rare now, and it is considered a piece of good luck to find them. The fragrant azalea is also said to have colored the side-hills in earlier times, on spots where they are now only found scattered here and there.

This is only one of many passages in which Cooper addresses the natural phenomena that are becoming increasingly rare or are already extinct in her region. Her concern centers on younger generations of people in her area never encountering species once familiar to that place. Even regional extinctions,

she seems to recognize, matter significantly, because they affect not only ecological health but also the human experience of a place.[22]

Cooper notices, for example, that certain plants are increasingly rare in her
area and even unknown to some area residents. This local loss of species, she
recognizes, results from cultivating and "improving" land. As she explains,
vegetated areas that experience a disturbance of some kind are often particularly abundant in plant life. She provides examples, contrasting a patch of
forest cleared long ago with more recently cleared areas that are intended for
development or cultivation. Through her presentation of this process, Cooper
illustrates the power of invasive species to alter a landscape.

First, she discusses an old forest grove that reveals a former disturbance but
is nonetheless relatively protected from more recent development. In "such
spots" as this old forest, "the soil is rich as possible," as evidenced by a profusion of native wildflowers circling the "mossy roots" of "mouldering old
stumps" that were "long since felled." In this forest environment, Cooper
delights in finding as many as "six-and-twenty" different plants—"all native."
At the time of this disturbance long ago, native species moved into the cleared
site. Second, she describes areas less protected, more recently disturbed, and
evidencing rapid loss of native plants and the obvious encroachment of exotic
species that, in her accurate estimation, "follow[ed] the steps of the white
man," "cross[ing] the ocean with him." These exotic plants, as Cooper again
correctly notes, fill in border areas such as roadsides and the edges of fields:
"they line our roads and fences, and the woods are no sooner felled to make
ready for cultivation, than they spring up in profusion." Cooper witnesses
here the patterns of plant succession as they are influenced by exotic species,
which can often become "invasives"—plants that colonize areas. Native plant
species can give way to nonnative, invasive ones—a process that often leads
to localized extinction of native species, and that potentially can lead to their
outright, global extinction. Even in Cooper's day, leading scientists noticed
her insightful treatment of these subjects: in an 1862 letter from Englishman
Charles Darwin to American botanist Asa Gray, Darwin asks Gray if he is
familiar with Cooper's "capital account of the battle between *our* and *your*
weeds."[23]

Contemporary scientists are beginning to better understand this process of
species colonization. Both intentionally and inadvertently, human settlers to
a region may introduce exotic or nonindigenous species into a native ecosystem. As ecologist George W. Cox explains, "exotic species" are those "whose
occurrence in a region is the result of human activities that have aided their
dispersal across geographical barriers or have created favorable conditions

for their establishment." According to Cox, scientists now see "that invasive exotics are not just additions to regional biota but are one of the greatest threats to native species and ecosystems." As vegetated areas are cleared for development or disturbed by either human or natural causes, "ruderal" species—what botanists call those plants that take over disturbed areas—move in and occupy the fresh soil. The reasons for the success of some nonnative species over native ones are complex and vary according to locale and species, but basically some exotics especially flourish because they have an advantage over their native counterparts: whereas the natives evolve on the site and tend to have more constraints on their population explosion (via natural controls in the ecosystem), exotics, which evolved in some other environment—with different predators, diseases, soil fungi, herbivores, and soil bacteria—lack their natural predators. Exotics therefore may find a convenient home in a disturbed area where there are few constraints on their growth, and their populations can freely explode, making them invasives. As Cooper noted, "The border of an old wood is fine ground for flowers." Sadly, however, these border areas, so susceptible to seed, were increasingly home to nonnative species. In her observations, Cooper anticipates the deep concern over invasive exotics and their role in plant succession that continues today.[24]

Contemporary biologist and nature writer Robert Michael Pyle's concept of "the extinction of experience" helps us understand Cooper's concerns. While we could never expect Cooper to have articulated a level of understanding of biodiversity comparable to that of twenty-first-century biologists, who now understand the global meanings of local species rarity, her sense of alarm at vanishing native species anticipates their concern. Pyle explains that local losses can have larger consequences than we might imagine: "Local extinctions matter for at least three major reasons." The first of these is that "evolutionary biologists believe that natural selection operates intensely on 'edge' populations," and "[l]ocal extinctions commonly occur on the edges." In other words, on the edges of forests or meadows, species' survival is especially important. Second in Pyle's explanation is the fact that local extinctions can be signals of larger problems: "little losses add up to big losses." Third, local extinctions can result in "a different kind of depletion," which Pyle terms the "*extinction of experience.*" As Pyle explains, "[T]he loss of neighborhood species endangers our experience of nature. If a species becomes extinct within our own radius of reach (smaller for the very old, very young, disabled, and poor), it might as well be gone altogether, in one important sense. To those whose access suffers by it, local extinction has much the same result as global eradication."[25]

Biologist Stephen Kellert describes this loss another way. In addressing the physical losses in biological diversity, he writes: "These losses certainly represent substantial threats to human well-being, but . . . far more may be at stake than just the diminution of people's material options. The degradation of life on earth might also signify the possibility of diminished emotional and intellectual well-being and capacity." Cooper's writings suggest the same ideas, albeit with different phrasing: if residents of a particular region never witness the presence of a pinnated grouse, then they have lost out on an experience peculiar to their regions. That is, the loss of the pinnated grouse is the loss of a potential insight into the varieties of life in the world. If we never see or experience the grouse, our experience of a particular place is reduced and impoverished. Similarly, the unlikelihood of local residents encountering a pitcher plant diminishes their experience of this particular place and likewise diminishes the levels of intergenerational connection between peoples in a place over time. The natural features that define the experience of one group of people are simply unknown to a later group. In this view, the local extinction of a species results in a diminishment of human experience.[26]

Cooper's expressions of grief over vanishing or decreasing species do not include many overt comments about the loss of potential experiences of nature. However, she does frequently express dismay at the local population's general ignorance of natural phenomena, thereby airing her concern about people's shallow knowledge of their surroundings. She is disturbed, for example, when area residents don't know the names of specific plants or animals; she advocates a system of naming plants that will be easy for even children to work with and remember; and she expresses regret at the lack of scientific attention given to several aspects of the natural world in America (birds, trees and other plants, and butterflies and other insects), believing that such attention would spread knowledge of the physical environment. In this regard, *Rural Hours* anticipates the conclusion reached by twentieth-century thinkers who assert that the ecological crisis is exacerbated by the degree to which Americans are removed from knowledge of the natural world. Particularly when she remarks on the rapidity with which people are clearing the forests, Cooper seems to anticipate what Pyle has called "a cycle of disaffection" in which individuals, and then communities, and then entire regions "grow more removed from personal contact with nature" and, as a consequence, "awareness and appreciation retreat." As species are lost, so is the potential for human experience of nature, which, in a vicious cycle, leads us to further neglect the degraded natural world.[27]

Cooper addresses this possibility of diminished humanity in a series of moving passages about forests. In these sections, she suggests not only that disappearing species and altered landscapes limit the human experience, but also that natural phenomena have an important role to play in our sense of what history is. History, she implicitly argues, should be "natural" in the sense that it should include the history of nature. These forest sections of *Rural Hours* are among the most widely anthologized and quoted sections of Cooper's work, which is no surprise, given her startlingly early expressions here of deep concern about deforestation and the importance of old growth forests to Americans. They are also remarkable, however, for their suggestion that history, as it is typically conceived, omits a tremendous amount by neglecting the story of nature. It is this aspect of history that she wants to revisit.

On July 23, Cooper describes a particular stand of trees on the edge of the village, "a remnant of the old forest" that is unique to the valley floor: "But although these old trees are common upon the wooded heights, yet the group on the skirts of the village stands alone among the fields of the valley." Each of these trees, she reminds readers, serves as "a monument of the past." While Cooper seems to accept the "wonderful" changes that Euro-American settlement has brought to the valley, she also laments that the old trees cannot communicate all the changes that they have "seen"—or that the region has witnessed. "There is no record," she says, "there is no human voice can tell" of the wild animals once resident there, of centuries of Native American settlement, or of the earliest incursions of the white settlers to the area. She describes the history of these many centuries as fully as she can with the very general information at her command, but the entire passage contains an eerie, nostalgic sense of loss at the prehistory to which the old-growth trees attest: "those calm old trees seem to heave the sigh of companionless age, as their heads rock slowly in the winds." The trees themselves are a form of history.[28]

Beyond noting their ancient presence, Cooper wants her readers to notice the anomaly that these ancient trees represent, since in their distinction from their surrounding environment, they serve as markers of long history. She remarks on the "wild dignity" of this grove, which consists of only "some forty trees, varying in their girth from five or six to twelve feet; and in height, from a hundred and twenty to a hundred and sixty feet." These old-growth trees are such a rarity, in fact, that they seem out of place: the grove "speaks so clearly of the wilderness, that it is not the young orchard of yesterday's planting, but the aged native pines which seem the strangers on the ground." Yet they serve as reminders of a history that precedes "American" history by scores of decades. The trees dwarf recent human accomplishments.[29]

Cooper expresses gratitude to the owner of the land on which the trees stand for allowing them to remain, for they make a unique historical contribution to this place: "no other younger wood can ever claim the same connection as this, with a state of things now passed away forever." Here she emphasizes the impossibility of recovering a story—a "state of things"—that will be forever lost when the trees are gone. She also suggests the inability of humanity to reconstruct this story when she admits that "all the united strength of sinew, added to all the powers of mind, and all the force of will, of millions of men" can do nothing to make a pine cone into an ancient tree. A tree simply must grow; humankind will never create an ancient tree. And if the tree should be felled, an aspect of the history of this place will be silenced, deadened. The tree *is* history, then, albeit an expression of history unlike those to which we are more accustomed. Natural phenomena attest to the long-term story—the identity—of a place. An accurate history thus depends on their survival as reminders of ages gone by.[30]

What we take from these passages devoted to history in its various forms is Cooper's concern that America's prevailing inattentiveness to the natural environment deprives the cultural memory of the full story of its homeland. One obvious result of this is a history that fails to account fully for the changes in the land. But a more disturbing implication of this gap in cultural memory is that it enables a disregard for environmental destruction. If Americans fail to notice the perceptible changes occurring in their environments, they are not likely to represent these changes—or their results—in their national consciousness. Through *Rural Hours*, Cooper seeks to reverse this tendency by representing the remnants of natural and cultural history that she observes in her surroundings. Through her attention to the history of nature, she both alerts her readers and calls attention to the dangers of altering significantly the physical environment—and, thereby, America's natural history.

Clearly, history plays a large role in Cooper's passion for nature. Cooper records the recent and ongoing history of seasonal change, the literary history of the natural phenomena that she observes, and the potential loss of history that accompanied disappearing species. Because all of these forms of history were important to the nation's identity, Cooper attends to them carefully, elucidating the losses that the nation faces even in this time, its mere infancy. In her view, a national story based on loss seemed inevitable but wrong. Recognizing nature's history—one aspect of its truth—revealed this regrettable story.

Observation

When in her July 23 entry on forests Cooper evokes a "state of things now passed away forever," we witness her interest in recovering the story of nature. In that entry, Cooper hopes to call to mind a time gone by, an increasingly irrecoverable story of her region; she hopes to give words to nature's story. In its various attempts to give words to natural phenomena and integrate them with the identity of the nation, *Rural Hours* seeks to establish an *environmental* history. This history depends a great deal on observation. Through *Rural Hours*, we recognize the crucial place of observation in Cooper's passion for nature. After all, close observation of natural phenomena informs us of what constitutes nature. As any glance at the pages of Cooper's book will reveal, observation is at the heart of her understanding of nature's meaning. Nature's truth lies in its particulars. However, Cooper's particular approach to natural history warrants comment, since she employs its techniques at a time when the genre was changing. Considering the natural-history context of *Rural Hours* helps us recognize Cooper's unique contributions to her society and helps us understand her particular style of writing.[31]

Essentially, natural history is a genre of writing about the nonhuman world; scientific in orientation, it has changed as the nature of science has changed. At the time Cooper wrote *Rural Hours*, the actual practitioners of natural history occupied a relatively small sphere in society. While there existed "a comparatively minute band of dedicated amateurs and professionals interested in systematically identifying, collecting, and often publishing discrete segments of the natural world," the vast majority of nineteenth-century Americans could not distinguish "a hawk from a handsaw," as Welch quips (borrowing a common phrase of the period). In this regard, Cooper was like some of her better-known scientific contemporaries, such as Audubon. As Welch explains, the works of such luminaries as Audubon "were ultimately based on individual observations often born of love for a particular locale and its natural occupants." However, "[t]hose apart from these nature observers and naturalists represented the bulk of the population." A woman pursuing natural history in rural New York State may have been relatively rare, but Cooper clearly saw the genre of natural history as a means of conveying her passion for nature.[32]

Especially in the later eighteenth century and the early nineteenth century, the genre of natural history had flourished in America as scientific-minded individuals sought to understand their physical environments through close study and analysis. At that time, natural history was "a broad area of scientific inquiry circumscribing the present-day disciplines of meteorology, geology, botany, zoology, and ethnology, [and the natural historian] took for [his] subject matter all of what they called the Creation. Any object within the natural order was a proper subject of natural historical inquiry; only man-made objects lay outside its scope." This emphasis on the natural world (as opposed to the human-made one) reflects the fact that natural history was also known as "natural philosophy" and "natural theology," terms that indicate the presumed interrelationships between studying nature, philosophy, and God. The study of God's creation was understood to be the study of God himself. While botany seems to have held a special place in the works of natural historians, they sought to observe all types of natural phenomena and then share their studies with others. However, by the close of the eighteenth century, the formal study of natural history was "waning," its prior characteristics giving way to one of two forms, depending on the education and goal of the practitioner: either increasingly scientific efforts to study nature, or artful, moral, or even fanciful considerations of the landscape and its nonhuman elements. These new pursuits were not necessarily theological in orientation.[33]

Several scholars provide helpful discussions of these adjustments to the genre, but for our purposes it is important to note that natural history was undergoing complex changes in the early decades of the nineteenth century—changes in its professional composition, its rhetorical form, and its philosophical approach to its subject: the nonhuman environment. In terms of its professional composition—who, that is, practiced natural history—advances in scientific understanding increasingly led to a distinction between "amateurs" and "professionals." Until this time, a natural historian might pursue his nature studies in addition to carrying on his "day job," as topics that we now deem "scientific" were considered to fall within the larger purview of knowledge, or "philosophy." As science advanced and, eventually, divided into discrete fields (such as geology, botany, and zoology), people began to segregate knowledge and to give increasing importance to scientific education and training. The amateur natural historian became rare as the century progressed, his concerns overshadowed in the dominant culture by an increasingly consumerist society that turned its attentions to economic prosperity rather than to the close study of nature. What was once a widespread undertaking in popular culture became the work of a few, specially educated, professional gentlemen.[34]

Susan Cooper's natural-historical pursuits illustrate some of these changes. Her work is scientific in orientation but certainly amateurish; her piety is present but not clearly as a unifying or motivating principle in her nature studies; and her purpose seems to be to represent in a literary form her detailed, informed observations of nature. Her work is neither purely scientific nor purely artful, moralistic, or fanciful, yet it exhibits a solid emphasis on description. Given the rising professionalization of the sciences in the nineteenth century, it comes as no surprise that the language and form of natural history writing also changed throughout her early life. However, natural history always had begun with observation and description. "At its most primitive," explains Pamela Regis, "natural history writing is description to accompany actual specimens. Words and things are linked by the actual presence of the thing described." The natural historian started his written record by observing a natural object, and then, especially following the rise of Linnaean nomenclature, naming that object as a means of asserting its identity. Cooper clung to this emphasis on naming what one observed.[35]

Naming the object is therefore a crucial step in making meaning in natural history generally, and in Cooper's work in *Rural Hours* in particular. Following the initial naming of a natural form or phenomena, the traditional natural historian might describe the species and then make references to other authorities' writings on the same subject under scrutiny. The natural historian held a faith in the "relation between things and the human eye," a relation that, as Michel Foucault explains, "defines natural history." A natural historian would likely begin an account by naming, move on to present other written records of the phenomena, perhaps discuss its presence in other cultural forms such as stories, folklore, or medicinal use, and then include remarks about the context in which the object had been observed. This form changed over time, and by the nineteenth century natural historians had also been influenced by exploration accounts and discovery narratives, so that their descriptions took on a narrative form as well. As Regis states, "[A] text . . . could verbally encompass the land." An entire book of natural history therefore might present an entire region.[36]

In his helpful analysis of the human sciences, Foucault asserts that eighteenth-century natural history is the "fundamental articulation of the visible." Its purpose, method, and emphasis are naming. According to Foucault, "its construction requires only words applied, without intermediary, to things themselves." Foucault explains that whereas today—and this was increasingly true throughout the nineteenth century as well—we recognize "not the sovereignty of a primal discourse, but the fact that we are already, before the very least of our words, governed and paralysed by language," in the eighteenth and early nineteenth centuries "[n]atural history finds its locus in the gap that is now opened up between things and words." As Foucault explains this natural history format, "every chapter dealing with a given animal should follow the following plan: name, theory, kind, species, attributes, use, and, to conclude, *Litteraria*. All the language deposited upon things by time is pushed back into the very last category." Roughly following this plan, Cooper often begins with her observation of a local natural phenomenon; moves on to a discussion of similar phenomena; proceeds to a discussion of related but different phenomena; and concludes with an overview and critique of representations of the phenomenon in other literature. The result could be educational, in the sense that natural historians could bring the components of a landscape to readers through language. As Regis argues, naturalists "used the language of natural history to make America intelligible to readers who had never seen any part of the Western Hemisphere." They also, like Cooper, might introduce their compatriots to their surroundings.[37]

Considering *Rural Hours* in this natural history context also helps us understand Cooper's prose style, which seems foreign to modern readers because it relies so heavily on straightforward description of her observations. This aspect of her book is part of what leads twentieth- and twenty-first-century readers of *Rural Hours* to find it "simple." Natural history writing largely has become a "lost paradigm," to borrow Regis's words. Closely observing—and then describing—our surroundings is not something that very many of us do. But to do so in Cooper's day was to contribute to an established manner of experiencing the natural world.[38]

Alongside her simple descriptions are her natural history–style meditations on natural objects of so many forms. On August 7, for instance, she notices the light on a stand of nearby trees, which leads her to discuss the particular bark of the ash tree, which happens to bear light beautifully. She then enumerates the types of ash found in the United States, their uses, and various stories from around the world that feature the ash. We can see this entry as an adaptation of the natural history essay form—moving from specific observation to a consideration of the species, and then to a discussion of the presence of the species in literature over time. Recognizing this context for the passage helps us realize that Cooper's purpose is educational even as it is celebratory: natural history provides a vehicle for attending to nature's impressive variety.[39]

There are many passages that exemplify the natural history form in *Rural Hours*, and while we would be remiss to say that all of Cooper's entries follow this form, a great many do. On September 9, for instance, we find Cooper following the expected natural history format in an entry on squirrels. She encounters a "chipmuck" (an earlier spelling of chipmunk) in the woods, and then she shares information about the red squirrel, gray squirrel, black squirrel, and flying squirrel, explaining where each lives, its preferred habitat, and its general behavior. She continues this encyclopedic approach to her subjects on September 26, when someone comes to her door with woodcock for sale, leading Cooper to express her concern over the "reckless extermination of the game in the United States." "Probably," she says, "the buffaloes will be entirely swept from prairies, once covered with their herds, by this generation." Right she was. But the reference to the woodcock brings on the expected inventory of fowl—this time, based not on proximity to her region but on the beauty of such birds. And on October 27, a passing flock of wild geese reminds her both of William Cullen Bryant's poem, "Water-fowl," and of the paths of migrating birds. Association is the basis of her writing, much as it is for the "professional" natural historian who conveys his observations.[40]

The simplicity and naiveté that readers have found in Cooper's prose are thus best understood not as evidence of her poor writing, but as evidence of her working within the conventions of a specific form of writing. Foucault explains that the "apparent simplicity, and that air of naïveté [that natural history] has from a distance" belies the complexity of its underlying philosophy of representation, whereby words evoke a thing. We can say the same of Cooper's nature writing. The "apparent simplicity" of *Rural Hours* proves to be its faith in description, its confident bridging of natural object and language. This approach to nature is all but incomprehensible to readers today, immersed as we are in our more modern philosophical and scientific systems that demand, respectively, "higher" metaphysical meanings and scientific conclusions. Records of observation for the sake only of observation strike many of us as meaningless. But when considered within this natural history context, we realize that such passages in *Rural Hours* function as more than "a simple record of little events." Through her simple descriptions, Cooper reconstitutes the natural environment before her readers' eyes. As Regis notes, "American natural historians were contributing to this cosmic order when they described and named the productions of their country." They were helping readers recognize the complexity and diversity of nature. Through *Rural Hours*, Cooper helped extend her readers' worlds by giving them her own.[41]

In 1848, when she began her work on *Rural Hours*, Cooper clearly believed that her culture was inattentive to its unique environment, that this neglect was resulting in a diminished place, and that she could employ traditional forms of natural history as a means of voicing her concern and awakening readers to the importance of knowing their surroundings. In a note within *Rural Hours*, Cooper suggests this ultimate purpose of her work: she expresses her wish that, while amateur in its approach to "simple matters," her book might serve as a "sort of a rustic primer" for "those whose interest in rural subjects has been awakened." She hoped that it might "lead them . . . to something higher." Simply by familiarizing them with the nonhuman world, Cooper might alert her readers to its value, which was—in her view—beyond mere human estimations of it.[42]

Through her example as witness to the history of her place, Cooper urges readers to observe the signs of nature's history that are present in the landscape. Her descriptions of her place suggest that the physical environment itself records its own story. Cooper's simple record therefore challenges readers to attend carefully to their surroundings. A passion for nature demands such careful observation, and, as Cooper would make apparent, careful observation requires humility.

Humility

Rural Hours helps demonstrate that for Americans to attend to the problematic changes occurring in their physical environment, they need to be humble in relation to nature. In several obvious ways, Cooper's narrative persona in *Rural Hours* embodies this humble posture. For example, Cooper rarely uses the word "I," preferring the more modest "we," and she maintains an unassuming persona even when she corrects the erroneous observations of others. She mentions, for instance, Martin Farquhar Tupper's *Proverbial Philosophy*, which contains a passing reference to a hummingbird flying into a tulip, presumably to feed, and she modestly corrects Tupper's account. The main subject in his passage is "Beauty," as Cooper explains, and not hummingbirds or tulips, yet Cooper advises readers that hummingbirds are not known to feed from tulips. The point stands corrected. She then admits, "The point is a very trifling one, no doubt, and it is extremely bold to find fault with our betters." Despite her humbling herself to her "betters" and her claim that the point is "trifling," she devotes a little more than a full page to the discussion.[43]

Cooper "corrects" misperceptions elsewhere in *Rural Hours*. For example, she points out that there are many types of trillium and that people should take care to distinguish them. In addition, during a discussion of the skylark and nightingale, birds that "are strangers on this side the Atlantic," she asserts that "[i]n some respects the nightingale differs from the common notions regarding it in this country." She proceeds to explain that the bird does not only sing alone at night, as is commonly thought, but that it also has been known to sing by day, and even in bustling large cities. Similarly, in her August 12 journal entry, Cooper corrects what she perceives as a widely held belief (held by both American and European readers, presumably) that August is a month when birds are especially quiet: "In short, many of our little friends [birds] are seen about the fields and gardens yet, and the country is by no means silent, though the most musical season is over. . . . But certainly August is not the voiceless month some people seem to fancy it." And in a similar vein of correcting common misconceptions, in the next day's entry Cooper explains that to refer to insects' "voices" is merely a figure of speech: insects produce their sounds "by friction, or by striking together hard substances of different parts of their bodies." She takes even Alexander Wilson to task. Wilson had written that Baltimore orioles did not prefer to dwell in pine forests, but early in *Rural Hours* Cooper points out that, in her experience, this is not the case: "they are common birds here—regular members of our summer flock; and we have remarked they are very often seen and heard among the pines of the churchyard." Indeed, she points out that the local churchyard "is quite a favorite haunt of theirs." Cooper recognized that published information could cause the widespread dissemination of erroneous beliefs about the natural world; and since many Americans did not engage in personal nature study, those misconceptions might be perpetuated for years. Cooper clearly felt that facts should be facts—even if these facts concerned something so seemingly insignificant as the variety of tree that a species of bird frequents.[44]

We also find Cooper's humility surfacing in the deprecating remarks that she makes about her own writing. For example, after referring in her preface to "the simple record" she will present, she characterizes its contents as "trifling observations." In a note to her text, she similarly describes her project as "a volume of the chit-chat, common-place character." Cooper's self-effacing remarks can be seen to reflect her proper behavior as a mid-nineteenth-century woman: modesty was a key virtue, and any female writer hoping to establish her propriety would play up her modesty to some degree.[45]

More profound, however, is Cooper's conviction of the need to remain humble in relation to nature, an idea that emerges subtly through *Rural Hours*. She ultimately suggests that the complexity and variety of the "real" natural world might elude human comprehension. To recognize nature's truth, then, required substantial humility, for one must accept an unverifiable, inherent value for nature that one cannot completely understand. To take this position is to admit defeat in the face of human reason or scientific insight, and to submit one's self to a power or life force indifferent to human existence. In other words, her view of nature is characterized by wonder and awe. Cooper's conception of this life force remains complicated: occasionally she expresses great gratitude to a traditional Christian God for the world of nature; at other times she figures nature's meaning as beyond the realms of understanding fostered by religion, government, and economics. Her Christianity therefore does not account fully for the value that she finds inherent in the natural world. Nature's meaning seems to exist beyond the one we would presume to accompany a conventional mid-nineteenth-century Christian piety.[46]

We find evidence of the sort of humility that Cooper deemed essential in her longest treatment of forests in *Rural Hours*—a passage that not only illustrates her belief in nature's inherent value but also anticipates twentieth-century concerns by explaining basic principles of forest succession and by ardently calling for the preservation of trees. In this passage, Cooper presents a hierarchy of values that she applies to the natural world. The ten-page treatise on forests represents Cooper at her most passionate; it also establishes her ideal relationship to nature based on humility. The entry begins: "*Saturday, [July] 28th.*—Passed the afternoon in the woods." She then expresses "gratitude and admiration" for the "utility" and "beauty" of the forests and is especially thankful for the manner in which a forest breathes the winds and relaxes the spirit. Calling attention both to her Christian faith and to the tendency of humanity to elevate itself, she describes her response to such beauty: "the mind readily lays aside its daily littleness, and opens to higher thoughts, in silent consciousness that it stands alone with the works of God." Immediately, then, we are reminded of the "littleness" of human life. Indeed, Cooper points out the limits of human understanding: "Every object here has a deeper merit than our wonder can fathom; each has a beauty beyond our full perception." Her assumption that the meaning of the forest exceeds her capacity for either reason or perception signals her divergence from some of her contemporaries, for whom transcendence of the human condition permits just such understanding. Cooper views humanity as being more insignificant than this.[47]

The essay then evokes the irrecoverable story to which the old forests attest—the same story that she addressed earlier, when she suggested that the old pines on the outskirts of the village function in some sense as history themselves. She writes: "The forest lands of America preserve to the present hour something that is characteristic of their wild condition, undisturbed for ages." The loss of these forests would mean a loss of this "wild condition" of the country. The wood has value as a testament to these earlier times, which fade from cultural memory as the trees vanish from the landscape.[48]

Turning to her more scientific mode, Cooper describes in detail the types of trees in this particular forest and the fact that the forest, if left alone, will rejuvenate itself, new plants emerging from fallen ones. After this basic presentation of the principles of forest succession, Cooper remarks on the unlikelihood of newly planted forests ever achieving the natural state of regeneration and growth that she now witnesses: "It is to be feared that few among the younger generation now springing up will ever attain to the dignity of the old forest trees. Very large portions of these woods are already of a second growth, and trees of the greatest size are becoming every year more rare." The natural cycle of forest succession may cease, given new planting and logging practices. Continuing in this empiricist vein, Cooper remarks on the varying girths of old stumps and the difficulty of counting growth rings as a means of determining tree age. (The cores begin to rot, forbidding an accurate count, she explains.)[49]

Then the day's entry turns to more philosophical subjects and presents additional "values" of the trees, "independently of their market price in dollars and cents" and in addition to those addressed implicitly: their beauty and ability to soothe the busy mind; their reminder of God's "handiwork" and "gifts"; their testament to a history beyond current comprehension; their fostering of plant diversity. Her focus on the "unsparing race" of woodchoppers lends emotion to Cooper's elaboration of these "other values." The trees, she argues, "are connected in many ways with the civilization of a country; they have their importance in an intellectual and in a moral sense." The preservation of trees "marks a farther progress" that at "this point we have not yet reached." Cooper's conception of this "farther progress" emphasizes "simplicity, a quality as yet too little valued or understood in this country." She explains the forms that an ethic of simplicity might take in her area: "Thinning woods and not blasting them; clearing only such ground as is marked for immediate tillage; preserving the wood on the hill-tops and rough side-hills; encouraging a coppice on this or that knoll; permitting bushes and young trees to grow at will along the brooks and water-courses; [and] sowing, if need be, a grove on the bank of a pool." When people intentionally leave trees standing rather than wantonly or unthinkingly destroy them, Americans will have made this farther progress.[50]

Cooper then introduces yet another reason for preserving trees, and while she asserts this value in the context of her Christian beliefs, she also distinguishes it as a decidedly human undertaking. Pointing out that "the spirit of destructiveness" shows a lack of gratitude to God, she suggests that people move "above the common labors of husbandry"—the ethic of dominion typically associated with the account in Genesis of man's role in the creation. "There is also something in the care of trees," she asserts, that "speaks of a generous mind." Tending trees gives a gift to the future—to that portion of the story of the earth that will continue beyond our individual human existences. "[L]ong after we are gone, those trees will continue [to perform] a good to our fellow-creatures for more years, perhaps, than we can tell." A generosity of mind, then, humbles the individual to the passage of time and to the long-term health of the environment. We should preserve trees because the earth needs them in order to sustain life. We should preserve trees, in other words, because they are valuable to the long-term good of the natural world.[51]

In these passages on forests, Cooper gives us her fullest expression of her passion for nature and of its foundation in a conviction that the natural world has value that exceeds humanity's estimations. Such a perspective—such an assumption of humility—elevates the natural world beyond economic gain, human understanding, and even Christian tenets. Humans ought to seek the "farther progress" embodied in a environmental ethic rooted in humility: "Every object here has a deeper merit than our wonder can fathom; each has a beauty beyond our full perception." Thus, through her writing, Cooper urges readers to respect the natural world as much as their limited human abilities allow.[52]

Responses to *Rural Hours*

Cooper's humble posture served a moral purpose in her society. Through it, she models the benefits of learning one's surroundings, which will help advance civilization toward a higher state—one in which it recognizes its own humble position in natural history. An early anonymous reviewer of *Rural Hours* may have put it best when he or she referred to the "self-denial" required of such prose. In a November 1850 review, we find this sensitive assessment of Cooper's work:

> The great merit of this volume, and it has *very* great merit, is, that it is written
> "in perfect good faith." There is a style of composition, though few persons
> have nerve and self-denial enough to write in it, which always charms; it
> consists in honestly calling things by their right names. . . . We dwell upon
> this peculiarity of style, because we have not lately met with so good an ex-
> ample of this kind of writing as the present volume contains. Nor is it an easy
> matter to write in this way, though it might seem to be so: it requires minute
> observation, sound sense, refined taste, and a certain simplicity and sincerity
> of character.[53]

Writing in an age when the powers of human reason were believed to trump all others, Cooper provides a check for the capacity of the human mind. Partly because she adhered to a Christian vision, but also because she envisioned an ultimate value to nature regardless of human institutions, Cooper challenged much of the thinking about nature in her day. Whereas many of the intelligentsia of her nation dedicated themselves to mastering the natural world through the increasing professionalization of science and through their dominant ethic of progress, Cooper advocated a meek position in relation to the natural world. Bridging the natural history tradition with what we can now call a plea for environmental ethics, Cooper called for a new sort of passion for the natural world—one rooted not only in history and observation but also in a humble respect for natural phenomena.

Contemporary reviews of *Rural Hours* help demonstrate not merely that Cooper's text was seen as "good," but that her specific manner of representing nature served, in the minds of her contemporaries, "literary" purposes. Mid-nineteenth-century reviewers accepted her adjustments to traditional natural history as helpful contributions to their emerging culture. Indeed, when *Rural Hours* appeared in 1850, it garnered lavish praise for Cooper, and reviewers noted particularly her expanded sense of history, her skillful observations, and her humble narrative posture. Each of these aspects of Cooper's prose received specific comment from reviewers. Reviewers also commented on Cooper's position as the daughter of James Fenimore Cooper, the famous novelist. Significantly, even a quick glance at the reviews reveals that Cooper had distinguished herself from her father, whose literary reputation was firmly and internationally established—and undergoing considerable scrutiny—at the time *Rural Hours* appeared. A *Harper's* review of *Rural Hours* notes, "The author is stated to be a daughter of Cooper, the distinguished American novelist, and she certainly exhibits an acuteness of observation, and a vigor of description, not unworthy of her eminent parentage." This reviewer praises Susan Cooper's powers of "observation" and "description" particularly, and these are, in fact, the two traits most frequently praised in the reviews of *Rural Hours*.[54]

Even reviewers less inclined to find Cooper's relation to her father a favorable indication of her literary potential note her success in these areas. In *Graham's Magazine*, for example, we find these remarks: "To judge from the dedication, the authoress of this goodly duodecimo must be the daughter of Cooper, the novelist. She has much of her father's remarkable descriptive power, but is happily deficient in that fretful discontent which disturbs the harmony of his later productions." While this reviewer may have been taking advantage of this opportunity to slight James Fenimore Cooper's achievements during a lull in his popularity, the reviewer does so by asserting Susan Cooper's superiority to one of the most celebrated authors of the century: her father. She has his descriptive power, the reviewer claims, but she more successfully creates a "harmony" in her volume.[55]

In addition to commenting on the Coopers in relation to one another, the reviewer refers to other traits that lead to the conclusion that *Rural Hours* is a strong contribution to American letters: "The writer wins upon the reader's sympathies with every page. Her intelligence is clear and quiet, enlarged by intimacy with nature and good books, and elevated by a beautiful and unobtrusive piety. We hope this will not be her last production." Here we see some of the gender expectations of her time: that a female author will convey a persona that is "quiet" and "unobtrusive." But significantly, we also find here recognition of her wide reading and praise for her "intimacy with nature."[56]

Cooper's focus on nature invited attention in a variety of magazines, even those not devoted specifically to literary culture. Prepublication and publication notices appeared in such widely read journals as *Godey's Lady's Book*, the *Literary World*, and the *Home Journal*; following its publication, brief but positive reviews appeared in *Graham's Magazine*, *Harper's New Monthly Magazine*, and the *Knickerbocker*; and lengthy reviews, which included a number of excerpts from *Rural Hours*, appeared in the *Literary World* and the *North American Review*. Andrew Jackson Downing, perhaps the most prominent horticulturist, architect, and landscape designer in mid-nineteenth-century America, also noted Cooper's close relationship to the physical world in his popular magazine, the *Horticulturist*.[57]

Praise for *Rural Hours* recurs throughout these reviews. In the *Woman's Record*, a reviewer declared, "Miss Cooper has formed one of the most interesting volumes of the day." A reviewer for the *Literary World* went so far as to compare Cooper's "style and manner" to those in "the recently-published volume of Mr. Bryant's letters"—his 1850 *Letters of a Traveller*. William Cullen Bryant, then editor of the *New York Evening Post*, was one of America's leading men of letters at the time; the comparison was complimentary, to say the least, and certainly welcomed by Cooper, who would later dedicate her own *Rhyme and Reason of Country Life* to the famed literary figure.[58]

For many reviewers, Cooper's knowledge of and familiarity with nature indicate her literary ability; her "literary" accomplishments seem, in fact, to be equated with her acute knowledge of natural history and her ability to share that knowledge in a manner unaffected by her particular preferences or emotional reactions. Reviewers remark, for instance, on Cooper's "style of simple elegance, without a particle of affectation," and on her "plain, careful, and truth-telling" prose. The *Harper's* reviewer states:

> Without the faintest trace of affectation, or even the desire to present the favorite surroundings of her daily life in overdone pictures, she quietly jots down the sights and sounds, and odorous blossomings of the seasons as they pass, and by this intellectual honesty and simplicity, has given a peculiar charm to her work, which a more ambitious style of composition would never have been able to command. Her eye for nature is as accurate as her enthusiasm is sincere. She dwells on the minute phenomena of daily occurrence in their season with a just discrimination, content with clothing them in their own beauty, and never seeking to increase their brilliancy by any artificial gloss.

Clearly praised here are the qualities of honesty, simplicity, accuracy, and sincerity. What this reviewer regards as Cooper's specific "peculiar charm" is the lack of "affectation," "overdone pictures," and "artificial gloss" in Cooper's prose. Significantly, it is Cooper's prose that lacks "ambition," and not her literary endeavor. In fact, she "command[s]" her "charm" through her intentionally "simple" prose, which adheres quite directly to its subject. Her close attention to "the minute phenomena of daily occurrence[s]" in nature exhibits her "just discrimination."[59]

What seems to impress the reviewers about Cooper's descriptive style, then, is precisely her emphasis on observation. Cooper's contemporaries praise her prose because of its adherence to its subject—the natural world. As a reviewer for the *North American Review* wrote, "We particularly enjoy the naturalness and freedom of the style . . . and we are grateful . . . that she . . . opens our eyes to much that escapes any less intelligent and minute observation than her own." The reviewers also praise Cooper's objective prose style, "this holding up a mirror, and daguerreotyping for our deliberate examination" specific aspects of the natural world. Another reviewer—writing for the *International Weekly Miscellany of Literature, Art, and Science*—dubs Cooper's "the finest capacities for the observation of nature." We might say that Cooper's strength, in these reviewers' eyes, is her objective realism.[60]

A slightly later commentary on *Rural Hours* again notes that Cooper's readers valued her objective—or "simple"—prose. In his *Female Prose Writers of America* (1855), an encyclopedic overview of women writers, John S. Hart distinguishes *Rural Hours* from other literary representations of natural phenomena and praises its lack of "extravagant embellishment":

Miss Cooper has an observant eye, and a happy faculty of making her descriptions interesting by selecting the right objects, instead of the too common method of extravagant embellishment. She never gets into ecstacies, and sees nothing which anybody else might not see who walked through the same fields after her. Her work accordingly contains an admirable portraiture of American out-door life, just as it is, with no colouring but that which every object necessarily receives in passing through a contemplative and cultivated mind.

Here simplicity is again praised; indeed, here it seems to indicate Cooper's knowledge and careful observation, or her "contemplative and cultivated mind." While Hart neglects to define clearly "extravagant embellishment," it seems clear that he associated it with "ecstacies," which denote trancelike states during which the individual loses touch with his or her physical surroundings. In this specific context, "ecstacies" seems to indicate passages that take the reader away from the natural objects under consideration—objects that "anybody else" would likely also see in a field. Such "embellishment" or "ecstacies" would add a "colouring" that would prevent Cooper's attentive, careful, straightforward description.[61]

Clearly, these many reviews indicate that Cooper's style and narrative persona appealed to readers, and her descriptive attention to nature received favorable commentary. The reviews also indicate, however, that readers believed Cooper's literary achievement served her readers in specific ways: through its model of nature study, as a historical record, and as an impassioned plea for preservation. The *Knickerbocker* reviewer notes the advantages of attending to nature as Cooper does: "This volume is a striking example of the good that may be secured, the pleasure that may be enjoyed, by a mind gifted with acute observation . . . in the every-day life of the country." This reviewer notes that Cooper claims in her book no "merit" to her observations, and exhorts, "But they *have* merit of their own, and that of no common order." Cooper's observations of "[b]irds, trees, and flowers" are so carefully done, the reviewer claims, "that one cannot help but see that the writer's heart was in each record of her pleasant journal." The "merit" that *Rural Hours* has seems to be Cooper's scrutiny of the varied natural world around her. Clearly, Cooper's passion was apparent to her readers. Indeed, *Littell's Living Age* reprinted a review from the *New York Evening Post*, which claims that Cooper's "daily observation" of country life is "almost enough to make one in love with such a life."[62]

Other reviews remark on the book's historical value and preservationist leanings. Commenting on the historical value of Cooper's work, a reviewer for the *Literary World* wrote that Cooper's sketch of a rural farmer's household "will be read in future times for its historic value." Another reviewer remarks specifically on Cooper's interest in preservation, revealing that readers responded to her environmental concerns: "The forest, which, like its early denizens the deer and the red man, vanishes as civilization advances, is the most interesting and important of the great variety of themes touched upon in the author's note-book during the summer. It makes one sad, if not angry, to think of the cold-blooded destruction of gigantic pines and elms by ephemeral and short-sighted man, to give himself treble the space he can improve or enjoy." Cooper's pleas for preservation clearly affected her readers.[63]

Finally, a reviewer for *Southern Quarterly Review* helps us see that Cooper's contemporaries also recognized the educational potential of *Rural Hours*. After remarking on Cooper's "good taste, good sense, and occasional research," the reviewer suggests that other readers might benefit from Cooper's example, which is "calculated, not only to afford amusement and instruction, but to prompt to imitation." Following her example, readers might learn how to observe their surroundings as closely as Cooper did, and they also might be motivated to do so.[64]

When we consider it in its discursive context, then, we find that *Rural Hours* both responded to a number of popular interests and appealed to readers' tastes. These reviewers' declarations about how *Rural Hours* might benefit its culture deepen our understanding of the purposes of literary representations of nature in this era. Cooper's work was thought to provide a record of country life that was sure to have historical value; help readers recognize the pleasure one can experience through nature observation; and assert a more humble approach to the American environment. While many modern-day readers of Cooper's book may struggle with her prose, in her own era Cooper's particular aesthetics—unaffected nature description—allowed her to challenge America's trajectory of environmental degradation. Through close attention to her surroundings and adjustments to the traditional natural history form, she expressed her visionary, humble passion for American nature.

"A Farther Progress"; or, A New Passion for Nature

In *Rural Hours*, Cooper explored the potential of this new story of nature. She fills her prose with unembellished, simple, plain descriptions of what she sees, and she does not merely "look out of the window." She drives, walks, and rows through her region, stopping to count seed pods in plants, identify which species grow in which locations, distinguish rare birds from resident ones, and perform minor scientific studies of curious phenomena. Indeed, Cooper's focus on the realities of her surroundings clearly distinguished her passion for nature from that of many of her contemporaries. She advocated attention to the "real" over the metaphorical. Cooper uses this term—the "real"—just once in *Rural Hours*, but its appearance there provides much insight into her hopes for *Rural Hours*. She clearly intended her book as a contribution toward the "farther progress" that she had envisioned.[65]

We find evidence of Cooper's desire to attend to the "real" in a lengthy section of *Rural Hours* devoted to British treatments of autumn. In noting how the New York autumn stuns her with its brilliancy, she expresses surprise to find Old World treatments of the season a bit dull. In her typical natural-historical style, she reviews several of these treatments, quoting such authorities as Shakespeare, Pope, and Keats, among others. In the most recent texts she examines, Cooper sees a change toward a more realistic descriptive style that does attend to the qualities of the season. This "very decided change" in representations of the season reflects the changing times. Cooper posits that the "more modern" writer conveys more literal and factual representations—a result of a change in cultural aesthetics regarding representation: "Some foundation for the change may doubtless be found in the fact, that all descriptive writing, on natural objects, is now much less vague and general than it was formerly; it has become very much more definite and accurate within the last half century." She suggests that recent developments in landscape painting contributed to the change, but she also notes the "more natural style in gardening"—one less focused on the neoclassical geometric design—that perhaps has influenced writers toward a more objective descriptive style. "It is seldom, however," she admits, "that a great change in public taste or opinion is produced by a single direct cause only." Indeed, we might be tempted to suggest that the changes in scientific discourse had some bearing on these literary developments: with the rise of positivism during the nineteenth century, objectivity gained prominence.[66]

However, Cooper emphasizes the explanation to which she lends the most credence—and that helps explain why she represents nature as she does. She explains, "people had grown tired of mere vapid, conventional repetitions," suggesting that readers tired of clichéd descriptions of nature, and that they desired fresh language and images. Recognizing, for example, that autumn's traditional representation as a "melancholy wight" betrayed the true vitality and beauty of the season, authors "felt the want of something more positive, more *real*; the head called for *more of truth*, the heart for more of life. And so, writers began to look out of the window more frequently; . . . in short, they learned at length to look at nature by the light of the sun, and not by the glimmerings of the poet's lamp." Literary tradition failed to provide persuasive or meaningful representations of nature, and so authors looked away from "the glimmerings of the poet's lamp" toward the outside world as a source for accurate descriptions.[67]

In our own time, literary theorists discredit the possibility of capturing the physical environment in language, and even the idea that one could do so receives criticism. Timothy Morton, for example, calls any attempt to convey the material world in language (or, "ecomimesis") a "form of ideological fantasy." However, as Morton also notes, "the *idea* of nature is getting in the way of properly ecological forms of culture, philosophy, politics, and art." Cooper saw the aesthetics of the "real" as a possible way of alerting people to their problematic "idea" of nature.[68]

In writing the "real" in *Rural Hours*, Cooper provides a different sort of story for her readers—one that attests to the value of nature's history, revitalizes the literary natural history tradition, and stretches Christian piety in order to assert nature's value beyond its function as a manifestation or reminder of the deity. Significantly, Cooper believed that the potential change she saw in literary representation could improve both art and human culture: "And a great step this was, not only in art, but in moral and intellectual progress." This new literary fashion improved culture through its closer adherence to truth—to the fact, in her experience, that traditional representations of autumn belied the season's grandeur. Cooper herself also sought this ideal in nature description, seeking to avoid "mere vapid, conventional repetitions." Such objective description also enabled her to model her sense of nature's value: by writing about nature "simply," she could illustrate her dominant culture's distance from the natural world.[69]

From Cooper's perspective, this dominant cultural story of nature had become one of abstraction; that is, natural facts had little value outside the scientific community. Most Americans, including many intellectual and cultural leaders, told a story of nature that had little to do with the real, physical environment. Indeed, several of their writings show us their preference for an abstract view of nature—one rooted in ideas rather than in nature itself. Most Americans did not devote time to learning the subtle changes of the seasons, recognizing different species of birds, or understanding the varieties of plants. Instead, the dominant story of nature in the early decades of the nineteenth century was based in metaphor.

To love nature as the "real," as Cooper did, was to diminish the power of pervasive metaphors that figured nature as evidence of national progress, human refinement, and intellectual achievements in reason. Nonetheless, some of Cooper's contemporaries were drawn to her unembellished style, as we have seen through their reviews of *Rural Hours*. Even Henry David Thoreau became increasingly convinced that "[m]ere facts & names & dates communicate more than we suspect," as he wrote in his journal in 1852.[70]

After *Rural Hours*

While I have concentrated here on Cooper's passion for nature only as she expresses it in *Rural Hours*, she devoted much of her writing life to this subject. Before writing *Rural Hours*, she had begun her publishing career with a domestic novel, *Elinor Wyllys, or the Young Folk of Longbridge*, which she published first in England in 1845 and later in America in 1846 under the unfortunate pseudonym "Amabel Penfeather." Although the novel met with a quiet reception, she continued her writing, and by the time of her death she had published in a variety of genres. Most of her major publications continued to pursue the subject of the natural environment. Following *Rural Hours* in 1850, Cooper edited and wrote substantial notes for an edition of the journal of British naturalist John Leonard Knapp; titled *Country Rambles in England; or, Journal of a Naturalist with Notes and Additions*, the volume appeared in 1853. In 1854 she came out with *The Rhyme and Reason of Country Life*, a sizeable anthology of nature poetry featuring poems clustered around various topics—all relevant to rural life and the natural world. In addition to publishing many other stories, essays, and historical writings, as well as several selections from her father's works, Cooper edited the *Appletons' Illustrated Almanac for 1870*. During these years, she also wrote essays about American landscapes, a small book that was sold to solicit donations for the restoration of Mount Vernon, and several biographical essays. Cooper also published an array of articles, short stories, and children's stories in magazines including *Harper's*, *Ladies Home Journal* and the *Atlantic Monthly*. Her final publication was a short story that appeared posthumously in 1895 in a children's magazine.

During the half century in which she published her many writings, Cooper also attended fairly frequently to new editions of *Rural Hours*. By 1876, the book had seen nine editions in the United States and England, some of which featured stunning illustrations and appeared in two volumes. Oddly, then, and despite the fact that she lived nearly until the close of the nineteenth century (she died in 1894), when Cooper published *Rural Hours* in 1850 she was both at the height of her career and at its relative beginning. For while she went on to publish several books, several stories, and many essays, we now see *Rural Hours* as her highest achievement in letters. She may have, too. Even at the late date of 1887, when she was in her mid-seventies, Cooper brought *Rural Hours* through yet another edition—but this time a substantially abridged one. Even if she had to do so in condensed form to appease the publisher, who had apparently expressed concern regarding the cost of such a lengthy book, she wanted to bring that book before readers once again. Her resolve attests to her belief that it constituted her signal literary achievement.

Despite the fact that *Rural Hours* remained Cooper's greatest success, her other works warrant revisiting. They were issued by major publishers and in leading periodicals of her day, and they demonstrate her lifetime commitment to being a writer in several genres. They also, however, attest to Cooper's lifelong interest in cultivating Americans' relationships to the natural world. Finally, they help us recognize the relevance that Cooper saw for her own master work years after it had appeared. In both a series of articles called "Otsego Leaves," which appeared in 1878 in *Appletons' Journal,* and an essay titled "A Lament for the Birds," which appeared in *Harper's New Monthly Magazine* in 1893, Cooper returned to her own *Rural Hours* as a source for information about birds. Using her own detailed observations of nests and birds from 1850, she constructed in 1878 and again in 1893 an argument about the loss of species then occurring in her region. As she expresses her grief over these mounting local extinctions, she helps us recognize *Rural Hours* as a potential source of environmental history. Whereas she had merely expressed concern over her changing landscape in *Rural Hours,* these later works offer full eulogies: in the course of less than half a century she had witnessed local extinctions, and were it not for her own *Rural Hours,* even she may not have had a record of these losses. By recording her surroundings in 1850, she had documented a landscape that would soon be changed radically. Her later publications, which point out specific biological losses in her community, suggest that she must have realized that, without her help, others were unlikely to realize these changes in their own land.

Readers continue to be drawn to Cooper's observations of the real. The detailed observations of *Rural Hours* have been helpful to current residents of Cooperstown who seek to understand how their home landscape has changed over time. Today, Cooperstown is best known as a quaint touristy village rich in forests and natural beauty, in addition to being the site of the National Baseball Hall of Fame and the source of the Susquehanna River. With its various tourist attractions and idyllic setting, Cooperstown draws many thousands of visitors each year. Twenty-first-century visitors appreciate the Glimmerglass Opera, the Farmers' Museum, the Fenimore Art Museum, and the New York State Historical Association's holdings and lovely grounds, which are located on land once owned by Susan's father. To be sure, the town bears many traces of its rich Cooper heritage: right around the corner from the Baseball Hall of Fame, one can find a large statue of James Fenimore Cooper marking the site of his final home, Otsego Hall. Local landmarks bear the appellations that the novelist gave to them in his Leatherstocking Tales, and the town's name itself attests to the pioneering work of Susan's grandfather, William, for whom it is named. Curious folks who ask around may make their way to the home that Susan Fenimore Cooper occupied as an adult; she called the place both Riverside Cottage and Byberry Cottage. But almost all visitors are impressed by the peace and beauty of Lake Otsego—Natty Bumppo's "Glimmerglass"—and its surrounding hills.[71]

Several of Cooperstown's residents keep a copy of *Rural Hours* at their bedside or on their coffee table, consulting it from time to time to compare the natural phenomena they witness on a given day to that observed by Cooper in hers. Cooper's attention to the real has also served contemporary biologists, who turn to her work as a record of environmental history. At suny Oneonta's Biological Field Station, which is located on the shores of Lake Otsego in Cooperstown, researchers consult *Rural Hours* as a sourcebook, looking to Cooper to tell them the story of the lake before its late nineteenth- and twentieth-century environmental degradation. With the assistance of her passionate account of her home place, they have discovered which fish species were native to the lake and which plants lined its shores in earlier times. Hoping to reverse the trends toward ecological imbalance in the region, they have reintroduced those fish that they could, learned about changes that would have affected botanical life, and sought—with her help—to improve the ecological resilience of the area.[72]

But even in its day, *Rural Hours* functioned in part as a lament for a wounded landscape. Pictures from Cooper's era attest to the rampant deforestation that she mourns in *Rural Hours*, and while Cooper certainly enjoyed the pleasures of her place in the mid-nineteenth century, she also took care to share with readers its waning native populations of flora and fauna. It was not the twentieth century only that brought drastic changes to this landscape. Even in the mid-nineteenth, these were changes that occupied Cooper throughout her writing days.

FIGURE 3. Cooperstown Looking West from Mt. Vision, ca. 1872.
Photograph by Smith and Tefler. Fenimore Art Museum, Cooperstown, New York.

FIGURE 4. Cooperstown Looking North from Augur's Hill, ca. 1885.
Photograph by Smith and Tefler. Fenimore Art Museum, Cooperstown, New York.

Abstraction

Cooper wanted the natural world to be considered more real by her contemporaries because she saw how abstract it had become in their lives. In this way, *Rural Hours* remains relevant to modern-day readers. When we "abstract" the natural world, we "consider it apart from its concrete existence," to borrow some phrasing from the *American Heritage Dictionary*. If many mid-nineteenth-century Americans abstracted the natural world by overlooking its particularity, twenty-first-century Americans do so even more thoroughly today: our dominant culture has grown particularly effective at abstracting the natural world. Neil Evernden has gone so far as to refer to nature in our day as "a cloak of abstractions." Indeed, these days our national economic and consumerist foundations seem to compel us to abstraction by blindly assuming the earth's endless abundance. When we buy gasoline for our cars, most of us do not customarily ponder the exact place of origin of the oil that contributes to the running of our cars, the processes, true costs, and peoples involved in getting it to our local pump, and the ways in which our use of that petroleum will affect the lungs of certain humans, the nervous systems of birds, the air quality of wherever the winds take our car's waste, or our personal contributions to global climate change. We do not consider the full context of that gasoline. Thinking this way is too hard—and, let's face it, too unpleasant.[73]

Instead, we live amid a culture that abstracts many of the products that we use from their "real" contexts in the physical environment. We see plastic bags as conveniences to carry groceries, not as yet another petroleum product—and certainly not as evidence of our culture's blind view of the earth as endlessly abundant. But when we buy gasoline, use plastic bags, and jet off on vacation, we are allowing ourselves to perpetuate our nation's myth of the earth's abundance. Or, if we do consider the full implications of our actions and the physical origins of our purchases, we make a conscious decision that our needs for gasoline, plastic bags, or a vacation outweigh the consequences of our purchase for the health of the environment—including, of course, our own health. But again, most of us do not think this way.

Susan Fenimore Cooper's *Rural Hours* and later writings urge consideration of abstraction on a different scale. Rather than focus on specific products such as plastic bags, which we can see as results of an abstract conception of the earth as endlessly abundant, Cooper's works invite us to focus on the faulty conception itself. Her writings attest to a form of abstraction very large in scope—one that informed the nation's vision of itself as a successful democracy boasting the finest in intellectual and artistic achievement. This abstraction allowed the natural world to serve as a means to metaphor. The following chapters consider three such metaphors that are prominent in the literature of the mid-nineteenth century: the inevitable progress of the nation; the potential to reach the highest levels of refinement, or good taste; and the intellectual capacities of the human mind. Each of these three metaphors enabled a sweeping vision of the American landscape by abstracting its biological reality in service to a particular story. Nineteenth-century Americans conveyed their metaphorical understandings of nature with eloquence and passion. With an eloquence and passion all her own, Cooper grappled with their potent stories.

Cooper's writings about nature provide a useful touchstone for a consideration of the metaphorical understandings of nature that pervaded the popular imagination of her time. Her many publications on the natural environment serve as fascinating and helpful points of entry into these metaphorical visions of nature, since in her writings Cooper both uses and questions these visions. In other words, even while they engage in these popular ways of knowing the natural world, her writings challenge these same modes of expression. Ultimately, there is a tension in Cooper's works that results from her adherence to the popular metaphorical stories of nature and her unmistakable desire to move beyond those stories.

This tension in Cooper's works demonstrates the limitations of the metaphorical conceptions of nature that circulated in mid-nineteenth-century America. For, as we have seen, Cooper believed that understanding the "truth" of nature necessitated learning natural history, observing nature's variety, and approaching the natural world with humility. The various visions of nature that were popular in her time, however, made very difficult her pursuit of nature's truth. Each of the three popular metaphors upon which I focus here limited Cooper in specific ways: understanding nature as a metaphor for American progress erased the possibility of considering the natural history that she valued so highly; seeing nature as a metaphor for refinement prevented one from observing its details and variety; and assuming the natural world to be a metaphor for human reason implicitly demanded abandoning humility in exchange for a profound faith in the ultimate powers of the human mind. Against these potent understandings of nature's meaning as symbol, Cooper told a revisionary story. Through her "simple record" of nature's events, she pursued natural history, observation, and an ethic of humility. The result was an understanding of the "real" that was based not in the abstraction of metaphor but in the literalness of the material world itself.

We may all, if we choose, open our eyes to the beautiful
and wonderful realities of the world we live in. Why should
we any longer walk blindfold through the fields?
SUSAN FENIMORE COOPER, Introduction,
Country Rambles in England

CHAPTER TWO

The Metaphor of Progress

Thomas Cole and the Improvements

of the American Picturesque

IN HER INTRODUCTION to her 1853 edition of Englishman John
Leonard Knapp's natural-historical account of his region of southern England,
Susan Fenimore Cooper suggested that *all* people could "open [their] eyes to
the beautiful and wonderful realties of the world" they live in. For Cooper,
as for Knapp, seeing these "realities" demanded a knowledge of natural history. As we have seen, knowledge of natural history was integral to Cooper's
sense of nature's truth. Natural history represented for Cooper not merely a
religious pursuit but, rather, the pursuit of the "real." One simply could not
understand the natural world without a solid sense of nature's history—its
native species, its seasonal cycles, and its changes over time. Because of her
belief in the inherent value of natural history knowledge, Cooper provided
in her edition of Knapp's book many detailed notes on the differences and
resemblances between those Old World species that Knapp discusses in his
book and similar species that American readers might encounter in their own
landscapes. Not wanting her readers to leave Knapp's book misinformed, she
took to educating them about natural history. Only with this sort of natural-
historical knowledge could one remove the "blindfold" preventing a clear vision of the "realities of the world we live in."[1] Knowing nature meant knowing
its history.

In emphasizing the importance of historical context to an understanding
of nature, Cooper entered a lively discourse surrounding the relationship of

history to the new nation's landscapes. This discourse informed several genres, the most important of which for our purposes were literature and landscape painting. In the early decades of the nineteenth century, both writers and artists pursued a unique American identity through their work, and they often used their talents to explore how the nation might distinguish itself culturally from its European parentage. At issue was the identity—or, the meaning—of the young nation, so the nation's progress so far—its nascent history—played a role in their efforts. We find many works from this period in which writers and artists suggest the inevitable success of the nation by figuring its history in positive ways. When they treated its past, artists and writers sought to establish the nation's promising future. In an odd sort of way, treatments of the young country's history suggested an inevitable future. To this way of thinking, America's story was both fated and guaranteed to be successful.

This mid-nineteenth-century formulation of history is a bit puzzling, in part because it is as much about the future as it is about the past: "history" functions to both explain the past and predict the future. Treatments of American history, in other words, told a story with an inevitably positive outcome: what had happened was preordained, and what would happen would be good and positive too, since America's course was assumed to be inherently right. In Cooper's time, then, "history" was nearly equated with "progress," and to reflect on American history was to reflect on national progress. As Joan Burbick states, "In the mid-nineteenth century, history was particularly significant to Americans because it explained the meaning of the new nation and predicted its manifest destiny. The history of civilized progress reassured the burgeoning American middle-class and engendered confidence in collective action." A contemplation of the past therefore became a contemplation of the future—and this look into the future told a story assuring success. For many Americans, history functioned as a means of endorsing the progress of the nation.[2]

"Progress" meant many things in the mid-nineteenth century. In the minds of Americans in this period, "progress" might mean industrial development, increased economic health for families and individuals, or improved working conditions for manual laborers. Progress could also indicate "agricultural innovation, inoculation for smallpox, [or] the organization of improvement societies," as Sara Gronim explains. In addition, progress might suggest improved literacy rates, increased educational opportunities, and thriving social justice movements, such as midcentury efforts on behalf of women's rights, temperance, and the abolition of slavery. A mid-nineteenth-century American might deem any or all of these evidence of social progress.[3]

However, the notion of progress that most concerns us here is the one that Tom Wessels addresses in *The Myth of Progress*. Wessels defines *progress* as no less than "our reigning paradigm" as a culture—an ideological understanding that structures our society, our political system, and our days, and that centers on a belief in the inherent goodness of economic growth. "[I]n order to progress," the thinking goes, "we need to keep growing the economy." Wessels suggests that this particular understanding of progress "was birthed in the nineteenth century" and continues to structure our culture. This particular notion of progress as economic growth assumes the good of "increasing consumption of resources" and, given its emphasis on resource extraction and landscape alteration, has harmful consequences for the physical environment. Certainly there can be benefits of the pursuit of progress through economic growth, as Benjamin Friedman has demonstrated. Nonetheless, there are also disadvantages, and in the mid-nineteenth century, this understanding of progress would have deemed as "good" the clearing of forests, the cultivation of lands, the rerouting of waterways, the raising of buildings, the establishment of the railways, and the general physical growth of "civilization." This understanding of American progress would have led many individuals, business owners, and political leaders to understand the American landscape as "a changing mosaic of landforms and resources," to borrow Richard Judd's words. To this way of thinking, the physical environment was "an unfinished landscape," the "development" of which is understood to be an improvement.[4]

Following this paradigm of national progress, the natural world can embody progress, as the landscape is shaped to reflect the increased consumption of resources that accompanies economic growth. What this meant in practice for mid-nineteenth-century writers and artists was that they figured nature in ways that testified to the inevitable, grand story of American achievement. As Angela Miller notes, "The paradox of landscape as a subject of art and a source of national culture was that it arose at a time when the United States was busily occupied in converting those same landscapes into commodities through industry and market capitalism." Through their works, writers and artists expressed a passion for the physical environment that celebrated progress as nature itself. Through their works, nature *is* progress: The natural world is represented as a symbol of the potential of economic growth through landscape alteration and resource extraction. Nature thus became a metaphor for progress.[5]

This understanding of nature as progress had profound consequences for America's relationship to its physical surroundings. In part, consequences resulted from the complex way in which this metaphor for nature functions.

On the one hand, "metaphor" is a rhetorical and conceptual tool that provides us with a means of making sense of—or organizing—our experience. Metaphors therefore help us create our experiences with the world. On the other hand, and as we all learned in grade school, metaphors are also vehicles for comparison. This means that as we create our experience of reality, metaphors can get in our way, because they can enable us to see things as other than they are. Thus, while comparisons can be useful tools in helping us sort out how we will relate to our surroundings, they also can limit us through their very framework. Through metaphor, we subtly impose upon one thing our understanding of something else.

In this way, our uses of metaphor can have consequences. This is certainly the case when we employ metaphors for nature. By understanding the natural world as a metaphor for progress, Americans were seeing it as a vehicle for displaying a presumed outcome: the economic success of the new nation. This meant that their ideal form of nature was a landscape that provided evidence of progress. As Daniel Philippon explains, "[M]etaphors gain currency . . . because they carry moral weight. They describe ideal states of the human relationship with the nonhuman world, which in turn have ethical implications. Metaphors are thus vehicles for our worldviews, carriers of our visions of the good." Therefore, the natural world is most valuable (or most good) when it has been altered in ways that might enable the economic and cultural stability—the flourishing—of the United States. Trees should be felled for agricultural fields, and meadows should be plowed or grazed. Waterways should enable the rise of industry, and clearings should be made for the establishment of centers of civilization. A good landscape was one that bore these changes. Not surprisingly, then, the natural world became a vehicle for displaying what many understood to be the inevitable, positive course of American development, and a landscape evincing progress was understood to be good.[6]

We discover evidence of this metaphorical view of landscape in several literary and artistic works from this period. These works employ a language (whether of words or images) that asserts the metaphor of progress. In some sense, we must expect the presence of metaphor in artistic works, since writers and artists must employ metaphor to represent their subjects. For writers especially, we recognize that at some level the very use of language involves metaphor. We employ words to invoke something else. As Ferdinand de Saussure established so effectively, words are merely signs for something other than words, so when we use language to express some aspect of nature, we immediately fall into the realm of metaphor; our language is a sign for nature. However, we can also recognize that some metaphors exercise control and dominance more than others. In her work on narratives of frontier exploration, for example, Kris Fresonke argues that "metaphors are our most habitual means of defining ourselves—by establishing a rhetorical relationship with the landscape, and more generally by mastering phenomena through language." Fresonke's choice of words here—"mastering phenomena"—helps us see the power of metaphor to shape our understandings. Even though we develop and employ certain metaphors through our use of language, those metaphors come to have a certain sort of power in our culture, especially as they become engrained and, as a result, unnoticed. For we live according to our metaphors. For instance, if we talk about the frontier as something that requires our "taming," we generally use such metaphorical language because we believe that the frontier requires taming, and, through our actions, we tame it. As Fresonke implies, as we use language, we distinguish ourselves from our subjects, and metaphors of domination especially assist in this separation. Even though language itself depends on metaphor, then, by using language in different ways we can shape and enact different sorts of relationships with our surroundings. In particular, we do so by shaping (and, arguably, then living in accordance with) different sorts of metaphors. Our metaphors have consequences.[7]

In the nineteenth century, the "picturesque" aesthetic served as one of the main vehicles through which the particular metaphor for nature as progress was expressed. This aesthetic informed both landscape painting and literature, and it provided the basis for the artistic vision of several prominent landscape painters, whose works helped establish what we now call the "American picturesque" and who comprise what has come to be known as the Hudson River School. Epitomizing this movement in the world of art was Thomas Cole, who remained "the foremost American landscape painter" of the nineteenth century, despite his premature death in 1848. We also find the picturesque vision in the poetry of William Cullen Bryant and in the novels of James Fenimore Cooper. Just as the American picturesque informed landscape painting, it informed literature. Through their words, poets and novelists figured the natural world as a canvas for displaying the nation's inevitable march toward greatness. In their writing and painting, artists of the picturesque employed what we might call a language of progress, although the elements of this particular language were not merely grammar and syntax. As John Conron argues, "[T]he American picturesque transforms nature—and art—into a grammar of forms or images." That is, through their representations of nature in both artistic renderings and linguistic description, artists transformed nature into a system of signs that conveyed and embraced the notion of progress. The result was that their art forms served to celebrate the transformation of the American landscape in the vague name of "improvement."[8]

Susan Cooper was among the many writers who experimented with the American picturesque, but her works suggest that she was troubled by how this sort of representation of nature affected people's experience of the history of American landscapes. Foremost among the consequences of understanding nature as progress was the erasure of aspects of the historical record that did not fit within the narrative of the nation's success. For example, in favor of assuring themselves of their rightful place on New World lands, most Americans silenced the stories of Native American extermination, betrayal, and relocation, deeming these aspects of history "inevitable"—if unfortunate—steps in the providentially designed progress of the United States. As Bruce Greenfield eloquently puts it, by the nineteenth century "Euro Americans were no longer coinhabitants of a continent whose people they had conquered; instead, they could see the primordial land itself as the explanation and justification for their presence in it." Similarly, this celebration of history as progress silenced the natural world. It implicitly encouraged representations of nature as a theater for displaying sweeping changes that epitomized the success of the new nation and discouraged considerations of cycles of seasonal change, native species, or losses in local landscapes. Throughout her works, Cooper gave voice to these overlooked aspects of nature's story, thereby challenging her contemporaries' vision of nature as a metaphor for progress. Her writings suggest that the picturesque's sweeping vision abstracts history from nature, preventing people from recognizing the true and rich history of America. Against this abstract vision, Cooper's works attest to the importance of natural history to an understanding of American nature. Ultimately, her works suggest that the prevalent passion for nature as a metaphor for progress was harmful to the young nation, its Native peoples, and its natural environment. Nature's truth was not progress but the rich history of nature itself.[9]

Thomas Cole and the American Picturesque

Thomas Cole's artistic vision grew out of the work of European artists and philosophers, including Edmund Burke, Claude Lorrain, and William Gilpin. However, in one particularly important respect, Cole and other artists of the American picturesque middle landscape were unlike their European counterparts, for whom the picturesque was propelled by a nostalgic longing for wild scenes no longer available to them because of the astounding progress of civilization. For American artists, the wilderness was available. Nonetheless, in its more common manifestation in the United States, the picturesque was nearly formulaic in its depiction of landscape scenes that also evinced evidence of thriving, rural settlements. Typically, a scene was "framed" by a rock outcrop or trees, and it usually contained at least one person, who signaled the ideal, domestic state of the scene pictured. Frequently, the viewer of the painting looked down on the scene—as if the artist had captured the scene at his feet from atop a hillside (as, indeed, he often had). This perspective was important to the picturesque, because it provided viewers with a sense of control over the landscape. The inclusion of ancient ruins was also integral. For practitioners of the picturesque in Europe, these ancient ruins were reassuring in that they signaled the immense strides of civilization. A nostalgic look back at ruins engendered confidence regarding the forward course of progress.[10]

Through his adaptation of the picturesque, Cole adapted this formula in order to celebrate the landscapes of the United States. Both his paintings and writings endorsed the view that a beautiful landscape—the ideal natural scene—evinced progress by signaling the land's development through depictions of landscapes altered in various ways to accommodate a growing civilization. Because the American wilderness discovered by the forefathers was giving way daily and visibly to cities, industry, and population growth, it therefore demonstrated the progress of civilization. One problem was that American landscapes did not boast the ancient ruins found in Europe, and this dearth of ruins was considered a detriment to the American picturesque, which Cole would discuss publicly. However, cleared hillsides, agricultural fields, quiet villages, individual smokestacks, navigable and harnessed waterways, roads, farms, churches, and factories all played important roles in conveying American progress. By including several such signs of progress in one scene, a painter could convey the "harmony" that was sought in the picturesque vision. "Harmony" and "variety" were essential characteristics of the American picturesque, and an artist might convey this harmony and variety in a landscape by including in a painting a balance of wooded lands, cultivated fields, settlements, lakes, rivers, or streams, and evidence of a peaceful and thriving (if quiet) settlement.

For the most part, Cole and his disciples in the American picturesque painted this balanced scene from life, by locating places that embodied this artistic vision. The artist produced a textured canvas that featured detailed depictions of natural forms with evidence of a human presence—sailboats on a river, frequently, or a dwelling in the distance. As a means of highlighting this progress, the artist might evoke the wilderness that was giving way to settlement by featuring a distant, pristine forest or a particularly wild-looking mountain. The contrast between the wilderness scene and the evidence of thriving settlement had the effect of asserting the stability and power of those domesticated spaces—displays of America's agricultural successes, economic growth, and seemingly inevitable tranquility. Through such a depiction of American progress, an artist might assure viewers that the nation's course was not merely right but even preordained. This was the story that many Americans longed to hear.[11]

We find this prescribed scene featured in several of Cole's works and in many paintings by artists who would emulate his vision. Cole's *View on the Catskill—Early Autumn* (1836–37) (plate 1), for example, features a view of a rolling valley below, complete with several signs of domestication: a mother and child passing leisure time on the bank of the river; a boater enjoying its calm waters; a home whose chimney attests to the warmth within; pasturage and agricultural fields; columns of smoke in the distance signifying some sort of milling or industry; and, in the bottom right corner, a fence—that ubiquitous reminder of the economic stability promised by the notion of private property. In this painting, the natural world functions as a cradle for this scene of domestication and progress.[12]

Intriguingly, Cole's *River in the Catskills* (1843) (plate 2) offers a similar depiction of the very same scene some years later, although the passage of time indicates how the picturesque will, of necessity, respond to the continual development of the American landscape. We witness more progress here. Through its central figure, who stands above the scene at his feet, perhaps signifying his command over all, we are reminded of the work that accompanies this narrative of progress: the axe in his hand and the stumps surrounding him suggest that he is merely taking a break from the work demanded by this story. Several critics have noted the mournful tone of this piece: its central figure could be admiring his handiwork as easily as lamenting its impact on the land. Indeed, Cole likely had a mixed emotional response to the development of this particular area, as Oswaldo Rodriguez Roque explains: Cole depicts here environmental changes that occurred near land belonging to his family. The changes occurred forcefully in 1835, "when the Catskill and Canajoharie Railroad began laying down tracks just beyond his property." Although these tracks existed when Cole painted his first version of the scene (in the 1836–37 *View on the Catskill*), he had chosen to omit them from his painting. We might imagine his figure in the later *River in the Catskills*, where the railroad appears prominently, as Cole's grieving self. Nonetheless, the scene is tranquil, featuring the many telltale signs of harmony that we have come to expect, each indicating just a bit more progress than the first painting: the boater and the figure in the distant field signify the leisure of economic success; several comfortable homes figure prominently, rather than just one; there are larger areas for pasturage and significantly broader tracts of agricultural lands across the river; distant smoke trails speak of nearby industry; and this time the railroad cuts across nearly the center of the picture. The painting may signal a lament over an altered landscape, but it simultaneously conveys the comfort that accompanies progress by figuring the physical environment as the seat of domesticity. An individual rows quietly in the river, homes sit peacefully along the road, and a man tends animals in the field.[13]

The complexity of Cole's relationship to the landscape becomes clearer when we consider his beliefs concerning "wildness." In an 1835 address at the annual meeting of the National Academy of Design in New York City, which he gave before the New York Lyceum and which was published the next year in the *American Monthly Magazine* as "Essay on American Scenery," Cole both celebrated the American picturesque and lamented that one crucial ingredient of the European picturesque that evaded landscape artists in America: ancient ruins. The absence of Old World ruins from the American landscape truly concerned both artists and writers, who saw such ruins as necessary to beauty. In this address, however, Cole offered Americans an alternative to this crucial ingredient. His goal was both to quell anxiety over America's dearth of ruins, which would testify to its ability to succeed as a civilization, and to offer a substitute ingredient for painters of American scenes. The alternative that he offers provides us with more insight into the American picturesque's abstract view of the natural world, for Cole suggests that artists embrace the "wildness" of American landscapes as the basis of its unique version of the picturesque. However, Cole's suggestion that Americans base their passion for nature in wildness is fraught with contradictions, for what he means by "wildness" is, apparently, evidence of progress. "Wildness" figures in this version of the American picturesque as the future site of progress.

Cole's presentation of this ahistorical wildness is subtle, for it occurs amid a celebration of American scenes. He first offers a full prescription for a typical picturesque American scene, emphasizing the elevated perspective and several signs of domestication, prosperity, and progress that are necessary for achieving the ideal vision. "Seated on a pleasant knoll," he writes in his essay, "look down into the bosom of that secluded valley, begirt with wooded hills—through those enamelled meadows and wide waving fields of grain, a silver stream winds lingeringly along—here, seeking the green shade of trees—there, glancing in the sunshine: on its banks are rural dwellings shaded by elms and garlanded by flowers—from yonder dark mass of foliage the village spire beams like a star." Cole could nearly be describing the scenes that he would paint as *View on the Catskill—Early Autumn* and *River in the Catskills.* As expected, perhaps, he mentions the importance of perspective and of the harmony evinced by the scene: the viewer gazes down on such signs of progress as "wide waving fields of grain," "rural dwellings," a church "spire," and a peaceful stretch of water: "a silver stream wind[ing] lingeringly along."[14]

In addition to assuring his readers of this potential for displaying progress through the American landscape, Cole acknowledges that many of his contemporaries are of the opinion that American scenery, in comparison with that of the Old World, "possesses little that is interesting or truly beautiful" because of its lack of ancient ruins. American lands could not attest to the wondrous progress of human civilization through the presence of ancient ruins of castles and amphitheatres, crumbling columns, and centuries-old churches, and so they could not affect a viewer as powerfully as scenes complete with such "vestiges of antiquity." Cole, who had himself toured Europe for more than three years, assures his audience that he has no intention of berating such Old World scenes, but he does want to urge a new view of the matter:

> I am by no means desirous of lessening in your estimation the glorious scenes
> of the old world—that ground which has been the great theatre of human
> events—those mountains, woods, and streams, made sacred in our minds
> by heroic deeds and immortal song—over which time and genius have
> suspended an imperishable halo. No! But I would have it remembered that
> nature has shed over *this* land beauty and magnificence, and although the
> character of its scenery may differ from the old world's, yet inferiority must
> not therefore be inferred; for though American scenery is destitute of many of
> those circumstances that give value to the European, still it has features, and
> glorious ones, unknown to Europe.

What he goes on to argue in his essay is that Americans might embrace the country's "wildness" itself—its untamed, undomesticated lands—as the foundation of the nation's distinct identity and natural beauty. By depicting

American wilderness, artists might celebrate America, advance American art, and provide an important contribution to national identity.[15]

According to Cole's description of this potential focus for representations of American nature, it seems possible that the particularities of American nature might receive some attention. Representing "wildness," after all, would seem to entail representing native species, natural processes, and particularized, local environments. Indeed, Cole painted many particular American scenes, celebrating their unique topography and biological detail. Several of his early works, such as *Falls of Kaaterskill* (1826), *Sunrise in the Catskill Mountains* (1826), and *The Clove, Catskills* (1827), portrayed specific American scenes. Furthermore, Cole's paintings frequently depict with great accuracy the particular flora of a region. For example, scholars have noted that he completed a painting that is now among his best known works, *The Oxbow*, only after consulting detailed notes that he had made three years earlier as he stood surveying the view he would commemorate in the painting: the perspective of the Connecticut River that one gains from atop Mount Holyoke. In his painting of the scene, Cole would take care to include the elm trees that he noted along the river, as well as the corn fields and the meadowlands below. Clearly Cole possessed knowledge of the distinct natural features of individual locales, and his paintings could be seen as celebrations of America's unique landscapes.[16]

This attention to detail motivated several of Cole's artistic disciples who headed west so that they might capture America's unique wild landscapes on their canvases. However, many painters remained dedicated to the more domesticated scenes that Cole also painted. For these practitioners in the Hudson River School, "wildness" would be represented by allusions to pristine nature amid domesticated settings. In such paintings as Cole's *View on the Catskill—Early Autumn* and *River in the Catskills*, the details of flora, fauna, and natural history are secondary to a narrative of progress. Even distant, forested areas on distant, faint hillsides appear destined for domestication. If we look closely, we find that the natural scenes presented by many of Cole's works are not very natural at all; rather, they seduce us, even today, into believing that we are viewing "nature" while what we are viewing is more accurately called "progress." Natural settings, in other words, come to represent the promise of American progress—a vision that obscured the particularities of native species, natural historical detail, and even Native American history in favor of a sweeping, idealized vision of nature that presumed its meaning to be American progress itself. This particular passion for nature abstracts the natural world in order to tell a different story.[17]

PLATE 1. Thomas Cole, American (born in England), 1801–48. *View on the Catskill—Early Autumn*, 1836–37. Oil on canvas, 39 × 63 in. (99.1 × 160 cm). The Metropolitan Museum of Art. Gift in memory of Jonathan Sturges by his children, 1895. 95.13.3. Image © The Metropolitan Museum of Art.

PLATE 2. Thomas Cole, American (born in England), 1801–48. *River in the Catskills*, 1843. Oil on canvas, 27½ × 40⅜ in. (69.85 × 102.55 cm). Museum of Fine Arts, Boston. Gift of Martha C. Karolik for the M. and M. Karolik Collection of American Paintings, 1815–1865, 47.1201. Photograph © 2009 Museum of Fine Arts, Boston.

PLATE 3. Thomas Cole. *The Course of Empire: Savage State*, n.d. Oil on canvas, 39¼ × 63¼ in. 1858.1. Collection of The New-York Historical Society.

PLATE 4. Thomas Cole. *The Course of Empire: Arcadian or Pastoral State,* n.d.

PLATE 5. Thomas Cole. *The Course of Empire: Consummation of Empire*, ca. 1836. Oil on canvas, 51¼ × 76 in. 1858.3; Collection of The New-York Historical Society.

PLATE 6. Thomas Cole. *The Course of Empire: Destruction*, ca. 1836.

PLATE 7. Thomas Cole. *The Course of Empire: Desolation*, 1836.
Oil on canvas, 39¼ × 63¼ in. 1858.5. Collection of The New-York Historical Society.

PLATE 8. Thomas Cole, American (born in England), 1801–48. *View from Mount Holyoke, Northampton, Massachusetts, after a Thunderstorm—The Oxbow*, 1836. Oil on canvas, 51½ × 76 in. (130.8 × 193 cm). The Metropolitan Museum of Art. Gift of Mrs. Russell Sage, 1908. 08.228. Image © The Metropolitan Museum of Art.

Cole's works therefore contain a paradox that remains at the heart of American identity: the nation loves its wild lands, but it loves them to death, as it were. Many of Cole's works endorse this paradox, and those are the works that concern us as we consider the nineteenth-century fascination with nature as a metaphor for progress. Cole's "Essay on American Scenery" conveys the complexity of this paradoxical aspect of American identity:

> A very few generations have passed away since this vast tract of the American continent, now the United States, rested in the shadow of primæval forests, whose gloom was peopled by savage beasts, and scarcely less savage men; or lay in those wide grassy plains called prairies. . . . And although an enlightened and increasing people have broken in upon the solitude, and with activity and power wrought changes that seem magical, yet the most distinctive, and perhaps the most impressive, characteristic of American scenery is its wildness.

Notice that Cole equates "savage beasts" with "savage men," distinguishing both from the "enlightened and increasing people"—Anglo Europeans—who exercise their "power" to make "magical changes" in the land. The history of human inhabitation of "this vast tract of the American continent, now the United States" begins with the European arrival on a land characterized by "solitude." In this way, Cole illustrates Kris Fresonke's recent characterization of the picturesque: "The effort in the picturesque is to escape ideology and to appear free from history." The oxymoronic thinking runs deep: a land that was "peopled" is nonetheless a land of "solitude," and this new aesthetic of "wildness" is the result of "changes that seem magical"—changes that, ironically, threaten the wildness at the core of this prescription for landscape appreciation. Indeed, this passion depends on substituting present hopes about the future for the natural environment.[18]

We witness this substitution of future progress for nature again when Cole discusses how the Hudson River might serve an important function in the American picturesque. After suggesting some resemblances between the Hudson and the European Rhine, he explains, "Its shores are not sprinkled with venerated ruins, or the palaces of princes; but there are flourishing towns, and neat villas, and the hand of taste has already been at work. Without any great stretch of the imagination, we may anticipate the time when the ample waters shall reflect temple, and tower, and dome." This passage helps us see the degree to which Cole's ideal landscape depends on its own demise. American wildness will give way to the development of civilization, with the attendant changes to the land that such development entails. These paradoxical elements of Cole's argument demonstrate the blindnesses inherent in this particular passion for landscape. One does not see the landscape for what it is; one sees evidence of a predetermined story of progress there.[19]

Through his "Essay," Cole advocates a passion for the American landscape that depends simultaneously upon erasing the history of Native American inhabitation and accepting sweeping changes to the land as preordained. As Cole writes, in tones reminiscent of religious revelation: "[I]n looking over the yet uncultivated scene, the mind's eye may see far into futurity. Where the wolf roams, the plough shall glisten; on the gray crag shall rise temple and tower—mighty deeds shall be done in the now pathless wilderness; and poets yet unborn shall sanctify the soil." We hardly have time to think of lamenting the wolf's disappearance, since Cole's language elevates what follows the wolf's relocation (or, more likely, local extinction): "the plough shall glisten." Using this sort of formal, apocalyptic language, Cole averts the reader's attention from the loss of wilderness that is certain to accompany what his language suggests is a holy transformation. This line of thinking allows one to assert a passion for "wildness" as the basis for cultural identity while simultaneously celebrating massive development of those same wild landscapes. The reality of losses and changes in the landscape occupies no part of this story of American nature. In this story, the physical environment is celebrated for its ability to accommodate a new civilization.[20]

This was a passion for nature based on a progress assumed to be good: here the natural world is "culturally redemptive." Nature functions to ratify progress. As William Cronon puts it, "Not only did artists record on canvas Americans' most dearly held beliefs about the meaning of national progress; they discovered those meanings embedded right in the landscape itself." The American landscape *was* progress.[21]

We find this vision repeated in many of Cole's works, as well as in those of his disciples in the Hudson River School. The story of nature is always the same—regardless of the unique flora, fauna, or long-term history of the location pictured—and that story always centers on nature's potential to accommodate Euro-American progress. This aesthetic "dulls the mind, in its repetitions, toward what nature might contain," to borrow Fresonke's phrasing. The specific details of natural phenomena matter not; instead, the story of progress takes over the land. The "real" natural world upon which Cooper would focus in *Rural Hours* becomes, through the imposition of metaphor, progress.[22]

The Literary Picturesque

Cole's 1836 "Essay on American Scenery" is valuable to us today because it helps us see how a passion for nature can become a passion for humanity. Through his aesthetic theory, a passion for nature was a passion for progress—a prescription, in other words, for an ahistorical vision that disregarded the particularities of natural processes and phenomena. This passion for nature conjoins landscape depiction with the nation's need for reassurances about what America might become. Clearly, then, the American picturesque reflects the larger cultural effort in the United States at this time to alleviate the anxiety that accompanies new nationhood by creating a distinctive focus for the cultural identity of the country. The focus of this national identity was on the country's manifest destiny—its fate as evidenced by its surroundings.

Like the picturesque aesthetic, the national consciousness of the 1830s and 1840s centered on the doctrine of "Manifest Destiny"—that ideological framework that would shape the nineteenth and twentieth centuries, and that arguably continues to propel our nation's course. The term "manifest destiny" first appeared in print in 1845, but the spirit captured by the phrase pervaded American life for at least a decade before the formal coining of the phrase. This was the spirit of justified, rightful development of a nation sanctioned by divine right.[23]

The particular rendition of manifest destiny that we find in the picturesque aesthetic impelled the fine arts in America for several decades in the nineteenth century and had great influence on American letters. In fact, the preoccupation with a properly balanced landscape took the world of art and literature by storm—so much so that it is difficult for the modern viewer to trace the paths of influence among the artists engaged in its pursuit. Cole painted scenes from James Fenimore Cooper's novels, William Cullen Bryant wrote poetry focused on Cole's artistry, Cole's writings on art contain quotations from Bryant's poetry, and the elder Cooper wrote resounding reviews of Cole's masterpieces. Their works were imbricated in each other's artistic visions. Susan Cooper was not exempt from these circles of overlapping influence: she dedicated her fourth book to Bryant (and included some of his poems in it) and contributed an essay to a volume dedicated to the famous landscape painter, Asher Durand, who was an admired colleague of both Bryant and Cole. In fact, in a painting that would become one of the most celebrated of the era, Durand depicted a landscape scene featuring Bryant with his writing tablet and Cole with his easel, both overlooking a stunning forested vista. (The painting is called *Kindred Spirits* [1849].) These various artists—both painterly and literary—produced works that were as enmeshed in each other's artistry as were their creators' shared passions for landscape. Together, however, their works largely silenced natural variety and history in pursuit of a vision of progress.[24]

In Bryant's 1834 poem "The Prairies," for example, we find a meditation on a specific landscape that purports to celebrate its unique identity and history but that has the end effect of ratifying progress. At first the poem celebrates this natural landscape and its history of resident Native peoples. The prairies are "unshorn fields, boundless and beautiful," whose grasses "stretch, / In airy undulations" and display through shadows the clouds moving through the sky. This is a land of "prairie-hawk" (northern harrier), wild flower, and the "magnificent temple of the sky." The poem's speaker recounts for readers the history of humans dwelling on these lands: the mound builders, presumed by Bryant to have "long . . . passed away," were followed by "[t]he red man," whom the speaker describes as "hunter tribes, warlike and fierce." At this point, the poem strikes readers as a celebration of this particular place and its relatively localized history, but the poem shifts in its final lines and becomes an anticipation of Euro-American settlement of the region.[25]

This shift occurs by means of two important sections in the poem: one devoted to a discussion of the seemingly inevitable disappearance of races of people, and the other devoted to positive images of the domesticity that European settlement will bring to the area. First, the speaker explains the absence of Native Americans on the scene: "Thus arise / Races of living things, glorious in strength, / And perish." Of the Native Americans who have left the area due to disease, murder, and political pressure, the speaker states: "The red man, too, / Has left the blooming wilds he ranged so long, / And, nearer to the Rocky Mountains, sought / A wilder hunting ground." This idea that Native peoples "sought a wilder hunting ground" may strike modern readers as nearly comical, given our knowledge that relocation was hardly a matter of choice for Native Americans. For the speaker of "The Prairies," however, this notion of a people "vanishing" or "fading away" as if the change had been ordained by God was a means of arguing on behalf of the presumed superiority of Anglo-European peoples over Native peoples. The passing away of one people to make room for another was, in this poet's thinking, natural. As the poem states, "Thus change the forms of being."

The second part of the shift occurs in the poem's closing lines, when the speaker subtly endorses settlement of the wild scene. He imagines the sounds that will accompany settlement of the area: a bee's "domestic hum" calls to mind "the laugh of children, the soft voice / Of maidens, and the sweet and solemn hymn / Of Sabbath worshippers." Also present in the speaker's reverie are the "low of herds" and "the rustling of the heavy grain," both indications of the agricultural promise of the region. All of these positive images of domesticity suggest that the prairies will not only accommodate settlement but will welcome it. Settlement is deemed inevitable: "that advancing multitude" is most certainly on its way. While "The Prairies" serves as a testament to the history of this land and its peoples, it does so in order to justify and even celebrate the progress that will take place imminently. Its nostalgia for an earlier landscape and its displaced peoples hardly seems very deep. This is a landscape of promise and progress.

While this romantic but cursory nostalgia for a people and natural environment appears in much literature of this period, perhaps no one better exemplifies this early nineteenth-century passion for American nature as progress than James Fenimore Cooper, whose series of novels known as the Leatherstocking Tales (1823–1841) ratified progress even as it appeared to celebrate Native Americans and the American wilderness. As the most famous living novelist in the nation, Cooper was widely credited with alerting the Western world to the rich literary potential of the American land. Especially through his Leatherstocking Tales, however, Cooper told a story endorsing America's early settlement by celebrating the ability of the natural world to accommodate the progress of the new nation.

Cooper's five-part, epic series focuses on the life of Natty Bumppo, a character who has come to seem more fact than fiction due to his ability to serve as a representation of mid-nineteenth-century national consciousness. Natty Bumppo's tale is now seen to represent the virtual erasure in the nineteenth century of ethical obligations to the natural world and to the Native Americans who peopled this continent at the time of "discovery." Alternatively called the Pathfinder, Deerslayer, and Hawkeye, Natty represents a wilderness lifestyle that simply must make way for American progress. He befriends Native Americans, defends his beloved home against the white settlement by resisting its emphasis on private property and law, and eventually, like so many Native Americans of Cooper's time, leaves his homeland in the east to head west beyond the Mississippi River, a place presumed to be beyond the march of progress. In other words, Natty is, as Philip Fisher puts it, a "surrogate" for national history. The course of his fictional life represents the fate of the nation's natural landscapes and Native peoples: he holds nostalgically to a way of life and to a people (Native Americans) representing the early history of American settlement, and it is always understood that progress will win out over his desires, which are figured as quaint and unrealistic.[26]

Because American progress is figured as inevitable in Cooper's Leather-stocking Tales, they serve as an endorsement of the path that American history has already taken. We find this sense of the inevitability of progress even in Cooper's Native American characters, who are nearly sacrificed to make way for white civilization. In the final sentences of *The Last of the Mohicans* (1826), for example, a Delaware chief named Tamenund seems to sanction his own culture's demise: "The pale-faces," he exclaims, "are masters of the earth, and the time of the red-men has not yet come again." While Tamenund's words seem to promise hope for the "red-men"—their time, he suggests, *may* "come again"—the plot of the novel all but assures readers of the death of traditional Native American cultures. After all, Tamenund laments through his words the destruction of the Mohican tribe. As if to confirm the ultimate destruction of Native peoples, and even indicate their complicity in their own cultural genocide, Cooper's Tamenund says, "My day has been *too* long." Apparently, he is ready to go.[27]

Cooper's treatment of his character enacts the same paradoxical view of history and landscape endorsed by the painters of the Hudson River School: the prehistory of the land, while mourned for its passing, must give way to the progress of the new nation, which is deemed right, inevitable, and inherently better. As Lucy Maddox argues, Cooper perpetuates the master narrative of the period, which portrays and sanctions the "inevitable" vanishing of both the "red man" and the American wilderness. His novels endorse American progress, and they presume that this progress requires a seriously diminished Native American presence. In James Fenimore Cooper's words, Natty is "a witness to the truth of those wonderful alterations which distinguish the progress of the American nation." This vision left little room for expressions of genuine grief over peoples, cultures, or native species that were wounded, displaced, or destroyed in the process of Euro-American cultivation. Instead, this was a passion that deemed nature the site of progress and depended on some major and crucial disregard for historical reality. This was the passion, in fact, of empire.[28]

Regret and *The Course of Empire*

It is possible that Thomas Cole recognized the problematic aspects of his landscape aesthetic; both his writings and certain of his paintings suggest that he struggled with its endorsement of progress in various ways. In his writings we find him lamenting the changes inflicted on American lands in the name of the nation's progress, and in some of his paintings we witness his concern that the course of America's development may have negative consequences for both its lands and its peoples. However, like William Cullen Bryant's lament for the changes on America's prairies, Cole's expressions of concern seem ultimately ineffective. To him, American progress was inevitable, if regrettable, but probably right.[29]

We find Cole's nostalgic acceptance of progress in his 1836 "Essay on American Scenery," where he expresses reservations about the destruction of natural life that will accompany American progress but then accepts that progress as natural. In the essay, Cole joins "those who regret that with the improvements of cultivation the sublimity of the wilderness should pass away," and he shares his own grief:

> I cannot express my sorrow that the beauty of such landscapes are quickly passing away—the ravages of the axe are daily increasing—the most noble scenes are made desolate, and oftentimes with a wantonness and barbarism scarcely credible in a civilized nation. The way-side is becoming shadeless, and another generation will behold spots, now rife with beauty, desecrated by what is called improvement. . . . This is a regret rather than a complaint; *such is the road society has to travel.*

While Cole laments these changes to nature, he clearly sees them as inevitable. By deeming his sorrow the result of "regret" rather than complaint, Cole registers his acceptance of the course of progress. Through this sorrowful acceptance, he foregrounds the insidious nature of the rhetoric of manifest destiny. In the name of "improvement," the nation watches its beloved lands "pass away," as if physical environments are prone to mortality in human terms or on a human scale. Nobility gives way to desolation, civilization to barbarism, and beauty to desecration. "[S]uch is the road society has to travel." Such was the course of empire.[30]

We also find Cole struggling forcefully through his paintings with some of the implications of his vision. We especially see this struggle in his epic series, *The Course of Empire*. Here too, Cole's expressions of grief were ineffective. Fault for this, however, may lie more with Cole's contemporaries, who craved endorsement of their nation's progress, than with Cole himself.[31]

Completed in the same year that "Essay on American Scenery" appeared in print, *The Course of Empire* comprises a set of five large canvases that depicted, in Cole's words, "the history of a natural scene as well as [the] epitome of Man." In a word, the subject of the paintings was progress. In his proposal to his patron, Luman Reed (who, incidentally, would not live to see the series completed), Cole explains that his "philosophy" for the paintings "was drawn from the history of the past, wherein we see how nations have risen from the savage state to that of power and glory, and then fallen, and become extinct." Rather than represent one specific, rural, picturesque scene, this monumental series would depict what Cole saw as the natural course of entire human civilizations. As Cole looked to history, that story revealed again and again the inevitable failure of even the most successful civilizations. This series would seem, then, to be Cole's warning to his contemporaries: America, despite its rapid progress as a developing nation, would one day fail. The paintings could urge Americans to be cautious in their national development; even the most successful civilizations of the past had fallen.[32]

Cole's method was to depict one landscape setting over time, with each of five depictions displaying a different stage in the progress of a nation. The five paintings would feature one location so as to explore what might occur in one specific location during the course of a civilization's rise, success, and inevitable fall. By featuring the same landscape in each painting, Cole's series might also alert Americans to the effects that their doctrine of progress would have on the physical environment—to what Perry Miller has called "the inescapable logic of a nationalism based upon the premises of Nature." America's passion for nature would not be able to govern or constrain itself. As the nation continued its course, the beloved landscape would be profoundly altered. These radical changes to the landscape would surely anticipate the fall of civilization. By depicting this story, *The Course of Empire* would serve as a sort of "moral history lesson for a young government and country," encouraging a cautious approach to changing the land and a vigilant guard against luxury or complacency. Through his art, Cole might warn the nation about the rapid, seemingly thoughtless development that now defined the nation.[33]

The culmination of Cole's vision is staggering. Cole's *Course* "would constitute the most ambitious artistic undertaking yet conceived by an American artist." Even today, the series is brilliant in its color, detail, and size. The first painting, *Savage State* (plate 3), features several apparently indigenous people running through a wild landscape, with only a small circle of clearly temporary tents, around which other Natives gather by a fire. *Arcadian or Pastoral State* (plate 4) features the same scene, now cleared by grazing sheep and marked by a nearly cloudless sky, allowing the viewer to see a larger mountain behind the smaller rocky hill that appears in each painting. In this second painting, Anglo-European children play near their mother, a couple dances under the trees, and a man sits and calculates figures in the dirt with his stick—the mark of an emergent civilized society. In the distance appears a public structure, classical in style and form, indicating Cole's inspiration squarely in the picturesque aesthetic. This is a happy, domestic scene.[34]

The third and fourth paintings, *Consummation of Empire* (which is an astounding 51¼ by 76 inches) and *Destruction* (plates 5 and 6) feature what appear to be European, Romanesque cities. In the former scene, people in lavish dress move on foot and boat through a series of white marbled buildings marked by columns, statues, and classical urns. In the latter scene, we witness the same city with bridges down, people drowning, and all the expected signs of hell, fire, and brimstone, including smoke, mutilated bodies, and a foreboding sky. Columns are shattered, and the statue figures are beheaded. In the final scene, *Desolation* (plate 7), no humans appear—only the wild scene from the first painting, marked now by no sign of humanity except for ruins covered in plants that are attempting to make their way again in this desolate land. In Cole's words, this final canvas served as "the funeral knell of departed greatness." While the sky is clear, the moon sets on the deserted scene.[35]

Cole's *Course of Empire* told an important story: human civilization may "succeed," but its success would deface the natural landscape and end in decadence and violence. While the natural world would recover from the foolery of generations, those particular civilizations die out. So, presumably, would the Natives who had inhabited the land in the first place. The message seems especially dark to us now, and Cole presumably intended it to be so.

Despite the clear intent of Cole's series, many members of his nineteenth-century American audience could not recognize its relevance to their world. One reviewer for the *New York Mirror* noted Cole's accomplishment in showing "what has been the history of empires and of man," and then asks, "Will it always be so?" Taking the view of so many of his contemporaries, he answers his own question with a "No." Although human history has taken this course in the past, he argues, "[p]hilosophy and religion forbid" that it will continue to do so: "[T]he progress of the species is continued, and will be continued, in the road to greater and greater perfection, when the lust to destroy shall cease and the arts, the sciences, and the ambition to excel in all good shall characterize man, instead of the pride of triumph, or the desire of conquests." It was, in fact, Cole's choice of architectural style that may have prevented his American audience from recognizing the warning implicit in this series. His depiction of European-style ruins reminded them of European landscapes, so they may have deemed the series irrelevant to their new nation in this new land. Whatever the reason, most nineteenth-century viewers of *The Course of Empire* did not heed its warnings.[36]

Americans were not ready for the suggestion that their civilization could travel the course that so many others had throughout history. American progress, they presumed, would escape this seemingly natural fate. "Nature" in America, after all, was progress itself.

Lessons from *The Oxbow*

As Cole worked toward the completion and exhibition of *The Course of Empire*, he undertook a painting of a specific, well-known spot in New England in hopes of making a quick sale. In this painting, *View from Mount Holyoke, Northampton, Massachusetts, after a Thunderstorm—The Oxbow*, which was also completed in 1836, Cole depicted what might look to be a traditional, picturesque scene (plate 8). Indeed, *The Oxbow* seemed to tell Americans the story of nature that they were prepared to hear. That is, the artist assumed a perspective atop a hillside and overlooked a rural scene at his feet that bore the traces of the developing nation. This is the story that we have seen in *View on the Catskill—Early Autumn* and *River in the Catskills*: the story of the landscape embodying American progress, the hopes of the new nation, and the beauty of wildness giving way to human cultivation.[37]

Atop Mount Holyoke overlooking a bend in the Connecticut River, Cole found the perfect vista from which to convey this story. His painting from this vantage masterfully depicts the passion for landscape that he had recorded just recently in his "Essay." Looking into the Connecticut River Valley, Cole could see many of the telltale signs of American progress. He portrays lands cleared for orchards and agricultural fields, winding roads alongside the river, pleasant homes surrounded by groves of trees, sailboats enjoying the languid waters, and even children playing by the shore. The hillsides attest to the hard work that this lovely scene requires: cleared patches appear amid thick forests. Indeed, the hills are quilted—patches of trees separate clearly demarcated logged sections. Faint smoke in the background suggests the possibility of growing industry, and clear skies over the valley suggest the promise of the future. Again, we find balance and harmony in the landscape. Through *The Oxbow*, Cole is able to express a popular passion for nature by painting the seemingly ideal scene of progress that he sees at his feet.

When we look closely at this painting, however, we find evidence of Cole's concern about the nation's progress. Just as we find Cole ruminating on the typical course of human history through his *Course of Empire*, in *The Oxbow* we find a struggle with the implications of this apparently idyllic scene. As other critics have noted, his creation of a divided canvas signals this conflict. In addition, the central (but obscured) figure in the foreground of the painting also communicates his concern.[38]

The divided sides of the canvas offer, however, the most obvious indication of Cole's sense of imbalance. Against the idealized scene of the right side of the canvas, the left side features the wild promontory that enables his elevated perspective. This side of the painting includes dark storm clouds, a deeply forested hillside, and a small grouping of trees and shattered stumps, all of which suggest the harsh conditions of this wilder state. On this side of the painting, we do not find much of the harmony typical of the landscape aesthetic in which the right-hand side seems to participate. Instead, this portion of the painting represents the wilderness condition that must give way to accommodate the idyllic rural scene. That idyllic scene comes at a price: the destruction of wilderness. Indeed, there seems to be a conflict here.[39]

We find this conflict epitomized by the small human figure in the near foreground of the painting. He stands at an easel, his umbrella and knapsack lying nearby. Somewhat oddly, considering that this *is* a painting, the figure is a representation of an artist who is, himself, painting from the same vantage point that Cole obviously has. The presence of an artist figure in a picturesque landscape painting is not all that unusual, a fact to which Durand's famous *Kindred Spirits* attests. What does seem unusual here is that the artist figure is both engaged in his work and facing the viewer of the painting. We might interpret this surrogate artist as Cole's reminder that the scene is an idyllic construction, a fabled representation of the landscape. In this sense, the artist figure amplifies the conflict embodied in the storm clouds on the left side of the painting. This is no simple, idyllic scene of progress, as the clouds and artist figure suggest: rather, the scene of progress depicted to the right depends on a violent "storm" of landscape destruction and on an idealized presentation by a painter. The painting therefore offers intriguing commentary on the production of this seemingly idyllic landscape: seeing the landscape as a testament to progress demands an imaginative act.

Or perhaps the presence of the artist suggests that an artist who seeks to capture such a view may meet with other artists doing the same. This redundancy implies the artistic commercialization of landscape, suggesting that celebrating the scene as a testament to progress is common, even an industry. It also attests to the degree to which rural vistas such as this one are growing more difficult to find. Such an interpretation is corroborated by the existence of other paintings and drawings of this same scene. In other words, the artist figure in the painting calls attention to the fact that our own view of that "real" place is mediated. Most fascinating in this regard is the way in which the artist figure poses in the painting. He faces the viewer, looking outside of the painting, as if we are intruders on this scene. Once we recognize the artist looking directly out of the picture at us, we are startled. In looking back at the viewer, the figure implicates him or her in creating this false sense of the scene. The scene is a fiction, or an idealized vision.[40]

While Cole's depiction of the Connecticut River Valley seems a fairly mimetic representation, the presence of an artist within that landscape suggests that the very landscape he represents is to some degree deceptive—that it is the result of his craft. From the top of Mount Holyoke, Cole has to blend the real land with its idealized role in America's passion for landscape. This crafting requires that he celebrate the real development of those lands and idealize them by silencing, as indeed the landscape has, the bloody history of the early settlers wresting those specific lands from Native Americans and the loss of wilderness that has accompanied their celebrated development. Through its points of tension and conflict, Cole's painting signals that it silences aspects of the real. The Oxbow thus calls attention to the necessary blending of the real and the ideal in this picturesque scene. Seeing the scene through the eyes of the artist demands silencing the real story: that there is an artist who has rendered the scene in such a way as to celebrate its beauty rather than to mourn its losses.[41]

The silencing of history that is integral to the traditional picturesque vision becomes more obvious still when we consider a later depiction of the same scene done by another artist—William Bartlett's View from Mount Holyoke (ca. 1838). In Bartlett's drawing, the perspective shifts slightly, so that we see not only the valley to the right of the hill but also the landscape to its left (figure 5). What occupies the left-hand side of Bartlett's scene is not the wilderness that will give way to progress but a strong sign of domestication: a structure that, as early as 1821, offered tourists shelter and a resting place atop Mount Holyoke. The imposing grandeur of the mountain in Cole's representation appears here as merely a well-trammeled hillside, and Cole's contrast between wildness and domesticity gives way to a unified depiction of an afternoon's recreation and entertainment. The "natural landscape" of Bartlett's vision is progress itself: villages, industry, clearings, and, even on apparently remote hilltops, touristy centers for afternoon picnics. Bartlett likely did not intend the painting in this way; but when it is seen today alongside Cole's The Oxbow, View from Mount Holyoke seems a testament to both the American yearning for an idealized view and the rapidity with which natural landscapes became domesticated in the Northeast in the nineteenth century.[42]

FIGURE 5. William Bartlett. *View from Mount Holyoke*, ca. 1838. From *American Scenery: or, Land, Lake and River Illustrations of Transatlantic Nature* (1840), by Nathaniel Parker Willis. AC8.W6795.840aac. By permission of the Houghton Library, Harvard University.

The popularity of Bartlett's image in the nineteenth century helps us recognize how Americans accepted this sort of progress. As Martha Hoppin notes, "Bartlett's prints were republished numerous times, lending them an unprecedented authority and providing a ready model for the many trained and untrained artists who produced images of [the scene] during the nineteenth century." Perhaps the most influential appearance of *View from Mount Holyoke* was in Nathaniel Parker Willis's 1840 *American Scenery*, a two-volume celebration of particular American scenes that also featured dozens of engravings based on Bartlett's drawings.[43]

By contrast, few nineteenth-century Americans would have encountered Cole's *The Oxbow*, despite its prominence today in the history of American art. After its initial 1836 exhibition at the National Academy of Design, it was exhibited only three times in the century, and it was not reproduced as an engraving. The popularity of Bartlett's image suggests that rather than understanding images such as Bartlett's as expressions of grief over changed lands and displaced peoples, we might instead understand them as celebrations of both lands that were uniquely American and a natural environment that was accommodating development. As Angela Miller notes, "If for Cole nature and nation remained antagonists, for those who followed[,] the United States *was* nature's nation." For Bartlett this seems to be the case: from atop Mount Holyoke the landscape could be equated with progress.[44]

Cooper's Revisionary Picturesque

Like Cole, Susan Fenimore Cooper had a complicated relationship to the picturesque aesthetic, and especially to its idealized, sweeping vision of landscape and history. In her work she directly addresses the ways in which the passion for nature as a metaphor for progress silences the real. She does so by both engaging and disrupting the traditional picturesque vision through her writing. On the one hand, Cooper celebrates the expected components of a picturesque rendering of a rural scene. Indeed, in *Rural Hours* and elsewhere she positions her narrator on hilltops and provides for readers a painterly view of the valley below. Similarly, we see throughout her works that she was capable of participating in the necessary idealization of landscape that this particular passion for landscape entailed. She appreciated a "harmonious" landscape as much as did her contemporaries. On the other hand, however, Cooper's writings at times question the assumptions implicit in this popular mode of loving the natural world. Through her attention to the specific natural life forms in her area, Cooper invites readers to take a closer view of natural phenomena than the popular landscape aesthetic allowed. At other times, her writings call into question the ways in which that popular vision idealizes the land so that viewers are enticed to overlook its history in order to celebrate American progress. While on the surface, then, her writings may seem to emulate the picturesque vision of nature, ultimately they problematize its sweeping vision by calling attention to the ethical implications of its metaphorical view of the land.

Specifically, Cooper's work grapples with some of the same problems that Cole himself recognized as inherent in this popular way of conceptualizing the new nation's physical environment. Cooper's writings, even more forcefully than Cole's works, alerted her contemporaries to the fact that by practicing this vision of the land, they were robbing it—and themselves—of its true, complicated, age-old history. Viewing the landscape as the site of American progress meant abstracting that landscape from its past and overlooking the rapid transformation of that land—a process that, for Cooper, had disturbing consequences. In this view of nature, the "real" upon which Cooper focused so carefully in *Rural Hours* gave way to metaphor. Cooper was not as willing as many of her contemporaries to silence natural and human history. To help her contemporaries understand the implications of their vision, Cooper borrowed their techniques and painted through her words alternate scenes for them to contemplate—scenes that evinced an alternative passion for nature.

In some passages of *Rural Hours*, we witness Susan Fenimore Cooper becoming a sort of landscape artist in the traditional vein of the American picturesque. As she fashions her words into sentences, she shapes for the reader a well-crafted scene, and through its detail we behold a painting that has been created through prose. On one summer day, for example, she recounts her view from the lake, where she rows in the heat of early June. From her perspective in the boat, she sees "hills and forests, farms and groves, encircling a beautiful sheet of water." Notice as she dons the language of an artist painting a picture and as she emphasizes—as an artist might—the "harmony" of the scene:

> Our own highland lake can lay no claim to grandeur; it has no broad
> expanse, and the mountains cannot boast of any great height, yet there is a
> harmony in the different parts of the picture which gives it much merit, and
> which must always excite a lively feeling of pleasure. The hills are a charm-
> ing setting for the lake at their feet, neither so lofty as to belittle the sheet
> of water, nor so low as to be tame and commonplace; there is abundance of

wood on their swelling ridges to give the charm of forest scenery, enough of tillage to add the varied interest of cultivation; the lake, with its clear, placid waters, lies gracefully beneath the mountains, flowing here into a quiet little bay, there skirting a wooded point, filling its ample basin, without encroaching on its banks by a rood of marsh or bog.

Cooper begins this particular description by alerting the reader to the humble scale of the scene (the "lake can lay no claim to grandeur"), but throughout the remainder of the passage she assures us that the humble nature of the scene is part of its value. In fact, the scale of the various components of the scene contributes to its idyllic beauty and artful balance.[45]

Cooper brings to her description a fine sense of what constitutes an appropriate balance of scenic elements: the height of hills are proportionate to the lake, the hillsides feature trees such that they are neither barren nor overcrowded, and the lake edges are varied enough that they are not monotonous, but not so varied as to include sections of swampy ground. Proportion and balance are the themes of her prose painting: "there is a harmony in the different parts of the picture." Cooper's emphasis on "harmony" suggests that she brought to her description a prescription of sorts—one involving a set of established criteria for rural scenes. This especially seems the case as the passage continues and Cooper contrasts the human-made aspects of her view with these balanced, natural features:

> And then the village, with its buildings and gardens covering the level bank to the southward, is charmingly placed, the waters spreading before it, a ridge of hills rising on either side, this almost wholly wooded, that partly tilled, while beyond lies a background, varied by nearer and farther heights. The little town, though an important feature in the prospect, is not an obtrusive one, but quite in proportion with surrounding objects. It has a cheerful, flourishing aspect, yet rural and unambitious, not aping the bustle and ferment of cities; and certainly one may travel many a mile without finding a village more prettily set down by the water-side.

Again, Cooper emphasizes balance and "proportion," and the passage reads almost like a travel brochure. Indeed, Cooper seems intent on proving that Cooperstown and its environs meet up to some preestablished criteria for rural scenes. And this is, in fact, just what she is doing here. In this passage we find Cooper engaging in the American picturesque vision and, thereby, demonstrating the pervasiveness of its landscape aesthetic, including its celebration of progress as a necessary element of a beautiful scene.[46]

But Cooper also drew for readers other pictures through her words—ones that invited readers to heed more carefully both the history and natural phenomena of their lands. In her *Rural Hours* entry for Wednesday, June 27, for example, she urges attention to the details of development that are discernible in a landscape, thereby suggesting that the historical progression of America's development is at least as important as the result of such development. She calls attention to *process* rather than *progress*, inviting people to dwell on the alterations to nature that enable progress.[47]

She begins by contemplating the degree to which the cultivated landscapes around her home hide the recent history of their cultivation, leading a passerby to "[look] in vain for any striking signs of a new country." In fact, "as he passes from farm to farm in unbroken succession," he will find that "the aspect of the whole region is smiling and fruitful." The scene, that is, could be interpreted as an idyllic, picturesque one—balancing homes with cultivation, progress with rurality. In her discussion of this particular scene, however, Cooper forbids an easy capitulation to this idealized vision. She invites readers to look closely at the scene so as to discern the signs of history that, though faint, indicate a more complete story of this land. The region may seem "smiling and fruitful," and indeed it may be productive, but Cooper wants readers to know that there is more going on here than what meets the "untrained eye."[48]

She begins by suggesting that people may miss those signs of history for several reasons: first, "the advanced state of civilization" allows for substantial changes to be made without many remaining signs of toil; second, the "natural features of the country itself" accommodate these changes without appearing much altered. These facts combine to create a scene that enables people to overlook the history of the development of this specific place and to see it, instead, as a mere sign of progress.[49]

What Cooper illustrates, however, is that this scene testifies to progress only to those individuals content with not truly seeing the details of the scene. The picturesque vision, of course, encourages such blindness, and she means to correct it. In the paragraphs that comprise her June 27 entry, she subtly instructs her readers on how to "read" the landscape. As she looks out over a "few miles of country in sight at the moment," she describes her view and suggests that a scrupulous eye can perceive many stages of cultivation—"widely different conditions"—in this one scene.[50]

Here we again experience Cooper's surroundings by means of her painterly eye, but in this particular vision we receive a lesson in landscape history rather than a celebration of American progress. She begins: "[W]e amused ourselves by following upon the hill-sides the steps of the husbandman, from the first rude clearing, through every successive stage of tillage, all within range of the eye at the same instant." Cooper then points to several indications of the area's cultivation: remaining tree stumps, signs of some fallen forest, and topography indicative of ancient pathways for water. Within view is also "an opening in the forest marking a new clearing," its black ground the site of "charred stumps." And "on a nearer ridge" appears an area cleared and fenced, although not yet plowed or planted with crops. Cooper laments the tendency that she sees around her to clear land but then let it lie fallow, noting that "it frequently happens that land is cleared of the wood, and then left in a rude state, as wild pasture-ground." Documenting her disapproval, she calls this "an indifferent sort of husbandry . . . in which neither the soil nor the wood receives any attention." Progress merely for its own sake is not acceptable to Cooper. When informed by the clear vision that she models here, one sees not only promise in the landscape but also its unnecessary destruction.[51]

As Cooper goes on to point out, even cleared fields look different, revealing their varied pasts: "Those wild pastures upon hill-sides, where the soil has never been ploughed, look very differently from other fallows." The "heaving, billowy character" of the hillside pastures results from the small hillocks that form over the remaining roots of the trees felled to clear the hillside. The remains of an ancient forest thus announce themselves through the texture of the topography. There are other, "softer touches . . . telling the same story of recent cultivation," touches that most observers would miss. Seeing these subtle marks requires an attentive eye: "It frequently happens, that walking about our farms, among rich fields, smooth and well worked, one comes to a low bank, or some little nook, a strip of land never yet cultivated, though surrounded on all sides by ripening crops of eastern [Old World] grains and grasses." Cooper shares her preference for native plants as she explains: "One always knows such places by the pretty native plants growing there," the "gyromias and moose-flowers, sarsaparillas, and cahoshes, which bloomed here for ages, when the eye of the red man alone beheld them." Progress threatens native species, which serve, in Cooper's estimation, as clear reminders of prior inhabitants of this place. Not content only to distinguish the native from invasive plants, Cooper further elucidates the history of the region by reminding readers that other peoples once dwelled on these developed lands. When one sees sarsaparillas or moose flower, one is in the presence of rich history.[52]

Understanding this place necessitates heeding its detail and variety—not merely reading a well-proportioned scene as evidence of the nation's destiny made manifest. On the contrary, what's "manifest" in this passage is the cultural extermination of a people, silencing "ages" of their history, and a displacement of native plant species with foreign ones.

What we find, then, in this passage from *Rural Hours* is Cooper tending to the variety in her line of vision. Rather than merely idealize her landscape as one of progress and promise, Cooper alerts readers to the history of change to which the landscape attests. She thereby encourages a more finely tuned understanding of the land than the picturesque vision of nature allowed. She also expands cultural memory by demonstrating the evidence of natural history available from even one point of observation. By assuming the position of someone who reads the signs of history in the land, Cooper echoes the painterly techniques of her artist contemporaries; but rather than idealize progress, Cooper points to the ways in which progress masks both human and natural history.[53]

Dissolving the Picturesque View

Cooper revisits her complicated interest in the picturesque in a later essay titled "A Dissolving View," which is both an exercise in the narrative picturesque and an analysis of the picturesque preoccupation with progress as it is revealed through a landscape. On the one hand, Cooper uses her essay to contemplate the beauty of autumn while perched on a hillside overlooking the valley beneath her, much as a landscape painter might do in her day—though Cooper uses words rather than paint. In this sense, she celebrates the traditional picturesque vision, even engaging in a fantasy view of the scene that enables her to pepper it with Old World ruins. On the other hand, she offers through her essay a sophisticated explanation of the role that ruins play in Old World landscapes and considers the general absence of such ruins in the New World; ultimately she suggests that the picturesque has little role to play in this New World landscape. Her essay lays open the possibility that the picturesque aesthetic is inappropriately applied to American nature. Once again, her writing functions to challenge the popular passion for landscape based in metaphor.

"A Dissolving View" appeared in an 1852 collection of essays and drawings, *The Home Book of the Picturesque*. This beautifully illustrated volume features a series of essays celebrating the American picturesque. As a modern commentator has observed, its list of illustrators "reads like the honor roll" of the finest Hudson River School painters. Indeed, the volume featured the most famous names in both literature and art: we find the words of James Fenimore

Cooper, William Cullen Bryant, and Washington Irving alongside engravings of works by Thomas Cole and Asher B. Durand, among other prominent artists. After its initial publication in 1852, the book appeared again under different titles later in 1852, later still in 1868, and again, in a slightly different form, in 1872. Its reception attests to the popularity of this particular manner of loving nature.[54]

Cooper's contribution to the volume has four distinct parts, each featuring a different sort of writing: she begins with a contemplation of American autumn based on her picturesque view from a hillside on a fall day; proceeds to a discussion of the historical preference for ruins in a landscape; offers an analysis of her New World landscape in the context of this preference for ruins; and finally shares her imagined vision of an alternative scene in the valley beneath her, which is the result of a fanciful "game" that she plays that introduces Old World–style ruins into her view. The blending of genres in the essay—picturesque description with analysis of an obviously storied landscape—allows Cooper to analyze the ways in which landscapes attest to different stories of human culture.

"Autumn is the season for day-dreams," she begins. Such days "arouse the fancy to unusual activity," allowing the "caprice" to exercise itself, as the "softening haze of the Indian summer" contributes "the illusory character of the view." It is "the brilliant novelty of the scene" that invites such day-dreaming. The essay thus begins with a celebration of American autumn—a topic she had treated at some length in *Rural Hours*. Cooper plays up the fanciful mood brought on by the season, explaining that the autumnal woods seem to change color each year. Borrowing a tool in perspective from contemporary landscape painters, she describes herself as seated on a lookout over the countryside below her. From atop the "projecting cliff which overlooked the country for some fifteen miles or more," the scene before her unfolds. As she describes her view—her "magisterial gaze"—we feel as though we are viewing a landscape painting—perhaps even a portion of Cole's *The Oxbow*. She describes "the lake, the rural town, and the farms in the valley beyond" that lie at her "feet like a beautiful map." Here she celebrates the traditional American picturesque.[55]

Cooper continues in this vein in the essay's second part—her discussion of ruins—where she suggests that even the magnificence of an American autumn scene benefits from the presence of humanity. Here we see Cooper engaging in the landscape aesthetics so celebrated in her day by the Hudson River School painters. She asserts that views of fall foliage are enhanced by some marks of civilization, such as a clearing, a village, or an agricultural field:

"A broad extent of forest is no doubt necessary to the magnificent spectacle, but there should also be broken woods, scattered groves, and isolated trees; and it strikes me that the quiet fields of man, and his cheerful dwellings, should also have a place in the gay picture. Yes; we felt convinced that an autumn view of the valley at our feet must be finer in its present varied aspect, than in past ages when wholly covered with wood." The ideal landscape bears the traces of humanity: "The hand of man generally improves a landscape," Cooper asserts. "Generally the grassy meadow in the valley, the winding road climbing the hill-side, the cheerful village on the bank of the stream, give a higher additional interest to the view." However, Cooper carefully qualifies her pronouncement that the "hand of man" benefits the landscape when she explains, "where there is something amiss in the scene, it is when there is some evident want of judgment, or good sense, or perhaps some proof of selfish avarice, or wastefulness, as when a country is stripped of its wood to fill the pockets or feed the fires of one generation." The signs of humanity that improve a view, then, are quiet ones, not large-scale alterations or damage to the environment.[56]

After establishing that signs of human civilization (ancient ruins) enhance one's view of a landscape, Cooper then addresses the privileging of ancient ruins in the picturesque vision. She suggests that we find such improvements to the land even in lands formerly occupied by humans of the "most savage condition." She reminds readers that even the prairies of her "new" country bear the traces of prior cultures in the form of mounds built by ancient peoples. While these ruins may not look like the ancient ruins of Europe or Asia, they nonetheless function to remind us of earlier dwellers: "These lasting and remarkable tumuli, or mounds, although they produce no very striking effect on the aspect of a country, yet have an important place in the long array of works which give a peculiar character to the lands." While the mounds may strike a viewer as subtle marks of history, Cooper argues that they nonetheless lend it a particular "character" or uniqueness. She seems interested in making readers aware that the aesthetics of contemporary landscape painting and viewers' expectations, all of which have been informed by the European experience, fail to take into account the specific, New World version of "ancient ruins."[57]

Cooper celebrates the particular landscape of her new nation by featuring its nontraditional ruins. Marking the distinction between Old World and New with an exclamation point, she exclaims, "How different from all this is the aspect of our own country!" This exclamation signals the start of the third section of Cooper's essay, in which she addresses the newness of her nation:

"[T]he fresh civilization of America is wholly different in aspect from that of the old world; there is no blending of the old and the new in this country; there is nothing old among us." The American landscape is bereft of ruins, but even if there were any, Americans would likely erase their presence in the name of progress: "If we were endowed with ruins we should not preserve them; they would be pulled down to make way for some novelty." This would reflect the fact that "we are the reverse of conservators in this country." The American way is to make room for the new.[58]

In this regard, Cooper criticizes her fellow Americans: the "civilization of the present" is "less dignified, and imposing in aspect. It would be comparatively an easy work to remove from the earth all traces of many of the peculiar merits of modern civilization." She gives several examples, all attesting to the elusive quality of the achievements of the age: light suspension bridges, railways, steam-powered ships, the telegraph, and the achievement of Daguerre in creating the daguerreotype. In contrast to earlier ages and Old World places, the present American era seems to delight in structures and achievements that are ephemeral: "look, in fact, at any of the peculiar and most remarkable of the works of the age, and see how speedily all traces of them could be removed." If a barbaric group of people were to try to destroy all traces of her civilization, Cooper argues, they could do so easily, leaving no "monuments of our period." Significantly, given the concern that she expresses in *Rural Hours* for nonnative, invasive plant species in her region, she speculates here that the only remaining presence on the New World landscape of Euro-American culture would be nonindigenous plants: "Perchance, as regards America, the chief proofs that eastern civilization had once passed over this country would then be found in the mingled vegetation, the trees, the plants, ay, the very weeds of the old world."[59]

Nonetheless, a benefit of the American tendency for development is that among its landscapes, "there is little territory which can be called really sterile." Even America's unshorn hillsides and dense forests "give it naturally a cheerful aspect." The adjectives that Cooper uses to describe American landscapes and architecture also emphasize her positive view of them: "cheerful," "pleasing," giving of "satisfaction," and providing a "general air of comfort and thrift." While American landscapes possess their own forms of beauty, they are beautiful nonetheless. Cooper therefore has redefined what makes a landscape beautiful. American nature is made beautiful not by marks of progress, such as ruins, but by its unique features.[60]

Upon establishing the unique attractiveness of the American landscape and the reasons for its dearth of ruins, Cooper returns in her essay to her position on the hillside "overlooking the country." Here in the fourth and final section of the essay, she plays "a sort of game of architectural consequences." She imagines the scene at her feet through the idealized picturesque lens, engaging in its passion for nature; she then quickly escapes her imagined vision, leaving behind that aesthetic for her preferred, uniquely American scene. Once again, she rejects the picturesque.[61]

Cooper's "game" begins as she waves a sprig of "wych-hazel"—associated with magic in folklore—over the valley at her feet and fantasizes a "razing" of the village. Its bridge, homes, and other village buildings disappear quickly, as if her witch-hazel-induced fantasy were the work of a barbaric race intent on erasing the Euro-American settlement from the region. She waves the sprig again, and the old-growth forest returns to the valley, "in the same stage of autumnal coloring with the woods" surrounding her. Another wave of the witch-hazel brings to the valley "a spectacle" indeed: a vision of the valley as it would look "had it lain in the track of European civilization during past ages." This transformation is so severe that "it required a close second scrutiny" to determine that the view now in sight was truly the same place now settled into a picturesque village—"every thing was so strangely altered."[62]

Cooper's "game of architectural consequences" is not unlike Cole's vision as expressed in *The Course of Empire*. There, Cole allows certain physical features of the land to appear in each painting, thus ensuring that the viewer realize that she is witnessing different versions of the same scene. Cole's high, rocky outcrop appears in each of the five paintings, and in all but *Consummation* and *Destruction* the same kinds of trees appear in the foreground. Just like Cole, Cooper fixes her gaze on geographical features to ensure that she is witness to the same location. As she sees the valley in its Old World guise, she determines "that all the natural features of the landscape remained precisely as we had always known them; not a curve in the outline of the lake was changed, not a knoll was misplaced." Familiar plants remain, and the autumnal woods retain their bright hues. Other than these similarities, however, "all resemblance ceased."[63]

First, Cooper notices that many of the hills "had been wholly shorn of wood." She then provides a detailed account of the "mere hamlet" that remains: its cottages; a central green sporting a large, stone cross; an inn; one old church; a few shops; a stone—as opposed to wooden—bridge; the ruins of a tower, and narrow roads lined with hedges in the English style. A country estate lies just outside of the village, and on its outskirts are a castle, a convent that has been converted to a farmhouse, the ruins of "feudal castles," and a "whispered" ancient Roman road that had once led to a villa on the site of the convent-farmhouse. In the distance are eight other hamlets, all within view. Cooper describes what seems to be a pleasant view, if one that is decidedly different from the view at her feet or those depicted by her painter contemporaries devoted to particularly American scenes.[64]

Then, as quickly as her fantasy game begins, it ends. A bee visits her witch-hazel sprig and stings her, awaking her to reality. The bee is not native to America, and to Cooper's imagination its presence signals the passage of time—and of the progress associated with Anglo-European settlement. The arrival of the bee as an end to imaginative musing was a familiar trope in American literature at this time: a bee's hum wakens William Cullen Bryant's speaker from his landscape reverie in "The Prairies," and, as Duncan Faherty notes, we encounter bees as signals of future domestication of wilder spaces in both Irving's *A Tour on the Prairies* and James Fenimore Cooper's *The Oak Openings*. At the close of her essay, Cooper drops the sprig (which now also carries the bee), and "the spell was over; the country had resumed its everyday aspect." Given the course of this essay, we can take Cooper at her word and assume that this last section of the essay is what she claims it to be: a game. Having discussed the New World landscape in relation to the Old, she simply launches into an imaginative redrawing of the land.[65]

But this is a game with a context: the picturesque aesthetic as represented by the Hudson River School painters. The picture that Cooper draws tells a different story of the land than the one they typically depicted on their canvases. Through her vision, we are witness to the Roman conquest, the history of religious conflict between Catholics and Protestants, and a highly stratified society. Her New World landscape tells a different story altogether. As she remarks in the middle of this piece, "there is not in those old countries a single natural feature of the earth upon which man has not set his seal," and her whimsical description of the European version of her valley bears this out. When she says upon first viewing the imagined scene that many hills were "wholly shorn of wood," we cannot hear these words as preferential, especially if we read them within the context of Cooper's other passionate discussions about deforestation.[66]

Indeed, her treatment of European ruins and their New World counterpart suggests the possibility of a new aesthetic, one based in New World landscapes and on the realities of the new nation's physical environment. After all, it is the European landscape that "dissolves" in the course of her game, giving way to the pastoral reality at her feet. Whereas Cole's *Course of Empire* moves from the savage state to an unpopulated, "destroyed" scene, in "A Dissolving View" Cooper takes readers from her rural countryside surroundings to the nation's prehistory, with its old-growth forests, and then to the imagined European scene, only to return again to the genuine vision before her. The reality of the scene at her feet bookends her fantasy visions of it, which "dissolve," impossible—and perhaps not preferable—as they are. While Cooper engages in the techniques of a landscape painter as she sprinkles her fantasy scene with ruins and other reminders of an Old World history, she takes care to emphasize that her creation of that vision is a game. To assume that course for the new nation is to erase its distinctions. As Calvin Luther Martin points out, "Human monuments" are often "a means of preempting the stories inherent" in the landscape. Cooper's essay indicates the need to recover those stories.[67]

"A Dissolving View" suggests that what should "dissolve" is a landscape aesthetic that, while producing beautiful art by American artists, imposes Old World expectations on the New World landscape and hurries "progress" toward a goal that, while no one says it, seems European in origin and outcome. Indeed, earlier in the essay we find Cooper chastising humanity for its tendency toward "rivaling the dignity and durability of the works of nature" through its monuments, columns, and arches, arguing instead for its inherent superior beauty. Here, she quietly endorses the primacy of the literal view that she does have, rather than the one that can be imagined through the picturesque.[68]

Finally, then, "A Dissolving View" engages the picturesque aesthetic in order to examine its applicability to the New World. The essay suggests that this aesthetic depends upon an understanding of landscape that is foreign to America—or on what Robert Abrams has called "a set of representational and discursive practices rooted in European interests, economic priorities, and cultural assumptions." The traditional elements of the picturesque landscape do not fit within Cooper's New World setting, and so she dissolves the scene before her. Cooper's essay takes us through a series of impositions onto the landscape—a trying on of alternatives, as it were: a wilderness scene, Europeanized nostalgia for a landscape with ruins, and, finally, the rural valley alive with autumn's colors. This aesthetic tour suggests that the moral and historical significance of the American landscape awaits representation. The new nation's lands require an aesthetic that attends to the reality of the land: its species, seasonal cycles, and history of change. Once again we find Cooper's passion for nature based in the real.[69]

As we have seen, Cooper's contemporaries in the picturesque held a different sort of passion for American nature. They represented landscapes as scenes evincing the good that accompanies progress. This meant that they frequently ignored the negative effects of the nation's development and silenced the history that predated European settlement of the area. In "A Dissolving View," Cooper called attention to this tendency toward erasure by imagining and then dismissing certain types of scenes in favor of the scene at her feet: the literal landscape. In this way, she championed a passion for nature based on attending to nature's variety.

Manifest Losses

In *Rural Hours*, Cooper had also carried on this revision to nature's meaning: she urged her contemporaries to dwell on both the evidences of natural history that one could witness in the landscape and the history of the Native peoples who had lived in these lands. As she demonstrates, consideration of these displaced peoples complicated an ethic of progress by forcing one to recognize the losses that Native Americans had incurred as a result of American development. Through *Rural Hours*, Cooper calls the attention of readers to what we now call the "prehistory" of the United States—that portion of history that precedes the written records of Europeans and that the popular picturesque vision silenced. Not only does she do this by invoking the natural history of landscapes; she also does so by prompting readers to dwell on the role that Native Americans have played in the country. Rather than contemplate a landscape as a testament to progress, as some of her contemporaries did, she contemplated a landscape as a testament to loss.

In devoting pages in her writings to the tendency of American history to silence the realities of Native American presence in the landscape, Cooper necessarily faces head-on the historical vision and popular legacy of her father's work. James Fenimore Cooper, after all, had popularized the story of the inevitable demise of Native peoples as a result of the European settlement of the North American continent. In the works of James Fenimore Cooper, the land is "pictured . . . as ready for life," as one scholar notes: the prehistory of the land "has ended." As Lee Clark Mitchell and Lucy Maddox expertly demonstrate, the stereotype of the noble savage who had "vanished" from eastern lands permeated nineteenth-century American culture, and at times we find Susan Cooper's language echoing this unfortunate stereotype. Yet despite the fact that she uses terminology that strikes modern-day readers as degrading, Cooper's writings about Native Americans suggest that she was sympathetic toward them and that she mourned their displacement in the name of white civilization.[70]

In several places, Cooper gives sustained attention to the sense of loss that she experiences as she considers their displacement from the land. In one particular passage in *Rural Hours*, we find Cooper seemingly endorsing the view of Natives that her father and Bryant had advocated even as she sympathizes with them. In the midst of an overview of the history of her particular valley, she writes:

> At length . . . the white man came to plant a home on this spot, and it was then the great change began; the axe and the saw, the forge and the wheel, were busy from dawn to dusk, cows and swine fed in thickets whence the wild beasts had fled, while the ox and the horse drew away in chains the fallen trunks of the forest. The tenants of the wilderness shrunk deeper within its bounds with every changing moon; the wild creatures fled away within the receding shades of the forest, and the red man followed on their track; his day of power was gone, his hour of pitiless revenge had passed, and the last echoes of the war-whoop were dying away forever among these hills, when the pale-faces laid their hearth-stones by the lake shore. The red man, who for thousands of years had been lord of the land, no longer treads the soil; he exists here only in uncertain memories, and in forgotten graves.

Here Cooper echoes the treatment of Native Americans popularized in her father's novels. Hearthstones replace tomahawks, and all seems well with the land.[71]

Elsewhere Cooper wrote more sensitively about the history of Native Americans. Between February and June 1886, she published thirteen articles in *Living Church* magazine conveying with care and sympathy the history of the missions to the Oneida peoples. In addition, we know from extant letters that Cooper intended to publish a book called *The Shield*, which she planned to be a fictionalized rendering of early Native American history. A letter from George P. Putnam to Cooper indicates plans to begin printing *The Shield*. While Putman issued prepublication notices for the volume, *The Shield* has not been found in either book or manuscript form. Nonetheless, these letters reveal Cooper's intention to devote her writings to Native American subjects. Ultimately, it seems that she represents the Native American presence on these lands differently than her father. This fundamental disagreement between father and daughter must have been difficult for Susan Cooper, as undoubtedly she felt a debt of gratitude toward her father that acknowledged more than his role as the mere facilitator of her publications.[72]

Cooper's references to Native Americans in *Rural Hours* take various forms. Sometimes she makes a passing comment about Indian traditions—

that maple sap was an important source of sugar to them, for instance, or that they ate passenger pigeons seasonally and hung gourds for the benefit of flocks of purple martins. She also wants readers to understand the importance of certain aspects of the physical environment to the Natives: they used the black ash for their baskets, ate many of the local mushrooms, used the feathers of the wood duck and porcupine quills for ceremonial purposes, and, she presumes, considered whortleberries precious eating.[73]

In several passages, Cooper educates her readers about the Natives of her particular area, sharing both her own encounters with Oneida peoples and information that she has gathered from others. On one particular summer day, she describes her past encounter with Native American basket makers, who moved through the village every now and again trying to sell their goods. She had received three basket sellers in her home and, later that afternoon, visited their encampment near the river. In this same entry, she recounts a visit of a larger group to her home and writes a brief essay on the obligations of American civilization to the Native peoples: "It is easy to wish these poor people well; but surely something more may justly be required of us—of those who have taken their country and their place on the earth." "But such is only the common course of things," she says as she closes her entry. Capitulating to the belief that the Natives will eventually benefit from Euro-American civilizing influences, Cooper closes her entry with the expected refrain: "they suffer from the vices of civilization before they learn justly to comprehend its merits."[74]

There is a real tension in Cooper's discussions of Native Americans that readers cannot ignore. On the same summer day that she recounts the visit of the basket makers, she records in a particularly powerful paragraph her contemporaries' ignorance about Native Americans:

> There are already many parts of this country where an Indian is never seen. There are thousands and hundreds of thousands of the white population who have never laid eyes upon a red man. But this ground lies within the former bounds of the Six Nations. . . . [W]hen it is remembered that the land over which they now wander as strangers, in the midst of an alien race, was so lately their own—the heritage of their fathers—it is impossible to behold them without a feeling of peculiar interest.

In part, Cooper's "peculiar" interest seems to center on educating her readers as much as possible about the "remnant of the great tribes" that remains in her area. But she seems equally intent on disrupting nationalistic assumptions by inviting readers to contemplate the morality of Native American displacement. In this passage she claims the lands on which she lives as "their own—the heritage of their fathers." Given that Cooper's own grandfather, William Cooper, had carved the village out of the wilderness, and that her own father had celebrated that pioneering spirit in his fictional works, Susan Cooper's willingness to attribute "the heritage of their fathers" to fathers other than her own is remarkable. She seems perfectly willing to cast doubt on her own right to occupy this ground.[75]

We find her unwillingness to endorse progress in other passages as well. For Thursday, May 30, Cooper writes about the natural springs in her area, which are "all full to overflowing" at this time of the year. After discussing their wide presence in the village and its surrounding fields and forests, as well as noting the typical properties of their waters (some are particularly sulfurous, others touched with limestone), she remarks on the pleasure of encountering springs on one's walks. On this particular day, she attests to coming across "more than a dozen distinct fountainheads within a distance of a mile." In the penultimate paragraph, she focuses on the pleasures of springs, and in particular on their "purity" and the humility with which they make their sounds in the landscape as their waters rise to the surface of the land: "There is a quiet beauty about them all which never fails to give pleasure. There is a grace in their purity—in their simplicity—which is soothing to the spirit; and, perhaps among earth's thousand voices, there is none other so sweetly humble, so lowly, yet so cheerful, as the voice of the gentle springs, passing on their way to fill our daily cup." Here, within the last two paragraphs of the day's entry, Cooper does a remarkable thing.[76]

After her tribute to the pure beauty of springs, she immediately offers a striking treatment of the subject of loss. While the entry up to this point could be seen as superficial in its appreciation of this form of natural beauty, here in the final paragraph, Cooper lends both moral and historic significance to her observations. She expresses her awareness that the "daily cup" of villagers and travelers who now enjoy the waters from the springs has replaced the daily cup of others who are now—and suddenly—removed from this place. She refers here to the Native Americans who once lived in much larger numbers in the region and also to the wild animals who have been displaced by the growing numbers of Euro-American inhabitants in the area. Her words are moving, in spite of her use of terms such as "savage" and "red man," which modern readers will find degrading:

> When standing beside these unfettered springs in the shady wood, one seems
> naturally to remember the red man; recollections of his vanished race linger

there in a more definite form than elsewhere; we feel assured that by every
fountain among these hills, the Indian brave, on the hunt or the war-path,
must have knelt ten thousand times, to slake his thirst, and the wild creatures,
alike his foes and his companions, the tawny panther, the clumsy bear, the
timid deer and the barking wolf, have all lapped these limpid waters during
the changing seasons of past ages.

Not content merely to admire the springs for their beauty and utility, Cooper
invests them with history. And she goes on to invest that history with moral
significance for her readers.[77]

She does this first by alerting Euro-American readers to their ignorance of
such springs. It is "quite possible," she says, that there "may still be springs
in remote spots among the hills of this region, yet untasted by the white
man and his flocks, where the savage and the beast of prey were the last who
drank." Through this sentence, she suggests that the recent settlers of the area
may not even *know* their home places; in making this suggestion, Cooper
implicitly questions whether they belong here and raises ethical concerns over
the various displacements that have resulted from American progress.[78]

However, she lends additional moral significance to her observations by
focusing on the issue of displaced history itself. Cooper describes the sounds
and sights that one imagines as one contemplates the springs: she envisions
a panther or deer advancing toward "the fountain at our feet," and hears the
rustle of leaves or breaking of a dry branch that might signal an approaching
"painted warrior." The springs, for her, function as a signal of former life in
this place—what Thoreau would call "Former Inhabitants" in *Walden*. As she
witnesses the springs, she recollects the many life forms that have lived in
their midst.

In fact, Cooper's entry suggests that the springs are inseparable from this
natural and human history. Her final sentence emphasizes this notion by insisting on the humanity of Native Americans while lamenting the lack of
evidence of their recent residence in these woods: "It was but yesterday that
such beings peopled the forest, *beings with as much of life as runs within our
own veins*, who drank their daily draught from the springs we now call our
own; yesterday they were here, today scarce a vestige of their existence can be
pointed out among us." In this one sentence, Cooper indicts her culture for
its presumed right to these lands, which were so recently home to a people
whose humanity—completely comparable to her own—is scarcely visible.
She also imbues the landscape with deep history and insists that her readers
recall losses as they pursue progress.[79]

The one sign of evidence that Cooper does see for the former prominence of other cultures in her area are the Native American names for things that remain scattered throughout the land. In a lengthy discussion of the need to name landmarks, towns, and natural features of the landscape, Cooper suggests retaining whenever possible Native American names. Language serves as a "monument" to the past, she claims. Native words are usually pleasant to the ear, she notes, but the real reason to use these original names is to keep alive the memory of the peoples to whom they attest. Again, she resists the subtle erasure of history by progress:

> There are many reasons for preserving every Indian name which can be ac-
> curately placed; generally, they are recommended by their beauty; but even
> when harsh in sound, they have still a claim to be kept up on account of
> their historical interest, and their connection with the dialects of the different
> tribes. A name is all we leave them, let us at least preserve that monument
> to their memory; as we travel through the country, and pass river after river,
> lake after lake, we may thus learn how many were the tribes who have melted
> away before us, whose very existence would have been utterly forgotten but
> for the word which recalls the name they once bore.

Although she employs the language of her day, which has reached the status of cliché in ours (the tribes have "melted away before us"), Cooper again insists on the importance of the landscape bearing testimony to its past. To the ear cognizant of origins, words can evoke history. The landscape bears few traces of displaced peoples, yet the language used to describe that land might. Again, Cooper's purpose is to convince her readers of a moral obligation to preserve the history of the landscape.[80]

But here we also witness her desire to attend to results of America's corrupting influences: "And possibly, when we note how many [tribes] have been swept away from the earth by the vices borrowed from civilized man, we may become more earnest, more zealous, in the endeavor to aid those who yet linger among us, in reaping the better fruits of Christian civilization." Referring, no doubt, to the debilitating effects of alcohol on Native Americans—effects now known to be exacerbated by different genetic tolerances of sugars—Cooper suggests her fellow countrymen's duty to help those peoples who remain. Modern day readers will likely experience a twinge of anger at Cooper's neglect to mention European disease, relocation, and outright murder as additional—in fact, the most potent—"vices" wrought by "civilized man" on Native Americans. Some readers will also find troubling Cooper's tendency to mingle the history of Native Americans with the history of nature, as if indigenous peoples are just another natural creature. Indeed, in her moving passages on forests, Cooper even seems to equate old growth trees with Native Americans by saying that the presence of one reminds her of the other. But for Cooper, both the "vanished savage race" and the "vanished" wild animals native to her home comprise the identity of her landscape. She is deeply troubled that the tendency in her day is to silence both the history of Native Americans and the history of the former animal inhabitants of her area amid a widespread celebration of progress. Against this popular vision, *Rural Hours* suggests through its overt pleas for preservation of native species and its reminders of the Native American history on the land that, increasingly, national progress is built upon significant loss. A passion for nature that overlooks this reality neglects the true history of the land itself—its displaced peoples, plants, and animals.[81]

We see Cooper pointedly questioning her nation's ethic of progress in *Rural Hours'* treatments of forests. In the passage from July 23, for example, Cooper suggests that a local stand of old-growth trees has historical value in that it serves as a reminder of a wilderness condition now passing away. After a moving description of a specific stand of old-growth trees and a consideration of how easily one human armed with an ax could fell them, Cooper suggests that even if the trees were replaced now with new trees that were allowed to grow indefinitely, the history that the old growth trees represent would be lost forever. The loss of wilderness is the loss of history. Changes in a landscape prevent people from realizing the history of that land:

> But allowing even that hundreds of years hence other trees were at length to succeed these with the same dignity of height and age, no other younger wood can ever claim the same connection as this, with a state of things now passed away forever; they cannot have that wild, stern character of the aged forest pines. This little town itself must fall to decay and ruin; its streets must become choked with bushes and brambles; the farms of the valley must be anew buried within the shades of a wilderness; the wild deer and the wolf, and the bear, must return from beyond the great lakes; the bones of the savage men buried under our feet must arise and move again in the chase, ere trees like those, with the spirit of the forest in every line, can stand on the same ground in wild dignity of form like those old pines now looking upon our homes.

Cooper enters the realm of preservationist rhetoric here, arguing eloquently that the old-growth trees should not be felled because they testify to a wilderness condition now altered forever. Cooper's thesis is not that the trees serve as a reminder of God's greatness, or even as a reminder of how quickly or remarkably human civilization has progressed. Rather, the passage paints a picture of the impossible, playing a "game" of "consequences" of the sort she plays in "A Dissolving View," imagining the forests swallowing up the fruits of the new nation in order to return to its wilderness condition. Of course, this is a vision that cannot be. Even if the thriving civilization growing in her valley should "fall to decay and ruin," there will remain "a state of things now passed away forever." But preserving this stand of trees amid her nation's ethic of progress will take hard work—work necessary, she argues, to preserving history.[82]

This passage, which again mentions in one breath Native Americans and wild animals, is clearly a lamentation for an irrevocably diminished quality of nature. Cooper's references to even the possibility of destroying the region's new civilization in order to bring back the state of native grace once found there suggests that she sees something troubling about the European colonization of this land, which has emphasized progress at the expense of natural history. She turns the landscape scene back on the viewer, forbidding an erasure of history. Nowhere does Cooper suggest that Europeans should not have settled America in the first place, but she recognizes that not only Native Americans have been colonized: so has the natural environment.

What is lost to progress is lost forever, and there can be no complete recovery of destroyed peoples or landscapes. Cooper wants her readers to recognize—and to feel—this loss to the land. She wants them to heed evidence of loss in the landscape, and to preserve evidences of that loss, which, she suggests, are valuable precisely because they testify to the rich history of these lands. Her passions for both nature and nation depend on this recognition and celebration of history.

Rewilding the Landscape

Cooper's emphasis on the literal history of the natural world and its peoples helps us recognize that the ethic of progress celebrated by her contemporaries led to a widely held passion for nature that depended on a metaphorical, abstract understanding of the physical world. As artists and writers expressed this passion for nature through painting and literature, they celebrated a vision that had little to do with the natural and human history of that landscape. By abstracting the land from its human and natural history contexts, artists and writers created a story for the land based on their hopes for the young nation. They fashioned this new narrative by figuring the natural environment as a manifestation of preordained history—as the site of assumed progress for human civilization. As Earl Powell puts it, the landscape came to serve "as a metaphor for the new country." More specifically, the landscape was a metaphor for the assumed, inevitable success of the new Euro-American democratic civilization now prospering on the North American continent. We see, then, that "manifest destiny" not only assumes as divinely sanctioned the progress of Euro-American civilization; it also abstracts history from an understanding of landscape.[83]

Through their insistent evocations of displaced peoples, flora, and fauna, Cooper's works incriminate what Robert Abrams has termed nineteenth-century America's "historical amnesia." People immersed in this particular passion for landscape did not see the "real" in nature. That is, they did not recognize the particularities of natural phenomena, natural history, or landscape history. Indeed, for many Americans, the landscape had become more *idea* than reality; as Angela Miller notes, "for many Americans, painted nature was more eloquent than the thing itself." Many Americans envisioned the natural world as a backdrop intended to accommodate and showcase the playing out of America's progress. The nation was well on its way to developing an identity that silenced Native American history and disregarded the flora and fauna of the new nation in favor of a blind endorsement of a future that was assumed to be good, right, and sanctified. While some nineteenth-century Americans certainly recognized the disturbing consequences of this ethic, the nation as a whole embraced it.[84]

Yet Cooper's particular passion for nature insisted on understanding the historical realities of specific landscapes. In her writings, she maintains that celebrating the New World landscape necessitates fully comprehending the history of the place and knowing intimately the natural history of an area. In characterizing her approach to landscapes, we might borrow a term from contemporary environmental historian James Feldman, who suggests that people can "re-wild" nature by telling stories about places that reinvest them with their true and full natural and human histories. Cooper "re-wilds" landscapes by inviting readers to consider "the natural and human reality" of places, as opposed to the "cultural myth that obscures much of what [Americans] most need to understand"—in this case, that the meaning of landscape does not lie in imported aesthetic expectations or in an erasure of history, but rather in the knowledge of the American landscape having "long been a place of human dwelling." Cooper does so by alerting readers to the reality of the indigenous presence on a land often depicted as empty or vacant before Euro-American settlement.[85]

Through her close attention to the land and its history, we might say that Cooper encourages what Daniel Philippon calls a "truly ecological" sense of identity: one that includes "both the individuality of particular organisms and the history of the communities of which they are a part." She seemed to recognize that an ecologically sensitive identity includes remembering "the species—and the people—that have lived here before," and she hopes "to preserve those that remain."[86]

To Cooper, it seemed as if most Americans walked around blindfolded, unaware of—and incapable of seeing—nature's astounding history and overwhelming variety. And if we are honest, we admit that her world is not far from ours. During her day, as in ours, powerful segments of the population spoke passionately on behalf of the nation's course, endorsing its erasure of natural and human history from the shared consciousness. They, like so many today, pursued a passion for nature that was a passion for progress; and they, like us, perpetuated the comforting falsehood that our nation's course, though perhaps regrettable, is excusable given our "progress" toward a clear, bright, right, enviable future.

Cooper's passion for nature's history revealed to her "the beautiful and wonderful realities of the world we live in." Some of these realities spoke of loss, and others spoke of wilderness conditions gone by. But all of nature's "realities" were important, she believed, to the nation's sense of itself. And they were certainly important to an understanding of the natural world. Instead of continuing their "walk blindfold through the fields" in pursuit of progress, Cooper's contemporaries might embrace her passion for nature's "realities"—those losses in natural and human history that were the result of America's unchecked progress.[87]

True, healthful refinement of head and heart becomes
more easy, more natural under the open sky and amid the
fresh breezes of country life.

SUSAN FENIMORE COOPER,
"Village Improvement Societies"

CHAPTER THREE

The Metaphor of Refinement

Andrew Jackson Downing and the

Moral Prescription for Landscape

MANY MID-NINETEENTH-CENTURY Americans believed that they
could prove America's virtues to the world by developing a refined, genteel
society. This pursuit of American refinement was reflected in many areas of
American life, as Richard Bushman's *The Refinement of America* attests. It also
influenced the nineteenth-century passion for nature, as a particular sort of
love for the land became a characteristic of refinement. In one manifestation of this passion for nature, people such as Ralph Waldo Emerson and
Susan Fenimore Cooper argued on behalf of "the country life," which they
felt was beneficial to the improvement of the individual, as opposed to the
corrosive, unrefined influences of the city. As Cooper once wrote, "There is
more of leisure for thought and culture and good feeling in the country than
amid the whirl of a great city." One might also demonstrate one's refinement
through gardening, horticulture, and landscape design—in sum, activities
that domesticated landscapes. Nature was understood to bear the imprint
of a refined humanity, and in this particular passion for nature the landscape
became a metaphor for refinement.[1]

We find initial evidence of the nineteenth-century association of nature appreciation with refinement in the columns of the May 1834 *New-York Farmer,
and American Gardener's Magazine*. This magazine was devoted to gardening
and agriculture, so not surprisingly it features articles with such titles as "To-
bacco for Ticks," "Lupines," and "On propagating the Purple Broccoli from

Slips, and on the Agency of Manure prepared from Sea Weed in improving various Vegetables." However, the magazine also contains articles on topics that bear little obvious relation to cultivating the soil. For instance, one called "The Enjoyment of Reading" discusses the civilizing function of reading—a subject that seems to have little connection to agriculture or gardening. Nonetheless, the hybrid quality of this periodical persists: placed between pieces titled "Tar on Sheep" and "Steam-Digging Machine" appears "Family Album," a brief note with suggestions for ensuring the development of morality in children. The presence of "The Enjoyment of Reading" and "Family Album" alongside articles on horticulture signals the relationship between nature appreciation and refinement in this period. Nature, in fact, served as the site of refinement, and its cultivation indicated the high moral status of its cultivator.

A closer look at "Family Album" helps us understand how readers of a gardening magazine would be concerned with refinement. This particular article, which is reprinted from (and attributed to) the *Portland Courier*, describes an open-topic essay assignment that an "excellent widowed lady of this city" gives to her children weekly: "A folio . . . is provided as a place of deposit, into which each member of the family is required to put once a week a piece of written composition, upon any subject that may suggest itself to the mind of the writer. Saturday evening the budget is opened and each piece read, criticized, and amended, in the presence of the family." The author goes on to recommend the activity to all families, declaring that "profligacy and low vice" are sure to be countered by the practice: "Give your children an early love for books, refine their taste by works of art, set them an example of religious excellence, of correct manners, and endeavor to make the domestic hearth always attractive, and you bar up all the great avenues to immorality." We readily recognize the article's concern with moral improvement: as the author of "Family Album" states, one goal of the family portfolio is to "refine [the children's] taste" in order to "bar up all the great avenues to immorality." In part, then, "Family Album" indicates the era's preoccupation with morality. In addition, however, this article's presence in a gardening magazine indicates that the era's concern with morality influenced interactions with the natural world. Good taste, it was assumed, would prevent immoral behavior, and discerning reading and informed gardening were the pursuits of a person with good taste. This meeting of agriculture and morality indicates the era's conjoining of nature and refinement.[2]

Clearly, in mid-nineteenth-century America, tending to the natural world and improving Americans' moral stature were concerns held by members of the same readership. Individuals with the financial resources and leisure time necessary for subscribing to and reading publications devoted to horticulture were likely also middle- to upper-class Americans intent on cultivating the morality of the nation's citizens. This population deemed intellectual activity, attractive landscapes, and informed gardening to be characteristics of gentility. These are the individuals whom Sarah Burns, a scholar of nineteenth-century American rural life, characterizes as "the power elite of the [increasingly] industrialized United States, the culture consumers who maintained or struggled to maintain, cultural dominance in a changing society."[3]

Like *New-York Farmer*'s editors, Susan Fenimore Cooper likely thought that articles on gardening practices, agricultural procedures, and moral cultivation were pursuing a shared goal—one that we might describe as "the refinement of America," to borrow Bushman's phrase. Through several of her own writings on nature and moral improvement, Cooper contributed to the large cultural project of improving America and participated in the ideological linkage of the cultivation of nature with refinement.[4]

We can see Cooper's contribution clearly in two particular essays. Amid her career-long work as a writer devoted to natural subjects, she published a seemingly aberrant essay called "The Talent of Reading Wisely." This piece recommends choosing one's reading material based on its potential for moral uplift, "shunn[ing] for conscience sake" those titles with questionable content. As Cooper writes, "[T]he passion for common fiction may become almost as dangerous as dram-drinking." (To drink a dram was to imbibe one-eighth fluid ounce of spirits. A dram-drinker was one addicted to this practice.) We also find Cooper's concern for moral uprightness in her 1869 essay, "Village Improvement Societies," which urges each rural American village to appoint a committee to oversee the architectural and landscape designs of its community. While the purpose of each Village Improvement Society is to ensure aesthetically pleasing surroundings, any reader of Cooper's essay quickly discerns her belief that a beautiful village signifies a morally upright citizenry. She aims to improve "the physical, moral, and intellectual good of the people" by shaping their immediate physical surroundings. According to Cooper, careful reading selections can bolster one's moral integrity, and tasteful villages can serve as a testament to American civility and refinement. Through these publications and others, Cooper reveals her endorsement of her society's tendency to conjoin an interest in nature with America's moral refinement.[5]

In addition to leading people to associate nature with morality, the widespread nineteenth-century faith in the restorative powers of the natural world took another potent form in the early decades of the century: the popular landscape design movement. This was a movement that would assume that nature's meaning lay in its ability to display human refinement, and it would attract figures such as Ralph Waldo Emerson and Cooper, as well as many other Americans of means. This mid-nineteenth-century landscape design movement was most forcefully led by Andrew Jackson Downing, who undertook a virtual campaign to beautify the rural Northeast through horticulture—the cultivation of fruits, vegetables, and ornamental plants. Through his books and his popular magazine, *The Horticulturist and Journal of Rural Art and Rural Taste*, Downing provided designs for homes and their surrounding landscapes that people might adopt, implement, and benefit from. These designs were understood to be related to the refinement of the American people. As Tamara Plakins Thornton explains, Downing was "convinced that the practice of horticulture would save America from materialism, restlessness, even intemperance, dangers that obsessed Americans of the antebellum era." Indeed, the trendy landscape movement of the period assumed that the area surrounding one's home signaled the state of one's morality. In droves, people sought to follow Downing's landscaping advice and home designs so that they might demonstrate their gentility.[6]

For Americans who cared about what others thought of them or who wanted to be assured of their own morality, the stakes were high. Bushman puts it this way: "All who aspired to simple respectability had to embody the marks of the genteel style in their persons and their houses." If one's garden did not look a certain way, then one's level of refinement was in question. Similarly, many believed that the area surrounding one's home should adhere to certain criteria in its outward form so that it could serve as a testament to one's refined taste. By making changes on the outside, such as exercising certain decisions about architecture, landscape design, or even home decor, people could demonstrate their high moral states. They worked, then, from the outside in, even as they worked from the inside out: they shaped their outer environments to reflect their inner tastes, and they demonstrated their tastes by shaping their environments. If it seems as though the logic underlying this landscape design movement is circular, that's because it was. The physical landscape reflected one's refinement, and one's refinement led one to shape the physical environment.[7]

The role that the natural world played in this formulation was complex, but clearly Americans were telling themselves a particular story about nature as they shaped their surroundings so that they might indicate their refinement. The particular details of that story, however, require some elaboration. At first glance, it might seem that the landscape design movement necessitated a faith in nature's inherent goodness and that at the base of this story was an assumption of nature's value. After all, assuming nature's refining powers would seem to entail valuing nature inherently. But under Downing, the story did not go this way at all. Rather than assuming the moralizing force of "natural" nature, midcentury Americans in pursuit of Downing's ideal grew increasingly convinced that it was necessary to shape their surroundings in order to demonstrate nature's highest moralizing potential. Through gardening or shaping the land in a certain way, an individual could reveal nature in its refined form. In other words, this story of nature assumed that nature needed the help of humanity. And, somewhat paradoxically, it needed this help in order to attest to the best in humanity. Nature served as a metaphor for refinement in that landscapes were seen as embodying certain qualities. The power of Downing's landscape design movement was its suggestion that natural phenomena must be shaped in certain ways in order to display this refinement. In a sense, then, passion for nature was passion for refinement.

In the popular landscape design movement of the nineteenth century, what was at issue was the sophistication of Americans—and of America. In a word, Americans were concerned with "taste." In fact, we can safely say that the middle decades of the nineteenth century were years when a particular group of influential Americans was consumed by thoughts of their own good taste. Perhaps because they were aware of their nation as young, inexperienced, and uncertain of its identity, people devoted considerable time, energy, and words to convincing others of how to demonstrate their high moral status, their intellectual accomplishment, and their civilized ways.

To understand Downing's popularity fully, one must also understand the philosophy upon which he based his program, since his success reflected not only the force with which he undertook his campaign for refinement but also the readiness of Americans to heed his urgings. Downing's influence was powerful because his followers understood his prescriptions for improving the American landscape as part of an effort to develop the good taste of Americans. This interest in taste was far-reaching in Downing's day. When the term "taste" was used during this period, its meaning and power were understood by most educated Americans to be rooted in a specific set of ideas that had been popularized by the Scottish "common sense" philosophers, and in particular by Archibald Alison. Alison's *Essays on the Nature and Principles of Taste*, which was originally published in 1790 in Europe, was enormously popular in the United States and appeared in several Americans editions in the early decades of the nineteenth century.[8]

The details of Alison's theory of taste are elaborate and compelling, but most important for our purposes is the fact that his entire philosophical enterprise rests upon the assumption of nature's symbolic meaning. Specifically, Alison's theory was rooted in his belief that natural phenomena do not have meaning in and of themselves but gain significance as humans attach thoughts to them. Good taste does not depend upon perceiving nature's inherent beauty or value; rather, it depends upon assigning symbolic value to phenomena. An object in nature, for example, is beautiful or valuable not in and of itself but because of the ability of an individual to ascribe it with meanings based in human experience. To exercise one's good taste with regard to nature, then, means for Alison to interpret nature as symbolic of some aspect of the human state.

Clearly, Susan Cooper was not exempt from the interest in refinement shared by so many of her contemporaries in the Northeast: her writings indicate that she held to certain elements of the passion for nature as a sign of refinement. In particular, her writings show us her belief in the possibilities of landscape to serve metaphorically as a signal for human refinement. In addition to publishing her essay on the importance of outwardly shaping a village so as to demonstrate the inward goodness of its inhabitants, she also writes in *Rural Hours* about architectural styles that signal the influence of Downing. More generally, in *Rural Hours* she models a certain type of genteel relationship with the natural world, as scholars have shown. For Cooper, as for so many other Americans of her day, nature functioned as a metaphor for her own good taste, and a landscape shaped in certain ways could attest to a highly refined society.[9]

However, Cooper's writings also point to some of the limitations of this prevalent understanding of nature's meaning. They challenge the idea that the natural world is better off when shaped by humanity. In addition, they struggle with an assumption that is foundational to Downing's thought—one central to the theory of Alison that underlay Downing's program: that matter is symbolic of humanity. Cooper's writings grapple with the metaphorical story of nature assumed by the popular landscape philosophy of her day. The assumption of nature's symbolic value inhibits Cooper's growing sense that meaning resides in natural phenomena themselves rather than merely in the associations that a human being brings to them. Once again, Cooper's works demand that we explore her society's view of nature's meaning.[10]

Archibald Alison's Moral Prescription for Nature

By 1845 the editor of the *Knickerbocker* magazine could be so certain of his readers' familiarity with Archibald Alison's work that he would remark, upon receiving yet another edition of the popular *Essays*, that it was "a work too well known to require comment." Indeed, Alison's book had shaped discussions of taste in much of the Western world: by the mid-nineteenth century, several editions of his book had appeared in the United States, and his theories grew so popular that his notion of taste became a commonplace. Andrew Jackson Downing's landscape design program would be based on Alison's theories, as would several other major cultural productions—including, to some degree, the writing of Susan Fenimore Cooper. As Donald Ringe states, "the influence of [Alison's] ideas is everywhere apparent in the prose and verse of the period," and several scholars have explored the ways in which Alison's theory is foundational to an understanding of this era.[11]

While several people have discussed the influence of Alisonian theory on even the most prominent of writers and artists, few have explored the role that his thinking plays in terms of mid-nineteenth-century understandings of the natural world. But in this regard, Alison's vision proved powerful indeed. Through a consideration of Alisonian theory, we are able to witness the process by which a widely held understanding of the natural world is based on assumptions concerning human taste. Alison popularized an aesthetic that proclaims a human-centered vision of natural phenomena as not just preferred—and not even just as the mark of a refined person—but as the basis of a moral individual. Through his *Essays*, Alison sanctioned a certain way of knowing nature as integral to being a moral person. This would have powerful implications for the American understanding of nature.[12]

Important to understanding Alison's theory is familiarity with several of his key terms—"taste" being, perhaps, the most important one. "Taste," according to Alison, relates to the perception of beauty in the world around us. What "taste" is, exactly, is the human aptitude for discerning that beauty. In other words, "taste" is the capacity of the human intellect to detect and delight in the beautiful.

Because human beings are fairly comfortable finding beauty in their surroundings, one might expect Alison's theory to be fairly straightforward. Indeed, Alison notes that beauty may be discerned everywhere and "in almost every class of the objects of human knowledge," making it seem as though exercising taste would be a very common occurrence for humans. But just what *is* beautiful, according to Alisonian theory, is not as obvious as we might think it would be, and just what happens when we experience "taste" is also surprising. This is largely because beauty, in Alison's estimation, is not inherent in things themselves. Rather, beauty adheres to what we bring to things through thought. In other words, we make things beautiful by bringing our thoughts to our viewing of those things.[13]

Alison calls this process of bringing thought to things "association," another term that is central to his *Essays* and to popular discourse in the nineteenth century. According to Alison, "association" is the mechanism by which we assign beauty to things, and we do so by means of our imaginations, which play a crucial role in Alisonian theory. Through imagination, we "associate" the thing in view with "a train of thought." This term "train of thought" is, like the term "association," central to Alison's rhetoric and appears in many forms in nineteenth-century writings. The "train of thought" is distinct from the sight that we see, although inspired by it; it works by "resemblance," whereby the object we see resembles some aspect of human experience or inspires impressions in our minds that "correspond" with other thoughts, and so we connect a "resembling thought" to the object, and then the train, as it were, takes off. Resembling thought leads to resembling thought until, finally, the train of thought *itself* is beautiful and leads us to feel the pleasure that is taste.

For example, I may see a calm lake surrounded by evergreen trees. I may "associate" this scene with my pleasant childhood experiences of spending the summer months at a similar lake in New England. My association of this lake with that of my childhood may lead me to a train of thought in which I contemplate the beauty of the scene, and then the beauty of my childhood, and then the beauty of childhood innocence, and, ultimately, the beauty of innocence itself. According to Alison, I am experiencing "taste." The "train of thought" is the series of "associations," and through the process of association we are enabled to recognize beauty, ascribe it to whatever we see, and thereby experience "taste."[14]

This seems relatively straightforward, and most of Alison's readers would likely feel confident that they were capable of experiencing taste and being a refined individual. However, Alison complicates the accessibility of refinement when he suggests that while all humans are capable of experiencing taste, not all will. Most frightening is the fact that people who think they have good taste may be fooling themselves. First, Alison explains that the capacity to experience taste is a "faculty of the human mind," an aptitude of each individual. Significantly, though, not just any train of thought will lead us to experience taste; rather, we have to be careful about keeping our minds in the right state so that we are capable of experiencing pure, or true, taste. As Alison explains it, we need to be in the right state of mind to discover beauty and experience taste: the "disposition" that we bring to our observations will affect whether we experience beauty correctly. Although the ability to experience taste is inherent in the human condition, one's ability or propensity to experience this feeling needs to be nurtured throughout one's life. And not nurturing one's ability may lead one to have false associations—trains of thoughts that seem to promise beauty but that, in fact, do not.[15]

As one proceeds into even the earliest pages of Alison's treatise, one cannot help but recognize that certain "emotions of taste" are proper while others are not. For instance, Alison warns that one must distinguish passing fashion—"the accidental prejudices of his age"—from "the uniform constitution of the human mind," or those commonly shared, most genuine, pure criteria that he assumes inspire taste. This distinction is especially crucial to the artist, who seeks to inspire true beauty and not merely a beauty that is deemed fashionable by a passing fancy of certain people. The distinction between passing fashion and genuine beauty is also important to the critic, upon whom the reading public depends to categorize art and literature as either truly artful or as merely trendy.[16]

This sense that certain associations are proper while others are not becomes very important to the American passion for nature as refinement. When we explore this aspect of Alison's theory, we come to understand that its assumption of nature's "truth" is frighteningly wrapped up in notions of refinement. What this will mean is that nature must be seen in certain ways to be experienced in a "refined"—or culturally sanctioned—way. In a sense, this theory regulates understandings of nature by deeming certain responses to it as appropriate, moral, and genteel. That nature's meaning relates to human gentility becomes especially disconcerting when we realize that Alison saw this gentility as itself natural. In fact, for Alison our proper responses to nature are assumed to be a natural human emotion in need of cultivation.

The possibility of experiencing taste correctly is further complicated when Alison makes the ability to associate properly dependent upon "the character of [one's] imagination": "The nature of any person's taste is, in common life, generally determined from the nature or character of his imagination, and the expression of any deficiency in this power of mind, is considered as synonymous with the expression of a similar deficiency in point of taste." Thus, a "deficient" sense of taste is due to a deficient imagination—an imagination that forms, we presume, faulty associations and therefore attributes beauty to things based on problematic trains of thought. We are now in danger of following a faulty train of thought not simply because we get off to a bad start but because our imaginations are flawed.[17]

The implications of a flawed imagination become clear if we consider the relationship between this imaginative capacity and "morality," as this term figures in Alison's theory. What we find is that a deficient imagination—or, an inability to experience taste—has to do with our moral capacity, or, as Alison would put it, our ability to *feel* properly. His theory explains "feelings" by means of positing—and this is perhaps the most interesting aspect of Alison's theory—that "taste" is an "emotion." As Alison explains it, when one recognizes beauty in something, "[t]he perception of these qualities is attended with an emotion of pleasure, very distinguishable from every other pleasure of our nature." As the individual discerns beauty, one feels a pleasure that is taste. This particular emotion—"the emotion of taste"—is an especially important emotion, Alison explains, because it shifts the mind from contemplation of the material world to the realm of the mind (or what Emerson will call the realm of "reason," as we will see in the following chapter). In Alison's words, the emotion of taste is a "superior and more complex emotion" than all others of which humans are capable, precisely because the "qualities that produce" the emotion of taste "serve to exalt the human mind, from corporeal to intellectual pursuits."[18]

Put differently, humans experience a certain pleasure in perceiving beauty, and as we perceive that beauty (and, therefore, feel the emotion of taste), our minds are "exalted," or engaged in an elevated pursuit. For Alison, taste enables us to transcend the merely material and enter the realm of thought. As I contemplate that lake that evokes my childhood summers, for example, my mind is elevated by my ultimate contemplation of the beauty of innocence. This pursuit of an idea—of something "higher" than the mere lake itself—is what makes the exercise of taste the mark of a particularly moral individual. It is also what makes Alison's theory particularly interesting to consider in its attitude toward nature, because it makes attention to nature a moral matter.

Through his elaborate theory, Alison makes the contemplation of nature a matter of morality by linking intellectual capacity with emotional health, and good taste with morality. If an individual considers him- or herself to be an intelligent, moral person, then he or she will have to value trains of association and abstract ideas over the physical world of nature. As Alison phrases it, taste is a matter of "moral affection," so if one cannot experience taste correctly, then one is not merely imaginatively impaired; one is also morally corrupt. In the mid-nineteenth century, being morally corrupt was not an option for anyone who hoped to be a respectable individual. The only choice one had was to value the abstract over the material. For anyone seeking acceptance in genteel culture, a passion for nature was, of necessity, a passion for refinement.[19]

Because Alison's theory demanded a narrow set of responses to the physical world, people seeking to exercise their good taste would need guidance toward those proper responses. Hence the need for Alison's book, which provides readers with virtual prescriptions that they can follow in their efforts to cultivate taste. Alison structures his book so as to help readers experience taste: for instance, its second "Essay" discusses how beauty is manifest through certain sounds, sights, colors, motions, forms, and shapes. Here the reader is instructed on which sounds should be associated with which thoughts, thereby interpreted as beautiful and, hence, productive of the emotion of taste. In a sense, then, his book serves as an instruction manual, suggesting which phenomena should garner which trains of association. By extension, the book also provides a framework for experiencing nature. As Gregg Camfield explains, through Alison's philosophy "human beings can objectify their reactions to the external world by comparing them with the reactions of others." By adhering to his formulas for association, one could rest assured and pursue taste in the correct, sanctioned manner. When viewing anything—be it a landscape, a flower, or even a human face—people could find beauty and "feel" taste when they were able to discover through their imaginations common trains of thought.[20]

Alison provides several frameworks of understanding that we can safely apply to whatever we see. We may experience the association of an object with the "beneficence of the Divine artist," or we may associate the object with some aspect of our own mind, including a past experience, a resemblance to some past event or social occurrence or to some memory especially dear to us. One mid-nineteenth-century writer, in urging associations with the divine, explained, "Human taste is a creation of GOD, and that taste finds its objects in the kindred works of GOD; that mind therefore which is in harmony with nature, dwells in the Divine idea." Whether associating phenomena with the deity or with some specific aspect of human existence, the objects we view must be seen to be "signs" or "expressions" of "mental qualities." (We can consider religious thought one such "quality.") As Alison states, association is most successful when it follows "analogies with the life of man."[21]

According to Alison, this process was one of science, not simply one of art or philosophy: he offered his readers a theory that promised a scientific understanding of refined individuals. Indeed, Alison referred to his theory as a contribution to "the science of mind," that field of study devoted to discerning the inner workings of the human intellect. Through his insistence on "moral affection" as science, Alison establishes his theory as a contribution to understanding humanity. To be a good, refined human was to associate one's way toward morality.[22]

Considering that Alison's notion of taste takes as a starting point the perception of a material thing or phenomenon, the natural world matters surprisingly little in his philosophy. However, his theory had a profound effect on the truth that Americans would assume for nature. Most significant to our purposes is the fact that the contemplation of the visible realm gains prominence as that contemplation leaves behind the material in pursuit of the cerebral or "intellectual" realm. Clearly, then, what is important to Alison's doctrine is not the physicality of the object, sight, or occasion that inspires taste; there is, in fact, little meaning in this physicality. He states outright that the delight one feels when experiencing taste is "very little dependent upon the object which excites it." Rather, what is important is the ability of the human mind to invest an object—or landscape, occurrence, or person—with meaning. The truth of nature, then, does not reside in its physicality, but lies in the human capacity for association.[23]

At the root of association is metaphor—a belief in the potential of the natural world to serve as a sign of some aspect of humanity. As Alison says, "[T]he qualities of matter are not beautiful . . . in themselves, but as they are, by various means, the signs or expressions of qualities capable of producing emotion." In other words, matter is symbolic of human emotion. It is not a flower in itself that is beautiful but rather "the signs or expressions of qualities" of the flower that encourage emotion in us by reminding us—through association—of something that makes us feel pleasure. We then invest the flower with beauty.[24]

This attribution of beauty to natural phenomena is especially crucial to the environmental implications of Alison's philosophy, because it prevents the possibility of finding intrinsic value in nature. It does so by attributing little meaning to natural phenomena apart from those human meanings that we should associate with those phenomena. At that moment, for instance, when we see the flower as beautiful—the moment, that is, of discovering the human-based association spurred by that flower—we invest the flower with meaning. And that meaning is, obviously, human centered, having little to do with the identity, structure, or function of the flower in terms of the *natural* world. The material world has meaning, according to this theory of taste, only when we can associate physical objects with something that causes us to think about ourselves.[25]

In this theory of taste, then, the material world has little meaning apart from serving as the means by which humans can reflect on themselves, their experience, or their God. As Alison puts it, "the qualities of matter" are most useful to us in terms of the degree to which they are "expressive to us of all the qualities of mind they signify." Association demands a leap of the imagination away from the material world.[26]

This convergence of taste, intellect, emotion, and morality is a potent force in the mid-nineteenth-century story of nature. Indeed, Alison's terms are present in a variety of forms in the discourse of the mid-nineteenth century, much of which assumes that the value of the natural world lies in its associative properties. As Camfield recently noted, "Alison gave America its most cogent and most popular exposition of aesthetics." And this was an aesthetics based on finding a common ground for responses to external phenomena. Indeed, Alison is considered a "common sense" philosopher because he, like the other Scottish common sense philosophers, advocated a sense "common" to all: the "moral" sense. This sense was "common" in that it was available to all humans, but Alison believed that it was exercised by only a few. Experiencing taste was therefore the mark of an elite segment of humanity—the most moral of human beings.[27]

Under Alison's philosophy, therefore, the aesthetic experience is to a large degree regulated, or at least agreed upon, by the members of a certain group of people who are concerned with taste. This aspect of Alison's work also informed nineteenth-century America's fascination with sentimentalism, a topic of great interest to both literary writers and other would-be arbiters of public emotion. Writers such as Harriet Beecher Stowe and Sarah Hale hoped to direct Americans' expressions of feeling so that they adhered to certain standards that the artistic and literary elite deemed proper. Within such discourse communities, individuals could check their associations against those of others, making certain that their responses are common and, therefore, true or moral. Through his powerful construction, Alison created what Elizabeth Maddock Dillon has called "a community of taste"—a version of beauty that is shared and perpetuated by a group of people. The value of nature became a part of this cultural practice. Natural phenomena are valuable to the degree that they inspire "analogies with the life of man." In order to be a moral person, one had to view nature in prescribed ways—ways demanding that nature be valued in terms of humanity. This means that in order to be a moral, refined individual one had to abstract nature, wrenching its meaning from its physicality and locating it, instead, in the human mind. Under Archibald Alison's theory of taste, nature had become a metaphor for the refined human mind.[28]

Somewhat paradoxically—given his emphasis on "reverie" as opposed to close observation—Alison's theory of taste left much work to be done by artists and writers. These creative figures could help cultivate taste in others by crafting scenes suitable to the experience of taste. This meant crafting scenes that inspired thoughts about humankind: as Camfield explains, "Alison tells the artist not to copy the essences of external reality but rather to copy the essences of human subjectivity." This was because, as Camfield puts it, "[n]ature to Alison merely symbolizes these internal states, and, therefore, an artist tries in copying nature merely to copy the symbolic representations of human characteristics." Artists and writers were doing their most valuable work when they created visions of humanity.[29]

Artists might create these visions of humanity-in-nature in several ways. Making historical associations in one's art was an especially effective way of meeting Alison's prescription for the artist. Since the picturesque aesthetic drew upon historical landmarks as a means of indicating the powers of humanity to shape a place, it became a popular means of expressing Alisonian associations. In the *Columbian Magazine* of 1844, a brief essay accompanies an engraving of an idyllic scene featuring a rock outcrop adorned with a classical building towering over rowers who are enjoying the view. This "View near Coldspring," readers are instructed, "should fill the mind and heart" with specific sorts of thoughts, "suggesting to one thoughts of praise and adoration." As Alison had explained in his *Essays*, by placing an ancient building or an "old tower in the middle of a deep wood, a bridge flung across a chasm between rocks, or a cottage on a precipice," an artist could inspire thoughts relevant to the human condition. The tasteful observer would be sure to associate the view with appropriate, human-centered ideas. A view of a sunset could also suffice, because it could inspire thoughts of the passage of time and the fragility of human life. Alison's theory thus elevated the artist to the position of being an arbiter of taste. Through his works, the artist might cultivate the morality of his viewers.[30]

The popularity of this pursuit of good taste manifests itself in the rhetoric of the magazines of the day, in large, coffee-table-style books featuring pictures of civilizing landscapes, and in written descriptions by those successfully living the genteel, rural life. For example, by merging art with the book form, Nathaniel Parker Willis participated in celebrating the Alisonian approach to landscape art: in 1840 he published his anthology of steel plate engravings,

FIGURE 6. W. L. Ormsby's "View near Coldspring." *Columbian Magazine*, July 1844. Courtesy of the Rare Book, Manuscript, and Special Collections Library, Duke University.

American Scenery; or, Land, Lake, and River. The introduction to that lavishly illustrated book openly states that the volume's focus on picturesque scenes stems from the fact that "[t]he picturesque views of the United States suggest *a train of thought*" that is unique and important, and that allows the viewer to "[rid] himself, as far as possible" from lesser "*associations.*" Clearly, Willis provided these beautiful scenes to readers so that they might practice their ability to follow the proper trains of thought and associations, prescribed by Alisonian theory.[31]

There was therefore a "pedagogical quality" to Alison's aesthetic, as Dillon terms it: one could learn to perceive beauty in the manner that he suggests while bolstering the general level of refinement in one's community by providing opportunities for others to exercise their taste. Taste could "be taught as a means of creating a moral community." As one mid-nineteenth-century American said, "The moral good of the community requires the cultivation of the public taste," and "advantage can be taken of the law of association." Many people joined in and became instructors of taste, avidly pursuing nature's abstract associations. One consequence of this was the simultaneous, if inadvertent, obscuring of the material world of nature that accompanied association. Natural phenomena became valued and meaningful not in and of themselves but as means to "taste." As people pursued a passion for nature within this philosophical system, they pursued not close knowledge or observation of nature but their own capacities for refinement.[32]

Association and Cooper's "Simple Truths"

Susan Fenimore Cooper's relationship to association becomes clearer when we consider its tremendous popularity at the time when she was writing. We can see association informing discussions of nature in several mid-nineteenth-century popular magazines. There are two basic ways in which the magazines demonstrate the popularity and pervasiveness of Alisonian theory. On the one hand, nature is understood to be a moral, refining force—a general premise of Alison's thinking. On the other hand, natural phenomena is associated with specific feelings—specific examples of proper trains of thought.

In nineteenth-century periodicals, botanical study in particular is seen as an avenue for association and, therefore, moral refinement. As H. T. Tuckerman wrote for *Godey's Lady's Book* in 1850, the study of flowers could lead one to thoughts of the human condition. One might contemplate flowers and make associations with the gratitude one should feel at being given life; or one might recognize the resemblance between the short life of a flower and the brevity of human life: "These two ideas—that of the gratuitous offering of nature in the advent of flowers . . . and the thought of their brief duration—invest flowers with a moral significance that renders their beauty more touching and, as it were, nearer to humanity, than any other species of material liveliness." Tuckerman demonstrates to his readers the associations that they might make between flowers and themselves: "Flowers are related to all the offices and relations of human life."[33] Again, we find that nature serves as a means of human refinement.

Similarly, another writer for *Godey's*, Margaret Cooke, encouraged parents to teach their children about flowers as a means of guaranteeing their "moral culture." An education in flowers could help the children learn to associate the flowers with religion: "these fair blossoms are but the embodying of ideas which originated in the mind of God." Even the title of Cooke's piece demonstrates the degree to which botanical study was associated with moral development: "Floral Lessons in Morals." Clearly, a specific knowledge of natural phenomena was not at issue here; an education in "morals" was.[34]

A brief review of periodicals from the mid-nineteenth century also attests to the popularity of certain associations. For example, people routinely associated autumn with melancholy. This particular association comes right out of Alison's pages. As an example of a common association of natural phenomena with "the life of man," Alison had mentioned in his *Essays* that contemplating an autumnal scene led one to experience taste by associating the scene with melancholy. He likely drew this association from the many literary accounts that had presented the season as gloomy—perhaps the same texts that Cooper would turn to as she, in *Rural Hours*, recounted literary representations of that season.[35]

We commonly find this association in mid-nineteenth-century magazines. One contributor to the *American Agriculturist* began a somber essay on autumn with these depressing statements: "Nothing more insensibly saddens and affects the heart, than the first impression made on us by the gradual approach of the fall of the year. A tinge of melancholy is abroad over the landscape." Similarly, in an issue of *Knickerbocker* in 1845, a poem called "November" by one A. M. Ide Jr., laments autumn as a gloomy season and associates it with the "autumn" of human life. Later in the year, that same periodical features W. T. B.'s "The Coming of Autumn," which likewise represents the season as melancholy and woefully claims, "O, life, it is tearful!" And in 1848 "Corolla" offered a poem called "Autumn Musings" to the readers of *Godey's Lady's Book*; autumn there is a season "of the earth['s] decay," reminding one that "we/Like all the rest, must pass away!" From these accounts, it is surprising that nineteenth-century Americans did not commit mass suicide on September 21. Clearly they associated autumn with the gloomy fact of human mortality.[36]

Throughout *Rural Hours*, Cooper reacts to particular popular associations and to the common emphasis on nature's refining force at the expense of close observation of nature. In one instance, she experiences disappointment upon realizing how few children in her area know the names for specific plants. While this is discouraging news, more disconcerting still is the comparable ignorance of adults: "their elders are generally quite as ignorant as themselves in this way." Even rural dwellers seem shockingly ignorant of the plants that they come upon in their daily lives:

> It is really surprising how little the country people know on such subjects. Farmers and their wives, who have lived a long life in the fields, can tell you nothing on these matters. The men are even at fault among the trees on their own farms, if these are at all out of the common way; and as for the smaller native plants, they know less about them than Buck or Brindle, their own oxen. Like the children, they sometimes pick a pretty flower to bring home, but they have no name for it. The women have some little acquaintance with herbs and simples, but even in such cases they frequently make strange mistakes; they also are attracted by the wild flowers; they gather them, perhaps, but they cannot name them. And yet, this is a day when flower borders are seen before every door, and every young girl can chatter largely about "bouquets," and the "Language of Flowers" to boot.

While the language of flowers may have dominated cultural discourse, a knowledge of which plants grew in one's immediate surroundings did not.[37]

In another instance, we find Cooper taking issue with the common association of autumn with melancholy—an association that, in her view, obscured the reality of nature's seasons. Her literary treatment of autumn in *Rural Hours* suggests that she wished to displace the conventional association of autumn with one based more squarely in the vibrant natural phenomena of the season. She wished that people would find a meaning for autumn through observation rather than association: "Some persons occasionally complain that this period of the year, this brilliant change in the foliage, causes melancholy feelings, arousing sad and sorrowful ideas, like the flush on the hectic cheek. But surely its more natural meaning is of a very different import." Quite to the contrary of the traditional association of autumn with melancholy, Cooper finds autumn vibrant, exciting, and beautiful. And, she happily reports, some of her contemporaries had also changed their tune about autumn. The basis for her assessment, however, was neither literary history nor the tradition of associations with the season; rather, she based her judgment on her own close observations. She notices the "[m]ild, balmy airs" of fall, the "[c]lear skies and cheerful breezes," and the ripening of fruits that accompanies the chillier, energizing temperatures. And she notes that "colors so brilliant and so varied hung upon every tree." Thus the "track of truth" has led her and others to represent the "native dignity" of the season rather than to rely on the traditional associations of the season that have left it "tricked out in conventional devices of man." Rather than pursue "convention" as she contemplates autumn, Cooper wishes to pursue its "natural" truth.[38]

Alison's philosophy left little room, however, for the sort of close observation of nature that clearly interested Cooper. Taste was best experienced, he explained, when the individual was in a "powerless state of reverie," being "carried on by our conceptions, not guiding them." But Cooper's model naturalist depended upon guiding his or her eye, resisting an adherence to "conceptions" or preconceived ideas, and remaining quite powerful, rather than powerless, over flights of fancy. As Cooper's writings demonstrated to readers, attending to one's physical environment demanded fine skills of observation, close attention to detail, and a willingness to watch in order to discover meaning. Applying preconceived notions was dangerous. Doing so, and failing to observe closely, could lead to an erroneous understanding of one's surroundings—such as when people held to the old notion that swallows spent the winter hibernating "in caves and hollow trees," or, worse yet, that they spent the winter "under water" in the mud of rivers and lakes, a belief that Cooper mocks. Simple observation, she explains, can help correct these misunderstandings.[39]

The problem, Cooper suggests, is that people have such little value for these sorts of truths about the natural world. "It would be difficult," she says, "to understand how sensible people could be led to maintain such opinions, were it not that men, both learned and unlearned, often show a sort of antipathy to simple truths." Indeed, it would seem that Alison was one such individual. In his *Essays*, Alison had disparaged the sort of close observation upon which a close knowledge of one's surroundings depends:

> There are many, whom the prospect of such appearances in nature excites to no exercise of fancy whatever; who, by their original constitution, are more disposed to the employment of attention, than of imagination, and who, in the objects that are presented to them, are more apt to observe

their individual and distinguishing qualities, than those by which they are related to other objects of their knowledge. Upon the minds of such men, the relation of resemblance has little power; the efforts of their imagination, accordingly, are either feeble or slow, and the general character of their understanding is that of steady and precise, rather than that of enlarged or extensive thought.

In Alison's theory of taste, the natural historian is urged away from finding meaning or beauty in things themselves. Rather, he or she is urged toward "enlarged and extensive thought," which does not accompany close observation—the discernment of "individual and distinguishing qualities" of phenomena. The individual prone to close observation is deemed "feeble and slow." Alison's teachings thus remove meaning from phenomena themselves and place all meaning in imaginative association. His philosophy has no regard for the "steady and precise" observation required for Cooper's "simple truths."[40]

If there is anything that we take away from Cooper's writings about the physical environment, it is that she believed in the value of what Alison had disparaged as "steady and precise" observation. Indeed, *Rural Hours* serves as a compendium of her search for nature's truths in her immediate surroundings. It served to curb Cooper's contemporaries' growing contentment with relations to nature that had little to do with nature and much to do with human associations—or metaphors.[41] *Rural Hours* urges readers to notice the truths of the physical world through observation.

Andrew Jackson Downing's Analogies

Alison's theory not only influenced popular writing about nature; it also influenced the shape of the American landscape in the mid-nineteenth century, particularly through his comments on gardening. In his *Essays*, he had extolled the virtues of gardening—not because it was an activity that brought one closer to natural phenomena or taught one about plants, but because it enabled one to shape the landscape in a manner best suited to inspiring taste. Through gardening one could improve upon original nature and alter it according to the principles of taste. The landscape designer, while not as empowered as the landscape painter, who can adjust elements of a scene for effect, or as the writer, who can start from scratch and create natural phenomena out of thin air through words, nonetheless exercised considerable influence: he could work with nature's raw materials and thereby create a scene that would cultivate refinement.[42] This promise was Andrew Jackson Downing's call to arms.

Downing was the most prominent American spokesman for rural refinement in the 1840s and early 1850s. His *Treatise on the Theory and Practice of Landscape Gardening* (1841) quickly established him as the premier "apostle of taste" in America. Although interest in refining rural life was generally high in the middle decades of the nineteenth century, as even a brief survey of book titles from the period attests, Downing quickly established himself as the leading voice of his day with regard to rural landscapes. His *Treatise* preached a lifestyle abundant in cultivated landscapes and advocated landscape gardening as a means of refining America.[43]

Downing defined landscape gardening as at once "the development of the Beautiful" and "the embellishment of nature," definitions that immediately signal his assumption that, by manipulating a landscape, an individual could improve nature. This improvement depended upon making a particular scene embody an ideal, one that Downing defined for his followers. Fascinatingly, Downing claimed that this program was based on "tasteful simplicity." "Simplicity" seems decidedly inaccurate, given that his landscape designs frequently meant altering the shape and botanical composition of an area. Given that his notion of "simplicity" depended upon "embellishment," we see that Downing's program was hardly simple at all.[44]

Similarly, it was hardly natural. Nature was best when shaped, altered, and improved upon. As Adam Sweeting states, "No one who reads Downing can fail to recognize the environmental determinism implicit in his writings. Tasteful houses and landscaped grounds are moral catalysts; by their appearance alone they can improve one's soul." Indeed, as Downing himself wrote, "In rendering [one's] home more beautiful, he not only contributes to the happiness of his own family, but improves the taste, and adds loveliness to the country at large." Through his program to beautify rural America, Downing promised to heighten the taste and morality of the nation.[45]

Not surprisingly, given his emphases on refinement and morality, Downing earned many converts. The widespread mid-nineteenth-century endorsement of his philosophy has led one recent historian to refer to Downing as having, "more than any other individual, shaped middle-class taste in the United States during the two decades prior to the Civil War." Even during the nineteenth century, Downing's contemporaries recognized the degree and breadth of his achievement; writing just after Downing's untimely death in 1852, one commentator claimed that his influence "was wide as the country," remarking that "no individual, probably, has contributed more largely than he to the improvement of the public tastes."[46]

As this commentator's phrasing suggests, Downing's philosophy was grounded in the widely held theory of "taste" that had been informed by Alison's *Essays*. Downing, like Alison, was concerned that people failed to exercise their taste—and, thus, to develop morally—because they lacked the ability to see properly the forms of beauty in their physical surroundings. Alison had urged his readers to train themselves to experience this ubiquitous beauty more often; he had written, "Whatever is great or beautiful in the scenery of external nature, is almost constantly before us; and not a day passes, without presenting us with appearances, fitted both to charm and to elevate our minds; yet it is in general with a heedless eye that we regard them, and only in particular moments that we are sensible of their power." His concern, then, was with improving the "heedless eye," which he did by helping people develop a discerning vision that might allow them to experience the refining shift from the material world to the imaginative one that accompanied the emotion of taste. Building from this philosophical base, Downing launched his program to improve Americans' taste by urging his fellow citizens to create scenery and homes that were most likely to awaken the intellectual capacity for taste.[47]

His method entailed producing many publications. Downing issued not only multiple editions of his *Treatise* but also books offering specific advice on the architecture of country homes and cottages and on the fruit trees that thrived in the rural Northeast. Almost immediately he saw the results for which he had hoped. By 1848, just seven years after his initial publication of the *Treatise*, Downing commented in the *Horticulturist* on "the rapid increase of taste for ornamental gardening and rural embellishment in all the older portions of the northern and middle states," a cultural change that he saw as a mark of "the progress of refinement" in the nation. And in the preface to his 1850 edition of the *Treatise*, he commented, "[T]he public taste in Rural Embellishment has, within a few years past, made the most rapid progress in this country." Downing's refinement of America had caught on.[48]

Undoubtedly part of his success was the bald fact that people appreciated his useful tips on what would grow well in their gardens. Indeed, in just one issue of his *Horticulturist* one could find advice on everything from ornamental trees to winter pears, from climbing roses to asparagus, and from strawberries to trellis designs. But Downing's success also stemmed from his assumption that, as one of his admiring contemporaries phrased it, "[o]utward life is a manifestation of inward life." Downing could capitalize on this belief and assert that the shape of one's home landscape bore a direct relationship to one's morality.[49]

It would follow, then, that Downing's advice for shaping landscapes should emphasize similarity. That is, a "moral" landscape would likely shape the environment into a uniform vision as people copied the advice that he set out in his publications. Downing hoped to address what he called the "incongruity" of American landscapes. Following his advice, Americans could help others by providing inspiring scenes to passersby, and they could also demonstrate their own taste—their own "disposition to follow out the train of thought which such objects naturally produce." Of course, the irony of Downing's program is that the "following out" of "thought" was hardly natural at all: by making uniform nature's variety, humans imposed upon it a philosophical ideal and a value system that had little to do with the particularities of nature that people like Susan Fenimore Cooper struggled to preserve. For Downing, as for Alison, the beauty of the natural world had to be enhanced by humanity, and as this occurred the human mind was refined. In pursuit of this refining vision of nature, Andrew Jackson Downing put Alison's ideas into practice and set before Americans of means the possibility of an aesthetically ideal landscape that could illustrate their good taste and contribute to the further refinement of American culture. While not all Americans could afford to pursue Downing's ideals, people of all classes could admire the idyllic yards and estates of those who could.[50]

While much of Downing's philosophy depended on the abstraction of nature, much of his advice as it appeared in his books and magazine was quite concrete. For example, with regard to architectural designs, he offered numerous specific plans, copies of which appeared in popular periodicals of the time. Similarly, he offered advice about particular varieties of plants that flourished in certain soils. Downing was quite aware, after all, that "taste" was not "a natural gift, which springs heaven-born into perfect existence—needing no cultivation or improvement." Taste needed to be cultivated, so he offered specific plans to his readers. In addition, Downing described particular locales at which readers might see his ideals applied.[51]

Following Alison's theory that the best way to cultivate taste was to experience it in sure-fire settings, Downing offered readers a list of specific locations where they could see good taste in action: at these sites one could "study trees" and "landscape gardening, on a large scale, and in its best sense," and even see "the best kept and most extensive lawn in the Union." We get a sense of the economic status of Downing's assumed audience when he suggests that one can witness "that species of suburban cottage or villa residence which is

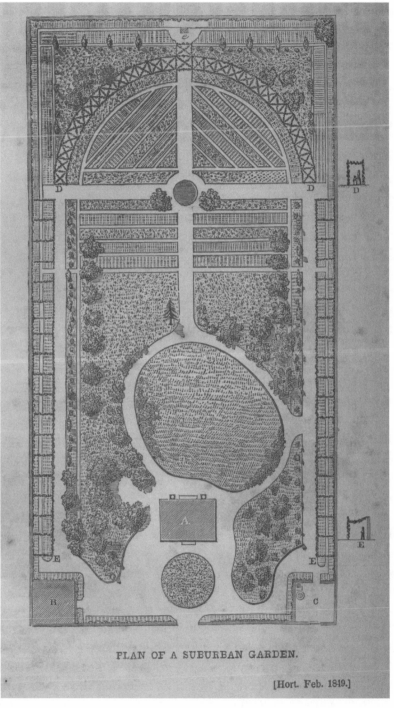

PLAN OF A SUBURBAN GARDEN.

[Hort. Feb. 1849.]

FIGURE 7. "Plan of a Suburban Garden." Frontis, *Horticulturist* 3, no. 8 (February 1849). Courtesy of the Rare Book, Manuscript, and Special Collections Library, Duke University.

most frequently within the reach of persons of moderate fortunes" by visiting some estates that occupy "from five to twenty acres." The "tasteful improver" would not be wasting time or money in visiting these locales; rather, "he will undoubtedly save himself much unnecessary outlay." More important, by studying cultivated, tasteful landscapes in order to emulate them, "he will be able to avoid the exhibition of that crude and uncultivated taste, which characterises the attempts of the majority of beginners." Downing recommends that "before they lay a corner stone, or plant a tree," people should "visit and study at least a dozen or twenty of the acknowledged best specimens of good taste in America." Part of Downing's plan, then, was what we might call the regularization of the American landscape. By emulating specific "specimens of good taste," Americans could turn the countryside into a continuous, if homogenous, testament to American refinement.[52]

Visiting model estates had as much to do with abstraction, however, as it had to do with seeing concrete applications of Downing's design plans. One quickly gains the sense when perusing Downing's writings that what was most at issue in his plan to improve the American landscape was refinement, not the state of the physical environment. As Thornton argues in her historical study of mid-nineteenth-century Boston's interest in horticulture, attention to the landscape stemmed not from a genuine desire to understand more accurately the natural environment of the young nation. Rather, members of the upper and middle classes believed in "the rich symbolism of rural pursuits." While Downing largely assumed that his tasteful followers would cultivate a close knowledge of their domesticated plants, this was not always the case. He seems not to have been aware of the extent to which horticultural pursuits could be removed from an understanding of the realities, or natural history, of the American environment.[53]

Yet Downing did define his profession as "the embellishment of nature," and his program clearly focused his would-be tasteful followers on an ideal, rather than a real, understanding of the natural world. Downing explains in his *Treatise* that one attains "the Beautiful," or "our *ideal* of a rural home," by "the removal or concealment of everything uncouth and discordant, and by the introduction and preservation of forms pleasing in their expression, their outlines, and their fitness for the abode of man." As David Schuyler asserts, Downing's ideal landscape was a "controlled" one that "bore the impress of civilization": "The landscape garden was not untouched nature but nature improved by art." Landscape gardening, when done in "pure taste," Downing claimed, delivered "*a more refined kind of nature.*" In his *Treatise*, Downing explains the means to this ideal: "Landscape Gardening . . . [embraces] the whole scene immediately about a country house, which it softens and refines, or renders more spirited and striking by the aid of art. In it we seek to embody our *ideal* of a rural home." Downing's plan thus requires altering nature and then characterizing the result as a symbol of refinement.[54]

What the popular understanding of Downing's recommendations neglected, however, was a recognition of the environmental costs of his proposed rural "ideal." Susan Fenimore Cooper recognized this particular drawback of his philosophy, and in *Rural Hours* she attacked it head-on. While Downing's was ultimately a philosophy based on abstraction and refinement, Cooper's was based on the observation of nature's particulars.

A More "Natural" Refinement

Downing worked throughout his career to persuade Americans that the outward appearances of their rural homes and landscapes reflected both their personal virtue and the nation's cultural refinement. As David Schuyler asserts, Downing was "[c]onvinced that there was an intimate connection between taste and social order"; he thus "believed that well-designed homes and gardens were the outward mark of cultivation and a measure of the nation's cultural as well as material progress." While Cooper seems to have agreed with this general sentiment—that orderly domestic settings symbolized gentility and the improvement of America—in *Rural Hours* she sought to extend the relationship that Downing assumed existed between morality, virtue, and the design of landscape and architecture to include a more "natural" element. Cooper hoped to convince Americans that direct observation of nature was crucial to America, that knowledge of natural history should also be a quality possessed by a cultivated person, and that the conservation and preservation of rural landscapes was perhaps even more crucial to refining America than improving the current fashion in gardening and landscape design. Whereas Downing hoped to refine Americans through their homes and gardens by cultivating their taste for architecture and landscaping, Cooper hoped to refine Americans "naturally," that is, by cultivating their observation and knowledge of the literal, physical world.[55]

Cooper's revision of Downing's philosophy of nature depended on her belief that American civilization could not progress without more attention to its attitudes toward and uses of the natural world. This meant, for instance, that in order for individuals to become truly virtuous citizens, they must move beyond the cultivation of fashionable gardens by deepening their knowledge of the physical environment. In Cooper's view, the morality and integrity of Americans depended upon their gaining accurate and respectful understandings of nonhuman life forms. She encouraged, therefore, "appreciation" of the physical environment in the manner advocated by D. W. Meinig: not to signal "approval," but to signal perceiving "distinctly," or being "keenly sensible of or sensitive to." As Meinig would have it, "Environmental appreciation therefore is akin to music and art appreciation in the fullest sense of a long-term training of the mind and attunement of the senses to grasp, to penetrate, to experience to a more than ordinary degree." Such an appreciation depends on understanding nature in and of itself.[56]

Therefore, underlying much of Cooper's critique of her culture in *Rural Hours* is her understanding of the underpinnings of America's infatuation with shaping the natural to please aesthetic and consumer desires, an understanding that led to a rather thorough analysis of her culture's behavior. She recognized that her nation's dedication to altering the natural world resulted from the belief that humanly cultivated life-forms were superior to natural ones. Thus, America's apparent mania for shaping gardens and lawns and for "improving" the countryside somewhat paradoxically belied the nation's radical distance from its surrounding natural environment. America's passion for nature as a sign of refinement had little to do with a *natural* nature; rather, it depended on a highly shaped, modified environment.

For example, whereas Downing claims that horticulture "transforms what is only a tame meadow and a bleak aspect, into an Eden of interest and delights," Cooper counters that leaving the meadow to itself and learning the myriad plant forms indigenous to it would make one recognize the meadow as the "Eden" it already is. She writes that "a meadow is a delicate embroidery in colors, which you must examine closely to understand all its merits; the nearer you are, the better." She further remarks that "the sweet and fresh perfume" that the many flowers of a meadow produce "increases daily *until* the mowers come with their scythes." For Cooper, Eden does not need to be created by "culture"; it exists already in "nature." Whereas Downing recommended that Americans need gardens to "[contain] the mind and soul of the man" who tends them, Cooper recommends becoming well acquainted with the larger natural world, which in her view does not necessarily reflect what Alison would have called "analogies with the life of man."[57]

Cooper struggles with several aspects of Downing's philosophy—in particular its assumption that the natural world should be altered to accommodate the refining vision of society. While she occasionally comes forth with a damning reference, as to the "unsparing race" of woodchoppers, she more often offers remarks about preservation that are reserved and understated. The reader has to work a bit to recognize her concern over modifying the natural environment. Cooper often lays out all of the pieces of an argument and depends upon the reader to draw a logical conclusion. For example, in her brief mentions of porcupines—an animal that was becoming increasingly rare in her area due to habitat destruction—Cooper quietly suggests that the local race for hemlock bark may lead to their local extinction. But recognizing her preservationist leanings can be a challenge, since Cooper's argument is essentially an implicit one. She merely sets out three facts and leaves it to the reader to draw the conclusion to which they point. First, she mentions the genial nature of the porcupine, establishing it as a creature generally harmless to humans. Second, she points out that hemlock wood is disappearing from the area at an alarming rate, as it is being used to make roads and sidewalks: "A vast amount of hemlock timber must have already been worked up for our highways, and for paving village side-walks; and probably all that is left will soon be appropriated to the same purposes." Third, she follows her full discussion of hemlock trees with this brief reference to the porcupine: "The porcupine is said to have been very partial to the leaves and bark of the hemlock for food." Thus, while Cooper never openly advocates preservation of either hemlock or porcupine, she provides readers with the bases of an argument that, if taken to its logical conclusion, suggests that hemlocks must be preserved in order for porcupines to recover in the area. Similarly, she does not write that building roads and sidewalks is not necessary, but she laments the tree loss that will bring about these improvements.[58]

In passages such as these, Cooper seems to criticize American culture's interest in rural pursuits as a genteel activity that rests upon the prevalent conception that the nonhuman world exists solely to serve the human world. Shooting game in the countryside with fellow gentlemen as a sport may make one appear a genteel member of the most prominent, elite circles, but understanding the effects of such activities on local ecosystems—that ruffed grouse had been exterminated in areas, for example—leads one to examine more closely the effect of one's actions on the environment. Similarly, insisting on sidewalks might associate one with the most fashionable and dignified of citizens, but recognizing that one's sidewalks have led to the local extinction of porcupines—"gentle, harmless" creatures—might diminish some of that self-regard.[59]

In one of her March 27 entries, Cooper takes issue directly with one of the philosophical underpinnings of Downing's movement: that improving culture necessitates enculturing nature. Specifically, Cooper makes a statement regarding the superiority of natural flowers over cultivated ones: "We admire the strange and brilliant plant of the green-house, but we love most the simple flowers we have loved of old, which have bloomed many a spring, through rain and sunshine, on our native soil." This passage establishes a continuum of emotional responses that humans have to natural life forms—a continuum that runs from "admiration," on the one hand, to "love," on the other, with "love" clearly superior to "admiration"; the natural flower displays a purer grace than the cultivated one. While this idea that natural flowers are superior to those from the "green-house" might seem innocent enough, Cooper further develops the sentiment and ultimately condemns the cultural enterprise of seeking to embellish nature through the human control of it.[60]

Following a discussion of many flowers coming into bloom in the woods and meadows, Cooper claims that human cultivation of flowers robs them of their native beauty:

> [H]ow all but impossible for man to add to their perfection in a single
> point! . . . Pass through the richest and most brilliant parterre in the country,
> with every advantage which labor, expense, science, and thought can bestow,
> and you will find there no one plant that is not shorn of some portion of
> its native grace, *a penalty which it pays for the honors of culture.* . . . . . Go out
> [instead] in the months of May and June into the nearest fields and groves.

Cooper's sarcasm about the "honors of culture" suggests that many of her contemporaries would celebrate what she saw as a negative form of cultural appropriation. For Cooper, culture—in its attempts to control and replicate, and then to better or embellish nature—detracts from the grace of natural forms. Similarly, in a discussion of the beauty of wild roses, Cooper remarks, "[T]here is, indeed, a peculiar [that is, particular] modesty about the wild rose which that of the gardens does not always possess." Of the popular practice of grafting roses for gardens, Cooper states, "It is a cruel thing in a gardener to pervert, as it were, the very nature of a plant."[61]

While Cooper certainly did not object to gardening per se, she did object to what she saw as a subtle form of environmental imperialism and evidence of a larger cultural tendency to appropriate the natural for the sake of the cultural. The "penalty" that nature suffered for being colonized by culture was too great, whether one was speaking of an individual greenhouse flower or of an increasingly altered American landscape. The cultural appreciation of the environment was evident in a taste for greenhouse flowers, in the perversion of wild species, and in the lack of general knowledge about nature among the majority of American people.

Mutual Admiration

Although Cooper clearly disapproved of certain foundational aspects of Downing's popular landscape design movement, there was also much to attract her to his teachings. In a very tangible way, she apparently appreciated his architectural sense; when she and her sister built in the 1850s the home in Cooperstown that they would share until their deaths, Cooper chose a design remarkably reminiscent of Downing's "Country House in the Pointed Style," the plans for which had appeared in his *Cottage Residences* and *The Architecture of Country Houses*. Cooper also admired Downing's dedication to encouraging Americans to tend to their native lands. In *Pages and Pictures*, she noted her father's passion for landscape gardening, and in an article titled "A Glance Backward" she similarly noted James Fenimore Cooper's pursuit of the "new art in America." While her beloved father's devotion to improving the landscape predated Downing's work, it nonetheless prepared her to appreciate the latter's call for Americans to tend to their physical surroundings.[62]

These contemporaries shared additional interests as well. Like Downing, Cooper adhered to the belief that "taste [could] be taught as a means of creating a moral community." She dedicates herself in *Rural Hours* to alerting others to the value of observing one's natural surroundings. In addition, Cooper, like Downing, valued the picturesque as a means of perceiving landscape; both were strong proponents of the picturesque vision. In all, Cooper and Downing shared a great deal, and she acknowledges as much in a note in *Rural Hours* where she thanks Downing both for his publications and for his "kindness in directing her course on several occasions."[63]

Especially appealing to Cooper, however, would have been Downing's particular hopes for the relationship that American women might share with the New World landscape. Downing believed women needed to spend more time outdoors, especially in their gardens and on their lawns. In an editorial essay that he published in the April 1849 issue of the *Horticulturist*, "On Feminine Taste in Rural Affairs," he had issued a call for women to increase their involvement in gardening. There he posed the question: "*What is the reason American ladies don't love to work in their gardens?*" Calling on women to display their patriotism through horticulture, he urges them to nurture their own connections to "mother nature." His concerns are specific, however, to the activity of gardening. He was not encouraging women to tromp through the forests or countryside: "Everything which relates to the garden, the lawn, the pleasure-grounds, should claim [American women's] immediate interest. . . . [N]ot merely to walk out occasionally and enjoy it; but to

FIGURE 8. Riverside (or Byberry) Cottage, the home of Susan Fenimore Cooper. Drawing by A. M. [de Peyster?], 1889. Courtesy of the Cooper family.

know it by heart; to do it, or see it all done; to know the history of any plant, shrub, or tree, from the time it was so small as to be invisible to all but their eyes. . . . [T]o live, in short, not only the in-door but the out-of-door life of a true woman in the country." Upon a first reading, this seems a rallying cry for women not only to begin their gardens but also to study nature. "Know the history" of the plants, Downing exhorts. However, Downing's emphasis here is on the history of the plants one has in one's garden. He encourages knowledge of domesticated plants, rather than wild or native ones. Significantly, Downing advises that one—at the very least—"see" a garden "done," and we might suppose that he means one should have one's servant tend the garden. Again, one may experience the moral influences of horticulture simply by watching. In either case, this relationship with natural phenomena is domesticated and, ultimately, quite distant from what Cooper understood to be the "real" natural world.[64]

Given Downing's desire for women to be "true wom[e]n in the country," it should not surprise us that he lavished praise on Cooper's book. In his September 1850 issue of the *Horticulturist*, he printed an excerpt from *Rural Hours* that contains some of Cooper's most overt pleas for the preservation of trees. In the next issue he published a review of *Rural Hours*. There he praises Cooper's book for its ability to bring readers to the neglected world of nature. He focuses his comments on the importance of being restored from the ills of society by heeding "the good teachings" of nature. *Rural Hours*, he wrote, "is the exact counterpoise which so many of our young people need for their overexerted imaginations"—"overexerted," that is, by preoccupations with business and by urban life in general. Downing rebukes those readers who may object to the absence of a plot in the book: "Yes, you are quite right. There is no story, but the story of the earth—the oldest of all story books—and no incidents but the incidents of nature—God's incidents. But do you think such incidents too trifling and commonplace for your attention?" *Rural Hours* offers a model for humble engagement with the physical environment.[65]

Downing particularly focuses his review on Cooper's gender, claiming that Cooper's volume provides the "first proof of an intelligent, genuine, feminine fondness for nature." A memoir of Downing's life informs us that he also emphasized Cooper's gender in discussions with his friend, the Swedish writer Frederika Bremer. In speaking with Bremer about *Rural Hours*, Downing had stressed the potential of Cooper's book to influence American women in rural matters. According to Bremer's account of their conversation, Downing "spoke with great satisfaction of Miss Cooper's work, 'Rural Hours,' . . . and expressed again a hope I had heard him express more than once, that the taste for rural science and occupations would more and more be cultivated by the women of America." Downing's reactions to *Rural Hours* clearly centered on Cooper's ability to influence American women as gardeners and on the ability of the book as a whole to bring readers closer to the "calms" of nature.[66] In all, it seems that Downing received Cooper's book as a contribution to his efforts, for Downing recommended that people read *Rural Hours* as a means of escaping the ills of society, experiencing nature's repose, and bolstering what was ultimately *his* program: refining America through gardens.

Both Downing and Cooper suggest that American civilization will be improved as its citizens tend closely to their physical surroundings. However, Cooper took Downing's concern beyond the realm of domesticated nature. By addressing the importance of old-growth forests, wild and native plants, and disappearing species, she suggests the necessity of close observation of nature in a refined America. A passion for landscape, she insists, must include an appreciation for native natural forms, as well as knowledge of particular phenomena. Hers was no garden-variety refinement.

The Paralysis of Complexity

The fact that Cooper's book both endorses and challenges Downing's philosophy of taste should not surprise us, and we should not interpret this aspect of *Rural Hours* as either weakness or ambivalence. Rather, we should see Cooper's simultaneous enjoyment of Downing's work and her concern over the enculturation of natural phenomena as part of her complex passion for nature. Indeed, the complexity of her passion for nature is one of the signal strengths of *Rural Hours*: it demonstrates the degree to which cultural productions—texts, paintings, philosophies, even individuals—are, quite literally, products of culture. Our ways of using language, our landscape or home designs, and our levels of natural history knowledge are deeply embedded in cultural value systems and assumptions. *Rural Hours* demonstrates the degree to which these popular ways of understanding the natural environment can shape our relationships with it, even when we are, to some degree at least, hoping to see or move beyond those culturally limiting bounds. Cooper embraced certain portions of her culture's popular understandings of nature even while she struggled to articulate alternative ways of loving it: through close observation, natural history knowledge, and humility. She calls attention to the significance of native species, the losses that accompanied development, and the ideological dangers of altering nature in the name of culture. For Cooper, improving American culture meant asking the nation's citizens to consider the means of their refinement, which struck her sometimes as very unnatural indeed.

Like Susan Cooper 150 years ago, many of us hope to move beyond the paralysis in which we so often find ourselves—comfortable in our refinement but inclined to challenge the values and false visions upon which our refinement depends. Also like Cooper, many of us struggle against a powerful cultural adherence to shaping the natural environment in order to display certain values. We water our lawns in the desert in order to demonstrate our refinement, and we hope for increased attention to biodiversity even as we pursue lifestyles that perpetuate its destruction. In this sense, Cooper's passion is our passion: tasteful, refined, safe, domesticated—and, sadly, paralyzed.

We claim, in this age, to be more especially in quest
of truths—how, then, shall we ever find them, if we
are busy throwing obstacles in each other's way?
SUSAN FENIMORE COOPER, *Rural Hours*

CHAPTER FOUR

The Metaphor of Reason

Ralph Waldo Emerson's
Transcendental Dominion

LIKE MANY OF her contemporaries, Susan Fenimore Cooper believed that nature could serve as an elixir to heal an increasingly diseased
civilization. She had hinted at this state of affairs when she suggested in 1853
that many of her contemporaries were walking "blindfold through the fields."
In her view most Americans paid little attention to the realities of the natural
world in their daily lives, and Cooper believed that the nation's culture was
paying a price for this neglect of the physical environment. In 1855 she wrote,
"Probably there never was a people needing more than ourselves all the refreshments, all the solace, to be derived from country life in its better forms."
The reason that people failed to attend to nature was reflected in the spirit of
the day, which Cooper characterized as gripped with "the fever of commercial
speculations," "the agitation of political passions," "the rapid progress of science," "the ever-recurring controversies of philosophy," "that spirit of personal
ambition and emulation so wearing upon the individual," and "idle ostentation and extravagant expenditure." Urban centers were growing, affecting the
quality and pace of life for many citizens of the nation. In this day and age,
Cooper argued, "[w]e need repose of mind," and the experiences of nature
available outside America's bustling cities could provide this repose.[1]

Cooper was not alone in her concern about this trend toward urbanity.
Throughout the century, many people spoke on behalf of attending more
closely to nature as an antidote to what were seen as the poisoning influences

of civilization. A leader of this crusade to improve American society through nature was Ralph Waldo Emerson, whose lectures, writings, and philosophy profoundly influenced American letters and eventually gained for him a prominent position in literary history. Like Cooper, Emerson was concerned that Americans were not paying attention to their surroundings—that they were walking blindfold through the fields. As Emerson wrote in his 1836 essay *Nature*, "To speak truly, few adult persons can see nature." Like Cooper, Emerson hoped to adjust the course of American life by calling attention to the uplifting properties of the natural world. We might say, in fact, that Emerson and Cooper were two American authors who devoted their careers to improving American society by pointing people toward the truth that could be found in nature: they both wanted to help Americans *see* nature.[2]

However, what Emerson and Cooper saw in nature was very different. As they urged readers to heed nature's positive influence, Emerson and Cooper led them toward distinct sorts of relationships with the physical environment. Both writers believed that nature was a "moral influence," to use Emerson's words, and both writers relied on language as a means to expressing their vision. Nonetheless, they held different concerns about how language might be used to convey the natural world. More fundamentally, while they both understood nature as a source of truth that could benefit humanity, their beliefs about how humans might access that truth were poles apart. Cooper, as we have seen, believed that nature's truth was best recognized by learning and observing its particulars while accepting the humble role of humanity. For Cooper, the power of the sense of sight—of *not* "walking blindfold through the fields"—involved humility in the face of nature's variety and history. The truth of nature resides in the physicality of the natural world. For Emerson, in contrast, the natural world serves only as a means to truth. Sight was important because it could lead to insight, and nature merely provided the means to insight. Put differently, Emerson's use of nature as a source for revealed truth assumes that nature is a vehicle for that truth, which is something higher than nature itself—something beyond the material world. One studied nature in order to exercise the capacity for insight, and the most valuable insights bore little relation to the humility that Cooper valued. Rather, the most valuable insights were those that illustrated the seemingly unlimited capacities of the human mind. For Emerson, the truth of nature was its ability to lead humans to exercise reason in its highest form. Cooper, however, envisions nature as truth itself, and not as a vehicle for anything other than *what it is*. When one sees nature, one sees truth. For Emerson, nature is a means to an end; for Cooper, nature is means *and* end.[3]

In Emerson's works, and especially in *Nature*, we see how passion for nature could become a passion for human reason. We also see that nature served Emerson primarily as a metaphor for reason itself. However, before examining how Emerson establishes nature as a metaphor for reason in *Nature*, it is worthwhile for us to consider the similarities between Cooper and Emerson, for an examination of their shared contexts and distinct conclusions affords us the opportunity to see how a foundational passion for nature can result in very different relationships to it. What we find through close study of these two writers is that seeing nature as a source of truth can lead to relationships to nature that are as different as night and day, depending on how one supposes that truth is accessed—and on the degree to which one assumes an individual is capable of discerning that truth. We find that when nature is a metaphor for human reason, as it was for Emerson, it is possible to overlook the details of the physical environment. On the other hand, when one envisions nature as truth itself, as Cooper did, the specificities of biota and natural cycles are most significant. An exploration of Cooper's and Emerson's concerns and assumptions helps us see the mid-nineteenth-century struggle to answer the very basic and crucial question of how human beings might best relate to the natural world.

Shared Foundations

In addition to a desire to improve American society, Cooper and Emerson shared deep roots in Christianity, an understanding of nature rooted in the natural theology tradition of the eighteenth century, a fascination with the methods of contemporary natural history and in the rising scientific study of nature, and a concern with the relationship between language and nature. Emerson and Cooper also shared an interest in the books of the day's leading scientists. They both mention popular scientists in their writings, and scholars have argued on behalf of their efforts to "affiliate" with scientific pursuits, to borrow Nina Baym's term. All of these elements contributed to their respective passions for nature. Strikingly, though, Emerson and Cooper valued different aspects of these various enterprises. Emerson especially adjusted his basic assumptions about nature due to his studies of romanticism. Cooper would remain more squarely rooted in the eighteenth-century natural history tradition while developing a sense of nature's value as residing in its materiality. If we explore how and where Emerson and Cooper diverge in their thinking, we can begin to see how Emerson could divorce nature's truth from its physicality. In order to see this, we need to reconsider the changing role of natural theology at this time and, in particular, how it responded to romanticism.[4]

Eighteenth-century natural theology maintained that the natural world revealed the truth of Christianity—and the existence of God—through its variety and intricacy. The "design" of the world was a testament to the existence of God. In the words of Kris Fresonke, "In its simplest terms, the [design] argument goes like this: from the manifest design of the world, we can infer the presence of a designer." This belief in design was seen as compatible with scientific pursuits well into the nineteenth century, leading "natural theology" and "natural history" to be nearly synonymous. By studying nature, one grew closer to God and his truth, since nature was merely God's design for the world. As one discerned the natural world, one discerned the truth of God. In the first decades of the nineteenth century, therefore, most of America would have assumed this connection between the moral and physical "spheres of creation."[5]

During these early decades of the nineteenth century, however, other philosophical and scientific developments challenged and supplemented the basic design argument. Romanticism was one such development. Under the influence of the leading European romantics, who included Kant, Goethe, Wordsworth, and Coleridge, proponents of American romanticism urged a relationship to nature based on faith in the human imagination. Specifically, they emphasized the powers of the mind to intuit truth. In large part, romantic thinkers relied on the doctrine (or theory) of correspondence in order to bridge the distance between the human mind (or imagination) and truth. As Laura Dassow Walls explains it, the doctrine of correspondence "healed the gap [between the physical world and the mental realm] by making mind and nature aspects of each other." In discovering correspondences—or analogies—between the human mind and the material world, the individual gained a deeper knowledge of both; this in turn led to a deeper knowledge of truth, or of some divinely unifying law. The doctrine of correspondence, Walls illustrates, is a logical step from a belief in design: "it centered all inquiry in the deep embrace of a divinely designed universe which excluded the unknowable by fencing in certainty with the guarantee of coherence." As the individual contemplated the universe, he or she discerned the correspondences (analogies, connections) between things, believing that more study led to more truth. Ignorance was impossible in this theory that guaranteed coherence by assuming that what one learned from nature was both a lesson about the self and an insight into ultimate truth.[6]

This romantic faith in the powers of the human mind had implications for theories of both knowledge and God. The basis for human knowledge was no longer basic sensory perception, as Lockean empiricism had posited, but the exercise of reason, which promised a higher end. Through the powers of reason, an individual could discern—through intuition and imagination—not only knowledge of the material world but also of its unifying laws and ultimate truths. Knowledge therefore depends on "the mediation of mind," a step far beyond an initial processing of sensory perception. The imagination and human intuition gain center stage.[7]

While the imagination gained prominence in romantic philosophy, so did beliefs concerning the ultimate potential of the self. Some thinkers went so far as to suggest that the human imagination (much like the divine powers) was infinite in its capacities. In fact, some said that the purpose of human life is to better understand the self and its relationship to divinity. Through close study of the physical world—understood as the evidence and assertion of God—one might more fully realize one's own likeness to God. This belief took various forms and, for obvious reasons, seemed blasphemous to conservative Christians, for whom the creation was God's work—not humanity's. But romanticism shifted the spiritual quest for divinity from a pursuit of evidence of the divine in the world beyond the self (nature) to a pursuit through nature of the divine within the self. No longer merely the site of evidence of God, the natural world becomes also the locus of the individual's pursuit of the divinity within the self.[8]

This sort of attention to the natural world was a far cry from traditional natural theology. As Leon Chai explains, "Whereas traditional theology had professed to see the nature of God in the external world, Romanticism now asserts its presence within the soul. To be sure . . . even the external world continues to possess a sacrality of its own. This sacrality, however, belongs not to its forms but to its substance, which is now pervaded by the divine presence. As a result, all matter becomes sentient with spirit." The romantic pursuit of nature was thus the pursuit of the divine in the self, and the physical world was assumed to be sacred due to its being the site or occasion for the mind to do its mediating work—its discovering of correspondences between the external and the internal: "Romanticism claimed to detect, by intuition, rather more about God in nature than the fact of coherent and universal craftsmanship." According to romantic thought, then, the individual could employ his imagination in the highest form—reason—to intuit the bases of morality and the highest forms of truth. The creation is thus "a means by which the self shall finally realize its own divine nature." For many romantics, including Emerson, studying nature was akin to studying the self, and realizing the truth of nature was akin to realizing one's own divinity.[9]

Emerson was deeply immersed in the romantic philosophy of his day and, in the eyes of some scholars, was responsible for advancing a specifically American form of romanticism. Cooper, however, held to a different view of things altogether. Nowhere in her works does she grant the individual the type of power to discern divinity that Emerson assumes through romanticism. In fact, compared to Emerson's view, Cooper's understanding of God in relation to nature seems quite tame and old-fashioned. Whereas Emerson takes the assumption of natural theology to its radical, romantic conclusion, Cooper sticks more closely to the original natural-theological premise: nature "furnish[es] the principal evidences of religion." Starting from this premise, Cooper focuses on the role of humanity in God's creation, significantly positing nature as a reminder of the humble position of humanity on earth. For Cooper, nature's truth overpowers mere human truths, suggesting the ultimate truth of nature itself. Emerson, on the other hand, sees nature's truth in terms of the power of human reason. Because of his belief in the primary importance of reason as a tool for cultivating the self, he assumes that nature exists in order to aid humanity's quest for reason. Nature's truth lies in its function as a means to reason.[10]

For the sake of clarity, I have just drawn a deep line in the sand between Cooper's and Emerson's understandings of nature. This line—though useful for our purposes in understanding these authors' relationships to nature—is not quite this clear when we examine all of these authors' works. For instance, we find Cooper flirting with romanticism's notions, especially in her concerns with artificiality. "Artificial" was a loaded term in the middle of the nineteenth century, and it is therefore not surprising that both Cooper and Emerson employ it. For romantic thinkers, the artificiality of modern life was one of its largest shortcomings. The natural quality of rural life was giving way to what was seen as the artificiality of city life, and the natural powers of human reason had been masked by the artificiality of Lockean empiricism. Even the methods of science created an artificial separation of what was increasingly believed to be a natural, organic whole: the physical environment. Emerson and Cooper both were concerned about the "artificial" classification system of natural history—Emerson with its disregard of the principle of connectivity, and Cooper with its use of words that bore little connection to what they named. Both authors were concerned with the artificial role that language might play in natural history. Their different views concerning how language should be employed in relation to nature inform their understandings of nature's truth.[11]

For Cooper, natural history nomenclature should enable people—common people—to have a working knowledge of their surroundings. Children should be able to easily learn and memorize the names of plants, for instance, and mothers should be able to instruct their children in those names. Natural history should enable a close relationship with nature so that we can better know the creation so as to be ever more impressed with its complexity and variety. Recognizing nature's diversity humbles us, which is a good thing, according to Cooper. Clearly the language of natural history—and the understanding of nature that this language enables—is important to Cooper in that it allows one to know where he or she *is*. Natural history serves as a means of grounding the self in a specific place.

For Emerson, natural history exists as a tool for helping us realize our highest intellectual capacities. As he wrote, "The use of natural history is to give us aid in supernatural history. The use of the outer creation is to give us language for the beings and changes of the inward creation." The study of outward things aids us in our quest to understand ourselves.[12]

Clearly, both Emerson and Cooper are interested in how humans are connected to the natural world, and both focus on language as a vehicle for that connection. They believe that some uses of language enable a more genuine relationship with one's physical surroundings and that, conversely, certain uses of language contribute to the corruption of society. Both authors, then, make the integrity of language an important component of their proposals for an improved human relationship to nature. But they take this concern in different directions.

Emerson understood language as a means of transmitting the spiritual truths that are conveyed through the phenomena of the natural world. Nature, in other words, serves as the basis of language but also as the path toward truth. Therefore, when Emerson expresses apprehension regarding the integrity of language, he is voicing concern about the degree to which humans are conscious of the origins of language as they use it. Awareness of language's roots is important to Emerson because he assumes that language originates in the natural facts that are symbolic of spiritual truths. Using language well, then, attests to a heightened awareness of truth.

Cooper's writings nowhere suggest that she held to this particular tripartite relationship between language, nature, and truth. When she shares her anxiety about how language is being used by her contemporaries, her worries focus on the ease with which language enables a working knowledge of the specifics of the organic, nonhuman world. Her concern lies in the difficulty of memorizing the names of plants, for instance, and in the degree to which names of places bear little relation to the geography or history of the places themselves. Like Emerson, then, she hopes that language can be "close" to nature—that is, that words can correspond to the physical environment. But unlike him, she holds this hope because she wants Americans to be able to recall natural history through their words. As we see throughout Cooper's writings, language is ideal—or most true—when it enables one to name, with some degree of specificity and detail, one's surroundings.

In spite of all of the historical, philosophical, religious, natural-historical, and scientific contexts that Cooper and Emerson shared, they developed understandings of the self in relation to nature that have different effects on how humans conceptualize themselves in relation to their physical surroundings. Ultimately, Emerson tells a story of nature that features the grand saga of human reason—a story in which nature serves humanity—while Cooper tells a story of the wonder of the physical creation itself. Cooper's passion led readers to focus on cultivating humility in the face of nature, whereas Emerson's led them to focus on cultivating their minds while using nature as a vehicle for that self-cultivation. In other words, one author focuses on the primacy of the natural environment, and the other on the primacy of the individual. Each of their forms of passion for nature has its strengths in terms of bettering American society, and we stand to learn much from them both. Undoubtedly, however, Emerson's vision remains more prominent in American culture today.

Ralph Waldo Emerson and Dominion over Nature

Emerson's *Nature* arguably remains his signature piece—the fullest statement of his beliefs about the role that the physical environment should play in the lives of Americans. In *Nature* he attempts to inspire his contemporaries toward a revitalized society by writing a treatise on the meaning that the natural world should hold in their lives. Through this work, Emerson composes a new story for nature, and he does so with admirable passion and force. The essay emerges from his deep grief about the state of society. At the start of *Nature*, he outlines his concerns: "We are now so far from the road to truth, that religious teachers dispute and hate each other," thoughtful men "are esteemed unsound and frivolous," and people "grope among the dry bones of the past."

Society seems filled with the din of unnecessary arguments and an unquestioning adherence to traditional ways of thinking, believing, and living. The time has come, Emerson asserts, for change: "There are new lands, new men, new thoughts," he exclaims, suggesting that people "demand" their "own works and laws and worship." He believes in this new nation, and especially in its tremendous potential for revitalizing religion, law, poetry, and philosophy. This revitalization will center on nature. Emerson's essay is nothing less than an instruction manual on nature's meaning—the truth that people can and should recognize as a means for saving their society from stagnation.[13]

We can read *Nature* as a prescription for healing society through a new understanding of nature's meaning. As we analyze how Emerson constructs and presents his theory of nature, we watch him abstract nature to a degree we have not yet seen in other nineteenth-century expressions of passions for nature. Through Emerson's diction and imagery, his powerful little book removes the meaning of the material world from any consideration of its physicality and proposes instead a marriage of "Matter" and "Mind," or, in other words, a direct relationship between the human capacity to reason and the presence of material reality. As we will see, Emerson compels his readers to recognize the physical world as a mere means to a heightened intellectual state. Nature becomes "the road to truth"—the vehicle of reason. Nature is thus a metaphor for the human capacity to reason, and in inquiring into nature's existence we are inquiring into our own.[14]

In order to make this theory clear to readers, Emerson starts with the most basic but potent of questions: "to what end is nature?" Here at the outset we realize that Emerson's passion for nature rests in his belief that "we have no questions to ask which are unanswerable" by "the order of things"—that is, by the physical environment. His purpose in *Nature* is none other than to "inquire" about "the end" of nature. The magnitude of this proposed undertaking warrants comment, as its goal is to investigate the purpose—or function—of nature. Since his 1836 essay, which his most recent biographer terms "a wholly audacious inquiry," no other American has pursued this broad undertaking in his or her writing. The question—To what end is nature?—is astounding not simply in its scope and boldness, but also in its assumption that a human being could discern the "end" of nature. But Emerson's courage in this undertaking reflects the accepted purpose of scientific endeavor in his day, which he also explains in his introduction to *Nature*: to develop "a true theory" that will "explain all phenomena," including nature.[15]

In some sense, therefore, Emerson's philosophical project was also a scientific one. Indeed, scientists of his day believed that through a thorough study of nature, they might arrive at a theory that explained all of life, and Emerson wrote a book of philosophy as a means of arriving at this explanation. The purpose—or "end"—of the natural world can be taken fairly directly, Emerson believes, from the creation itself. Its "forms and tendencies"—or its appearances and propensities—show us its purpose. Here Emerson attests to his unwavering faith in what he calls "the perfection of the creation." He also points to the abstraction of nature upon which his philosophy will depend. "Seeking" nature will mean searching for some truth that lies outside of its materiality. If we can see it correctly, we can discern ultimate truth. *Nature* represents Emerson's attempt to do so.[16]

Here at the outset we recognize two crucial components of Emerson's goal in explaining the significance of the natural world to his readers. First, Emerson depends on the sensory perception of the eyes. If nature demonstrates her purpose through her forms and tendencies—her design—then by looking closely at the natural world we can discern that design and, hence, nature's purpose. Indeed, sight will be the crucial human sense for Emerson, not merely throughout this one essay, but through all of his writings. Seeing nature's design will allow us to understand its truth. Second, Emerson assumes that there is an "end" to be discerned here. His entire project in *Nature* presupposes not only that humans can discern the purpose of nature but that there is a purpose to be discerned. Even more important, he takes for granted that nature's purpose has something to do with humanity discovering the one truth that "will explain all phenomena." This most significant aspect of Emerson's work helps us realize, from the start, that his relationship to nature is utilitarian. In other words, his approach to his subject assumes that nature exists, at least in part, to serve humans by providing evidence for them of a truth. As he will state later in the essay, "Nature subserves to man."[17]

In answering his broad question concerning the end of nature, Emerson proposes that nature serves four basic functions for humans, which he discusses in the order of their increasing importance: commodity, beauty, language, and discipline. As he develops each section, it becomes increasingly clear that each of these four functions is anthropocentric—that each works in service to human beings and their abilities to reason. Put as simply as possible, nature serves humans by 1) providing basic commodities that enable life; 2) meeting the human desire for beauty in our surroundings; 3) inspiring the words that we use, thereby making our words "signs"—or symbols—of nature, which is itself, according to Emerson, symbolic of "spirit"; and 4) teaching us through its ways, and in fact serving as a sort of academic "discipline" or means to education. Of these four "uses" of nature, the third one—nature's function as "language"—is the most complex; as other scholars have pointed out, understanding it is crucial to understanding Emerson's essay. Recognizing this aspect of Emerson's theory is also vital to understanding his particular passion for nature. By the close of his essay, nature has become reason itself—a reflection of the human capacity for higher thought. But we should not get ahead of ourselves, because *Nature* offers us a detailed explanation of each of these four, basic functions.[18]

Examining the particulars of Emerson's discussion of each function enables us to recognize the degree to which his passion for nature and his sense of its truth have little to do with its material reality. At each step of his argument, we find him traveling deeper and deeper into the human mind; perhaps for this reason, *Nature* often baffles first-time readers. Its structure, however, is deceptively simple: Emerson elaborates the four lower uses of nature by giving a few pages to each, and he orders his discussion in terms of the growing significance of each of nature's uses. Nature's function as beauty, for instance, is more important than nature's function as commodity. Although he presents us with this hierarchy of nature's use for humans, the hope of humanity rests on a thorough understanding of each one. Therefore, Emerson explains each thoroughly.

Nature's most base, "low" function—as commodity—is, Emerson claims, "the only use of nature which all men apprehend." Nature's function as commodity is so obvious to Emerson that he does not give many examples of it, and we do not need many to follow his drift: nature provides the stuff that makes it possible for us to live. Nature provides us with air, water, sunlight and soil for growing our food, and fruits and grains and wood with which to feed and shelter ourselves. From nature's basic commodities, humans build "cities, ships, canals, [and] bridges." What astounds Emerson is the fact that humanity is so often miserable—despite these ample forms of "divine charity" that "nourish man" and "the steady and prodigal provision that has been made for his support and delight on this green ball which floats him through the heavens." Here, then, is one cause for Emerson's concern that men are not seeing nature very well: they neglect to recognize even this most "mercenary benefit" of nature: its function as commodity. Notice that even in this, Emerson's fullest consideration of nature in terms of its material existence, nature serves humanity and inspires our thoughts by suggesting through its forms how we might improve upon it (via shelter, canals, or cities).[19]

A "nobler want" of humankind is served by nature's ability to feed our desire for beautiful things and inspire our spirits to imitate its beauty. This is nature's next function: "beauty," which takes a few forms. On the most basic level, the natural world pleases our eyes: "the primary forms, as the sky, the mountain, the tree, the animal, give us a delight *in and for themselves*; a pleasure arising from outline, color, motion, and grouping." Indeed, "almost all the individual forms are agreeable to the eye," and so people feel compelled toward imitations of these forms through sculpture, painting, gardens, dishes, wallpaper, and woodwork. "[T]he simple perception of natural forms is a delight," and nature serves us because it is "medicinal and restores" us. Furthermore, Emerson explains, nature's beauty is important because human actions acquire additional force and meaning through the beauty of the scenes in which they are set. Conversely, beautiful human actions augment the foundational beauty of the world. The "beauty" of the hero's deed enhances "the beauty of the scene," and nature's brilliance "sympathize[s]" with great human actions. In other words, a heroic deed grows nobler when it takes place in a lovely setting, and a landscape becomes more beautiful when a heroic deed occurs in it. Both of these first two forms of nature's beauty serve humans.[20]

Finally, the beauty of the world is significant in a third way that clearly abstracts nature from its physical context: it is "an object of the intellect." That is, the grace of the natural world inspires humans to seek beauty intellectually—not only through heroic deeds, but also through the cultivation of "Taste." The result of this inspiration is art: as Emerson puts it, "The creation of beauty is Art." Nature's beauty therefore functions to arouse the creative energies of humanity. As with Archibald Alison's interest in nature as a means to "taste," this particular function that Emerson gives to nature has little to do with the material world itself. Nature's beauty becomes, in this treatment, a vehicle for human creativity.[21]

Emerson acknowledges as much in his "Language" section, where he states, "Nature is the vehicle of thought." This one statement is essential to Emerson's entire conception of the relationship between nature and the human mind. He believes that nature functions as the great enabler—making it possible for humans to survive in comfort (through "commodities") and to experience and create beauty. Here we realize that nature also enables thought, which, in Emerson's view, is potent only when it achieves expression through language. As he explains this important function of language, we see how nature's meaning is wrenched from its physicality and placed instead in an abstract or symbolic realm.

Emerson elaborates his theory of language first by stating three seemingly simple points:

1. Words are signs of natural facts.
2. Particular natural facts are symbols of particular spiritual facts.
3. Nature is the symbol of spirit.

He then enlarges upon each point in order to establish how it is that nature is thought's vehicle. At base, he explains, every word has its roots in a physical fact or phenomenon. In his words, "Every word . . . if traced to its root, is found to be borrowed from some material appearance." This is the case not only for simple nouns but also for "moral and intellectual" facts: "*Right* originally means *straight*; *wrong* means *twisted*. *Spirit* primarily means *wind*; *transgression*, the crossing of a *line*." While we may not think deliberately about the roots of the language that we use, he explains, the rootedness of language in nature is a fact.[22]

This point is fairly easily digested. Next, however, Emerson makes a leap in logic—as well as a leap in faith. It is here that many students of Emerson lose sight of his assumptions about the human relationship to nature, and understandably so since his notion of nature grows increasingly abstract. This "origin of all words that convey a spiritual import,—so conspicuous a fact in the history of language,—is our least debt to nature," he claims. Again creating a hierarchy within his already established hierarchy of nature's uses, he states: "It is not words only that are emblematic; it is things which are emblematic. Every natural fact is a symbol of some spiritual fact. Every appearance in nature corresponds to some state of the mind." Here Emerson asserts that the stuff of nature serves as a mirror, reminder, or signal of some potential feeling or idea in the human mind. At one level, this means that human thoughts and emotions are in tune with nature, or that nature enables us to have a certain thought or feeling: "Who looks upon a river in a meditative hour, and is not reminded of the flux of all things?" But at another level, this theory suggests a specific relationship between humans and nature's truth, and it is this aspect of Emerson's philosophy that he explains in the remainder of the "Language" section and to which he returns throughout the remainder of *Nature*: nature's truth, he suggests, is its embodiment of reason.[23]

Emerson adheres to a belief in a divine presence "wherein . . . the natures of Justice, Truth, Love, [and] Freedom, arise and shine." He calls this divine presence "Spirit" and explains here that humans can access this divine spirit through what he calls their "Reason." This capacity of mind depends on more than merely exercising the senses; it depends, rather, on searching out the analogies or correspondences that exist between the physical world and the world of the mind. Here we especially see romanticism's influence on Emerson. According to Emerson, discovering analogies—between nature's beauty and human nobility ("Beauty"), for example, or between the stuff of nature and man's means of living ("Commodity")—allows us to achieve the heights of human intellectual capacity: reason. As we exercise reason, we partake of the divine spirit.

But Emerson's notion of this divine spirit has little to do with the humility that would have traditionally accompanied an encounter with divinity. In fact, this meeting can occur through language, which constantly exhibits humanity's ability to convey spirit. As humans speak and write, they give voice to those aspects of nature that *are* the divine spirit. Language, when intentionally and discerningly used, permits the individual to transcend his mere existence in the senses and enter the world of spirit. Because "man is an analogist, and studies relations in all objects," the highest of intellects will seek the relations between things—between mind and matter, and between nature and thought—as means of reaching the one truth, which Emerson refers to as "Spirit," "the Creator," and the "universal soul" alike. The material world of nature exists to enable this achievement of spirit.[24]

Given that nature, for Emerson, is the vehicle of spirit and a theater for the playing out of human reason, it should come as no surprise when he claims here in "Language" that "[t]he world is emblematic" and that "the whole of nature is a metaphor of the human mind." In other words, the world reflects human truths and exists as an emblem of the potential heights of reason or intelligence. Language thus plays a crucial role in enabling humans to transcend their physical existence and enter the realm of truth. This claim is striking because it subsumes the entire physical creation under the category of humanity—positing the natural world as an imagistic construction. This is an idea, however, that Emerson will come back to later in *Nature*, when he asks "whether nature outwardly exists." For Emerson, nature's material reality is incidental. We will return to this idea later, as Emerson develops this premise at length in the "Idealism" section. For now, we will note that Emerson states as fact what his theory has been assuming all along: the major purpose of nature is to function as a grand mirror for human thought. Nature is "emblematic," then, in the sense that it is symbolic of a divine truth that, apparently, *is* the human mind.[25]

Emerson says in his discussion of the fourth item on his list of the "ends" of Nature, "Discipline," that it includes "the preceding uses, as parts of itself." In other words, nature's function as discipline includes its function as commodity, beauty, and language. By "discipline," Emerson intends a mode of learning, as in the "academic disciplines" that comprise a university or college curriculum. From Emerson's perspective, nature itself is one such discipline. Indeed, we can fairly easily recognize that nature teaches us by means of its being a commodity (we learn to eat from its plenty, for instance), by means of its beauty (we learn to emulate its beauty through our art and culture), and by means of its being a source for our language (we make language based on nature's lessons). But Emerson moves beyond these three basic uses of nature, pointing out that nature also functions as a discipline in the sense that "[e]very property of matter is a school for the understanding." That is, beyond commodity, discipline, and language, all aspects of the natural world teach human beings, giving us "sincerest lessons" and urging us onward to higher thought.[26]

The remainder of *Nature* considers "Idealism" (whether the physical world is formed by ideas or material), "Spirit" (the use of nature that sums up all the rest), and "Prospects" (thoughts about the future). It is here in these sections that Emerson's passion for nature becomes most apparent and his metaphoric use of nature most forceful. In "Idealism," he considers what was at the time called the "ideal theory" of nature. This theory, which Emerson found in the works of his contemporaries but which reaches back to Plato and was present also in the work of Berkeley, held that ideas are the basis of reality. In other words, the "idea is more real—more important—than the physical product" or the natural world. In *Nature*, Emerson takes this idea so far that he concludes: "Whether nature enjoy a substantial existence without, or is only in the apocalypse of the mind, it is alike useful and alike venerable to me." His understanding of the "ends" of nature stands unshaken even by the possibility that the physical universe does not exist "outwardly." Whether the natural world is material or merely constituted by ideas, it is useful to him.[27]

This is largely because, as he says in "Spirit," "all the uses of nature" may be "summed [up] in one:" "It always speaks of Spirit." In all of its functions, nature attests to the divine spirit: "It suggests the absolute." Whether the material world is in fact material or whether it exists merely as a set of ideas in the human and divine mind is irrelevant to him. To readers today, it may seem ludicrous that Emerson would even inquire whether nature is real, since we now recognize the results of attending inadequately to the real condition of nature—results such as global climate change, species extinction, and large-scale human health problems. But this was not Emerson's perspective, and even if he had had these facts at his fingertips, they may not have concerned him, because his inquiry is philosophical, not material. That is, his purpose is to determine nature's function for humanity's pursuit of the improvement of human intellectual culture. Above all, nature serves humanity by inviting, feeding, inspiring, and exhibiting communion and union with the spirit.[28]

In "Prospects," the reader gets a final glimpse at the degree to which Emerson's theory of nature relies upon abstraction. This occurs amid Emerson's vision of what might happen if the mind's power is achieved, or, in his words, if "the apocalypse of the mind" is allowed to unfold. First, Emerson warns that his society seems far off from achieving this ideal relationship to nature. "At present," Emerson chides, "man applies to nature but half his force [of reason]." This is the "reason why the world lacks unity, and lies broken and in heaps." Because Emerson believes that individuals are applying merely half of their force to understanding nature, he can claim that "man is disunited with himself." But Emerson holds onto hope. As man pursues his own mind in his relations with nature, he will arrive at truth. And this truth will reveal to him the full powers of his own mind, the "kingdom of man over nature."[29]

The promise of Emerson's vision is remarkable: it assures an overturning of the balance of power in the world. Rather than being subject to the powers of material nature, Emerson promises that humankind, provided it can see nature correctly, will also discover its own potential for reason. Through reason, humanity will attain clear insight into the relations between all things, the laws of the universe, and humanity's true power. As one scholar of romanticism puts it, the "genius" that is promised here is none other than "re-creation of the world." "[T]he whole direction of *Nature*," insists Laura Walls, "and of Emerson's work right to the end, was to reimagine nature as the instrument of human will, such that ultimately all nature would be nothing more nor less than our living 'double,' our second self reconstructed in the image of our desire." Emerson's promise is dangerous, because it offers humanity the possibility of controlling and dominating the physical world by defining nature as an embodiment of reason. He assures his readers that the "kingdom of man over nature" will be grand beyond our imaginations. What this promised Americans was nothing less than a material world remade in light of the desires of the human mind. In the words of Elisa New, "*Nature* had promised Americans breadths of possession commensurate with their scope of imagination." For Emerson, achieving this ultimate expression of the imagination resulted in the ultimate of revelations: We could control the natural world. For readers in the twenty-first century, we see the frightening results of such a philosophy: a society that conceptualizes the natural world through such abstraction that it destroys the life upon which it depends. Such a philosophy results in the deaths of species, ecosystems, and peoples.[30]

Any person who feels that the material world is an embodiment of human reason is bound to experience some trepidation—and Emerson does. The capacity of the individual that he describes is frightening in its potential, and it is this fear that leads Emerson to note the "certain reverence" and "alone[ness]" of the most memorable experiences he has had in nature. He indicates that he is "daunted by the immense Universe to be explored," and that he experiences some anxiety as he contemplates "the fearful extent and multitude of objects." This fear, however, results from Emerson's belief that nature's variety is indicative of man's capacity. He is overwhelmed, in other words, by his own potential power: the multitude and variety of nature's forms are, after all, emblems of human capacities.[31]

The fear that Emerson expresses, while real and genuine, seems to give way in *Nature* to his fascination with human potential, which he describes in several places as "power." In its allusions to power, *Nature* suggests the seductive aspect of Emerson's understanding of nature as a metaphor for reason. As Emerson explains, the individual increases his "domain of knowledge" through the discernment of nature's objects and their relations to truth, and he thereby acquires additional "weapon[s] in the magazine of power." By using language associated with the militia, Emerson helps his readers see the radical force of their potential power. With their weapons of knowledge, they might reorganize the world.[32]

To be fair, for all his attention to what we cannot help but see as an abstract philosophy, Emerson does attend to actual experience of the natural world. He did so in his private life, and even in *Nature* he devotes paragraphs to describing genuine natural phenomena, including flower species and winter sunsets. However, even these passages devoted to "real" phenomena end up displaying the power over nature that he assumes for humans.[33]

First, he suggests, one must adopt an attitude of "reverence" in order to see nature rightly. The feelings of reverence that accompany us when we take time to contemplate the stars on a clear night are feelings that we should bring to every encounter with nature. This approach to nature has certain qualities: being "alone," not in a literal sense, necessarily, but in the sense of recognizing that even common objects of nature are ultimately "inaccessible." Emerson's example is the stars, toward which nearly any thinking and feeling person experiences a sense of wonder when contemplating their mysterious light; he explains that this "poetical sense in the mind" can accompany any viewing of any natural object. "The flowers, the animals, the mountains" can

all evoke this reverence. Emerson suggests that we bring this "certain reverence" to our encounters with "all natural objects," which are bound to "make
a kindred impression, when the mind is open to their influence." Adopting
an approach to nature that is "poetical" is necessary to "[distinguish] the stick
of timber of the wood-cutter, from the tree of the poet." In other words, the
power of nature to move us resides in large part in our own approach to it.
This approach—this willingness to be moved, to be "poetical," to experience
"reverence"—is the skill that Emerson fails to find in his contemporaries. It
is this sense of mind that so many of us lack, and that lack prevents us from
truly seeing nature. In this context, he makes his pointed claim about the de-
ficiencies of his contemporaries: "To speak truly, few adult persons can see nature." "At least," he goes on to qualify, "they have a very superficial seeing."[34]

But this type of seeing depends not on concentrating on the outward;
rather, it depends on concentrating on the inward—on the feeling that accompanies the seeing. In this poetical state of mind, one encounters natural
objects with "a perfect exhilaration," a gladness that borders on fear. ("Almost
I fear to think how glad I am," Emerson says.) In the sublime, we return to
a childlike state, donning "the eye and the heart of a child," and adopting a
state of "perpetual youth," even the innocent "spirit of infancy." What Emerson describes here is the romantic sublime—that emotional response to
nature characterized by an overwhelming sense of awe in the face of nature.
The experience of the sublime necessarily leads one to feel "alone" and to recognize the "inaccessible" nature of outward things, because one has the sense
that nature means more than we can know, that the design of the universe
reflects a power greater than ours, and that we are insignificant in comparison
with both the design and the designer.[35]

This is a mysterious union between man and nature, Emerson admits,
one beyond human comprehension: "an occult relation." Yet through this
experience, which only the man willing to don the spirit of a child—or of the
poet—can experience, "we return to reason and faith." This return to reason
and faith is best described by the famous but elusive figure of the "transparent
eyeball," that potent image of unhampered, omnidirectional, divine sight.
What Emerson means by this "return" remains mysterious, and many scholars have proposed readings of this most-cited of Emerson's paragraphs. In this
state, we embody perhaps the ultimate paradox, becoming everything and
nothing at once: "all mean egotism vanishes," yet "I see all." "I am nothing,"
yet "I am part or particle of God."[36]

This most influential image, through which Emerson intends to convey
the best way to see nature, points us to the highly abstract quality of the

Emersonian passion for nature. Oddly enough, this ideal moment in nature has little to do with the physical environment. There is, in fact, practically nothing physical about the experience. It's all *mind*. Emerson's ideal self-in-nature becomes "transparent," is filled with "currents of the Universal Being," and experiences "reason and faith." He is pure mind, and yet he has achieved the most that he can be. The result is not that he can see more clearly those aspects of the physical world around him; rather, the result is insight into the capacities of the self: in nature "man beholds" something "as beautiful as his own nature." And what he beholds is his own capacity for divinity.[37]

Emerson's philosophy is certainly empowering. It places man "in the centre of beings" and insists upon what he calls a "radical correspondence between visible things and human thoughts"; it is founded upon what Emerson calls "the great doctrine of Use," which he defines as "a thing is good only so far as it serves [humanity]." At every step in *Nature*, Emerson assumes that the physical world exists for the benefit of humankind. The fact that nature exists as commodity is nothing compared to the human ability to make "reproductions or new combinations" of these commodities through his intellect. Nature's munificence exists in order that people may create higher forms of meaning. "A man is fed, not that he may be fed," Emerson chides, "but that he may work." Nature's function as commodity provides for us, but does so in order that we may make and shape a more genial environment in which to live. Human power over commodity is far more worthy of celebration than the "temporary and mediate" benefit of nature-as-commodity itself. Similarly, in Emerson's explanation of nature's function as "Beauty," "Language," and "Discipline," it is the human being who has the most power. In "Beauty," the person who creates art "throws a light upon the mystery of humanity" by crafting "the result or expression of nature, in miniature." The artist gathers all of nature's beauty into one expression: "Thus is Art, a nature passed through the alembic of man." Of the ways in which nature functions as beautiful for humans, this is the highest: to enable man to become a creator himself. With regard to "Language," the "use of the outer creation is to give us language for the beings and changes of the inward creation." And pertaining to "Discipline," the most common events teach "the lesson of power": that the individual "can reduce under his will, not only particular events, but great classes, nay the whole series of events, and so conform all facts to his character." Nature serves as "the raw material" for man's ever-increasing discovery of—and then imposition of—his will in the world. Luckily, the "ethical character" of nature leads always to truth, so this developing will is characterized by only good things.[38]

In each and every regard, then, Nature's purpose is figured in terms of humanity, its needs, its desires, and its potential—and above all, its quest for the ultimate self through reason and nature. "Nature is thoroughly mediate. It is made to serve." In his or her position of dominance, the individual has the capability to realize the degree to which the outer world is not merely a service provider in the quest for truth but is an actual reflection of the individual will: "the world becomes, at last, only a realized will,—the double of the man." Man (the term is Emerson's) may use his reason to become one with the spirit, the divine, nature, truth. Interestingly, nature functions in these various "base" ways on behalf of humanity, but nature depends on humans to make the best use of its functions. In other words, nature serves these several functions for man, and then each of those functions is overcome—or augmented—by man's intellectual powers.[39]

Later, in an essay called "The Poet," Emerson would put it this way: "The Universe is the externization of the soul." But here in *Nature*, as if to make the point of nature's service to man palpable, Emerson baldly states: "It receives the dominion of man as meekly as the ass on which the Saviour rode." This is Emerson's story of nature—what Walls terms his "imperial vision." Nature is to humanity what the ass was to Jesus—a vehicle for carrying out the divine purpose of the self. And while that purpose is truly empowering and champions the powers of the self, the particulars of natural phenomena, seasonal changes, and individual species have no place in it.[40]

Cooper's Lessons in Concreteness

Given the general disregard for concrete aspects of the natural world in Emerson's philosophy, we are not surprised to realize that Cooper's version of nature's truth differed considerably from his. As we have seen, she attended very closely to specific natural phenomena. Cooper's reason for encouraging this closer familiarity with natural phenomena centered on what she saw as the injurious influences of modern life. While these negative aspects of society were not unique to the United States, Cooper expresses her belief that Americans are especially vulnerable to their harmful effects:

Probably there never was a people needing more than ourselves all the refreshments, all the solace, to be derived from country life in its better forms. The period at which we have arrived is rife with high excitement; the fever of commercial speculations, the agitation of political passions, the mental exertion required by the rapid progress of science, by the ever-recurring controversies of philosophy, and, above all, that spirit of personal ambition and emulation so wearing upon the individual, and yet so very common in America, all unite to produce a combination of circumstances rendering it very desirable that we should turn, as frequently as possible, into paths of a more quiet and peaceful character.

Fascinatingly, these corrosive aspects of society relate as much to intellectual advancements (science and philosophy, in particular) as they do to commerce, politics, and "personal ambition," those aspects of modern life commonly accused of distracting people from what matters most. Cooper suggests that nearly all components of American society were conspiring against the "repose of mind" that could be gained through time spent in natural environments.[41]

The "repose of mind" that Cooper recommends for her contemporaries differs considerably from the flights into reason that Emerson suggests people seek through nature. The lessons to be acquired through time spent attending to the physical environment are, according to Cooper, intended to both quiet the mind and enrich the spirit by turning our attention *away* from ourselves—not toward ourselves and our powers of mind, as in Emerson's recommendation. Cooper suggests that "we need the flowers, to soothe without flattery; the birds, to cheer without excitement; we need the view of the green turf, to teach us the humility of the grave; and we need the view of the open heavens, to tell us where all human hopes should center." With each turn of phrase, Cooper suggests the humbling truths to be taught by the natural world: nature soothes and cheers, but it does so without flattery or excitement. The natural world indicates that human life is brief and not as significant as our self-aggrandizing, bustling culture would have us believe. The stimulations of commercial society, a politically engaging democratic society, and intellectual advancements have little bearing on the world of nature: this is the point that Cooper wants her readers to recognize.

Certainly Cooper's understanding of the temporary place of humans on earth is framed in terms of her Christian beliefs: "human hopes should center" on the "open heavens," since they offer the promise of an afterlife. By connecting nature's humbling powers to her belief in God, Cooper sees nature through a lens that we might term one of "reason." Christianity is, after all, a product of the human intellect and therefore of human reason. However, if we focus only on the Christian context of her remarks, we miss the way in which her relationship to nature centers on the natural—and secular—world itself. This tension in Cooper's works—between her Christian faith and her belief in the importance of fidelity to the real details of nature—yields a rich contribution to American environmental thought. Through it, she insists that human pursuits on this earth are virtually insignificant. At every step of the way, our physical surroundings remind humanity of its temporary, even incidental, place here.[42]

We have already seen that Cooper's story of nature includes as essential components the natural and human history of specific places. What we recognize now is that this historicized and particularized nature is its truth, in Cooper's view of things. We see this in part through what she chooses to write about as she represents the physical realm for readers. Unlike Emerson's abstraction of nature in pursuit of truth, Cooper's writings focus on her non-human surroundings in order to record observations of particular species, seasonal progressions, and recurring or cyclical phenomena—and in order to suggest the relative insignificance of human beings in this larger scheme. By recording nature in such detail and with such precision, she suggests that there is value inherent in what she sees of nature around her—value that exists regardless of the human imagination. Nature bears recording in and of itself, and not only as a means to some higher truth, even if that truth is that of Christianity. The truth of nature lies in its very materiality. Nature's truth is the story to which it attests through its very being: the story of its history, of its vast variety, and of its alteration or disturbance. This is the story that Cooper tells of nature. This is her version of nature's truth. The result of this truth—its meaning for humanity—is moving in its implications: humans should feel honored to dwell on this earth and should recognize and live out their gratitude. In some sense, they should inhabit gratitude. And inhabitation of gratitude can lead only to humility.

Through her many works, Cooper encourages readers to attend closely to the truth of nature, to live graciously, and to recognize their humble positions in relation to nature. The first step in doing so was to attend closely to nature. As we have seen through *Rural Hours*, she believed that her society would benefit from attentiveness to the physical environment. We can also see her participation in the crusade to better America through nature in two of her later works: the introduction to her edition of Englishman John Leonard Knapp's *Journal of a Naturalist*, which was published as *Country Rambles in England; or, Journal of a Naturalist* (1853), and her sizeable introduction to *The Rhyme and Reason of Country Life* (1854), a substantial anthology of nature poetry that she edited. Both works attest to Cooper's passion for educating readers about the benefits of rural life and the recognition of nature's truth.

They also, however, demonstrate her commitment to understanding the role that the natural world had played in the literary history of the Western world and the role that language could play in leading to nature's truth. In these two works, as in *Rural Hours*, Cooper shared her passion for the truth that is nature.

According to Cooper, what does it mean for nature's truth to lie in its concrete details? There are many ways in which she develops this notion. Certainly one of the most potent lessons that readers glean from Cooper's writing concerns the truth of rural life itself. Unlike Emerson's philosophy of nature, which leads him to focus inward, Cooper's understanding of nature turns outward: her works inform us about what it means to reside in her particular version of rural America. As Nina Baym has argued, Cooper wrote in order to convince her contemporaries that one could spend time wisely and productively in rural America—that country life was not merely for the poor, the uneducated, and the unrefined. Indeed, we find this message especially in *Rural Hours* when Cooper explains several significant aspects of dwelling in a rural area, including: the particularly demanding role of the housewife during the winter season, when farmers are occupied with the slaughtering of their pigs; the arduous work that accompanies gathering wood during winter months; the village frenzy associated with spring cleaning; the custom of burying the dead in isolated cemeteries rather than in church-yards; and the role that maple sugaring plays in the rural economy of the Northeast. As she addresses topics such as these, Cooper teaches her more urban readers about the pleasures, satisfactions, and toils peculiar to country living.[43]

But Cooper clearly had an additional reason for representing the natural world so thoroughly during her writing career. She did so, as she wrote in *Rural Hours*, so that readers might be led "to something higher." Given her comments elsewhere on this matter, I suggest that we call this "something higher" "truth." What is difficult, though, about Cooper's concept is her assumption that the truth of nature lay in its very physicality. Unlike Emerson, she does not view the phenomena of nature as a means of attaining a different, higher, philosophical end—in spite of her use of the phrase "something higher." Cooper's nature does not require translation. Instead, she sees what she sees, documents its occurrence, considers the mere fact of the phenomena to be inherently valuable, and accepts her experience of that phenomena as a lesson in truth. That truth is based in the wonder of nature, which leads her, again and again, to feelings of gratitude and to the acceptance of the insignificance of humanity. It is a truth that would prove of great significance in the twentieth century for the science of ecology.[44]

An understanding of the literary-historical context in which Cooper participated helps explain her particular version of nature's truth. We can discern this context through her own characterizations of *Rural Hours*, the way in which her publishers marketed her book, and her later writing projects, which clearly continued in this tradition. Cooper envisioned herself as a participant in the long tradition in English literature of representations of nature. This tradition, as Cooper saw it, had matured in the last century and, as a consequence, had been informed by Christianity, and, in England in particular, by the Anglican Church. As a lifelong, active member of the American version of the Anglican Church—the Episcopal Church—Cooper understandably maintained that the physical world is the creation of a Christian God. Throughout her works, she peppers her prose with expressions of wonder and gratitude at the generosity of her Christian God. However, what is striking about her references to her religious beliefs is how little they have to do with the meaning that she assumes for nature.

In this regard, Cooper's position is complicated, and I do not wish to make light of her deeply felt religious convictions. Yet, while nature is always and everywhere in Cooper's work the result of God's handiwork, she does not adhere completely to the assertion put forth in Genesis, capitalized upon by Baconian science, and endorsed by Emersonian philosophy: that humanity holds dominion over its creatures and soils. On the one hand, she does make the assertion that humanity "is lord of the earth and of all its creatures." On the other hand, she consistently maintains that humanity must be grateful for these gifts and that, significantly, humanity is "responsible for the use of every gift." Similarly, while she describes humans as "the steward[s]" of the earth, she also insists upon the "humility" that should accompany the human presence on earth. It is a humility that she sees as especially necessary in light of the needless alteration and disturbance of land, "as when a country is stripped of its wood to fill the pockets or feed the fires of one generation." Her ambivalence on these points is indicative of her emerging ecological sensibility. She adheres to her belief in nature as God's creation while also conceptualizing the physical world as an entity, a material realm, a reality in and of itself, governed by its own laws—laws that twentieth-century thinkers would call the laws of ecology.[45]

Cooper had models to follow as she considered nature in this way, but her models were not those of romanticism. One model that she indicates very early in her writing career—in her preface to *Rural Hours*—is the Anglican priest and author of *The Laws of Ecclesiastical Piety*. Cooper explains in the preface that she writes in hopes of "giv[ing] pleasure to any who, like the honored Hooker, love the country, 'where we may see God's blessings spring out of the earth.'" Significantly, this quotation of Richard Hooker's does not come from his theological writings but from a letter that he wrote to the church leaders, in which he asked that he be relocated to a rural church setting, where he might "see God's blessings spring out of the earth." While Cooper invokes a church authority, she does so in order to summon his love for the natural world and his endorsement of the benefits of attending to it. Her *Rural Hours* preface indicates that she envisions herself as participating in a long tradition of attending to the wonders of natural life from a position of piety.[46]

In providing readers with a detailed introduction to her rural surroundings, Cooper also continued in the vein of Gilbert White's *The Natural History and Antiquities of Selborne* (1789), a popular book that had inspired John Leonard Knapp and that would soon move Henry David Thoreau to live deliberately while getting to know the physical environment of one particular locale. In *Selborne*, White, who was curate of his village, explores his rural village and its environs, conveying through his representations of nature his religious feelings. His "long commitment to place expresses itself in affectionate bonding to landscape particulars." John Leonard Knapp would follow White's lead, writing with care about the physical environment surrounding his rural village. White's and Knapp's books, Cooper assures us, "stand side by side, on the same shelf, in the better libraries of England." Given this comment, it's hard not to believe that she hopes to complete a trilogy on behalf of nature through *Rural Hours*.[47]

Cooper therefore had solid forebears to emulate in maintaining her religious feelings while expressing the variety of the natural world. Like White and Knapp, she proceeded according to the basic assumption of natural theology, namely, that the natural world "was a centerpiece of the revelation of religious truth to humanity." In entering this tradition, she hoped to contribute to what she describes in *Rural Hours* as a literature that pursues "the track of truth"—expressions "endeavoring to paint the works of the Creation in their native dignity, rather than tricked out in conventional devices of man." She hoped to give language to her physical surroundings for their own sake. As we have seen, she believed that this literary tradition was especially needed in America, where people were increasingly living in cities and spending little time in rural areas. As she explained in *Rural Hours*, people needed a literature of nature that is "more real," that has "more of life" and "more of truth."[48]

To some degree, Cooper's attention to aspects of daily rural life—to spring cleaning or to chores on a farm—can be seen as part of her "more real" representation of her region. That is, she deliberately educates readers about the realities of living in the country. However, given the degree to which Cooper includes detailed descriptions of natural phenomena in her writings, and given the nature of her later essays on the subject of a literature of nature, we also must see her records of natural history phenomena as substantial parts of her endeavor to establish in America a truthful literature of nature. She wants readers to look closely at their natural surroundings and to recognize that what they see there is, in and of itself, a form of truth. Discerning this truth requires a careful eye and a careful study of natural history.

Cooper's version of nature's truth demands attention to the particularities of nature—and not Emersonian leaps to the heights of reason. Whereas Emerson concentrates on the power over nature that humans can achieve through reason, Cooper focuses on the necessity of humbling oneself to the unique facts of natural phenomena—not as a means of gaining power, but as a means of understanding its physicality and detail. As an example of her interest in this sort of truth, we might turn to her May 19 entry in *Rural Hours*, where we find Cooper alerting readers to distinctions between certain flowers that are commonly lumped together and erroneously referred to as "trilliums." The following paragraph appears after one in which she explains that she had gone on a walk through a nearby meadow on a particularly lovely evening:

> The evening air was delicately perfumed throughout the broad field, but we could not discover precisely the cause of the fragrance, as it did not seem stronger at one point than at another; it was rather a medley of all spring odors. The June-berry is slightly fragrant, something like the thorn.
>
> We found numbers of the white moose-flowers, the great petals of the larger sorts giving them an importance which no other early flower of the same date can claim. There are several varieties of these flowers; they are quite capricious as regards coloring and size, some being as large as lilies, others not half that size; many are pure white, others dark, others again are flushed with pale pink, or lilac, while one kind, with white petals, is marked about the heart with rich carmine tracery. Now you find one pendulous, while another by its side bears its flower erect. Botanists call them all *Trilliums*, and a countrywoman told me, the other day, they were all "moose-flowers." Each variety, however, has a scientific name of its own, and some are called nightshades; others wake-robins, both names belonging properly to very different plants. The true English wake-robin is an arum. The difference in their fruit is remarkable.

She goes on to explain that the flowers of these plants, "so much alike to the general observer," are followed by berries that are distinguishable, and she describes how to discern their unique characters.[49]

The truth to be found here is the truth of precision, of the subtle variety of nature, of the importance of attending to nature's specificity for the sake of acknowledging its multiplicity. Hers is a passion for the natural realm that dwells profoundly in detail. Whereas Emerson situates the reader in nature in order to guide him or her toward the pursuit of reason through that material realm, Cooper submits her reader to fine detail, to nature's every feature. Cooper particularizes her environment.

We might see Cooper's edition of John Leonard Knapp's *Journal of a Naturalist*, which had been published in England in 1829, as a continuation of the project that she had begun in *Rural Hours*: spreading the truth of nature. In the introduction to her 1853 edition of Knapp's book, which she titled *Country Rambles in England*, Cooper explains that Knapp recorded in detail the natural phenomena of his immediate surroundings. He writes about the trees, grasses and other plants, birds, butterflies, animals, and seasonal changes, much as she had, of course, in her own *Rural Hours*. She prepares his volume for American audiences as a means of offering an example of an individual who is knowledgeable about his physical environment. Such knowledge, she explains, serves to "honor" God by heeding his physical creation. "We Americans, indeed, are peculiarly placed in this respect. As a people, we are still, in some sense, half aliens to the country Providence has given us; there is much ignorance among us regarding the creatures which held the land as their own long before our forefathers trod the soil, and many of which are still moving about us, living accessories of our existence, at the present hour." Unlike Knapp, many Americans are unable to name their surroundings.[50]

Why she chooses to use a British naturalist to educate her American audience is interesting: Americans, she claims, often have through their *reading* a better working knowledge of the landscapes of England than of America. That is, through the study of literature, Americans may have at their fingertips the names of specific plants and animals, but they are unaware that those names bear little or no relation to the biota of the New World. Cooper explains the predicament in which this state of affairs leaves her fellow citizens:

> Thus it is that knowing so little of the creatures in whose midst we live, and mentally familiar by our daily reading with the tribes [or, natural species] of another hemisphere, the forms of one continent, and the names and characters of another, are strangely blended in most American minds. And in this

dream-like phantasmagoria, where fancy and reality are often so widely at variance, in which the objects we see, and those we read of are wholly different, and where bird and beast undergo metamorphoses so strange, most of us are content to pass through life.

So it is that many Americans move through their days referring to plants and animals by incorrect names and assuming that they know what they do not know. Cooper goes on to suggest that while there are similarities between species of the Old World and the New, few animals or plants are truly the same: "[M]any of us are ignorant of the very striking, leading fact that the indigenous races of both hemispheres, whether vegetable or animal, while they are generally more or less nearly related to each other, are rarely indeed identical. The number of individual plants, or birds, or insects, which are precisely similar in both hemispheres, is surprisingly small." "But there is a pleasant task awaiting us," she insists: the learning of the truth of American nature.[51]

Her edition of Knapp's book becomes, then, a textbook in the discernment of native species. Through substantial notes—nearly fifty pages of them—that she has composed to accompany Knapp's writings, Cooper explains to readers the distinctions between the natural phenomena that he describes and what American readers might see around them. She culls her information from the writings of prominent scientists and other sources, and she gives special attention to birds—that aspect of the natural environment that seems to have interested her most. In reading *Country Rambles in England*, one receives a fine introduction to the uniqueness of the American environment, and especially to the species with which Cooper was most familiar: those residing in her region of New York State.[52]

Paying this sort of detailed attention to one's physical surroundings demands a language attentive to nature's variety, and in *Rural Hours* especially, Cooper expresses her concern that language in America is not adequate to the task. Whereas Emerson had urged readers to recognize the emblematic powers of language, Cooper urges readers to ground their words in nature itself. Her concern is twofold: the names for things bear little relation to their natural context, and, sometimes as a result, people cannot learn them easily. Some of her concern is with aesthetics (some names are simply ugly), and some of it reflects her patriotism (language evoking the Old World takes a hard rap). For example, she claims, "The Republic itself is the great unnamed," and she laments that "[t]he citizens of the United States are compelled to appropriate the title of the continent, and call themselves Americans"—after Amerigo Vespucci, with whom "our mistakes began." But for the most part,

Cooper believes that language should reflect nature itself—its particularities and its indigenous history. Indian names for rivers and lakes are especially suitable, she says, listing several of which she approves: Mississippi, Altamaha, "Susquehannah" [sic], Ontario. "[T]hey have a claim to be kept up on account of their historical interest, and their connection with the dialects of the different tribes," she explains. Again, then, we find Cooper intent on reminding Americans of the unique history of their lands.[53]

But when it comes to naming the landscape and retaining historical significances, Cooper has little affection for the names of European explorers and heroes. Just as she holds the name "America" in great disdain, she believes that, for features of the landscape, individual's names should not be used; instead, "another class of words appears much better fitted to the natural features of the land, its rivers, lakes, and hills." This is the case because "no private individual would seem to make out a very clear claim to bestow his name upon a vast, rocky pile." With regard to the custom of naming mountains after individual men, Cooper quips, "generally it must be admitted that this connection between a mountain and man, reminds one rather unpleasantly of that between the mountain and the mouse." Men aspire to a self-important grandeur when they impose their names on the landscape. Rather than this arbitrary and proprietary method of naming, Cooper advocates "learning the true character of a country in its details" and naming locations accordingly. Once people discern the particular character of a place, they can better determine the precise "fitness" of a name. To aid in this process, Cooper provides a list of words that evoke aspects of the landscape and suggests that people combine them as they name new settlements.[54]

Cooper similarly criticizes the use of Latinate names for plants, arguing that such names are "clumsy" and that they "[pervert] our common speech." "Why," she asks, "should a strange tongue sputter its uncouth, compound syllables upon the simple weeds by the way-side?" Part of what Cooper reacts to here is the "artificial" discourse of natural history, which she and many of her contemporaries regarded as separating people from their physical surroundings. Science seemed to be making even the most basic knowledge of one's surroundings unnecessarily complicated. But Cooper also responds here to the divorce of object from context. She suggests employing "natural names" that are preferable for the degree to which they reflect the season or location in which they bloom, the habitat preferences of a specific plant, or the particular uses to which a plant is put. "Spicy gilliflowers," for example, are named for the month in which they bloom ("gilli" being a corruption of July), and "primroses" gain their appellation because they bloom in the early spring. The term "hare-bell" recollects the fact that the flower "loved to hang its light blue bells about the haunt of the timid hare," and "carnation" serves as a version of "coronation," since that flower was sometimes worn in a wreath. Such names, Cooper argues, are closer to nature. They enable a more accurate attention to its particulars.[55]

The Latinate names increasingly used by botanists pose two particular problems for the young nation: they are difficult for people to learn and recall, and they are nearly impossible to include gracefully in literature. In order to ensure that people attend to their surroundings, "we should have names for the blossoms that mothers and nurses can teach children before they are 'in Botany,'" when those children will learn the Latin appellations in a formal course of study. Furthermore, "if we wish that American poets should sing our native flowers as sweetly and as simply as the daisy, and violets, and celandine have been sung from the time of Chaucer or Herrick, to that of Burns and Wordsworth, we must look to it that they have natural, pleasing names." Since she hopes that common people will be able to name their surroundings, and that the young nation will be able to produce a meaningful literary tradition, Cooper encourages a process of naming nature based in its materiality.[56]

A language that adheres more closely to the environment will enable Americans to realize nature's truth by recognizing—and being able to name—its variety. But using this language depends on seeing nature accurately, and in *Rural Hours* Cooper expresses her concern that her contemporaries are not seeing very well. In this regard, she urges readers to "see" in a very different way than Emerson proposed. She advocates "seeing" in a literal sense, since she feels that her contemporaries are not heeding the material reality around them. Cooper addresses this concern through her detailed accounts of what she sees and by distinguishing the subtleties between certain species and others, alerting readers to native versus nonnative species, and describing exhaustively the phenomena of one year. But she also does so by addressing the occasional tendency to associate human feelings with natural occurrences—to substitute other emotions for the gratitude and humility that she assumes should accompany seeing well.

The Relinquishment of Power

We find Cooper's tendency toward gratitude throughout *Rural Hours*, where she states her wonder at the mystery of nature again and again. We especially see it in her lengthy passage on autumn, where she distinguishes American autumn from that of the Old World, reviews literary treatments of the season, and, as we saw in the last chapter, tackles head on the Alisonian association of the season with "gloom." In particular, we notice her interest in being true to the season and in urging people to feel gratitude through their experience of the season's truth:

> Some persons occasionally complain that this period of the year, this brilliant change in the foliage, causes melancholy feelings, arousing sad and sorrowful ideas, like the flush on the hectic cheek. But surely its *more natural meaning* is of a very different import. Here is no sudden blight of youth and beauty, no sweet hopes of life are blasted, no generous aim at usefulness and advancing virtue is cut short; the year is drawing to its natural term, the seasons have run their usual course, all their blessings have been enjoyed, all our precious things are cared for; there is nothing of untimeliness, nothing of disappointment in these shorter days and lessening heats of autumn. As well may we mourn over the gorgeous coloring of the clouds, which collect to pay homage to the setting sun, because they proclaim the close of day; as well may we lament the brilliancy of the evening star, and the silvery brightness of the crescent moon, just ascending into the heavens, because they declare the approach of night and her shadowy train!

Here Cooper urges people away from the tendency to see nature, as so many romantics did, in terms of human emotion (a sort of pathetic fallacy, as Ruskin would later term it, or anthropomorphism, as we now commonly say). Instead of ascribing to nature some human feeling, she suggests that people rely more directly on their vision to guide them to its "more natural meaning." Note her use in the following passage of words that invoke several varieties of seeing:

> *Mark* the broad land glowing in a soft haze, every tree and grove wearing its gorgeous autumnal drapery; *observe* the vivid freshness of the evergreen verdure; *note* amid the gold and crimson woods, the blue lake, deeper in tint at this season than at any other; *see* a more quiet vein of shading in the paler lawns and pastures, and the dark-brown earth of the freshly-ploughed fields; *raise your eyes* to the cloudless sky above, filled with soft and pearly tints, and then say, what has gloom to do with such a picture?

If people would only see clearly what is before them, Cooper intimates, they would recognize the irrelevance of their gloom to nature's autumnal display. Much more appropriate to what we see in autumn—and to nature's truth—is gratitude, she concludes: "Tell us, rather, where else on earth shall the human eye behold coloring so magnificent and so varied, spread over a field so vast, within one noble view? In very truth, the glory of these last waning days of the season, proclaims a grandeur of beneficence which should rather make our poor hearts swell with gratitude at each return of the beautiful autumn accorded to us." Cooper instructs readers to leave their feelings behind as they contemplate the natural world, and to reflect upon its physical variety. Such reflection will lead to emotion, to be sure, but to the one emotion that Cooper imagines as "true" to nature: gratitude. In the face of nature's multitudinous forms, one can only feel grateful.[57]

Given her attention in *Rural Hours* and elsewhere to the intricacies of nature and to what seems to be its infinite variety and forms of beauty, we must recognize that Cooper believed that one of the most significant functions of nature—the most significant function, I would argue—is to humble humanity. This humility depends upon people relinquishing the self-aggrandizing power toward which Emerson—and so many other influential cultural and social figures—led them. This humility involved assuming a lowly position in relation not just to God and his creation, but to a very earthly nature. Unlike Emerson's sense of nature's truth lying in its service to human reason, Cooper believes that its truth demands relinquishing power. Nature may lead to "something higher," but for Cooper that "something higher" "speaks of a generous mind." Nature's truth points her to gratitude, not to the powers of human reason.[58]

When Cooper appeals to this generous mind, she indicates her valuation of nature's bounty in ways that transcend Christian teachings about nature's role in human life. Indeed, she points to the value inherent in the physicality of nature itself: "in planting a young wood, in preserving a fine grove, a noble tree, *we look beyond ourselves*" to the other life forms of the planet—"the band of household friends"—and to the future of humanity and of nature itself: "to our neighbors—ay, to the passing wayfarer and stranger." In recognizing that preserving nature serves not merely ourselves but the larger circle of life, Cooper states that we will experience gratitude. "[I]t becomes a grateful reflection that long after we are gone, those trees will continue *a good* to our fellow-creatures for more years, perhaps, than we can tell."[59]

Beyond a moral good associated with Christianity, Cooper posits here an ethic that we would now call ecological in orientation: an insistence that good is inherent in nature's preservation. Thus, her approach to nature, while compelled by one of the most potent ideological systems in human history—Christianity—enabled a more persistent attention to the real and, hence, to a relationship with nature that attended closely to actual life forms. Such a relationship renders the truth of nature—and the truth of nature is bound to improve American society.

Toward an Ecology of Humility

Examining side by side Emerson's and Cooper's beliefs about nature's powers to cure America's ills demonstrates that despite their foundation in some shared assumptions about nature, they end up in very different places. Both regret America's ideological course away from the natural world, which was having, they both felt, very disturbing consequences. In reorienting readers toward nature, however, they point toward paths leading to quite distinct truths. A comparison of their preoccupations with language and nature affords a view of the distinct and subtle connections that each writer makes between imagination and nature, or between mind and world. Cooper's view is more influenced by a conservative Christian vision, and Emerson's by the tenets and methods of romantic philosophy, but both grapple with the power of words to name and with how language might unite the individual and nature. In the end, Cooper particularizes her environment, and Emerson transcends his through metaphor as a means to power. She suggests that we relinquish power in preference to humility; he invites us to claim it through reason.[60]

Neither Cooper's nor Emerson's views promise the solution to the current American alienation from nature. Missing from Cooper's vision is a concrete plan for improving environmental health, and missing from Emerson's philosophical vision is the absolutely essential insight into fragility, the recognition that the integrity of the nonhuman environment depends upon careful attention to just that flower, and to just that species of fish—not because they serve man, but because they are valuable in and of themselves. Nonetheless, both authors had insights that inform ecological thinking in the twenty-first century, and both suggest necessary components of a sustainable ecological vision of humanity's relationship to the natural world. On the one hand, Emerson's philosophy enables ecological thinking by appreciating the unity in nature. Recognizing the organic whole of nature has been crucial to current-day efforts to understand the basis for the earth's health. In addition, we need the rationality provided by Emerson's vision, as calls for humility alone do not solve environmental problems. On the other hand, Cooper's philosophy of nature enables a crucial attention to particulars. While her metaphysic bears traces of eighteenth-century natural theology, it also values nature's elements for their own sake and asserts that the truth of nature resides in its very physicality. As modern scientists have come to realize, we need to study the particulars in order to tend to the whole. Approaching this study with wonder and humility can open our eyes to new ways of understanding.

Important to our purposes here, however, is that Emerson's vision emphasized metaphor to such a degree that his expressions of passion for nature become, in the end, expressions of passion for the capacities of the human mind. He never truly let go of his belief that nature "subserves" man: as he wrote in "The American Scholar," "[I]n the mass and in the particle nature hastens to render account of herself to the mind." According to Emerson, the meaning of nature has more to do with the use that man can make of "the account" through reason than with the details of nature themselves. In fact, with regard to nature's details, he asks, "But what is classification but the perceiving that these objects are not chaotic, and are not foreign, but have a law which is also a law of the human mind?" In his estimation, knowledge of nature for its own sake is pedestrian. The goal is to make "the impressions of the actual world . . . fall like summer rain, copious, but not troublesome, to thy invulnerable essence." Ultimately, Emerson promises in "The Poet" that Americans will claim the material realm, as if the national culture itself were a god: "Thou shalt have the whole land for thy park and manor, the sea for thy bath and navigation, without tax and without envy; the woods and the rivers thou shalt own; and thou shalt possess that wherein others are only tenants and boarders. Thou true land-lord! sea-lord! air-lord!" According to this version of nature's truth, the goals of humanity are dominion and power. But for Cooper, any human being who claims to be a "lord"—or who, in her words, "rise[s] above his true part of laborer and husbandman" and "assumes the character of creator"—is "apt to fail." Rather, people should "give life and spirit to the garden." They must strive for what she called "conceptions of nature independent of man," by which she means a recognition of nature in and of itself.[61]

Whereas Emerson's philosophy enabled him to recognize the power that humans had in the environment, it also compelled him to co-opt the natural world for purely philosophical and metaphoric ends, in a way that we can see as "ideological" in the sense that Paul de Man uses that term: "the confusion of linguistic with natural reality." That is, the way in which Emerson talks about nature allows him to assume for it an identity as other than the thing-in-itself. This is the imposition of ideology on the landscape, or, to put it another way, the ideological appropriation of the landscape, which enables metaphors to permeate and construct the national consciousness.[62]

Through Cooper and Emerson, we see very clearly that the mid-nineteenth-century preoccupations with nature's truth—and its developing passion for nature—could take deeply divergent paths, each of which could provide a distinct American relationship to nature. Emerson's philosophy, in the words of Walls, became "wind under the wings of America." As Emerson's *Nature* demonstrates, and as contemporary society proves, if the natural world is understood as a means to power, then the variety of nature does not matter as much as its connectivity—or the human ability to make philosophical meaning of it: as commodity, as form of beauty, as food for the spirit, or even as a basis for language. This is the utilitarian vision of nature that we live amid today. While many contemporary Americans dedicate themselves to environmental concerns, the will to dominion and power currently characterizes the nation's dominant relationship to nature, as evidenced by our comparatively slow responses as a nation to pressing issues such as dependence on oil and global climate change. Walls beautifully captures the contemporary relevance of Emerson's vision, arguing that, "[i]ronically, *Nature* includes a manifesto for modern industrial progress." Indeed, Emerson provides "marching orders to scientists and poets to join ranks and remake nature according to what will become, increasingly, a nationalist vision. . . . The material world we inherited from the twentieth century, for better and for worse, has gone far toward fulfilling Emerson's vision of making the world 'only a realized will,—the double of the man.'" Emerson is certainly not to blame for this; his was merely one voice amid many. But our current losses in habitat, biodiversity, and climate health are a testament to the dangerous potential of such a vision.[63]

Cooper provided another possible path for her culture. Amid this empowering vision, this Emersonian celebration of intellectual possession that would grip the nation well into the twenty-first century, Cooper, through her quiet cataloging of nature's truth, proposed a philosophy of concreteness. In nature's variety was Cooper's truth, and if variety is truth itself, then preservation is crucial. Once you notice the variety of nature, she suggests, you are bound to experience wonder and, hence, to feel gratitude. That gratitude leads to humility, and that humility can lead to preservation.

As Susan Fenimore Cooper wrote in the middle of the nineteenth century, "There still remains much for us to do" in terms of educating ourselves about the truth of nature's particulars. She had faith, however, in her young nation: "[I]t lies in our power to advance the national progress in this course," she believed.[64] So must we.

At last, we know not what it is to live in the open air, and
our lives are domestic in more senses than we think.
From the hearth to the field is a great distance.

HENRY DAVID THOREAU, *Walden*

CHAPTER FIVE

Passion for Nature beyond Metaphor

From Walden *to Henry David Thoreau's*

Late Natural History Projects

ON AUGUST 23, 1845—nearly two months into his stay at Walden
Pond but nine years before he would publish the book about that stay—
Henry David Thoreau intended to spend the afternoon fishing. He set out
for Fair Haven Pond but was stopped by a heavy rain that, after soaking him,
led him to seek the nearest shelter. He found cover in the humble home of
"John Field," the "shiftless Irishman" who would occupy some memorable
pages in *Walden*. On this August day, meeting Field sets Thoreau to thinking
about how to live meaningfully and well. Thoreau craves a life of "ventures &
perils," of "enterprise and discovery." In his journal entry recording his day's
adventure, he writes with passion about making every moment count. To
live well one must find the meaning that accompanies each moment. These
thoughts lead Thoreau to write about the potent meaning that he finds in all
things but that seems to elude most men: "In all the dissertations—on language—men forget the language that is—that is really universal—the *inexpressible meaning* that is in all things & every where with which the morning
& evening teem. As if language were especially of the tongue. . . . The rays
which streamed through the crevices will be forgotten when the shadow is
wholly removed."[1] For Thoreau, natural phenomena have a "meaning" typically "forgotten" by humanity—forgotten, perhaps, because this meaning resists representation in conventional uses of language. He believes, however,
that this meaning deserves recognition and even some sort of representation,

a new sort of "language," some method of conveying the "inexpressible meaning" of "all things."

This thought challenges the transcendental philosophy that Thoreau was avidly exploring with the help of his friend and neighbor in Concord, Ralph Waldo Emerson, who assumed that conventional language aids the human quest to know nature as a means to human reason. In spite of its challenge to transcendentalism, Thoreau's interest in a meaning for nature that evades language persisted in his thinking. As he expresses it on this August day in 1845, he believes that natural phenomena hold a "meaning" that humans generally fail to recognize. Thoreau's understanding of nature's "inexpressible meaning" invites us to think beyond our common uses of the term "meaning," which we typically associate with the specific significance that human beings ascribe to something. Key to our common use of the word "meaning" is the fact that we generally think of this "specific significance" as something generated by human beings; that is, we presume that human minds determine the significance of things, thereby determining their meaning. Because we humans are the meaning-makers, we can typically articulate the meanings we create. We make meaning, and then we name it in language. As Thoreau suggests here, however, his particular understanding of nature's meaning centers on its *being*—a being beyond human expression. As he says, this sort of meaning resists conventional representation in language but is, instead, "the language that *is*" (emphasis added). In spite of Thoreau's use of the word "language" here, the notion of "meaning" that he employs resists language because it presumes that existence is significance, or that being brings along with it a value—even if that value is "inexpressible."

Such a notion of meaning also subverts the idea that humans determine meaning. If, as Thoreau argues, meaning resides in the existence of things, in the particularity of forms and phenomena, then the significance of the natural world is beyond the powers of human expression. This is because, according to this view, the significance of nature (its meaning) is its physicality, and physicality evades expression—except, of course, by means of its very physicality. For Thoreau, nature's meaning is its being, the mysterious presence of its particularity, and his own humility and wonder in the face of its multiple phenomena. In this view, perhaps the closest humans can come to experiencing this aspect of the natural world—the "language that is"—is to study natural phenomena closely, attentively, and humbly, to revel in nature's physicality.

Thoreau's pursuit of nature's meaning was lifelong, involving countless rural walks, several ambitious journeys into wild places, innumerable moments of close observation of natural phenomena, and thousands of written pages. His quest for knowledge of nature also entailed a sensitive and probing analysis of how language works on nature's behalf. Reviewing Thoreau's decade-long analyses of language could occupy a scholar for a lifetime, but two passages in his writings provide us with an introduction to two points central to his theory of language and nature.[2]

We begin with Thoreau's enigmatic remark about "the inexpressible meaning that is in all things & every where," found in his journal entry of August 23, 1845, which provides the first key to Thoreau's understanding of nature: human language, as it was commonly used, failed to communicate the natural world. As he had written in 1845, the "meaning that is in all things" could not be conveyed by conventional language, since a language "of the tongue" eluded that meaning. Thoreau believed that through their very existence, natural events and phenomena had a meaning of which most of human society remained ignorant, and he sought a way to communicate this meaning. For example, Thoreau found great value in such things as "[t]he rays which streamed through the crevices"; he thought that they spoke a "language" through their very occurrence. The question of how to capture this meaning for himself and others would occupy Thoreau throughout his life. Although "the meaning that is in all things and every where" was both "inexpressible" and often "forgotten," Thoreau would dedicate his days to trying to "publish" its inexpressibility through his public and private writings. He indicates his reason for pursuing this paradox—publishing the inexpressible—in the 1845 journal entry: this was the language that provided the fundamental connection between human beings and "all things and events" of their world. This alternative language was "universal" and, Thoreau was certain, crucial to understanding nature's truth.[3]

The second key to Thoreau's sense of the limitations inherent in language is found in a section of *Walden*. This passage represents a reworking of the August 23, 1845, journal entry. (Such reworkings were common for Thoreau; he revisited journal writings and revised them for publication.) In his revision of the journal passage for *Walden*, Thoreau insists, amid a discussion of language, reading, and listening to nature, that "all things and events" speak a language. This claim echoes directly the language of the earlier journal passage. However, in *Walden* he elaborates on the "inexpressible meaning" that he had named in his journal by describing it as a language "*without metaphor.*" In naming "metaphor," Thoreau calls attention to that tool of language that frequently appeared in his culture's discourse concerning the natural world. Metaphor, he wrote in this key section of *Walden*, had become "copious and standard"—so much so that men remained "in danger of forgetting the language" that things "spoke" *without* metaphor. That is, metaphor had become so pervasive in cultural discourse that few people realized that it obscured and limited their vision. Metaphor, Thoreau suggests here, had become a limiting habit of thought—a way of perceiving the world that seemed as natural as nature itself but that prevented thorough understanding.[4]

Thoreau's decision to revise his 1845 journal passage to include a specific discussion of metaphor suggests that he believed that in his immediate circle in Concord and, perhaps, more generally in his culture, metaphor was overwhelming language and the human ability to understand the natural world. As we have seen, metaphor informed how nature was understood in Thoreau's era: his contemporaries employed metaphors for nature in various cultural pursuits, and Susan Fenimore Cooper struggled with those metaphors. However, as far as I know, few people directly discussed this tendency to see nature through metaphor and, thereby, to create distance from nature. Yet Thoreau does. In this way, he is unlike Cooper, whose writings acknowledge and resist the dominant metaphors for nature but do so only implicitly. Cooper challenges the tendency to see nature as a metaphor by suggesting that nature's truth emerges through the facts of natural history, observation, and a humble approach to phenomena; her works thus demonstrate both the power of metaphors for nature within her culture and her own consequent desire to learn nature's more authentic, historicized, material meanings. Nonetheless, Cooper's disruption of these metaphors remains subtle. Thoreau, on the contrary, cites metaphor overtly as a problematic aspect of the ways in which, as he describes it, "our lives are domestic in more senses than we think."[5]

While Thoreau was certainly familiar with the techniques and influence of landscape painting, with the popularity of shaping landscapes to exhibit good taste, and with the Emersonian faith in the powers of reason, he grappled less with the specific metaphors for nature upon which these aesthetics were based and more with one significant effect of such approaches to nature: their abstraction of the physical environment. Thoreau wrestles with the fundamental issue of the role that language plays in the human relationship to nature and, more specifically, with metaphor as an overwhelming force in conventional language and thought. He struggles ultimately with humanity's tendencies toward anthropocentrism and abstraction.[6]

Precisely because the metaphors for nature that informed landscape painting, landscape design, and Emersonian philosophy obscured "the inexpressible meaning that is in all things," they served as powerful instruments in shaping cultural understandings of nature. Just how they did this warrants some explanation. The ways in which literary and artistic aesthetics shape cultural understanding is a slippery subject that has been explored by many scholars—though definitively by none. Still, most scholars agree that, although most artistic productions tend not to be direct instruments of power over people, they do give expression to currents of thought in a society and, thereby, participate in cultural change by means of giving specific expression to ideas circulating within society. Consider, for example, Harriet Beecher Stowe's *Uncle Tom's Cabin*, which did not literally start the Civil War but was widely credited with giving voice to widespread concerns and, thereby, inspiring people to act. Such works of art are agents of change. Cole's, Downing's, and Emerson's works are manifestations of a set of historical circumstances that made it possible, and perhaps even probable, that people would increasingly understand nature in anthropocentric terms. This set of historical circumstances includes the growth of industry and resource extraction that accompanied the rise of capitalism, and that increasingly led to the commodification of nature; the felt need to "tame" the landscape so that it was suitable for productive, healthy living; and the anxiety accompanying the desire for American cultural independence at this time. Also relevant is the phenomenon that Lance Newman has recently described as central to understanding romanticism: the "changes in the balance of class forces in New England in the 1830s and 1840s" that accompanied the industrialization of the northeastern United States. The metaphors for nature employed by Cole, Downing, and Emerson (progress, refinement, and reason) did not themselves colonize the minds and language of innocent Americans and alienate them from the physical world. Rather, the metaphors employed by these figures grew organically out of their cultural moment, reinforcing attitudes toward the natural world that already had a place in cultural discourse.[7]

These metaphors enabled an aesthetics of alienation not because the particular men I examine here were startlingly "new" in their approach to nature, but because they helped perpetuate the distance from nature already present in discourses of nature. In doing so, they engaged in what Michel Foucault calls the discourse "practices" of a period. As Foucault explains, "[A] change in the order of discourse does not presuppose 'new ideas,' a little invention and creativity, a different mentality, but transformations in a practice, perhaps also in neighbouring practices, and in their common articulation." The metaphors for nature that we find in the works of Cole, Downing, and Emerson were particularly formative representations of nature—"neighbouring practices"—from this period when discourse concerning nature was undergoing such a "transformation." Drawing on their individual interests, concerns, and artistic talents, as well as on the ways of thinking about the natural world that were available to them at that time, each communicated part of what Jane Tompkins (following Foucault) has called "nodes within a network," or expressions of "what lay in the minds of many or most of their contemporaries." Of course, the particular forms that these men's aesthetic expressions took were "original"; yet some of the assumptions that informed their aesthetics drew from the currents of thought circulating in their society. The same currents of thought about the role that nature would play in America enabled Cole to express concern for the diminishing American wilderness, Downing to seek to capture a sort of wildness through landscape design, Emerson to imagine a new relation to nature through his philosophy, and Cooper and Thoreau to be concerned about certain aspects of their contemporaries' representations of nature. Clearly, some Americans were thinking about how to understand—and represent—the natural world in mid-nineteenth-century America. How these figures engaged and pursued those currents of thought, however, differed notably.[8]

Through our consideration of these three metaphors for nature—progress, refinement, and reason—we have glimpsed part of a transformation in a discourse practice: how expressions of passion for nature can become expressions of passion for something other than the physical world. In each of the three cases examined in the preceding chapters, passion for nature grew to be a passion for some aspect of humanity. Each metaphor became a way of conceptualizing the physical realities of the natural world in service to some humanly constructed vision—whether it be a vision of progress, refinement, or reason. For instance, we have seen that a concern about the nation's course could transform a desire to celebrate the landscape into an ardent expression of national progress. Similarly, we have seen that an inquiry into the capacities of human reason could shape a supposed passion for nature into a celebration of the intellectual powers of humanity. These metaphors suggest a troubling aspect of mid-nineteenth-century American culture: through certain cultural productions (landscape painting, landscape design, and Emersonian philosophy), the nation's proclaimed love for its physical environment became embedded in abstraction. Through these metaphorical understandings of nature, artists and writers revealed the nation's growing alienation from the natural settings that it purportedly loved so passionately.

The common ingredients of these metaphors warrant some comment. The metaphors share these key components: 1) their assumption of the centrality of humanity in understanding the natural world; 2) their effect in distancing the natural world from the realm of human concerns; and 3) their illusion of providing humans with control over nature. At first glance, the first two components may seem at odds with each other, but this is not the case. If we consider each of these key components in turn, we see that each of the metaphors participates in a story about nature's meaning in the lives of human beings. Similarly, each story places human beings at center stage: nature's meaning, as well as its ideal state, is circumscribed by human identity. As Emerson had written, "The Universe is the externization of the Soul." If we consider his words as they pertain to these three metaphors for nature, we might say that each of them served to "externize" some aspect of the human condition.[9]

As each metaphor was put to work, then, it functioned ideologically. From the perspective of nature-as-progress, the natural landscape could be read as a symbol of the rightful march of civilization across the continent. Nature was a metaphor for American progress, and when nineteenth-century Americans envisioned the landscape as a testament to the success of their young nation, they were assuming for nature a meaning that reinforced their preferred vision of themselves. Similarly, when followers of Andrew Jackson Downing's landscape philosophy shaped their surroundings to display their gentility, they took for granted nature's function as a vehicle for the development of their own good taste. And, when Emerson and his fellow transcendentalists contemplated analogies between the natural world and the human intellect, they assumed that nature existed as a means to self-expression and self-cultivation. Each of these metaphors figured nature in terms of a meaning that had more to do with human preoccupations than with nature itself.

In this way, these metaphors had the effect of distancing the natural world from the realm of humanity—the second of the key components mentioned above. Precisely because humans imbued their understandings of nature with their own concerns, humanity became alienated from the physical world. Once we assume a meaning for something that has more to do with our own affairs than with the particularities of the thing under consideration, we prevent ourselves from knowing it directly. When nineteenth-century Americans saw their natural environments as means of expressing their own refinement, they increasingly failed to see those environments for what they were: particular ecosystems, each with its own biological diversity, unique flora, and ecological challenges. As they disturbed various unique ecosystems in hopes of transforming the landscape so that it might fit their vision of a "refined" space, people silenced the meaning of nature that Thoreau sought— that meaning being its physical particularity. And as they developed their human-centered (or, anthropocentric) meanings for nature, they distanced themselves from it—inadvertently, perhaps, but definitely and powerfully.

For most of Thoreau's contemporaries, nature's meaning became its ability to display good taste. Alternative meanings of nature, such as those that Thoreau or Cooper found in its materiality, became more difficult to uncover.

Most important, perhaps, these metaphors achieved what I have identified as their third key ingredient: they provided the illusion of having control over nature. In some ways, of course, having control over nature was not an illusion at all: as Carolyn Merchant reminds us, early Americans made massive and nearly irreparable changes to watersheds, ecosystems, and landscapes, seriously challenging the ecological integrity of many bioregions. Americans of the nineteenth century built railroads and engines, countless factories and mills, and lasting dams and cities. As several historians have noted, the physical landscape of America that we now know came of age in the nineteenth century. Metaphors of progress, refinement, and reason clearly did provide control over the land, and these are the physical changes that have led writer Bill McKibben to predict the "end" of nature. As we have come increasingly to understand, these changes to the physical environment have resulted in human beings having merely the illusion of control over nature, for these changes to nature are eventually changes to humanity—a species that is, of course, a part of the natural world. Indeed, the illusion of control over nature masks the reality that we have failed to understand certain aspects of what we might call nature's "truth": its (and our) need for preservation, sustainability, and ecological integrity.[10]

The metaphors upon which these works rest have become part of the "common articulation" of nature. In addressing landscape painting, for example, Kenneth John Myers argues that "in the second quarter of the nineteenth century . . . the mental practices necessary to the objectification of particular environments as picturesque landscapes became so commonplace among leading elements of the northeastern elites that they were reconceptualized as natural rather than learned abilities." As individuals lose sight of the "learned" nature of our understandings, they lose sight of the origins of those understandings and, hence, of their ignorance concerning the physical environment. Once an established part of American cultural identity, the aesthetics upon which those understandings are based would become increasingly difficult for people to recognize; they would have difficulty hearing that alternative type of "language" that Thoreau had identified—the one with which nature "teemed" its meaning. In this way, these particular metaphors shaped understandings of nature.[11]

If we acknowledge that each of these metaphors became a powerful tool in shaping the American relation to nature, we recognize that together they would grow more powerful still. Indeed, it is likely that in the middle of the nineteenth century, individuals did not employ one single metaphor for nature in their speech or thought, and most of them likely gave little deliberate thought to how their relationship with the natural world embodied the metaphors inherent in their understanding of nature. Most of us are not that conscious of our assumptions and language, at least not on a regular basis. Instead, it seems likely that some mid-nineteenth-century Americans held a passion for nature that embraced several ways of understanding nature through abstraction and metaphor, and that such metaphors easily and frequently mixed and merged with one another. For example, Downing's landscape philosophy mixes an understanding of landscape as a metaphor for refinement with a set of assumptions similarly rooted in metaphorical conceptions of nature: a refined landscape signified the rightful progress of the nation, as well as of the individual. In this way, an adherent of Downing's philosophy could easily embrace the landscape as metaphor for refinement and for American progress. Similarly, one who saw nature as a metaphor for human reason could also adhere to an understanding of nature as American progress. Such an individual would conceptualize the natural world as the promise of a particularly American form of intellectual power. For this person, nature would be evidence of America's intellectual superiority.

These metaphors for nature fit well together, as a passage from Emerson's *Nature* illustrates. Emerson's words reveal his assumption that those persons most refined and closest to "truth" would be able to discern the "relation between the mind and matter" that Emerson claims "stands in the will of God." He explains: "A life in harmony with Nature, the love of truth and of virtue, will purge the eyes to understand her text. By degrees we may come to know the primitive sense of the permanent objects of nature, so that the world shall be to us an open book, and every form significant of its hidden life and final cause." These words merge an understanding of nature as metaphor for reason with nature as metaphor for refinement and American progress: Emerson proposes here a nature that opens itself to a refined, progressive American culture. Such an understanding of nature would provide an attractive story for the young nation to embrace: it promises America a providentially designed path to ultimate knowledge. These metaphors for nature help create assumptions about the human relationship to nature that could structure a national ideology. In each version of the story, nature "subserves," to borrow Emerson's word, to humankind.[12]

Another way of saying this is to say that the natural world became the human world. Its processes, systems, and various phenomena were largely overlooked as Americans increasingly conceptualized the landscape as the site of a human civilization, without regard to a specific physical setting. On the one hand, it could appear that Americans were highly aware of their physical surroundings: the American lands were depicted in landscape paintings, shaped into tasteful estates and parks, and written about extensively by romantic writers. Furthermore, Americans could be said to be highly aware of their physical landscapes as evidenced by their very success in altering those landscapes: after all, environmental engineering requires some understanding of the physical world. But on the other hand, we could also see mid-nineteenth-century American culture as having very little to do with the physical world at all, since these cultural productions of the landscape—whether paintings, parterres, or poems—were highly dependent upon abstracting the landscape from its natural life and conceptualizing it in these specifically human terms.

Henry David Thoreau recognized the difficulties inherent in expressing passion for nature, so much so that he would spend much of his writing life teasing out the precise relationship between himself and his world. As he wrote in his journal in August of 1845, Thoreau would seek, especially through his private writings, to express "the language that is—that is really universal—the inexpressible meaning that is in all things & every where." He would quest beyond metaphor, seeking his version of the truth of nature.[13]

The Pursuit of Nature's Truth

The story of Thoreau's complex relationship to metaphor bears revisiting because it ultimately offers insights into his desire to use language to convey what he saw as nature's truth. It also sheds light on metaphor's role in shaping understandings of nature, or of what Cooper had called the "real." As Thoreau would write in his journal during the winter of 1846, he also pursued the real with a passion: "to keep [one's] eye constantly on the true and real is a discipline that will absorb every other."[14]

Here is a short version of the story of Thoreau's relationship to metaphor. As a young writer, Thoreau knew well its virtues; his neighbor and mentor, Ralph Waldo Emerson, was one of metaphor's strongest proponents. As we have seen, Emerson's view of language insists that words function to connect visible things to humanity through metaphor, and he found little value in language that sought to directly convey the details of natural facts without the added layer of allusion to human experience. He wrote, "I cannot greatly honor minuteness in details, so long as there is no hint to explain the relation between things and thoughts." For Emerson, correspondence through metaphor, image, or analogy was crucial to the success of discourse. Thoreau would eventually disagree. His challenges to Emerson began in the years preceding the publication of *Walden* (1854), as Thoreau thought hard about the best way to convey to others his relationship to nature. Eventually, he identified metaphor as a ubiquitous and problematic means of representing natural phenomena. There was clearly a debate at work in midcentury Concord over the relationship between nature and language.[15]

However, despite his concern over metaphor, Thoreau incorporated it into his published writings with extravagance and abundance. *Walden* in particular is saturated with metaphor: in what would become his most famous book, nature functions metaphorically, largely as a means to self-cultivation and as a symbol of the possibility of human enlightenment. Yet even as Thoreau prepared *Walden* for publication, he struggled in his private writings not only with metaphor but also with the larger question of whether language could serve him at all in his desire to convey nature's meaning. In his journal, Thoreau increasingly devotes himself to creating a record of natural phenomena that grants significance to the phenomena themselves.

While Thoreau was always a writer, and therefore one invested in the powers of figurative language, he seemed to make a change in his life in the spring of 1850—a general shift away from metaphor and toward conveying the literalness of natural phenomena through description. What we see through much of this later writing is Thoreau's struggle over the relation between things and thoughts. From 1850 until his death in 1862, Thoreau became increasingly occupied with this relation and with the close observation of natural phenomena. Toward the end of his short life (after *Walden* and his other major publications), Thoreau nearly—and tellingly—abandoned metaphor altogether in a large project that would use language in as simple a form as possible: here words simply recorded the phenomena of his world. He began to record in notebooks—in rather spare prose—the natural phenomena and natural history of his area. These charts, lists, and tables did not reach readers until recently (and most remain unavailable), but they demonstrate most directly Thoreau's passion for pursuing nature's inexpressible meaning. As several scholars have discussed, the ultimate goal of his copious, detailed study seems to have been nothing less than an account of all the natural phenomena of his area over a ten-year period. Some scholars refer to this project as Thoreau's "Kalendar," while others prefer the phrase "phenological charts." No matter what we call it, Thoreau's undertaking was monumental, though he would not live to see its completion. Upon his death, he left thousands of pages of notes, lists, and tables, all aimed, it appears, at charting nature's meaning.[16]

These later projects make clear that Thoreau's passion for nature, like Susan Fenimore Cooper's, led him to believe that natural phenomena had meaning in and of themselves, without regard for conventional human value systems. We might say that throughout his life, he moved toward a prose—and to a passion for nature—closer to Cooper's than to Emerson's. For Thoreau, as for Cooper, there was most definitely reason to "honor minuteness in details." Ultimately, metaphor, which he had referred to disparagingly in *Walden* as "copious and standard," was an impediment to expressing his passion for nature.[17]

That's the short version of the story. The long version, however, is much more interesting, for it helps us see Thoreau's arduous and painstaking struggle with the limitations of language in expressing nature. On the one hand, most of *Walden*—which remains his most celebrated work—is immersed in expression through metaphor. There it seems that Thoreau shaped his language in ways that he believed would impress his fellow transcendentalists, as well as in ways that would appeal to his audience. We might see the frequent use of metaphor in *Walden* as an implicit testament to the difficulty of evading metaphor in an age when metaphors for nature pervaded cultural discourse as the increasingly industrialized America grew evermore alienated from the natural world. On the other hand, the Thoreau of *Walden* is not the whole story of Thoreau's understanding of metaphor—or of nature.

An examination of Thoreau's later writings shows us that increasingly, and even as he was writing *Walden*, Thoreau expressed in his private works a desire to escape metaphor. Especially in his journal after 1850 and in his later natural history projects, Thoreau wrote *beyond* metaphor so as to record what he saw as nature's meaning. As Robert Kuhn McGregor argues, *Walden* should be seen as little more than a "progress report" in Thoreau's ongoing relation with nature. We find throughout Thoreau's works a passion for nature that wants to break through metaphor—to escape the convenient but confining cultural tendency to understand the natural world as always and already symbolic of something other than itself. We see this in his journal writings as early as 1845 and, in fleeting glimpses, even in *Walden*. Finally, Thoreau discovered a way to use language that better served his purposes in conveying nature's inexpressibility, which he had also referred to as the "language that is." This longer version of the story reveals Thoreau's pursuit of nature's meaning through a language that was as physical and concrete as nature itself.[18]

"Sounds" and a Language without Metaphor

There are several places in *Walden* where we witness Thoreau's struggle to convey his experience of nature without metaphor. Perhaps the most powerful is in the "Sounds" chapter, where he states his desire to perceive nature through a vehicle other than language, which itself rests on metaphor: words serve as linguistic signifiers of other things. While Thoreau examines many aspects of his contemporaries' relationships to nature throughout *Walden*, in "Sounds" the topic of investigation is metaphor itself. There he addresses head-on the limitations of knowing nature through metaphor. If we consider the chapter fully, however, we realize that it does not achieve much resolution; even this chapter that announces the limitations of metaphor clings to it.

Some context for Thoreau's "Sounds" discussion is useful here. Thoreau comes to his "Sounds" chapter from the one called "Reading," where he urges his contemporaries to "really hear and understand" the wisdom available to them through literature. Reading, he emphasizes, requires much work: the active discerning of truths applicable to our individual lives. While some of us are adept at such discernment, most of us, he strongly states, are not: "We are under-bred and low-lived and illiterate." Our illiteracy, however, could be cured by skilled reading. In fact, Thoreau suggests that there are works of literature that could alter our lives by revealing such truths as we have never dreamed of: "The book exists for us perchance which will explain our miracles and reveal new ones." Through reading, we may discover aspects of ourselves that we did not know existed.[19]

The "Reading" chapter concludes with a call of sorts for village improvement—but of the intellectual variety, and not the physical variety that Susan Cooper calls for in her "Village Improvement Societies." In his emphasis on improving a village's collective intellect, Thoreau cites the potential of the village to function in the United States as a center for intellectual culture, and he urges villages to invest financially, emotionally, and intellectually in the infrastructure that would enable this vision. He imagines his villagers hosting speakers on many themes, taking part in lifelong learning, and building a culture that endorses, celebrates, and even cherishes discerning, active reading. The entire village could be a sort of school—an "*uncommon* school."[20]

Following this pointed criticism of his society's disregard for lifelong intellectual activity in "Reading," Thoreau begins his next chapter, "Sounds," with the suggestion that another kind of reading—or, to think in Thoreauvian analogical terms, our experience of another type of language—is also neglected in his society. Thoreau begins the chapter with these words: "But while we are confined to books, though the most select and classic, and read only particular written languages, which are themselves but dialects and provincial, we are in danger of forgetting the language which all things and events speak without metaphor, which alone is copious and standard." Conventional human language, the language that relies on metaphor, is "copious and standard"—that is, customary and profuse, saturating our days. Here in his "Sounds" chapter, Thoreau alludes to the limitations of a language based on metaphor. These are limitations with which he would grow increasingly impatient throughout his life as an amateur naturalist. But he also promises the possibility of conveying this other type of language. He clearly imagines an alternative mode of communication: one "which all things and events speak without metaphor." While Thoreau never directly names this neglected, omnipresent language, the title that he gives to this chapter implies that this language is the language of sound. Just as Thoreau's contemporaries fail to read wisely and well, they fail to attend to the sounds that pervade their days. Listening is something his readers need to do more deliberately.[21]

In the course of the "Sounds" chapter, Thoreau helps his readers understand his complaint by describing the richness of the many sounds that accompany him during his stay at Walden Pond. These sounds include the falling of boughs in the spring, the "tantivy of wild pigeons," the splash of an osprey diving into the Pond for a fish, a mink's rush from the water in pursuit of an unsuspecting frog, the flitting of "reed-birds" (bobolinks), and, perhaps the sound most remembered by readers of *Walden*, the pervasive railway cars. Thoreau also notes the village bells, a distant, lowing cow, the calls of whippoorwills and various owls, and the bellowing of bullfrogs. These are the sounds that fill his days. However, Thoreau's accounting of the sounds that he typically hears relies heavily on metaphor. Indeed, in a literal sense, the chapter is filled with metaphors, analogies, and symbolism: as in most of *Walden*'s chapters, "Sounds" contains many figures of speech and extended analogies: the railroad is his "link" to society; the screech owls are "mourning women," and bullfrogs are "ancient wine-bibbers and wassailers." His paragraphs include metaphor upon metaphor: "the whistle of the locomotive" is a hawk's scream, a warning to the world, a symbol of the nation's economic system's rootedness in chattel slavery. ("Up comes the cotton, down goes the woven cloth.") And symbolism runs rampant: the hooting of owls suggests "a vast and undeveloped nature which men have not recognized." "They represent the stark twilight and unsatisfied thoughts which all have." In this sense, Thoreau proves his point very well: language without metaphor is nearly impossible.

Just what, then, is this "language which all things and events speak without metaphor"? While much of this chapter recounts many specific sounds, the direct and nonmetaphorical utterances of his world, much of the chapter has little to do with sounds at all. These other passages suggest an alternate meaning for this vague language. It seems, finally, that this "language which all things and events speak without metaphor" is the existence, the *being*, as it were, of things in and of themselves. It is the very existence of phenomena that Thoreau seeks to communicate and to which he believes people should attend, and he realizes clearly that to do so through conventional human language is impossible. While sounds are an important aspect of his relationship with the natural world, so are the unutterable, unnameable phenomena of the world: "The rays which stream through the shutter will be no longer remembered when the shutter is wholly removed." This elusive experience, which also evades conveyance in language, seems different from sound; it seems to be closer to the perception of a momentary occurrence of nature. "Looking always at what is to be seen"—being a noticer of natural phenomena—will bring true wisdom.[22]

Where this leaves Thoreau is in the position of recognizing a certain value to his experiences with the natural world that he cannot convey. And maybe that is the point: some aspects of that relationship are incommunicable. "Sounds" may be, therefore, poorly named. Perhaps the "language" that Thoreau fears we will forget is that aspect of the natural world that has no "purpose" in terms of human civilization, if human civilization is understood to relate to nature in an essentially utilitarian sense. The language that all things and events speak without metaphor may be the very life of the natural world—the existence of nature, which no language can account for or convey, and which only our senses can begin to understand. They can only be captured by his "being alert"—by sensing, observing, and heeding nature's details.

Clearly, Thoreau hopes to convey in this chapter of *Walden* the benefits of being "a seer" of nature. This seer, however, seems distinct from the Emersonian seer who creates all meaning through analogy or metaphor. Rather, Thoreau's seer suggests that nature's meanings may elude human systems of representation. And so Thoreau expresses briefly here his desire to capture this experience of the noumenal realm, which remains beyond the human ability of representation. For the sort of relationship with nature that Thoreau hopes to achieve, there seems to be no language adequate to the task. From this particular passion for nature, there is, in fact, "no path to the civilized world." Or so he tells us at the close of "Sounds."[23]

We also see Thoreau's struggle with metaphor in his famous loon passage from the "Brute Neighbors" chapter of *Walden*. The loon passage exemplifies Thoreau's grappling with the human tendency to shape the natural world—through metaphor—into human terms. What began as two distinct and moving experiences that demonstrated to Thoreau the elusive quality of nature's meaning to humans seems to become, through his own use of metaphor, a testament to the human desire to control nature. Ultimately, however, the passage points to nature's resistance to metaphor. Seeing this clearly requires a thorough examination of Thoreau's laborious construction of the loon passage.

A number of scholars have interpreted this passage as one of Thoreau's most effective representations of his simultaneous yearning for the wild and feeling of ultimate separation from the world of nature. While Thoreau's literal characterizations of the loon's wild voice and skilled diving emphasize his separateness from it, his rendering of the loon as symbolic of pure wildness allows readers to interpret his chase of the loon as a quest for wildness itself. Through his complex rhetorical maneuvers, Thoreau maintains the rupture between the perceiving subject (himself) and the object of his description (the loon). As H. Daniel Peck observes, "The entire scene emphasizes the independence of object from subject." Through his uses of figurative language, Thoreau underscores both his struggle for accurate perception and the difficulty of representing an aspect of nature in language. This is very useful, especially in alerting readers to their distance from nature.[24]

However, even while Thoreau communicates his distance from the loon and, implicitly, his humility in the face of the natural world, Thoreau's "astonishment, wonder, and disorientation"—characteristics Peck attributes to this section of "Brute Neighbors"—are rivaled by what I will call Thoreau's metaphor of the hunt. By incorporating the metaphor of hunting into his account of the loon, he complicates his presentation of the original understanding of nature's meaning that had accompanied his actual experiences, and he nearly replaces it with a sense of nature's value that is skewed toward human preoccupations. That is, through the metaphor of the hunt, nature's value is measured in terms of the degree to which humans can control natural phenomena. While Thoreau's passage demonstrates his separateness from the loon, it also momentarily abstracts the loon and appropriates it to human ends. Certainly this may not have been Thoreau's intention, but what emerges from his published encounter with the loon is a record of how easily one can abstract the sort of meaning for nature that Thoreau originally experienced.[25]

This interpretation of the loon passage in "Brute Neighbors" follows from a detailed consideration of its construction. The passage has two fairly distinct parts: preceding Thoreau's two and a half page account of chasing the loon appears a one-paragraph commentary on the Concord hunters' predations. This structure reflects Thoreau's composition process, which often involved bringing together loosely related passages from his journal and crafting them into one whole. Here, Thoreau used two distinct episodes from his journal: the first portion, which comments on the Concord hunters' pursuit of loons in autumn, he wrote in the fall of 1845, and it appears in the original manuscript version of *Walden*. This journal passage laments the loss of loons due to hunting in his area, and it reads as a plea for the preservation of loons and as a denunciation of hunting. The second portion of the passage originated from a different experience: it is a reworked journal entry from October 8, 1852, in which Thoreau records an actual encounter that he had with a loon on the surface of Walden Pond.[26]

The combined version of these originally separate writings—the one that appears in *Walden*—reveals neither the strong lament for the loss of these birds due to human hunting that Thoreau developed in his journal of 1845, nor the pure sense of wonder contained in the journal entry from 1852, which closes with a statement that reveals Thoreau's deep astonishment at the loon's diving abilities. Instead, the result of combining these passages is to transform hunting into a metaphor for Thoreau's wonder. That is, he figures his pursuit of his curiosity as a hunt for the loon, and the loon comes to serve—for a powerful moment—as a metaphor for his own enlightenment. Put simply, nature—in the form of the loon—functions temporarily as a means to celebrating humanity.

How Thoreau concocts this metaphor in *Walden* is complex. First, he writes about the "Mill-dam sportsmen," who become representatives of Thoreau: they are all "on the alert" to the loon's "wild laughter." The hunters' goal in hearing the loon is shooting it. Thoreau's is *knowing* the loon, much in the way that he is "determined to know beans" earlier in the book. By likening himself to the hunters, however, he creates a metaphor that represents his quest to know the loon as similar to the violent hunt of the sportsmen. Whereas the hunters arrive at the Pond "with patent rifles and conical balls and spy-glasses," Thoreau's chase of the loon on the water begins with arming himself with oars: "I pursued with a paddle." Thoreau's tools for pursuit clearly pose less danger to the bird, but he nonetheless emphasizes through his words the parallel aspects of the hunt and his own pursuit, and thereby suggests the domineering dimension of his pursuit of his "adversary."[27]

Part of Thoreau's description of the end of his hunt reinforces the notion that his is a quest on behalf of himself, and not for some authentic knowledge of the loon: both the hunters' mission and Thoreau's "game" of "a man against a loon" end with the pond being disturbed by a "wind" "rippling the surface of the water." Nature, as Thoreau puts it, seems to "[take] sides with all water-fowl," as the loon is "disappearing far away on the tumultuous surface." Both the hunters and Thoreau have failed in their pursuits: the hunters return to town to their "unfinished jobs," and Thoreau's job remains unfinished here at the Pond.[28]

When we consider the loon passage in this way, we find that Thoreau's chase of the loon is emblematic of his desire for a different sort of relationship with the natural world: one of domination and control. It is a huntlike quest for some sort of power over nature. Interestingly, Thoreau adjusts what could have been a clear call for the preservation of this form of wildness—the loon—and suggests implicitly to readers that nature be pursued quite literally, albeit in a form potentially less damaging than the hunter's gun. Thoreau's treatment of the loon serves as a testament to the degree to which even his vision of nature was immersed in the utilitarianism of his day: the loon becomes a means to understanding nature, not through Thoreau's mere encounter with it but through his metaphorical representation of that encounter. It is not enough for Thoreau to record his mysterious encounter with a loon; perhaps he feels that his reading audience demands that the encounter serve some purpose in his quest for selfhood. Through metaphor, the passage celebrates the possibility of individual transcendence over nature. In this way, Thoreau's loon passage seems to participate in the very story of nature that Thoreau hopes to revise though *Walden*. We should not expect differently. As Naomi Quinn argues, metaphors are often "selected to fit a preexisting and culturally shared model." His dance with the loon models a relationship with nature based on personal gain, rather than on attending to nature's more organic, alternative meanings. As William Mills has suggested, metaphors can work to "[break] through the bonds of customary vision, that is, those ways of looking at the world which have hardened into unanalyzed convention," but they can also work "toward the establishment of that customary vision." Thoreau's use of metaphor risks endorsing anthropocentric ways of relating to nature.[29]

The anthropocentrism is short lived, however, as the passage ends on a note that suggests the incapacity of metaphor to contain nature. Thoreau's game with the loon concludes when the loon evades him: the loon "balk[s]" Thoreau, the bird's sound "unearthly," as if indescribable in human terms. It "laugh[s] in derision of [Thoreau's] efforts" to reach him, and Thoreau finally catches the bird only through the vehicle of sight. The wind seems to help the loon escape even Thoreau's gaze: "I was impressed as if it were the prayer of the loon answered, and his god was angry with me." Thoreau again employs figurative language as he describes the more-than-human power that seems to aid the loon in its escape. Through this moment of metaphor, we are reminded that metaphors are just as likely to partake of culturally constructed systems of value as they are to convey fresh modes of perception: the metaphor of the loon's "god" helps Thoreau communicate his ultimate recognition of the bird as a creature beyond his human understanding, and one certainly beyond the abstracting powers of metaphor. "[S]o I left him," Thoreau records, indicating both his abandonment of the metaphor of the hunt and his surrender to his realization that the loon's meaning—nature's meaning—eludes his use of language. *Walden*'s loon passage finally suggests the incapacity of metaphor to convey fully this experience of the natural world. By conveying his encounter with the loon in this way, Thoreau subtly comments upon one aspect of the American relation to nature to which he clearly objects elsewhere in his writings: the human tendency to see nature through metaphor.[30]

In other sections of *Walden*, Thoreau more overtly engages predominant metaphors in hopes of shaking them up a bit. He particularly targets the buzz words "progress," "profit," and "business." Considering such metaphors, some recent critics argue that Thoreau's *Walden* often relies on metaphor precisely as a means of engaging readers and directing them toward the natural world. By figuring nature in terms more familiar to humanity, Thoreau's metaphors enable readers to recognize the correspondences between themselves and their nonhuman environment. Thus, while Thoreau often presents his observations of nature through the rhetorical forms of analogy, synecdoche, personification, and allegory, and while these narrative devices often result in Thoreau's addressing the natural world in terms more centered on humanity than on nature, some critics argue that Thoreau's goal in using these rhetorical devices is to familiarize his readers with the natural world. Lawrence Buell, for example, following Paul Ricoeur, argues that Thoreau's metaphors may initially take readers away from a natural subject and into the realm of the comparison, but that ultimately they serve to direct readers back to the original natural subject. Buell explains this "doubleness" of metaphor: "far from alienating the reader from the physical environment, these defamiliarizations seem meant to return us there with a new understanding and enthusiasm."

Figurative language certainly works to help readers reconceive or realize the object of a metaphor. For Thoreau, who wants to awaken his neighbors both to the wonders of their place and to the deadening aspects of their society, this rhetorical device often grants his Concord wilds a meaning more accessible to those living citified lives of quiet desperation. Through metaphor, Thoreau appeals to their way of knowing the world.[31]

Still, Thoreau's articulation of these goals did not come easily to him. He wrote, rewrote, and reworked *Walden* for many years, and the final product is large and difficult to categorize. This is primarily because Thoreau criticized through *Walden* the very foundations of American culture—its particular economy, especially, and the ways in which American enterprise was affecting people's daily lives. Thoreau's complaints were far-reaching, suggesting ultimately that Americans led lives that were quite *un*natural. People unthinkingly contributed to an economy that was destroying the New England landscape; and they were so caught up in demonstrating their refinement that they neglected to examine their inner lives. Finally, people were so removed from the natural world that they failed to recognize what they truly needed in life—what their necessities were, as opposed to the luxuries that cluttered their lives and ate away at their time. This helps explain why Thoreau comes across as a crank, especially in the opening chapters of *Walden*: he was attacking the foundational stories of American culture.

In the end, though, much of *Walden* is sufficiently immersed in metaphor that it leaves readers adrift in philosophizing to such a degree that the real natural world seems far gone. As H. Daniel Peck points out, Thoreau does not provide much specific description of his surroundings until 170 pages into *Walden*, where readers encounter the first "extended description of the actual landscape of the Pond." Even then, "insofar as landscape figures as an important mode of representation during the first half of *Walden*, it figures largely in an intermittent and strategic way"—one in "service of the larger argument" concerning "social reform." Here, 170 pages into *Walden*, Thoreau engages in what Peck calls "empirical observations" as opposed to the metaphysical ones that dominate the book. In spite of this attention to the landscape, most readers of *Walden* find it short on physical detail and long on philosophizing. Lance Newman, for example, notes its "hypostatization of nature into an unchanging transcendental reality," and suggests that in *Walden* "Nature has been materialized as a metaphysical ideal." Put differently, Thoreau's prose emphasizes his experience of symbol making of natural phenomena more than the literal phenomena themselves. The result is that, for many readers, his book calls more attention to him and his metaphor making than it does to the material world. This results in a natural world that seems, to readers of his text, elusive, dreamy, and even imagined. In *Walden*, nature frequently *is* subserved to man—serving as a vehicle for the making of allegory, analogy, and symbol. In terms of Thoreau's goal of realizing "the inexpressible meaning that is in all things & every where," this story of nature would not go very far.[32]

Thus, Thoreau meets with questionable success in offering an alternative relationship to nature in *Walden*. This may be exacerbated by the fact that many readers who know only the Thoreau of *Walden* unfortunately interpret his narrative persona as a misanthropic character who seeks the company of nature only as an antidote to the ills of culture. To this understanding, Thoreau's *Walden* endorses the very rift between civilized life and the natural world that he purportedly sought to heal by assuming the primacy of the self and envisioning nature as a retreat from the civilized world (rather than as an integral part of that world) and as the primary source of self-cultivation (or as the source of human reason). However, this understanding of Thoreau and his work fails to capture the range of his political commitments during his lifetime. Scholars including Sharon Cameron, Lance Newman, David Robinson, and Laura Dassow Walls point out that even in *Walden*, Thoreau undertook a profoundly social experiment. Newman explains that in writing *Walden*, Thoreau "was participating in a widespread movement of revulsion at the sudden explosion of class conflict in the industrializing northeast," making his undertaking primarily social in nature. Furthermore, he was a man deeply engaged in a range of social issues in his day, including aiding the abolition of slavery, protesting the Mexican American War, and celebrating the life of antislavery radical John Brown. Nevertheless, and notwithstanding the recent work of scholars to topple incomplete pictures of Thoreau's commitments to society, he remains in much of the popular imagination "America's great apostle of wilderness," a hermit who sojourned to the wilds of Walden Pond in order to escape society through isolated self-cultivation in nature.[33]

A True Expression of Nature: Thoreau's Journal

The well-known story of Thoreau's contribution to America's environmental imagination may end here—with his participation in the tradition of understanding nature through the dense metaphor that characterizes *Walden*. However, Thoreau's own pursuits of nature took him well beyond both metaphor and *Walden*, and to exclude these other parts of his work from our exploration of his passion for nature is to obscure both the man and his sense of nature's meaning. An examination of his journals reveals that Thoreau struggled overtly all of his life with the capacity of language to convey his experience of nature. To question the relationship between nature and metaphor is to question the function of language itself, which Thoreau did early on in his private writings. As Emerson had made clear, language functions by means of symbolism, which is simply a type of metaphor. What we find is that Thoreau realized that any expression about nature necessarily involves language, but that language ultimately compromises authentic expression to some degree, precisely because it involves metaphor.

But in addition to tackling this inherent problem of language's reliance on metaphor, Thoreau struggled with even more basic issues relevant to expressing his sense of nature's meaning. Could he best express himself through lecturing or through writing? Should he craft his ideas into words that others might read, or should he keep his writings private and to himself, thereby obviating the need to keep the needs of an audience in mind? More foundationally still, how should he experience nature? Should he spend time with others while he explored the natural world, or should he pursue his excursions in solitude? And when it came time to record his experiences with nature, was language up to the task? Could language ever convey his sense of nature's genuine meaning? A reading of Thoreau's journal reveals that he grappled with each of these questions.

First, let us consider how Thoreau addresses the general question of how he might effectively convey his experience through the medium of language. When it came to sharing his ideas with others, he had the choice between lecturing and writing, and he decided that writing was his preferred medium. He arrived at this decision after reflecting upon his experience as a lecturer. Speaking of what he saw as his feeble success at the podium, Thoreau commented on his frustration with having to shape his thoughts so that they were attractive to audiences:

> After lecturing twice this winter I feel that I am in danger of cheapening myself by trying to become a successful lecturer, *i.e.*, to interest my audiences. I am disappointed to find that most that I am and value myself for is lost, or worse than lost, on my audience. I fail to get even the attention of the mass. I should suit them better if I suited myself less. . . . I would rather that my audience come to me than that I should go to them, and so they be sifted, *i.e.*, I would rather write books than lectures. That is fine, this coarse.

The "coarse" form of lecturing forced him to appeal to his listeners, to shape his experience into a form that felt simply false to him. Writing was truer to his experience; it was a "fine" form. Yet even after he decided that the written word suited his purposes more fully than the spoken word, Thoreau continued to lecture.[34]

Thoreau also struggled with the function of language itself. We readily find passages in his journal where Thoreau contemplates the role of language in his life, and these discussions take several forms. On the one hand, we find Thoreau debating whether he is more effective at speaking to audiences or at writing to them; on the other hand, we find him discussing whether to have company in his experiences of nature or to go at them alone, without the distractions of society, and whether to craft his observations into prose for himself or simply record in his journal a more raw record of his observations—what he calls "[m]ere facts & names & dates." He clearly sought a language that might convey the essence of his experience of nature.[35]

Thoreau's frustration with the limits of language surfaces often enough in his various writings that it informs some of his most memorable, quotable utterances. In *Walden*, for instance, he had written that he desired "to speak somewhere *without* bounds; like a man in a waking moment, to men in their waking moments; for I am convinced that I cannot exaggerate enough even to lay the foundation of a true expression." Here Thoreau justified his prose style in *Walden*—at the edge of an expected or typical use of language, pushing the potential of prose to communicate different sorts of truths. Based on his "desire to speak somewhere *without* bounds," we can assume that Thoreau experienced a delight in being at the limits of language—at that point at which words might communicate truth by being broken of their typical uses. Yet as he reminds us here, Thoreau can not quite get to this place without bounds in *Walden*. He has a "desire" to speak in this manner, but he never suggests that he has achieved that desire. Rather, he writes, "I fear chiefly lest my expression may not be *extra- vagant* enough, may not wander far enough beyond the narrow limits of my daily experience, so as to be adequate to the truth of which I have been convinced." Here he suggests that language as it is typically used in prose is not the proper means to convey his particular truth. His may be a truth beyond expression.[36]

Clearly, the nature of these debates was complex; through them, Thoreau questioned social and genre expectations, the efficacy of language, and the getting of a living. (Thoreau did, after all, have to make some money, and the fact that he lectured and wrote for publication all of his adult life, despite his misgivings about doing so, attests to the threat of poverty overcoming even firmly held principle.) The debate itself, however, indicates the depths of Thoreau's struggle to communicate what he saw as the essence of his experience—an essence that had much to do with his own relationship to the physical environment. He did not want to compromise it through representation. Thoreau addresses this specific issue of how to communicate his particular experience of the natural world in the course of his journals. His dialogue with himself about these issues takes a set of interesting turns, but at the core of Thoreau's struggle is his desire to be faithful to nature's meaning. As he had suggested in August of 1845, he believed that meaning was "in all things & every where," but this meaning seemed ultimately "inexpressible." Communicating his experience through language would necessitate devising a new sort of language.

Attending to nature's meaning often meant going at it alone. Human company, Thoreau found, distracted him from his purpose of experiencing nature:

> By my intimacy with nature I find myself withdrawn from man. My interest in the sun & the moon—in the morning & the evening compels me to solitude. The grandest picture in the world is the sunset sky. In your higher moods what man is there to meet? You are of necessity isolated. The mind that perceives clearly any natural beauty is in that instant withdrawn from human society. My desire for society is infinitely increased—my fitness for any actual society is diminished.

While Thoreau wants the companionship of others and enjoys sharing nature's beauties and ways with others, he finds it impossible to do so. When contemplating nature's beauty and feeling as Thoreau does in such a moment, he finds no one who can possibly share his sense of his experience. To be true to nature—to "perceive clearly" that particular form of beauty—is to be removed from the world of human affairs. Thoreau thus holds a love for nature that removes him from the human community if he is to be true to it.[37]

Thoreau does not contrive this need for solitude. Rather, as he suggests on July 27, 1852, he believes that nature demands it, and he sees it as integral to discerning nature's meaning: "I am sure that if I call for a companion in my walk—I have relinquished in my design some closeness of communion with nature. The walk will surely be more common-place. The inclination for society indicates a distance from nature. I do not design so wild & mysterious a walk." The sort of attention that nature demands of Thoreau requires his solitude, and this is not by his "design." On the contrary, the experience of nature's meaning is "so wild & mysterious" that human company detracts from its fullness.[38]

This quotation from July 27, 1852, seems oddly incongruent with a remark that Thoreau also made in his journal during that same summer; on June 30 he had commented: "Nature must be viewed humanly to be viewed at all—that is her scenes must be associated with humane affections—such as are associated with ones [sic] native place for instance. . . . A lover of nature is preeminently a lover of man." One might read these lines as a confirmation of the prevalence of Alisonian theory in Thoreau's discourse; by associating nature with human emotion or experience, one could "view"—or find meaning in—nature. I do not think, however, that Thoreau's words ought to be read in just this way. What this remark meant for Thoreau was that understanding nature necessitated recognizing one's human perspective. He attempted to limit the degree to which his experiences in what he called "civilization" influenced, shaped, or mitigated his experiences in the natural realm. As Newman notes, Thoreau had long believed "that capitalist social and economic relations [had] destroyed humankind's immediate collective relationship with nature," and he now sought as genuine an experience of nature as possible. That is, Thoreau wished to know nature on its own terms. In the words of biographer Robert D. Richardson Jr., Thoreau recognized "the importance of the prepared eye and mind" in achieving such an experience, for as he knew all too well, the realm of "humane affections" cannot account for all of nature's meaning.[39]

Even the posthumously published "Walking" (1862), which Thoreau presented in earlier lecture forms as early as April 1851, expresses his desire for a language that communicates his sense of nature's meaning. He asks here, "Where is the literature which gives expression to Nature?" And he answers his own question with the assertion that such a literature does not yet exist because writers do not yet have a language that conveys nature directly: "He would be a poet who could impress the winds and streams into his service, to speak for him; who nailed words to their primitive senses, as farmers drive down stakes in the spring which the frost has heaved; who derived his words as often as he used them—transplanted them to his page with earth adhering to their roots." In the context of this discussion of a lack of true language or literature of nature, Thoreau will issue his assessment regarding the problem of passion for nature in his era: "There is plenty of genial love of nature, but not so much of Nature herself." People may express a comfortable, superficial appreciation for nature, but nature itself does not occupy a meaningful or substantial role in their thoughts or lives. No one has given expression to the natural world that Thoreau experiences: "I do not know where to find in any literature, ancient or modern, any account which contents me, of that Nature with which even I am acquainted. You will perceive that I demand something which no Augustan nor Elizabethan age—which no *culture* in short can give." Human culture seems thus far incapable of developing such an account of nature, because culture, he explains, has "affected" both "fancy" and "imagination" with a "blight . . . which it still bears." This "blight"—a wilting, dying, or withering of human imagination—stymies Thoreau's hopes for a passion for nature not limited by language and the conventions of society.[40]

What Thoreau calls for is a language outside of human culture, a relation to nature beyond civilization. Literally, of course, such things are impossible, as human beings cannot escape their human condition. But Thoreau wants to get as close as he can to this ideal, and figurative language serves him well. Through the metaphor of a blight affecting the imaginations of humanity, he calls attention to a paradoxical aspect of civilization: in Bradley P. Dean's words, in "insulating its inhabitants" from the dangers of the physical environment, "civilization risks denying its inhabitants the moral and intellectual benefits" of that environment. Dean explains in a recent analysis of "Walking," "One such benefit is a broadening of conceptions about humanity and our place in the universe. Conceptions developed within exclusively civilized frameworks generally and perhaps invariably reflect their insular, anthropocentric origin by falsely regarding humans as superior to or otherwise separate from nature." For Thoreau, one of the benefits of extended study of the natural world was that one could loosen the hold that civilization's frameworks had on the imagination, helping us to "realize our limitations."[41]

Resisting the blight of civilization meant adopting a posture of humility in the face of nature. In his private writings, we often find Thoreau acknowledging his sense of being merely one of many types of life forms on the earth—a position that humbles his humanity but that he finds comforting, even sacred. In a passage in his journal that might have helped him communicate his sense of the profound meaning inherent in natural phenomena, to which he had alluded briefly in "Sounds," Thoreau wrote of the significance of being reminded of his role as a biological being on the earth amid many biological beings. This passage begins to illustrate the power of nature's sounds to Thoreau's sense of being a member of the earth's community: "The creaking of the crickets seems at the very foundation of all sound. At last I cannot tell it from a ringing in my ears. It is a sound from within not without[.] You cannot dispose of it by listening to it. When I am stilled I hear it. It reminds me that I am a denizen of the earth." This reminder of the physicality of his existence gives Thoreau pleasure, reinforcing his humble place in nature's design. He cannot "dispose" of the sound; the sound is "from within." It humbles him by overwhelming his very being. This matters, because Thoreau expresses humility here as he celebrates his place as just another denizen of the earth.[42]

Thoreau found tremendous value in this relationship with nature; in fact, we might even say that his particular passion for nature was based on his recognition of his humble position in relation to the many phenomena of the physical world. He reveled in this humility. In his journal entry of July 25, 1852, he described the "more real profit" that his relationship to nature "yield[ed]," as over and against the "profit" earned by a typical man with a typical job in the workaday world. Just as he would say in *Walden* as he punned on the word "profit," Thoreau explains that he finds more value in devoting himself to spending time in the natural world than he does in gaining a living by more conventional means. He then offers a beautiful paragraph describing what he gains through his nontraditional employment. We might accept this paragraph and its contents as a representation of a day's "yield":

> The corn now forms solid phalanxes—though the ears have not set—& the sun going down the shadows even of cornfields fall long over the meadows— & a sweetness comes up from the shaven grass. & the crickets creak more loud in the new springing grass—Just after sunset I notice that a thin veil of clouds far in the E[ast]—beyond the nearer & heavier dark grey masses— glows a fine rose color—like the inner bark or lining of some evergreens. The clear solemn western sky till far into night—was framed by a dark line of of [sic] clouds with a heavy edge—curving across the N[orth]W[est] sky at a considerable height—separating the region of day from that of night. Lay on a lichen covered hill which looked white in the moon-light[.]

This passage represents Thoreau's "profit" of one afternoon—a profit that assumes that there is deep value in the sensory experience of natural phenomena. As Laura Dassow Walls writes, Thoreau's "desire [is] to close the gap between self and nature, to 'unsee' it, not by transcendence but by throwing himself bodily into it." Through his physical experience, he arrives at a sense of nature's value. It is as if Thoreau asked himself again and again: surely nature has meaning beyond our metaphor and analogies?[43]

At one point in his journal, Thoreau appears to have decided on an answer to this question. In considering the issue of whether he should continue his habit of crafting his journal passages into prose, he wonders in early 1852, "I do not know but thoughts written down thus in a journal might be printed in the same form with greater advantage—than if the related ones were brought together into separate essays." What is at issue here is the essence of his experience, which seems to get lost as he reworks his original observations for publication: "They are now allied to life—& are seen by the reader not to be far fetched—It is more simple—less artful. . . . Mere facts & names & dates communicate more than we suspect." The next day, he opens his day's writing with a similar sentiment: "Perhaps I can never find so good a setting for my thoughts as I shall thus have taken them out of." The authenticity of his experience seems compromised by artful prose.[44]

Thoreau's attention in his journal to the dilemmas of the composition process indicate his desire to find a more objective, simple language that might convey his observations. In fact, his later writing projects suggest that he came to believe that, to represent the natural world most effectively, one must move beyond an Emersonian adherence to a language of metaphor and toward a prose that conveys experience as accurately—and as literally—as possible, without the intrusion of metaphor. His later writings endorse what Thoreau had surmised in 1852: mere facts, names, and dates communicate more than we suspect.[45]

Nature's Authenticity: The Unfinished Kalendar

We find this more objective writing in one of Thoreau's final projects, one that he would not live to complete. Given its apparently huge scope and purpose, scholars even wonder whether this project—Thoreau's Kalendar, or phenological charts—was one unified undertaking or multiple ventures. As described by his biographer, Robert D. Richardson Jr., the project aimed at nothing less than a record of all natural phenomena in Thoreau's area. During the two years preceding his death, Thoreau created 750 pages of lists and charts recording the copious data that he had collected over a decade regarding certain phenomena. Richardson explains Thoreau's process and aim:

> [H]e worked at rearranging the natural history materials and observations he
> had been accumulating systematically for ten years. His working procedure
> now was to run through his journal entries for a single month, say April, of a
> single year, making a list of observations in a single category, such as leafing,
> in chronological order. Then he would go on to April of the next year and
> write down all the leafing data for that month. From nine or ten such lists,
> generally beginning with 1852, he would then compile a large chart, enabling
> him to track each item of April leafing across ten Aprils. He repeated the

entire process for flowering, again for bird sightings, again for different fruits, for quadrupeds, and for fish.

Whatever we call this final project, Thoreau's vision seems to have been a written record of his place. As Richardson points out, this was "a huge undertaking, a major effort, the general purpose of which seems to have been the distillation of ten years' observations into an archetypal year, not impressionistic, but statistically averaged." Accordingly, William Howarth calls Thoreau's natural history studies the "Book of Concord." This project was both art and science—or science with artistic design. He aimed for a record of nature itself, and through his collections he himself became a sort of participant in the natural world: as Bradley Dean puts it, "he amassed seasonal data so that he would be able to participate creatively, 'by expectation,' in nature's regenerative cycles." In this final project, Thoreau forgoes analogy in favor of merely recording natural occurrences. We might say that the potential Kalendar represents the ultimate record of nature in the least metaphorical language possible: mere facts and names and dates, together combined to express nature's own passion.[46]

It seems that here Thoreau, somewhat like Susan Fenimore Cooper, attempted to use language not as a vehicle for finding nature's "higher," human-centered meanings but as a way of humbly recording the meaning that he discerned in the physicality of nature itself. Thoreau becomes increasingly interested in the relationship between the noumenal and the phenomenal realms—increasingly interested, that is, in things-in-themselves in relation to the human ability to perceive those things. In his Kalendar, awareness and apprehension go backstage but depend upon his humble observations of natural facts.[47]

This is the Thoreau of his last years: the man who hoped to relinquish a language for nature based in metaphysics and metaphor for one that might "fasten words again to visible things" in a manner that Emerson neither envisioned nor practiced. In Emerson's eyes, perhaps Thoreau could not have been a true poet. In his essay "The Poet," Emerson had written, "Nothing walks, or creeps, or grows, or exists, which must not in turn arise and walk before him as exponent of his meaning." This view of natural life forms, which is arguably the view that permeates our culture today, assumes that the job of the individual is to create meaning for natural forms—a meaning that "speaks for, represents," or advocates some aspect of the human condition. In his Kalendar, however, Thoreau relinquishes traditional human meanings and assumes that nature's meaning is there in nature itself—in its facts and

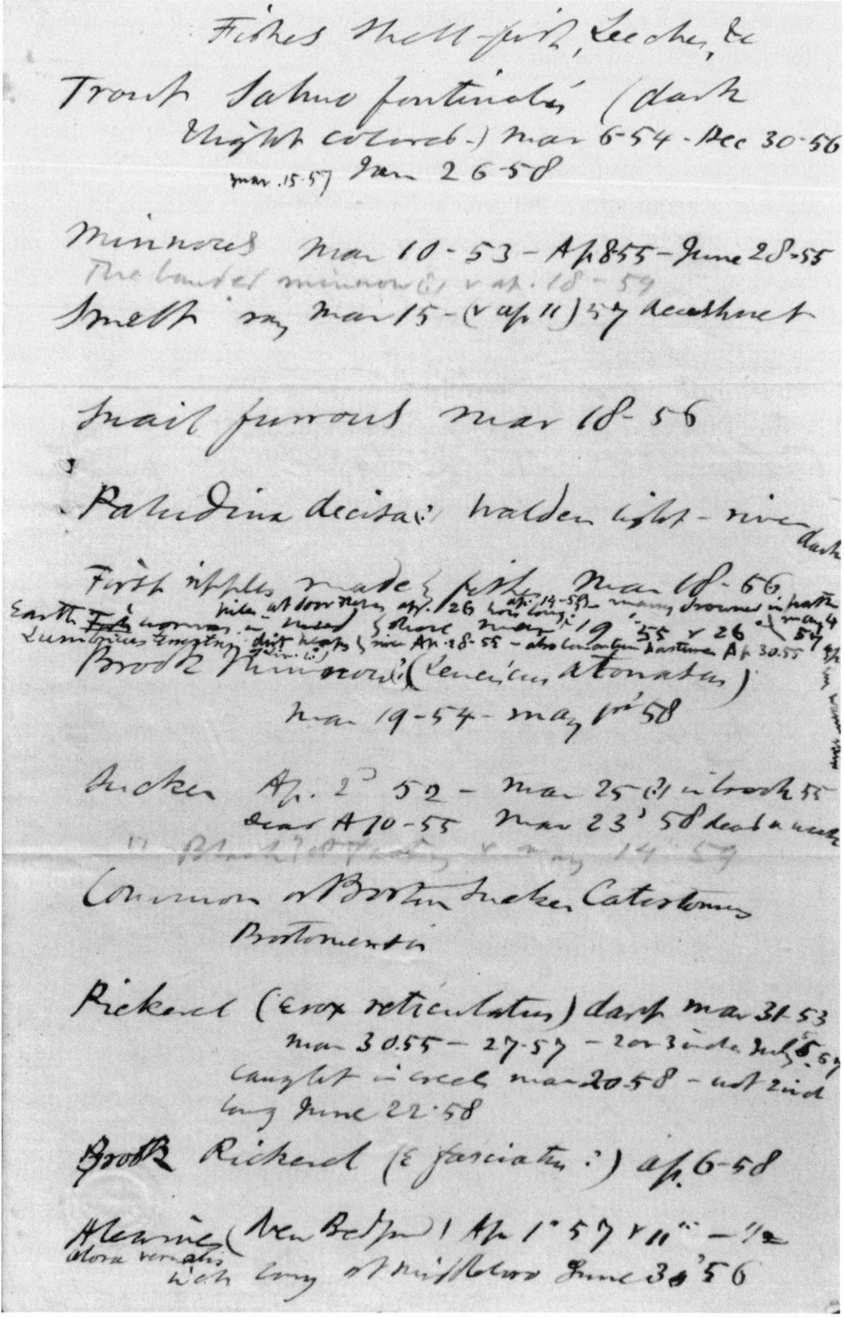

FIGURE 9. Henry David Thoreau, notes for the journal. "Fishes, shell-fish, leeches etc" (MS Am 278.5.20 [3]). By permission of the Houghton Library, Harvard University.

occurrences, and not in the ways in which a man could make nature "arise and walk before him as exponent of his meaning."[48]

Thoreau's intentions for his unfinished Kalendar remain unknown to us; tragically, he died while deeply engaged in this work. Some of his phenological charts inform several later lectures, and versions of some of those lectures were printed in his last years. This is the case for "The Succession of Forest Trees" (1860), "Autumnal Tints" (1862), and "Wild Apples" (1862), the latter two of which were published posthumously. We gain insight here into Thoreau's plans for bringing his nature studies to readers. Perhaps the best view of his goal, however, comes through *Wild Fruits* (2000), a recent posthumous publication of manuscript materials left by Thoreau at his death. Richardson suggests that the materials comprising *Wild Fruits* may represent "the next stage beyond the charts, the gathering up, in narrative form, of the vast materials." Here we might best witness Thoreau's final statements in his lifelong—albeit truncated—quest for expressing his passion for nature and his sense of nature's meaning.[49]

Wild Fruits is structured, first, according to different species of wild plants, and, second, by pertinent observations (usually arranged chronologically) about the plants. In his sections devoted to "Sarsparilla" and "Wild Gooseberry," for example, Thoreau notes the dates on which he has found the plants in fruit, and in a passage titled "Grains" he describes "the rapid growth of rye," noting when one can see the grain waving in the fields (May 14), when farmers generally gather corn for threshing, and when he hears the sound of the chaff being separated from the wheat. While incorporating the natural facts of his phenological data into prose will necessarily involve the use of figurative language, in *Wild Fruits* Thoreau's emphasis remains on the details of individual species, seasonal cycles, and natural history.[50]

Intriguingly, many of Thoreau's concerns in *Wild Fruits* mirror those expressed by Susan Fenimore Cooper in her works, especially in *Rural Hours*. There are differences in these two authors' works, to be sure, but they share the goal of connecting readers with specific natural phenomena, modeling a passion for nature grounded in close observation, and suggesting the value of a view of humanity as participating in a particularized natural environment rather than an abstracted one. Just as the daily and seasonal structure of *Rural Hours* emphasized nature's rhythms, so does the emphasis on individual species and their cycles throughout the year in *Wild Fruits*. Like hers, Thoreau's observations include references to community activities and to the appearance of specific phenomena in literary and natural history writing. Also like

Cooper, he notes locations around the globe where certain species may be found, and he identifies the origins of some species that are not native. And occasionally, as did Cooper, Thoreau lapses into rhapsody, overwhelmed by nature's plenty: "What bounty—what beauty even!" There are more specific connections between *Wild Fruits* and *Rural Hours*: Cooper offers a brief essay in *Rural Hours* on the local production of maple sugar; Thoreau offers a brief essay on the local production of cranberries. Cooper suggests that the American experience was being diminished by the gradual decline in native species; Thoreau similarly asserts that "there are many pleasures" that "he who walks over these fields a century hence will not know." Cooper laments the "penalty" that wildflowers paid "for the honors of culture" as they were cultivated and as wild populations were permitted to dwindle; she notes, "it is a cruel thing in a gardener to pervert, as it were, the very nature of a plant." Thoreau expresses a similar concern over the abstraction of plants that occurs as wild fruits are sold at market rather than picked in their native habitat: "It is a grand fact that you cannot make the fairer fruits or parts of fruits matter of commerce; that is, you cannot buy the highest use and enjoyment of them." Their value is less prone to commodification than their presence at markets would lead one to believe: "They educate us and fit us to live here." Both writers find value in experiencing species in their natural settings, and both thought that the likely inability of future Americans to do so (because of sweeping habitat changes) could only lead to ignorance and prevent what Thoreau called "a simple and wholesome relation to nature." Because both Cooper and Thoreau want to preserve natural habitats, both offer calls for their protection—and especially for the preservation of trees and forests.[51]

There are other striking similarities in their works. Cooper notes that trees "have other values" that are "[independent] of their market price in dollars and cents." Thoreau similarly argues in *Wild Fruits* that such "natural features" have "a high use which dollars and cents never represent." Whereas Cooper suggests that the preservation of trees and closer attention to nature will mark "a farther progress" in American culture, Thoreau states baldly: "It would imply the regeneration of mankind if they were to become elevated enough to truly worship sticks and stones." As a means to helping their readers toward these alternate forms of cultural improvement, Cooper and Thoreau share their experiences of the natural phenomena of their respective local environments. Cooper believes that Americans did not need "to walk blindfold through the fields" any longer, and Thoreau believes that most Americans were "still related to our native fields as the navigator to undiscovered islands in the sea." As one means to curbing this blindness and ignorance, Cooper includes a discussion of the phenomena of American autumn in her *Rural Hours*. Thoreau does the same in his "Autumnal Tints," where he suggests: "Objects are concealed from our view, not so much because they are out of the course of our visual ray as because we do not bring our minds and eyes to bear on them. . . . We do not realize how far and widely, or how near and narrowly, we are to look. The greater part of the phenomena of Nature are for this reason concealed from us all our lives."[52]

Both Thoreau's later natural history projects and Cooper's works exhibit the attempt to make something new of nature in language. They both encourage a tradition of nature representation that is scientific in orientation, that is based primarily on visual observation, and that employs language in a relatively simple manner: by naming what is seen. By attaching words to things in this way, and trusting the ability of language to name the thing and assert its value, they steer nature representation away from the course it was set upon by romantic thinkers such as Emerson. For most romantic thinkers, the meaning of the natural fact lies in its human analogue, and language serves to elucidate that analogy. But for Cooper and, increasingly, for Thoreau, the meaning of the natural fact is its very existence, its being—and language serves a much lesser role: the marking of that being, that existence, that phenomenon.

For Thoreau, and for his contemporary in loving nature's ways, Susan Fenimore Cooper, the facts of natural history were valuable in and of themselves. It was humanity's own hubris that insisted on marrying nature to humanity through metaphor. The habits of a plant are meaningful in and of themselves—although that meaning may escape the bounds of human language. But that meaning is there nonetheless. There is value in the thing itself—in the "mere facts & names & dates" of natural phenomena.

When one assumes that phenomena are meaningful and valuable in terms of their ability to shed light on the human condition, then language becomes a means of exploration, the primary mechanism for the elucidation of selfhood. Words are the means to the human understanding of itself. When one assumes that the phenomena in themselves are more meaningful than any analogy to be drawn from them, then language becomes a tool toward the comprehension of the physical world: it reinforces the primacy, legitimacy, and identity of the thing itself. Words are gifts in both cases—but the nature of the gift differs fundamentally. For the romantic thinker, words are gifts to the self, benefiting self-cultivation; for the natural historian such as Cooper or Thoreau, nature is itself the gift, and words merely serve to record the gift. The one perspective focuses on the individual person's discernment of truth of which he or she is the center; the other insists that the individual is incidental to the truth that is the noumenal world.

Like Cooper, Thoreau saw the need for humans to humble themselves in their views of civilization. In 1852, he recorded as much in his journal:

> It appears to me that to one standing on the heights of philosophy mankind & the works of man will have sunk out of sight altogether. Man is altogether too much insisted on. The poet says the proper study of mankind is man—I say study to forget all that—take wider views of the universe—That is the egotism of the race. What is this our childish gossiping [sic] social literature—mainly in the hands of the publishers? When the poet says the world is too much with us—he means of course that man is too much with us—In the promulgated views of man—in institutions—in the common sense there is narrowness & delusion. . . .
>
> In order to avoid delusions I would fain let man go by & behold a universe in which man is but as a grain of sand—. . . . Some rarely go outdoors—most are always at home at night—very few indeed have stayed out all night once in their lives—fewer still have gone behind the world of humanity—seen his institutions like toad-stools by the way-side.

What seems to be hampering humankind, Thoreau suggests here, is its own "egotism." Whether in philosophy, poetry, or daily life, humankind was too preoccupied with itself. People disregarded the world of nature—the "universe"—in favor of the "world of humanity." In order to escape this "delusion," Thoreau recommends adopting humility. As Robinson writes, Thoreau's later natural history writings "dwarf human measurement and challenge the human capacity to imagine. These cycles teach a humility that is essential to knowing nature, and also to living in accord with it." When the individual could see himself as "a grain of sand," as Thoreau had, then one might discern what Thoreau had called "the language that is," nature's inexpressible meaning.[53]

It is not clear whether Thoreau and Cooper were familiar with one another's work. Scholars have cited Thoreau's one journal reference to Cooper as evidence that he had read at least the opening pages of *Rural Hours*: amid his journal entry of October 8, 1852, which recounts his experience chasing the loon on Walden Pond, he writes, "A newspaper authority says a fisherman giving his name has caught loon in Seneca lake NY 80 feet beneath the surface with hooks set for trout. Miss Cooper has said the same." However, as Jeffrey Cramer has pointed out, when Thoreau read the account of the "newspaper authority," he would have encountered there a reference to Cooper having written about the depths to which loons can dive. So Thoreau need not have read *Rural Hours* to have known either Cooper's name or of her remark about loons. As for Cooper's part, her unpublished papers do not mention Thoreau or his publications, nor do her published works. However, Cooper and Thoreau traveled in similar circles—or rather their works did. Both published essays in *Putnam's Monthly Magazine*, both were avid readers of Humboldt, and both clearly hoped to improve American society through educating its citizens about natural phenomena. More important, both Cooper and Thoreau loved plants, birds, and the life of a naturalist. Whether they knew of one another seems immaterial, since their lives and literary careers demonstrate to us the presence in the mid-nineteenth century of two individuals dedicated to exploring a relation to nature of which they saw little evidence in their popular culture: a close attention to the natural phenomena around them. Passion for nature in nineteenth-century America is, ultimately, a complex meeting of nature and metaphor. Yet it is also these two writers working, in different locations, traditions, and influences, toward a different sort of "truth" for nature: a representation of the physicality of the material world.[54]

Through *Wild Fruits*, then, we glimpse the cultural work that Thoreau's Kalendar could perform: much like Susan Fenimore Cooper in her *Rural Hours*, Thoreau's passion for nature led him to inform people that understanding nature requires sensitivity to natural history, close observation of the natural world, and a humble approach to natural phenomena. By regularly studying the particulars of one's natural surroundings, they each practiced a close observation that, as a matter of course, led to an acknowledgement of seasonal cycles, the variety of life forms, and the regenerative nature of the physical world—realities of nature that led them both, invariably, to humility. Observing nature and seasonal time in this way might provide the bedrock of a new American identity. "By implication," Newman argues in this regard, "the rituals Thoreau represents in *Wild Fruits* will produce devotional experience on the land, which will in turn motivate the community to combine and take action in defense of what they will now see as the basis of their collective identity." Americans might embrace nature's meaning as their own—but not in terms of metaphorical understandings of progress, refinement, or reason. Rather, they might embrace a passion for nature based on nature itself.[55]

Of course, even early in his life, Thoreau had noted how language and civilization can prevent a recognition of nature's materiality. Contrary to the view that Emerson would delineate in "The Poet," Thoreau wrote in his journal in 1840: "The poet does not need to see how meadows are something else than earth—grass, and water, but how they are thus much." Natural phenomena did not need meanings beyond their being; their very being was meaning enough. When Thoreau writes in *Walden* that "we are in danger of forgetting the language which all things and events speak without metaphor," he sounds remarkably like the contemporary geographer Yi-Fu Tuan, who recently wrote, "We are in the habit of denying or forgetting the real nature of our experiences." Like Thoreau, Tuan writes in hopes of alerting readers to the "real nature" that is present in their lives—to the natural and physical processes and phenomena that accompany our days. And like Thoreau, Tuan considers it crucial "to increase the burden of awareness." Doing so, he suggests, is integral to "the humanistic enterprise." Therefore, Tuan praises the efforts of writers who seek to record the minutiae of their worlds, alerting readers to the vast diversity of life forms, the mysteries of natural processes, and the value of the thing in itself.[56]

Thoreau wrote, however, during an age that did not subscribe to the notion that nature has inherent value. He wrote at a time when his neighbor and one-time landlord, who just also happened to be one of America's leading writers, could say:

> All the facts in natural history taken by themselves, have no value, but are barren like a single sex. But marry it to human history, and it is full of life. Whole Floras, all Linnæus' and Buffon's volumes, are but dry catalogues of facts; but the most trivial of these facts, the habit of a plant, the organs, or work, or noise of an insect, applied to the illustration of a fact in intellectual philosophy, or, in any way associated to human nature, affects us in the most lively and agreeable manner.

Yet Emerson seems to have realized Thoreau's final purpose in studying the natural world. In his funeral oration in honor of his young friend who had died far too early, Emerson had praised Thoreau's abilities as a naturalist and as a thinker, calling him "the bachelor of thought and nature." Thoreau was, Emerson declared, "a speaker and actor of the truth," one who had the rare gift—the "unsleeping insight"—of seeing "the material world as a means and symbol." Significantly, however, Emerson could not say what, in Thoreau's mind and life, the material world served as a symbol of. While "none knew better than he that it is not the fact that imports, but the impression or effect of the fact on your mind," Emerson noted, "the meaning of Nature was never attempted to be defined by Him." The fact had meaning for Thoreau, Emerson saw; but that meaning was not one that anyone could articulate. Instead, "[e]very fact lay in glory in his mind, a type of the order and beauty of the whole." Each fact of nature, then, each phenomenon, life form, seasonal repetition, or occurrence in the material world, held meaning in and of it-self—as a testament to the living earth, "the order and beauty of the whole." This understanding was what led Emerson to call Thoreau "our naturalist." Upon Thoreau's death, Emerson would say, "Mr. Thoreau dedicated his ge-nius with such entire love to the fields, hills, and waters of his native town, that he made them known and interesting to all reading Americans, and to people over the sea." Even Emerson recognized that Thoreau's passion for nature led him to humility. To "barren facts" Thoreau had devoted the last of his days.[57]

Although the Thoreau who stands as the "icon of American environmen-talism" is the Thoreau of *Walden*—a book that has been called "the most central text in the ecocritical canon"—we now know the fuller story of Tho-reau, one that points us away from metaphor. Thoreau's days teemed with questions about nature's meaning: "for much of his adult life he was actively mediating between idealist and materialist accounts of the world, as well as between intuitional and empiricist modes of investigating it." The subtle ways in which these divergent manners of perceiving the world might shape hu-man experience would remain Thoreau's primary occupation until his death. Early in his career, he had written a sentence that has become famous among lovers of his works: "Let us not underrate the value of a fact; it will one day flower in a truth." The biographical context for Thoreau's remark is clearly his early interest in metaphor as it was used in transcendental thought. As we have seen through Emerson's *Nature*, transcendentalism valued nature as a means to developing human reason. Indeed, Thoreau would value natural facts throughout his career, but what we find is that his sense of nature's "truth" changes throughout his years. As David Robinson points out, we can see Thoreau's "intellectual life" as "a preoccupation with precisely this impera-tive, to see the convergence of fact and truth." This convergence is deeply rooted in Thoreau's understanding of the powers of metaphor, which under-went revision as he studied nature ever more closely in his last years. By the close of his days, Thoreau had found that a natural fact is valuable in its own right, rather than merely for what it suggests about the human condition.[58]

The Paralysis of Complexity, Revisited

Cooper's and Thoreau's diverse attempts to convey nature's meaning speak to issues with which we continue to struggle in environmental studies and in our culture at large. In twenty-first-century parlance, we might express their dilemma this way: they struggled with the relationship between nature and culture—a relationship that has remained contested in the environmental humanities. On the one hand, as both writers understood (although they would not have used these terms), recognizing the close ties between the human and nonhuman realms is central to a sustainable, ecological ethic. Humans are part of the natural world—we are natural life forms—and neglecting this fact can have very negative consequences for the nonhuman world. If humans view themselves as separate from the world of nature, then they are likely to promote an ideology and lifestyle that assumes that they can alter, develop, and control the natural world in ways that are ultimately detrimental to the well-being of species (including the human species). It is this ideological assumption that propels the belief that humans can completely control the planet, even the atmosphere, and that humans are not dependent on and part of those suffering systems. This attitude enables some people in our own century to believe that global climate change is no real threat to humanity, that the rapid, global decline in biodiversity has no relationship to American political and economic policy, and that environmental toxins are nearly irrelevant to rising cancer rates.

On the other hand, recognizing the ultimate distance between the human and nonhuman realms seems equally central to a sustainable, ecological ethic. Recognizing, that is, that we are both part of nature and frightfully separate from it (and powerful in terms of affecting it) is essential to developing policies, lifestyles, and attitudes that may help restore the health of the earth and ourselves. This recognition of the distance between the human and the nonhuman, however, needs to acknowledge our very dependence on the natural world. I do not mean simply realizing that we depend on the air, water, and earth for breath, sustenance, and shelter; I mean recognizing that, from an ecological perspective, all life forms hold the same value that each of our lives holds. As Thoreau put it, this "meaning that is in all things & every where" is "really universal." Embracing the fullness of nature would mean informing our every moment with the humility that must accompany this recognition. If we cease to understand human beings as the most valuable species on the planet, we might hear the universal language of nature. Finally, both Cooper and Thoreau offer this: with humility comes the selfless observation upon which an understanding of nature depends.

As if Nature could support but one order
of understandings . . .

HENRY DAVID THOREAU, *Walden*

CONCLUSION

The Canalization of Metaphor

NUMEROUS TWENTIETH- AND twenty-first-century thinkers suggest that many Americans are alienated from the natural world. In attempting to isolate a root cause for this alienation, some thinkers point to an economic system that abstracts physical objects from their natural origins by means of assigning value through currency, while other thinkers target Judeo-Christianity and its traditional emphasis on humanity's dominion over nature. Still others have proposed the growing gulf between scientific and humanistic intellectual circles in Western culture as a root cause of alienation from nature, and yet another group of thinkers has pointed directly to the rise of positivistic science as the most influential factor shaping America's current relation to the natural world. Clearly, however, the roots of the American distance from nature can also be found in pursuits associated with the humanities. As Barry Lopez has suggested of the state of the environment, "What we face is a crisis of culture, a crisis of character." In other words, the environmental crisis is as much a crisis of *humanity* as it is one of economic system, religious mythology, scientific pursuit, or positivism.[1]

As the preceding analysis of mid-nineteenth-century passions for nature suggests, an examination of cultural productions usually associated with the humanities (landscape painting, landscape design theories, and Emersonian philosophy) reveals that aesthetic pursuits seemingly devoted to the natural world can serve to alienate people from it. Early to mid-nineteenth-century America was an era when Americans sought to define the natural and cultural identity of the nation, and we can see that the nation's cultural identity was partially rooted in an abstraction of the material world in the name of humanity. Also present, however, was an alternate passion for attending to nature's materiality and for trying to communicate the value of doing so.

Passions for Nature leaves much work to be done. Worth exploring further are the degree to which this alternate passion for nature continues throughout the latter part of the nineteenth century—and into the twentieth and twenty-first; the ways in which this alternate passion for nature may have informed the preservation movements of that same period; and the degree to which American natural-history writing and literature develop the aesthetics of nature's materiality pursued by Cooper and Thoreau. One might ask how American poetry—from Walt Whitman through Wallace Stevens to A. R. Ammons and beyond—continues to pursue the alternate passion for nature that we find in the mid-nineteenth century. In addition, one might explore its earlier roots in the periods of discovery, settlement, and colonization. Further, one might explore how the American educational system has encouraged attention to nature's particularity, starting with the nineteenth-century botany primers, moving through the Nature Study Movement of the twentieth century, and continuing today in efforts to facilitate knowledge of—and experience in—the natural world in public education. Also worthy of much exploration is American culture's continued paradoxical relationship to the natural world; certainly America continues to celebrate the national landscape even as it generally disregards that landscape's particulars.

One might also pursue the ways in which this alternate passion might alienate individuals from the natural world, for, arguably, the passion for nature embodied in Cooper and Thoreau risks alienating people from nature as much as a passion for nature based on metaphor. Onno Oerlemans suggests as much: his analysis of British romantic writers and thinkers demonstrates that their attention to nature's materiality led them to feel alienated from the physical world. This alienation resulted from their feelings of insignificance in relation to nature and their recognition of their own inability to understand nature in its entirety. Attending to nature's materiality, in other words, filled them with awe and wonder to such a degree that they felt extremely humbled by—and ultimately alienated from—that materiality. This is another form of paradox: when they sought to understand nature's materiality, they felt alienated from it. Certainly we see this type of alienation in Cooper's and Thoreau's passions for nature, particularly through the degree to which they feel humbled as they study natural phenomena. But this is a very different type of alienation than the one that results from the passion for nature of their contemporaries (the one based in metaphor). Cooper's and Thoreau's alienation results from attention to nature's particulars, whereas the alienation that accompanies nature-as-metaphor results from the abstraction of nature's particulars. One leads to humility, whereas the other leads to disregard, at best, and arrogant self-absorption, at worst.[2]

Metaphors themselves, however, are not the problem—which is good, because we cannot avoid the presence of metaphor in our lives, our language, or our cultural productions. Metaphor is "pervasive in everyday life, not just in language but in thought and action"—so pervasive, in fact, that George Lakoff and Mark Johnson call metaphor "a natural phenomenon." They demonstrate that human experience, even "our ordinary conceptual system," is "fundamentally metaphorical." And metaphors can be very helpful tools in reorienting thought. As Lakoff and Johnson claim, "New metaphors have the power to create a new reality," and environmental thinkers and activists have relied on metaphor as they address pressing environmental problems. Several metaphors have served the environment particularly well in recent decades. For example, Deborah E. and Frank J. Popper have written about the success that their metaphor of "the buffalo commons" has brought to endangered areas in the Great Plains.[3]

If we take as a given, then, that human beings cannot avoid metaphor, we might accept the preceding analyses as suggesting that we ought to take great care with our metaphors associated with the natural world, since often those metaphors may deceive us into thinking that we are paying attention to nature for its own sake when we are, in fact, deeply embedded in an ethic of control and domination. Such is certainly the case in the particular uses of metaphors for progress, refinement, and reason that we have explored here. While we may not be able to escape metaphor entirely, given that human language is itself a form of metaphor (words are signs of things), and while we may not want to escape metaphors for nature, given that they can be helpful in certain forms, we certainly want to recognize when our assumptions about the natural world alienate us from our surroundings in ways that can cause harm to both ourselves and our world. The problem with metaphors for nature, then, comes when we allow our metaphors to define their subjects—when, in other words, the association developed through the metaphor begins to denote the original subject (the physical environment). In such cases, we risk losing sight of other potential meanings for natural phenomena. Rather than understand nature through natural history or observation of its phenomena, many nineteenth-century Americans envisioned it as the site of American progress, a means to expressing their refinement, or a vehicle for exercising human reason. By understanding the natural world in these ways, they created meanings for it that bore little relation to what H. Daniel Peck calls "the integrity of the world's own structures."[4]

The question remains as to what meaning one can draw from an acknowledgement of "the integrity" of natural phenomena. Cooper and Thoreau seem to have accepted humbly nature's meaning as something they could not know fully; in embracing their ignorance, they found meaning through their humility. I do not mean to suggest that they did not learn about nature, but rather that they continually realized that there was more to learn and that they found fulfillment in their very inability to discern nature's mystery and variety. Perhaps they found value in reinforcing their own ultimate ignorance and humility. The meaning of nature was, simultaneously, its own mysterious physicality and their own ignorance and humility. These concepts—ignorance and humility—can offer a compelling foundation for an approach to nature because they suggest that human understanding is not the basis of nature's meaning. Such a foundation is rare among approaches to the natural world.

Literary theorist Timothy Morton recently suggested that, since humans are as natural as "nature" is, the best we can do in terms of understanding nature is to recognize the space that is the gap between our consciousness (the "inside") and the world (the "outside"). Rather than suggest that there is some authenticity possessed by nature beyond this gap ("something more real beyond inside and outside"), Morton insists that there is only this inside-outside: "There is *not even nothing* beyond inside and outside." For Morton, attempts to convey nature's truth are "a form of ideological fantasy," because we cannot escape the fact that the most we can ever hope to represent is the inside-outside space where our consciousness, perception, and beings (the "inside") meet the world (the "outside"). That may be; perhaps *all there is* is the space where internal and external meet, meaning that there is not an "internal" truth or an "external" truth, but only the space of their meeting. Yet the pursuit of this space continues to privilege the primacy of individual experience, and Cooper's and Thoreau's alternate passions powerfully suggest that we might benefit from privileging the primacy of the physical world—and that one means to do this would be to embrace our ultimate ignorance of it. This approach encourages a tremendous humbling of selfhood, which may be valuable. As Kenneth John Myers argues, "[O]nce individuals learn to forget the role of the self in the production of environmental meaning they experience those meanings as impersonal or disinterested truths." Remembering the ultimate ignorance of humanity may provide a fine grounding for what Morton calls "a 'new and improved'" aesthetic.[5]

There are lessons here for us. Today, there are people who are pursuing a counteraesthetic remarkably like Cooper's and Thoreau's in hopes of altering more dominant, anthropocentric conceptions of nature. For many modern-day, revisionary thinkers, passion for nature must be rooted in a knowledge of natural history, close observation of nature, and an ethic of humility. These were the cornerstones, of course, of Cooper's and Thoreau's passions for nature. Still, our own cultural moment emerges from a history deeply embedded in discourses of environmental control, and the metaphors for nature that developed through the nineteenth-century aesthetics of alienation continue to inform the meaning of the natural environment in our lives today. All around us, we can see those metaphors at work. Arguably, they have come to define our dominant culture's relationship to nature, and they continue to prevent us from recognizing the integrity of natural phenomena and processes. Through its landscapes, its foreign policy, and its political rhetoric, the United States of America frequently tells a story for nature that centers on domination and control.

The Canalization of Metaphor

A term borrowed from the sciences perhaps best describes the extent to which the mid-nineteenth-century metaphors for nature examined here flow through American society today: "canalization." Canalization is a word used by both evolutionary developmental ("evo-devo") biologists and ecologists, and it refers, essentially, to the tendency of characteristics to remain fixed—to be, that is, entrenched as if in a canal or channel. More technically, in the parlance of evo-devo geneticists, "canalization" refers to the ability of a genotype to produce a certain phenotype, regardless of environmental (and even genetic) forces that might be expected to influence the process toward a different end. For ecologists, engineers, and landscape planners, the word is often used in a slightly different form—"channelization"—to refer to the process of modifying, usually by means of a concrete culvert, a stream or river course so that it follows a restricted, usually straight, path at a fixed depth. These are fairly specific uses of the word, but they are its most common. What attracts me to this scientific term, however, is its evocation of a directed, unchanging flow of things. It is this sense of the term that is emphasized by the *Oxford*

Dictionary of Ecology: "the holding of a developmental process within narrow bounds despite . . . disturbing forces." If I may be granted some poetic license, I would like to consider the canalization of metaphors for nature in American culture.

We might apply the above definition to contemporary understandings of the natural world. For example, we can consider as a "developmental process" the ongoing formation of American environmental attitudes. The "disturbing forces" threatening to throw these attitudes off track might be considered to be the degeneration of ecosystems, disturbances to native species, and developments in climate change, all of which signal environmental problems and ecological challenges. We might say that these disturbing forces threaten the "integrity" or "truth" of nature and indicate the early signs of an impending environmental "collapse," to use Jared Diamond's term. Despite these disturbing forces in the global environment, metaphors for nature are so canalized in Western culture that they—and the domination and control to which they lead—continue to misconstrue nature's truth in our lives. The "narrow bounds" of dominant understandings of nature ensure this entrenched course. Metaphorical understandings flow on, uninterrupted and undeterred. Because of historical precedent, habit, and hubris, American culture allows certain metaphors for nature to prevail. These pervasive, popular, potent metaphors lead our society to continually abstract nature, thereby avoiding any confrontation with—or response to—the disturbing forces that indicate serious problems with our current understandings of nature.[6]

I do not believe that American attitudes toward nature are permanently fixed. However, the concept of canalization allows us to envision their force and the work that will be required to alter their entrenched use. It also enables us to realize how controlling they truly are and that we cannot remain passive and expect them to change. As Neil Evernden suggests, we are simultaneously perpetrators and victims of our relationship to nature: "[I]f we would protect nature from the perils of the 'environmental crisis,' we must first acknowledge that those perils arose as a consequence of conceptual imprisonment." Nature's ills result from our conceptions of it—conceptions that imprison both nature and us. Evernden continues, "If we would save the world, we must set it free." In order to alter nature's meaning in our society and address the environmental crisis, we have to dismantle the assumptions through which we "imprison"—or canalize—nature's meaning in our culture. We need, that is, to recognize the powers of metaphors for nature in our lives today. We might be tempted to think that the three nineteenth-century metaphors that occupy the center section of this book belong only to history, and not to us: after all, they grew out of specific cultural movements that are, in some regards, finished. The paintings of the Hudson River School, the landscape designs of Andrew Jackson Downing, and the transcendental philosophy of Ralph Waldo Emerson remain things of the past. But the metaphors for nature upon which those specific cultural productions rest continue to inform our culture's current relationship to nature. They take slightly different forms, but we find echoes of them nonetheless in contemporary society's apparent sense of nature's meaning.[7]

Twenty-First-Century Progress

We have seen how nineteenth-century Americans believed that the nation's progress was both fated and guaranteed. The development of American lands, therefore, was interpreted as a mere means to this inevitably bright future. The physical environment served as a vehicle for displaying a presumably foreordained outcome: the success of the new nation. This celebration of the landscape of progress meant ignoring natural history, destroying some native species, and displacing others. Rather than find nature's meaning in its physical realities, Americans understood the natural landscape as the site of progress. Increasingly, the national landscape bore witness to this conception of nature: cities, railroads, and, eventually, high-rises and superhighways told the story of nature-as-progress.

In our day, American culture continues to assume nature's meaning as a testament to progress. At a basic level, we continue to view highly modified landscapes as evidence of achievement, even when they harm the integrity of local ecosystems, compromise the health of wildlife corridors, or harm local populations of native species. Like our nineteenth-century predecessors, we shape the landscape so that it serves as a testament to the grand story of American achievement and largely ignore the consequences.

For example, we are willing even to mark our most pristine landscapes with monuments to progress: as of this writing, at least thirty cell phone towers have been built in America's national parks. I see these cell phone towers not merely as causes of local disturbances to wildlife but also as evidence that our passion for nature is based more on the pursuit of progress than on any love for the facts or history of natural phenomena. Indeed, we are generally so removed from a consideration of the natural environment that we remain ignorant of the effects of our lifestyles. How many cell phone users consider the effect that their purchases have on the landscape of their "calling area"? How many consider the location of towers supporting their calls when they are "roaming"? If they knew these locations, would they still place their calls? In the name of progress, we compromise nature's integrity.[8]

In fact, our economic and political systems assume the validity of progress at the expense of the natural environment. In my home state of Idaho (as in many others), anyone suggesting a limit to growth is viewed as an enemy of progress and the future viability of the area. In some ways, of course, our society has taken measures to prevent large-scale environmental harm: legislation such as the Endangered Species Act ensures at least that endangered species will be protected. However, as any botanist, ichthyologist, or mammalogist will tell you, getting a species "listed" is a monumental challenge, and locally endangered populations of a nonlisted species receive no protection from this legislation. The legislation considers only global rarity, a loophole that prevents the preservation of many unique landscapes. So we witness progress through new housing developments, increased transportation infrastructure, and sprawling suburbs.

Others have noted the ways in which our remoteness from the natural world appears in our daily activities—activities that affect the natural world in ways of which we have little or no awareness. Jennifer Price, for instance, has provocatively described some of "the geographic and economic disconnections of modern American life." Such disconnections are also illustrated by Wendell Berry, who wishes to call attention to the ways in which our ethic of progress abstracts the natural world:

> We are involved now in a profound failure of imagination. Most of us cannot imagine the wheat beyond the bread, or the farmer beyond the wheat, or the farm beyond the farmer, or the history beyond the farm. Most people cannot imagine the forest and the forest economy that produced their houses and furniture and paper; or the landscapes, the streams, and the weather that fill their pitchers and bathtubs and swimming pools with water. Most people appear to assume that when they have paid their money for these things they have entirely met their obligations.

Like the mid-nineteenth-century audiences who responded to Thomas Cole's prediction of devastation through *The Course of Empire* by believing it was a tale about other lands, we turn a blind eye to real-life pictures that meet our eyes each day as we witness our landscape of progress. The American landscape is a virtual tale of our passion for progress.[9]

Twenty-First-Century Refinement

In the nineteenth century, Americans found nature's meaning in its capacity to display their own refinement. By altering natural phenomena, they shaped the landscapes around their homes in ways that they believed demonstrated their own good taste. In this way, the natural world was used to convey the story of American refinement. Nature served as a metaphor for good taste.

One of the most obvious ways in which we have perpetuated a relationship with our physical surroundings based on the metaphor of refinement is in our acceptance of green lawns and controlled gardens as the norm in land-scape design. More often than not, America's lawns and gardens depend upon threatened water resources, lawn mowers and weed cutters that rely on electricity and fossil fuels (which are in short supply), and herbicides, pesticides, and fertilizers (which, while ensuring a uniform appearance, profoundly affect wildlife, leach into the groundwater, and thereby affect our health, as well as that of our local ecosystem). We maintain such lawns and gardens for the sake of appealing to established aesthetic criteria, meeting the expectations of our neighbors or our neighborhood associations, and demonstrating our own good taste. That we are demonstrating our own refinement through our lawns is unlikely to occur to us, precisely because the association of landscape (and especially of "lawnscape") with refinement runs so deep in our society that it is nearly unrecognizable. We create and maintain such areas around our homes because we are expected to do so, and we rarely question that expectation. This landscape of refinement permeates our society so thoroughly that most of us neither see nor question it.

In my own community in southwestern Idaho, well-meaning citizens recently began a beautification campaign that illustrates how deeply entrenched is this expectation about landscape. Launched at a downtown community festival, the beautification campaign had a booth featuring petitions for folks to sign and placards to be displayed on lawns and in the windows of businesses. The signs read: "It's Everybody's Business." The campaign centers on encouraging people to beautify their lawns and gardens; so that people understood what the campaign instigators had in mind, they had at the booth a spiral notebook with pictures of tasteful lawns for others to emulate. The pictures featured meticulously manicured lawns of Kentucky bluegrass or similar nonnative, water-dependent grass species, with the occasional border garden featuring additional nonnative plant species. Just as Andrew Jackson Downing offered readers images of his tasteful landscape designs so that others could emulate them, the organizers of this campaign put forth through their notebook their images of tasteful lawns, in the hopes that they could achieve a uniform, controlled landscape—one that bears absolutely no relation to the realities of the southwestern Idaho physical environment: it is a sagebrush steppe (basically, a cold, treeless desert). Any knowledge of the area's natural history suggests that people should surround their homes with drought-tolerant plants. (Native species such as sagebrush, native bunch grasses, penstemons, and biscuitroots would do the trick; once established, they would eliminate the need for extensive irrigation, fertilizers, or herbicides.) Clearly, this campaign endorses a view of landscape that assumes its meaning only in human terms and through the metaphor of refinement. It also—through its emphasis on "Business"—suggests that such refinement is part of the "progress" associated with the nation's growth economy.

Across town I now see "It's Everybody's Business" signs. I am clearly more than a bit disgruntled by this campaign. I cannot get over the fact that these signs are meant to prod others—through social pressure and guilt—into following a uniform landscape plan, that they overlook the financial inequities of our community (which prevent some people from attending to their lawns in the way these petitioners would like), and that they do a terrible job of communicating what it is that they want (Who would read a sign that says "It's Everybody's Business" and know that they were supposed to pull weeds and call ChemLawn?). Regardless of these facts, the beautification campaign is most troubling because it endorses a vision of landscape that is steeped in ignorance, control, and domination. It assumes as "right" a landscape that is as incongruous in this physical environment as is a man on the moon.

Perhaps, late at night, I should run around town and scrawl on each sign, "Natural History Knowledge" above "It's Everybody's Business." In all seriousness, though, these signs are just one, relatively benign testament to a view of landscape as refinement. Rather than identify and maintain the uniquenesses of natural landscapes, we shape places into mere settings for our model vision. Our passion is for the model vision, rather than for the unique regional landscape that we modify in order to display that vision.

Moreover, we can look beyond our lawns and gardens for indicators that we abstract nature and understand it as a means of expressing our refinement; indeed, many aspects of our daily lives confirm our culture's pursuit of good taste. For example, in the name of comfort and refinement, we disregard the effects of our conveniences: that cell phones require towers across the landscape; that our suvs guzzle fuel and emit greenhouse gases not so that we can drive on the truly rugged terrain for which they are ostensibly built, but much more often so that we can cruise along superhighways and well-paved city streets; and that our large homes and immaculate lawns deplete aquifers, wells, and reservoirs while scientists warn us that water is in short supply. In this larger sense, the view of landscape as refinement has so permeated our culture that the natural world of our daily lives is replete with its manifestations, yet we remain blind to them. The integrity of nature's structures and life forms is threatened by our story of nature, which figures the landscape as a metaphor for American refinement.

Twenty-First-Century Reason

In the nineteenth century, "Nature" was understood by Emerson to be a means of pursuing human reason, and the pursuit of human reason was understood to be a route to intellectual power. One might develop analogies between natural facts and human experience, thereby using the natural realm to gain insight into the human capacity for higher thought. For Emerson, one pursued reason in order to transcend the physical world and enter the metaphysical realm. The goal was developing one's power—or "dominion," to use Emerson's word—over nature. The more analogies one recognized, the more one understood one's intellectual powers. In this philosophical scheme, the natural world functioned to encourage such analogizing, and its physicality was incidental to the metaphysical pursuits of humans. Nature was understood as the capacity for human reason itself, a means by which to achieve a human desire.

In our day, we find in certain intellectual circles a similar dismissal of nature's physicality in favor of the pursuit of reason. Such thinkers, like Emerson, engage in a process by which they abstract nature in order to pursue thought, all as a means of demonstrating their intellectual power. Some modern-day philosophers have critiqued this tendency, pointing to the degree to which Western intellectual culture obsesses over reason and metaphysics. Such intellectual pursuits, they argue, have had the effect of further distancing humanity from the physical realities of the natural world. Val Plumwood, for example, undertook a comprehensive examination of reason in relation to environment, arguing that "human-centredness permeates the dominant culture, fostering illusions of disembeddedness and invincibility." The pursuit of reason, in other words, so centers on humanity that certain thinkers ignore the natural phenomena and processes that permit all life. Similarly, Eugene Hargrove characterizes American intellectual history as "a history of ideas that supports a preference for mind over matter, thought and imagination over physical existence." In this view, the current preoccupation with human reason does not exactly figure nature as a metaphor for reason. Rather, in its twentieth- and twenty-first-century versions, the pursuit of reason tends to dismiss the physicality of nature altogether. Both Plumwood and Hargrove, however, are concerned with the degree to which the pursuit of reason dismisses humanity's dependence on the natural world by treating nature as either abstract or incidental—like Emerson did in *Nature*.[10]

Within our current academic culture, this abstraction of nature's physicality has been perpetuated also by twentieth- and twenty-first-century literary scholarship. Until very recently, literary theorists pursued representations of physical nature in literature largely as symbolic of metaphysical ideas. By interpreting representations of natural phenomena as symbolic of some aspect of human affairs, literary scholars perhaps inadvertently prevented readers from recognizing any value inherent in the physical world. Instead, literary scholarship has influenced generations of readers to understand literary representations of nature as having value only in the abstract. The dominant tradition in American literary scholarship has been to develop interpretive strategies that view representations of nature as symbolic, usually of some ideological force in the national culture. In other words, representations of nature are interpreted as symbolic of the dreams, ideals, and formation of America. Critics have rarely spent time discussing the realities of the physical environment.

As examples of such traditional interpretive strategies, we might consider some of the most influential titles in twentieth-century American literary scholarship. Amid these titles, we find a prominent practice of identifying representations of nature as symbols of the nation's ideological development. Nature as symbol or myth occupies the pages not only of Leo Marx's *The Machine in the Garden* and Henry Nash Smith's *Virgin Land*, but also of Myra Jehlen's *American Incarnation*, Annette Kolodny's *The Lay of the Land*, Bernard Rosenthal's *City of Nature*, Richard Slotkin's *Regeneration through Violence*, and Cecelia Tichi's *New World, New Earth*. In each of these influential studies, the author traces a symbolic, mythic, or metaphoric use of nature in American literature, and while these monographs contribute much to our understandings of American culture, they also perpetuate a tradition of inattention to the material world.[11]

Pursuing nature's symbolic meanings is not a bad thing in and of itself, but when this tradition in literary scholarship exists alongside so many other disembedded intellectual uses of the physical environment, it ends up contributing to a troubling cultural tendency: the abstraction of nature. In recognition of this, some literary scholars are developing alternative interpretive strategies in an effort to help literary scholarship participate in efforts to understand the roles of literature and language in the environmental crisis. Frustrated by the paucity of critical studies that focus on literal representations of the physical environment rather than on a humanly constructed version of it, Lawrence Buell posed the question: "Must literature always lead us away from the physical world, never back to it?" In recent decades, literary scholars have begun to imagine new ways to find meaning in literary representations of nature. They have even begun to consider natural history writing worthy of serious scholarly attention. Nonetheless, abstract understandings of the natural world are entrenched in American intellectual culture.[12]

Metaphors Mixed and Merged

In the nineteenth century, different metaphors for nature mixed and merged in cultural discourse, which increasingly reflected understandings of the natural environment that were deeply layered with metaphors of humanity. We find this same merging of metaphors for nature in our popular culture today. It appears in our popular discourse, as well as in our landscapes. For example, our refined lawns are as much signals of our progress as a nation as they are indicators of our refinement. Similarly, the academy's preoccupation with a disembedded reason reveals as much about our interest in human intellectual progress as it does our desire to demonstrate our refinement. The "best," most refined scholars of literature in the mid-twentieth century would hardly have deigned to attend to the natural facts conveyed in literature; to do so would have been considered pedestrian by most, as it still is by some. As in the nineteenth century, our understandings of nature reflect several decidedly human preoccupations.

Indeed, it seems as though in the United States today, there exists a popular culture whose passion for nature is so misinformed and abstract that we can hardly call it a "passion for nature" at all. Given the state of the American landscape—to say nothing of the impacts of the nation on other, foreign lands—we might say that America's passion for nature is now, more than ever, a passion for humanity. Ecologist Christopher Uhl has argued as much, suggesting that the basis for the nation's current story of nature is "humanity's inexorable march of progress." Indeed, in our preoccupation with humanity's advancement, we hold to an understanding of nature that deems it a theater for the playing out of human domination and control. Our physical landscape testifies to this tale of human dominion.[13]

Ultimately, however, I think that the American landscape testifies to the nation's anxiety. Arguably, the three nineteenth-century metaphors for nature that we have examined grew out of an anxiety gripping the nascent United States. At that time, many individuals were concerned with establishing an identity for the country, forming a national intellectual and creative culture of which its citizens could be proud, and negotiating the challenges posed by an increasingly citified landscape. Now we are faced with an anxiety of a slightly different sort. But like its nineteenth-century form, this anxiety also grows out of concerns about the future of the nation. At the present time, these concerns center on controlling foreign peoples and foreign lands as a means of ensuring the "security" of America.

This new concern is manifest in America's forceful imposition of democracy in faraway lands, its extraction of resources from other nations in order to support its own extravagant comfort and convenience, and its infiltration of foreign economies with American corporations and profit models. American anxiety over global control in support of its economic system is apparent in less obvious ways as well: in the distribution of waste and pollution to points and peoples distant from its homelands, for example, as well as in financial and political support for other nations' environmentally destructive practices so long as they promote American security and financial health. Granted, the typical uses of the words "security" and "financial health" rest on grossly distorted notions of America's well-being, as certain writers have pointed out.[14] Nonetheless, underlying America's relationship to the natural environment is a utilitarian approach to natural phenomena and processes, and a preoccupation with the country's comfort and convenience—to such a degree that the nation's vulnerability in terms of its dependence on nature is ignored. The result is a continuing environmental ethic of control and domination, and a landscape that bears the brunt of national anxiety. This anxiety prevents any accurate understanding of nature, its phenomena, its behavior, or its health.

As an example of the pervasive powers of this discourse of anxiety in the United States, we might turn to a speech given by the nation's president on September 15, 2005, in New Orleans, two weeks after Hurricane Katrina hit the city and the surrounding region. What we find here is that the representation of the natural world is not unlike what we would expect to find in a nineteenth-century speech on a similar occasion. The natural landscape is assumed to be all of these things: the site of a foreordained national progress;

a means to expressing American refinement; and a means to exercising human power—not through reason, but through sheer force. Hence, these three influential metaphors for nature mix and merge. Ultimately, the speech is a testament to a belief that, disturbing forces aside, the natural world will be made to accommodate this metaphorical vision. The physical realities of nature will be completely overlooked, and the landscape *will be* human progress, refinement, and power.

President George W. Bush called the hurricane a "cruel and wasteful storm," using language that insists not only that nature has evil intentions but also that such storms have no basis in thermodynamic and climatic realities. Rather than understanding the hurricane as a natural process that makes sense—albeit one that causes tragedies in human lives—Bush also referred to it as "a tragedy that seems so blind and random." He centered his speech, however, on the inevitable power of humanity: "The people of this land have come back from fire, flood, and storm to build anew—and to build better than what we had before. Americans have never left our destiny to the whims of nature—and we will not start now." The natural landscape of the Mississippi Delta will be rebuilt as a testament to progress; the City of New Orleans will be "better" than before (more refined); and nature's "whims" will not overpower America's will.[15]

This is an extreme statement of human power over nature and of nature's assumed meaning as being subject to human will, one that could emerge only from extreme fear and anxiety. Yet whatever one's political persuasions, one has to see President Bush's words as appealing to large segments of the citizenry and as at least somewhat indicative of popular sentiment. In this figuration of nature's meaning, natural processes matter not at all. The integrity of the area's deltaic lands, salt marshes, and water tables receive no mention, because in this understanding of nature, they simply do not matter. In fact, more and more people watch the reconstruction of New Orleans following the storm and wonder whether America's story of power over nature masks a more urgent story of the need for rivers to meander and for salt marshes to thrive. But Bush's speech spoke for the status quo—and of the probable future of American rivers and salt marshes: in the nation's misguided, anxiety-ridden quest to ensure its future, it will continue to ignore the realities of natural history, to silence observations about natural phenomena that threaten its canalized path, and to exercise hubris rather than humility.

Rachel Carson warned of this future in a 1952 speech. At that time, she said: "Mankind has gone very far into an artificial world of his own creation. He has sought to insulate himself, in his cities of steel and concrete, from the realities of earth and water and the growing seed. Intoxicated with a sense of his own power, he seems to be going farther and farther into more experiments for the destruction of himself and his world." This artificial world is our world, our rootedness in a relationship to our natural surroundings that is based on abstraction, symbolism, and metaphor—or, more precisely, on an obscuring of reality, blindness, and ignorance.[16]

Toward the Counteraesthetics

Many people grow increasingly alarmed at America's course, particularly as that course increasingly involves other nations, their peoples, and their lands. In the wake of Hurricane Katrina, for instance, more and more individuals have voiced a desire for new stories, both for America's national identity and its physical environment. Some of their concerns center on the degree to which America's current relationship to nature masks environmental realities. The words of Terry Eagleton effectively sum up this position: "Human beings are not mere products of the environs, but neither are those environs sheer clay for their arbitrary self-fashioning. If culture transfigures nature, it is a project to which nature sets rigorous limits." Indeed, humanity clearly has the power to exercise much control over nature, but our effects on nature are too problematic to ignore any longer.[17]

Arguably, of course, most human beings' passion for nature will privilege humanity. After all, humans are, as animals, instinctually inclined to protect themselves and to make the world a livable place for the procreation and success of their kind. However, the degree to which our relationship to nature centers on human concerns is something that we can, as creatures endowed with reason, control. We have the ability to imagine ways of ensuring our basic success while also recognizing more accurately the realities of nature's ways and needs. As Yi-Fu Tuan argues, "A human being is an animal who is congenitally indisposed to accept reality as it is. Humans not only submit and adapt, as all animals do; they transform in accordance with a preconceived plan. That is, before transforming, they do something extraordinary, namely, 'see' what is not there. Seeing what is not there lies at the foundation of all human culture." This capacity to "see" (or, phrased differently, to imagine) lies at the heart of current attempts to re-envision the dominant story of nature in America. People are imagining new stories in the hopes of disrupting the old ones. In effect, people are creating new, more environmentally sustainable metaphors for nature.[18]

These new stories are emerging in the world of art, landscape design, and intellectual culture. Emily Apter reports that a number of contemporary artists are featuring critical habitats in their works as a means of furthering "the politics of antiglobalization." In the field of landscape design and architecture, "green" buildings are increasingly the priority when new structures go up. More and more Americans, especially in the western states, are replacing their traditional lawns and realizing the different kind of beauty that can be found in yards that are xeriscaped (drought tolerant) with native grasses and other colorful, perennial plants. In my neighboring town of Boise, one might even say that a "refined" yard is one that is xeriscaped: people's definitions of "good taste" are changing as droughts worsen, water shortages increase, and water prices rise. And in intellectual culture, there have been great strides in recent years in fields such as environmental economics, conservation biology, and environmental studies, in addition to environmentally oriented literary criticism. Even *Newsweek* has featured an issue dedicated to the "Greening of America."[19]

Others make deliberate attempts to garner nature's meaning through close attention to specific phenomena. For example, the founders and editors of such publications as the *Journal of Natural History Education* seek "to foster a renaissance in natural history education." As another example, the National Science Foundation has funded "Project BudBurst," an effort to encourage individuals around the United States to pay particular attention to when individual plants bloom in their area. Inviting everyday citizens to engage in this type of scientific data collection that was so meaningful to Cooper and Thoreau may provide a way for scientists to "track" global climate change. In addition, increasingly local nature centers offer important venues for both children and adults to encounter natural phenomena.[20]

At the center of all of these endeavors is the recognized need to humble humanity to nature. Perhaps the most visible vehicle for the conveying of this new story of humility is natural history writing, which gains increasing visibility in our society through such publications as *Orion Magazine* and through the many book volumes dedicated to educating readers about local landscapes. Popular nature writer Terry Tempest Williams calls for people to develop "a fierce awareness of the forces outside of ourselves." Similarly, Gary Paul Nabhan claims, "We need to balance the internal with the external. A focus on something other than ourselves is probably healthy in this society, because we are so consumed with ourselves." And Scott Russell Sanders seems to challenge popular discourse such as that represented by Bush's September 15, 2005, speech when he states: "[T]he natural world was not made for our comfort and convenience. It preceded us by some billions of years, and it will outlast us; it mocks our pride, because it surpasses our understanding and control; it can be dangerous and demanding; it will eventually kill us and reclaim our bodies." Such writers are upsetting the canalization of problematic metaphors for nature.[21]

Like Cooper and Thoreau before them, all of these individuals—and so many others—are working toward a new story for nature. They believe, in the words of Daniel Philippon, that "[a]lthough we can never arrive at an essential 'nature,' we can nevertheless strive to listen to the 'voices' of nature," accessible by our only means of knowing our world: "direct experience." They are also arguably compelled to their words by anxiety, but theirs is an anxiety of a different sort. Their motivation is not specifically the protection of American security; rather, it is the preservation of the integrity of the natural world, which has been seriously compromised especially in the last century. They are anxious because so many people know so little about natural history and nature's phenomena. They are anxious because most Americans observe nearly nothing of natural processes and structures: curiosity about nature for its own sake seems all but dead in popular culture. And they are anxious because American hubris has done so much to conceal the beauty—and pleasure—to be found in humility.[22]

During his lifetime, Henry David Thoreau declared that nature could support more than "one order of understandings," and he dedicated himself to the humble pursuit of an "understanding" that differed from that of most of his contemporaries. Like Susan Fenimore Cooper, he located that pursuit in attention to the *real*. Nature's meaning was best understood, these authors demonstrated, by acknowledging its wondrous physicality. Through their writings, they demonstrate the distance between what Thoreau had called "the hearth and the field"—that is, between our habits of living in comfort and convenience, and a sensitivity to the realities of natural phenomena. They help us see that understanding nature through certain metaphors can mean robbing it of its inherent value—a word that has its roots in the word "strength" ("value" originates in *valére*, Latin for "to be strong"). Nature's "value," or its strength and health, lies in its materiality and processes. In many ways, then, Cooper and Thoreau offer early models for a relationship to nature based on a detailed knowledge of its particulars.[23]

Most significant in their works, however, is their development of what I call "an aesthetics of humility"—a celebration of the delight and beauty that is experienced by valuing nature's particulars and humbly accepting one's ultimate ignorance of nature's meaning. Like so many concerned individuals today, these mid-nineteenth-century authors offer us a path to understanding nature that embraces humility. Slowing down long enough to study nature is not mere work for Cooper, Thoreau, and their twenty-first-century counterparts; it is life's greatest joy. Cooper and Thoreau did their best to record their worlds. What they did not record so fully—but what we can see through their careful records of nature—was the exhilaration of recognizing humanity's small place in nature's long history, the ultimate mysteries that accompany each and every observation, and the empowering sense of responsibility that, ironically, accompanies a recognition of humanity's humble role on the earth.

The story of nature that might emerge from the aesthetics of humility will arguably also be based in metaphor. After all, metaphor is how humans think, how we make sense of our experience and surroundings. Even Cooper's and Thoreau's passions for nature understood the natural world through certain metaphors—harmony, resilience, and regeneration among them. All are part of their aesthetics of humility. We might now make them nature's truth for humanity, the passion inspiring our lives.

NOTES

1. Myers, "On the Cultural Construction," 60.
2. Richard T. T. Forman and Michel Godron, quoted in Odum and Barrett, *Fundamentals of Ecology*, 6.
3. Angela Miller, *The Empire of the Eye*, 20.

INTRODUCTION

1. Cooper, *Rural Hours*, 173–74. The marks that Cooper contemplates are very likely the lesions of a rust.
2. Stewart, *A Natural History of Nature Writing*, xvi; Buell, "Thoreauvian Pilgrimage," 175. The fullest consideration of Thoreau's influence on America's "environmental imagination" is Buell's *Environmental Imagination*. For discussions of Thoreau's influence, see Conway et al., who refer to Thoreau as the "patron saint of ecocentrism" ("The New Environmentalism," 10); Alfred Tauber, who argues that *Walden* has had a "formative effect on modern environmentalism" (*Henry David Thoreau*, 163); and Alan Hodder, who suggests that the Thoreau of *Walden* is a "cultural icon," and that "in thinking about him, we are inevitably thinking also . . . about ourselves, our values, and our culture generally" (*Thoreau's Ecstatic Wilderness*, xi and xii). As a corrective to our overemphasis on Thoreau, Michael P. Branch points to the limitations of treating him as if he gave rise to landscape writing: "reading the tradition of literary representations of North American landscapes as if that tradition began with *Walden* is akin to studying American history as if it began with the Civil War" (*Reading the Roots*, xvii).
3. See Kohlstedt, "Parlors, Primers, and Public Schooling." On women's sometimes "peripheral" but meaningful contributions to natural history study, see Baym, *American Women*; Kohlstedt, "In from the Periphery"; and Gianquitto, *"Good Observers of Nature"*. For a consideration of pre-nineteenth-century American relations to nature, see Sara S. Gronim's *Everyday Nature*, which documents a variety of ways in which residents of colonial New York had "everyday" familiarity with various natural (and supernatural) phenomena.

4. Jackson, *American Space*, 17–18. I draw the U.S. Census Bureau information that informs this discussion from two online sites: http://www.census.gov/population/census data/popctr.pdf; and http://www.census.gov/population/censusdata/table-4.pdf.

5. Jackson, *American Space*, 17.

6. Welch, *The Book of Nature*, 4 and 9.

7. Judd, 70, 72, and 7.

8. Welch, *The Book of Nature*, 9 and 8; Thoreau, "Walking," 208. On "nature-deficit disorder" and current concerns about intellectual deprivation caused by an absence of experience with the natural world in children's lives, see Louv, *Last Child in the Woods*.

9. de Tocqueville, *Democracy in America*, 461.

10. Undoubtedly, we need studies of the passion for nature held by many others at this time and in early America. We need the stories of more women and of minorities, including the many immigrants entering the country in these decades, the Native American peoples being displaced from so many areas, and the African and African American slaves and freemen of the North and South. In *American Curiosity*, Susan Scott Parrish has made a recent and important contribution to our knowledge of natural history as it was practiced across lines of race, gender, and nationality in the colonial British Atlantic world.

11. Snow, *Two Cultures*, 10, 5, and 15. Scholars have established that mid-nineteenth-century Americans did not assume the sort of distinction between scientific and humanistic ways of knowing that Snow describes as characterizing the twentieth century: see Walls, *Seeing New Worlds*, 5–6, and Jonathan Smith, *Fact and Feeling*, especially 45–91. Indeed, I am not arguing that a complete dichotomy existed between science and the humanities in the nineteenth century; rather, I am arguing that many forms of art—including literature, painting, philosophy, and landscape design—assumed a value system that abstracted the natural world even as they seemed devoted to expressing its authenticity.

12. Oerlemans, *Romanticism*, 12. For a recent and effective summary of these heated discussions, see Heise, "Hitchhiker's Guide."

13. Cronon, "The Trouble with Wilderness," 83. See Pattiann Rogers, "This Nature" for an entertaining and refreshing reminder of all that is "nature."

14. Heise, "Hitchhiker's Guide," 512; Philippon, *Conserving Words*, 15. Like I do here, Onno Oerlemans's recent *Romanticism and the Materiality of Nature* emphasizes some nineteenth-century writers' quest for nature's materiality; however, Oerlemans's focus is on British romanticism.

15. I discuss the history of natural history at more length in the next chapter; however, readers interested in this particular shift from natural theology to natural history might consult Knight, *Natural Science Books*, 47–62.

16. Kellert, *The Value of Life*, 217. While the traditional story of environmental history has omitted Cooper and these aspects of Thoreau's work, recent contributions suggest a possible shift of emphasis; Michael Lewis's new *American Wilderness: A New History* features a brief discussion of Thoreau's later work.

17. Levine, *Highbrow/Lowbrow*, 9 and 86; Lears, "The Concept of Cultural Hegemony," 574. Although Levine's study focuses on the cultural receptions of Shakespearean drama and of opera in the nineteenth century, it has fascinating implications for any consideration of "popular" pursuits in the period.

18. Buell, "Thoreauvian Pilgrimage," 175; ibid.; Tompkins, *Sensational Designs*, xi, xvi, and 195; Lears, "The Concept of Cultural Hegemony," 577. Relevant to the figures I discuss here are the following sources. On Thoreau: Buell, *Environmental Imagination*, 339–69; Meyer, *Several More Lives to Live*; and Dean and Scharnhorst, "The Contemporary Reception of *Walden*." Nearly any book on American art history demonstrates the continued importance of Cole; see Rainey, *Creating Picturesque America*, on the post–Civil War popularity of the picturesque traditions. On Downing, see Major, *To Live in the New World*; Schuyler, *Apostle of Taste*; and Sweeting, *Reading Houses and Building Books*. On Emerson, see Ruland, *The Rediscovery of American Literature*. Tompkins offered an early and illuminating discussion of the power of canons in her *Sensational Designs*, although she does not discuss any of my subjects.

19. For a full overview of the publication history of *Rural Hours* in both its American and British editions, see Johnson and Patterson, introduction to *Rural Hours*, xi–xv. This 1998 critical edition of *Rural Hours* marks the only twentieth-century publication of her full text. Cooper's entire publication history is also discussed in that introduction, and a listing of her publications appears as Appendix I in Johnson and Patterson, *Susan Fenimore Cooper*. The history of *Walden*'s reception has been discussed by several scholars; especially helpful is Teichgraeber, *Sublime Thoughts*, 222–66.

20. For more extensive comparisons of *Walden* and *Rural Hours*, see Baym, "English Nature"; Buell, *Environmental Imagination*; and Johnson, "Placing *Rural Hours*."

21. Nicholson, *Mountain Gloom and Mountain Glory*, 2; Kirwan, "Vicarious Edification," 14. For a discussion of various ways in which American women's writings about nature remain inaccessible to modern readers, see Kilcup, "'I Like These Plants That You Call Weeds'."

22. Sanders, *Writing from the Center*, 14.

23. Lakoff and Johnson, *Metaphors We Live By*, 145.

24. Ibid., 145, 146, and 156; Cronon, foreword to *Mountain Gloom and Mountain Glory*, xii. Kirwan makes a similar statement: "What we call 'nature' is ineluctably a story, one we have known since childhood, and the knowing of it since childhood is another story" ("Vicarious Edification," 243).

25. de Tocqueville, *Democracy in America*, 460. I am grateful to Laura Dassow Walls for calling my attention to the relevance of de Tocqueville's remarks to my argument here.

26. Cooper, *Rural Hours*, 208.

27. See Keeney, *The Botanizers* and Porter, *The Eagle's Nest* for discussions of amateur natural history in nineteenth-century America.

28. Slovic, foreword to *Greening of Literary Scholarship*, xi; Price, *Flight Maps*, xvi. This seems an appropriate place to say that I intend this book as a complement to several studies of literary history that have suggested that Americans created a unique national identity by turning to the land itself. Key studies in this vein include those of Jehlen, Perry Miller, Nash, and Tichi. In various ways and with various methodologies, these studies argue persuasively that American identity was nearly synonymous with the American land—with its vastness and displaced peoples, and with its wildness and the taming of that wildness. In this book, however, I wish to explore several influential meanings that Americans discerned for nature during this period and the aesthetic assumptions informing those passions.

1. Cooper, *Rural Hours*, 3.

2. Review of *Rural Hours*, *Harper's New Monthly Magazine*, 713. David E. Shi, in *The Simple Life*, provides a study of the changing understandings of simplicity and, in particular, of "a simple Life," throughout American history, beginning with colonial times. As he notes, because living simply has almost always been the professed goal of those who had the means and freedom "to choose their standard of living," those who have pursued simplicity have typically comprised "the intellectual and moral elite" in America (7). For his consideration of "the simple life" in Cooper's era, see especially pp. 100–24.

3. Cooper uses this phrase on page 208 of *Rural Hours*; I discuss the passage at some length below.

4. Cooper, *Rural Hours*, 4. See Thoreau, *Walden*, 12.

5. Cooper, *Rural Hours*, 4, 93, and 286.

6. Thoreau, *Journal* 4:296.

7. Cooper, *Rural Hours*, 4.

8. Ibid., 8, 9, 11, 174 and 329n27, 285, 330n34.

9. Thoreau, *Journal* 5:368; Cooper, *Rural Hours*, 4–5. See Bonaparte's reference in *American Ornithology*, Vol. III: 5.

10. Cooper, *Rural Hours*, 44.

11. Ibid., 202–07.

12. Ibid., 5.

13. Ibid.

14. Ibid., 42–43.

15. Ibid., 11–12, 34–36.

16. Ibid., 40–42, 60–61.

17. Ibid., 13–17, 12–13, 202–13. See Welch, *The Book of Nature*, 6, for a brief, helpful description of this cultural interest. See Spencer, *The Quest for Nationality*, for an account of the literary efforts at nation building from the colonial period through the nineteenth century. Baym's "English Nature" argues that Cooper wrote about her surroundings in order to demonstrate her own gentility. This reading of *Rural Hours* emphasizes Cooper "as a gracious lady of the manor" (180). Baym develops this reading of *Rural Hours* further in *American Women of Letters*, where she emphasizes Cooper's ability to make "social value" of her rural life (82). On the general role of female authors in educating the public about the many moral concerns of the day, see Cott, *The Bonds of Womanhood*; Epstein, *The Politics of Domesticity*; Kelley, *Private Woman, Public Stage*; and Welter, *Dimity Convictions*. On the specific use of botany in this pursuit, see Seaton.

18. Cooper, *Rural Hours*, 49–50, 76, 64–65, 328n9. Cooper's use of Torrey's *A Flora of the State of New-York* (1843) is evident throughout her book. Her specific reference to the dandelion refers to his volume 1, page 418.

19. Several twentieth- and twenty-first-century environmental historians and scientists offer discussions of the "ecological imperialism" that accompanied the European settlement of North America. Alfred Crosby's *Ecological Imperialism* discusses the ecological impacts of European expansion on a global scale from a historical viewpoint and includes a chapter specifically addressing weeds. George W. Cox offers a more scientifically

minded (but accessible) discussion of the impact of invasive species on North American ecosystems in *Alien Species in North America and Hawaii*. Kim Todd's *Tinkering with Eden* provides a highly readable, informed, and lyrical treatment of exotics in America aimed at the general reader; and Peter Coates's *American Perceptions of Immigrant and Invasive Species* explores the historical fears associated with nonnative species.

20. Cooper, *Rural Hours*, 9, 6, 6, 189–90 and 254, 254, 52, 139.

21. In "Thoreau's Notes," Philippon provides a helpful explanation of how we might see a record of natural phenomena as a work of environmental history. Philippon undertakes his analysis of Thoreau's notes on his 1861 *Journey West* to Minnesota in order to show "how to integrate the discipline-specific concerns of environmental history and environmental literature with ethical considerations about how human beings might best live in their various environments" (109). Philippon suggests that Thoreau's notes begin the work of creating an "ecological *community* identity" for a specific place—in this case, a section of Minnesota (109).

I borrow the phrase "nature's nation" from Perry Miller's book of that name. Cooper's vision of the landscape as revealing history reflects much of what D. W. Meinig describes as "the historian's" view of landscape. Meinig offers ten different ways of seeing and conceptualizing landscape, one of which is "landscape as history": "To such a viewer all that lies before his eyes is a complex cumulative record of the work of nature and man in this particular place" ("The Beholding Eye," 43).

22. Cooper, *Rural Hours*, 50. Biologist Robert Michael Pyle argues that twenty-first-century conservation biologists and the laws of our time primarily and problematically focus on complete extinction or endangered status at the expense of regional and local extinctions. Pyle notes, "outright extinction is not the only problem. By concentrating on the truly rare and endangered plants and animals, conservationists often neglect other forms of loss that can have striking consequences: the local extinction" (143). I am grateful to Michael P. Branch for pointing me to the connections between Cooper's concerns and Pyle's work on this topic.

23. Cooper, *Rural Hours*, 63, 64, 67. Coates cites the Darwin-Gray correspondence in *American Perceptions*, 71–73. I thank Tina Gianquitto for alerting me to this correspondence regarding Cooper's work, and Dan Philippon for pointing out Coates's particular reference to the correspondence.

24. Cox, *Alien Species*, 4 and 8; Cooper, *Rural Hours*, 49.

25. Pyle, *The Thunder Tree*, 144, 145 (italics in original), 145.

26. Kellert, *The Value of Life*, 7.

27. Cooper, *Rural Hours*, 82–83, 87, 330n33; Pyle, *The Thunder Tree*, 146. Pyle also writes, "I believe that one of the greatest causes of the ecological crisis is the state of personal alienation from nature in which many people live. We lack a widespread sense of intimacy with the living world" (145).

28. Cooper, *Rural Hours*, 116 and 118. This entire entry appears on pages 116–20 of *Rural Hours*.

29. Ibid., 120, 119, 118.

30. Ibid., 120.

31. Ibid., 120.

32. Welch, *The Book of Nature*, 8, 6, 9. Cooper was one of many "[i]ndividuals not

commonly associated with natural history . . . [who] devoted hours of intense effort [to] composing their commentary on the natural world" (Welch, *The Book of Nature*, 9). As Welch notes, "Resident observers, often as dedicated to the natural history discipline as . . . famed authors . . . also communicated their findings on the occurrence and habits of species. This information, gained through years of sightings and note taking, was made known through either publication . . . or direct communication with the major authors" (6–7). See also Regis, *Describing Early America*, on the ways in which natural history contributed to efforts at establishing a specifically American identity (especially 3–5). Such amateur "specific and localized efforts" as that of Cooper thus "balanced the grandly nationalistic ambitions" (Welch, 7) by providing records of lesser known locales. Welch also notes that despite the small number of engaged naturalists, natural-historical subjects nonetheless permeated the lives of middle- and upper-class Americans through hunting guides, flower books, amateur paintings, journal writing, and marginalia (9). However, Welch notes the divorce between genuine knowledge of real natural phenomena and these various forms of natural history discourse: early nineteenth-century natural history was "as 'learned' and highly artificial a discourse as any in Western culture. Natural objects in this discourse historically [had] not been portrayed as *part of everyday experience*, as the plants and animals are visually isolated from their environment and verbally described in erudite language" (5, my emphasis).

33. Regis, *Describing Early America*, xi. See Jenkins, *The Naturalists*, for a more comprehensive discussion of the natural history tradition; he begins with Pliny and explores the genre's mutations through the twentieth century, especially in illustration and, later, photography. As Regis points out, non-Anglo human beings were also frequently included by natural historians in this category of "nonhuman" nature, unfortunately (xii).

34. For overviews of changes in the natural history tradition, see: Bruce, *The Launching of Modern American Science*; Desmond, *Great Natural History Books*; Foucault, *Order of Things*; Larson, *Interpreting Nature*; Mayr, *The Growth of Biological Thought*; Outram, "New Spaces in Natural History" (especially 249); Porter, *The Eagle's Nest*; Thomas, *Man and the Natural World*; and Welch, *The Book of Nature* (especially 5). According to Sally Kohlstedt, the term "amateur" was not even used "to identify vocational scientific enthusiasts" ("In from the Periphery," 173). I emphasize "gentlemen" here because naturalists were, for the most part, male. However, Baym's *American Women of Letters* explores the ways in which amateur female naturalists "affiliated" with professional science in informal ways throughout the nineteenth century in order to lend their studies legitimacy. See also Gianquitto, *"Good Observers of Nature,"* Norwood, *Made from this Earth*, and Kohlstedt, "In from the Periphery" for studies of American women and their various relations to nature.

35. Regis, *Describing Early America*, 17. On the rhetorical forms of natural history, see also Jardine, *"Naturphilosophie,"* 233; Regis, *Describing Early America*, 15–18 and 20–22; and Hildebidle, *Thoreau*, 24–51.

36. Foucault, *Order of Things*, 133; Regis, *Describing Early America*, 39.

37. Foucault, *Order of Things*, 134, 131, 298, 129–30, and 130; Regis, *Describing Early America*, 14.

38. Regis, *Describing Early America*, xiii.

39. Cooper, *Rural Hours*, 146–47.

40. Ibid., 177–78, 190, 219–21.

41. Foucault, *Order of Things*, 132; Regis, *Describing Early America*, 14. From Cooper's essay "Small Family Memories," which she wrote in 1883, well after the publication of *Rural Hours*, we may also discern minor evidence of its natural history context. For Cooper, *Rural Hours* represented an outgrowth of her devotion to nature, which had its origins in her childhood experiences with her maternal grandfather. When she emphasizes the power of naming here, she alludes to the natural history tradition: "Grandfather [De Lancey] soon commenced my botanical education—being the eldest of the little troop, I often drove with him, in the gig, about his farms and into his woods, and it was my duty to jump out and open all the gates. In these drives he taught me to distinguish the different trees by their growth, and bark, and foliage. . . . He would point out a tree and ask me to name it, going through a regular lesson in a very pleasant way. Such was the beginning of my Rural Hours ideas" (32–33). This passage suggests that Cooper intends her book as a sort of "botanical education," "a regular lesson [delivered] in a very pleasant way." The "Rural Hours ideas" she refers to at the close of this passage might include educating others, pointing out differences in growth, bark, or foliage so that readers might also learn to identify specific plants. As her grandfather did with her, she hopes to heighten others' powers of observation.

42. Cooper, *Rural Hours*, 330n33.

43. Cooper, *Rural Hours*, 72. My count of the total number of times "I" appears in *Rural Hours*'s original 521 pages, including in Cooper's notes, is 59. Lawrence Buell has suggested that this aspect of Cooper's prose, along with her self-effacing narrator, results from her position as a nineteenth-century woman: "It reflects what pre-modern women were expected not to do (thrust themselves egoistically forward) and what they were supposed to do well (work with fine detail)" (*Environmental Imagination*, 177). But Buell also acknowledges that—regardless of its cause—Cooper's style clearly results in a humble presentation of her world, one more apparently biocentric. For fun, and as a means of comparison, Buell offers a rough estimate of the number of times Thoreau's "favorite pronoun," "I," appears in *Walden*: "an average of 6.6 times per page" in the first two chapters; 5.5 times per page in the next six chapters; 5.2 times per page in the next five, and 3.6 times per page in the final five chapters (122). While I agree with Buell's remark that these are "crude indices" of authorial humility, I also agree that they are somewhat instructive in conveying a sense of a narrative.

44. Cooper, *Rural Hours*, 49, 136, 155, 155, and 22.

45. Ibid., 330n33.

46. My discussion here does not offer a thorough analysis of Cooper's particular relationship to Christianity (a relationship that, in any case, we can only surmise, given the scant discussion of such matters in her extant biographical materials). Both Cooper's Christian beliefs and her dedication to her church warrant additional study. Here my goal is to draw special attention to the ways in which Cooper's writings demonstrate that she eschews an ethic of dominion, often associated with Christianity, in favor of an ethic of humility.

47. Cooper, *Rural Hours*, 125–26.

48. Ibid., 128.

49. Ibid., 131.

50. Ibid., 133, 125, 132, 133–34.

51. Ibid., 134–35.

52. Ibid., 125–26.

53. Review, *New Englander*, 653; emphasis in original.

54. Review, *Harper's*, 713.

55. Review, *Graham's*, 324.

56. Ibid.

57. Prepublication notices appeared in the *Home Journal* (July 27, 1850) and the *Literary World* (June 1, 1850, and June 22, 1850), and a publication notice appeared in *Godey's Lady's Book* (October 1850). See Downing, Review of *Rural Hours*.

58. Quoted in Allibone, *A Critical Dictionary*, 424; Allibone, "American Rural Life," 107.

59. Review of *Rural Hours* in *Knickerbocker*, 279; Allibone, "American Rural Life," 107; Review of *Rural Hours* in *Harper's*, 713.

60. "Female Authors," 171; Review of *Rural Hours* in *International Weekly Miscellany*, 72.

61. Hart, *The Female Prose Writers of America*, 413.

62. Review of *Rural Hours* in the *Knickerbocker*, 278–79; review of *Rural Hours* in *Littell's Living Age*, 414.

63. "American Rural Life," 108; "Female Authors," 173.

64. Review of *Rural Hours* in *Southern Quarterly*, 539.

65. Cooper, *Rural Hours*, 208.

66. Ibid., 207–8.

67. Ibid., 208; emphasis mine. Baym offers a discussion of nineteenth-century botanist Almira Phelps, who also urged women to "engage" with "the real world" (*American Women of Letters*, 25).

68. Morton, *Ecology without Nature*, 67 and 1 (my emphasis).

69. Cooper, *Rural Hours*, 208.

70. Thoreau, *Journal* 4:296. For a consideration of British romantic authors whose writings similarly reveal a "sheer appetite for the infinite physical presence of the world" and who, like Cooper, recognize "the value of resisting abstraction," see Oerlemans (201 and 200).

71. On the historical significance of Cooperstown, see Ravage's *A Region of Romance*; Taylor, *William Cooper's Town*; and James Fenimore Cooper, *Reminiscences*.

72. These comments are based on an interview that I had with Willard Harman, Director of the SUNY-Oneonta Biological Field Station, in which he described his team's use of *Rural Hours* to determine what he called "the state of the lake" in 1850.

73. Evernden, *The Social Creation of Nature*, 132.

CHAPTER 2. THE METAPHOR OF PROGRESS

1. Cooper, introduction to John Leonard Knapp, *Country Rambles in England*, 22.

2. Burbick, *Thoreau's Alternative History*, 1.

3. Gronim, *Everyday Nature*, 5.

4. Wessels, *The Myth of Progress*, xvi and xviii; Judd, 38. See Friedman, *The Moral Consequences of Economic Growth*.

5. Miller, "The Fate of Wilderness," 92.

6. Philippon, *Conserving Words*, 5–6. Building on the work of George Lakoff and Mark Johnson, Philippon uses metaphor in his study as a tool for analyzing late nineteenth-century and twentieth-century writings and their influence on the formation of five environmental conservation groups, arguing that "metaphor is the central figure of speech at work in the discursive frames that enabled these groups to succeed" (5). Mills, "Metaphorical Vision," also offers a consideration of important metaphors for nature throughout Western culture and history.

7. Fresonke, *West of Emerson*, 43.

8. Powell, *Thomas Cole*, 123; Conron, *American Picturesque*, 8. Cole's works actually combined aesthetic theories of the picturesque, the sublime, and the beautiful. By uniting these traditions with depictions of New World landscapes, he forged his particular contribution to the world of landscape painting. For my purposes, however, the influence of the picturesque on his work is most central. Conron offers a thorough and illuminating study of the American picturesque and its various manifestations in nineteenth-century American culture. Also see Driscoll and Lassiter for introductions to the Hudson River School. Roque, "The Exaltation of American Landscape Painting," explains the movement in relation to the quest for a cultural identity that gripped the country in the early nineteenth century (see pp. 21–22). Powell, *Thomas Cole*, provides an overview of Cole's career and his influence on Asher B. Durand, Frederic E. Church, and Jasper Francis Cropsey.

9. Greenfield, *Narrating Discovery*, 2. Lucy Maddox's *Removals* and Lee Clark Mitchell's *Witnesses to a Vanishing America* offer helpful analyses of, respectively, the nineteenth-century response to a "vanishing" Native American population and to a "vanishing" wilderness.

10. See Wallach, "Thomas Cole," for a helpful introduction to the picturesque (especially 29). Conron, *American Picturesque*, offers a detailed discussion of the range of elements typically found in a picturesque painting (see 67–86). With regard to the elevated perspective of the viewer, see especially Boime's study, whose title calls attention to this aspect of the aesthetic: *The Magisterial Gaze*. He explains: "The elevated point of view signified mastery over the land" (x). Conron also discusses the vista perspective in this way (118).

11. See Boime, *The Magisterial Gaze*, for a discussion of this formulaic quality of some of Cole's landscape paintings (49–50). On the changing ways in which the national landscape was depicted in American magazines from 1780 to 1820, see Lawson, "An Inexhaustible Abundance," who argues that by the early nineteenth century, landscape images functioned as "a crucial inspiration of cultural independence" (305).

12. Driscoll's *"All That Is Glorious Around Us"* provides several examples of artists who emulated this vision through their works.

13. Roque, "The Exaltation of American Landscape Painting," 39. Conron, following Novak's *American Painting*, offers an insightful reading of this painting and *View on the Catskill—Early Autumn* as, together, providing a narrative conveying "the violence of landscape domestication" (*American Picturesque*, 123).

14. Cole, "Essay on American Scenery," 108–9.

15. Ibid., 101. Cole was in Europe from June 1829 until the fall of 1832. See Powell, *Thomas Cole*, 49–61, for a discussion of his travels.

16. On these natural details in Cole's *The Oxbow*, see Hoppin, "Depicting Mount Holyoke," 31. Hoppin notes additional elements of the landscape that Cole included: the Hockanum ferry, the Mill River (a tributary), and Hulbert's Pond (33). As Hoppin also notes, however, "No one can exactly duplicate Cole's view [from Mount Holyoke] because in fact he altered reality" (59) by changing various aspects of the scene for his painterly purpose. These alterations that Cole made to the landscape have received much attention: Novak notes that even Cole's "realistic" depictions of landscape were composed (*American Painting*, 73), and Alan Wallach offers a thorough discussion of how Cole's painting departs from his notes ("Making a Picture"). Also see Bedell, *The Anatomy of Nature*, 19–20; Shepard, "Paintings of the New England Landscape"; and Ringe, "Painting as Poem" (especially 76–77) on the artist's "revision" of natural scenes.

17. The work of Albert Bierstadt perhaps best exemplifies this attention to the American West. I am grateful to Ian Marshall for conversations concerning Cole's representations of wildness which inform my argument here.

18. Cole, "Essay," 101–2; Fresonke, *West of Emerson*, 54.

19. Cole, "Essay," 106.

20. Ibid., 108–9.

21. Angela Miller, *Empire of the Eye*, 16; Cronon, "Telling Tales," 85.

22. Fresonke, *West of Emerson*, 10. Conron, *American Picturesque*, also notes that the American picturesque "comes to serve the status quo" (xxi).

23. John L. O'Sullivan first used the phrase "manifest destiny" in the 1845 issue of *United States Magazine and Democratic Review*. See Abrams, *Landscape and Ideology*, 75–84, for a discussion of the various elements of this national consciousness, which Abrams calls the "master narrative" (73). In this narrative, Americans are "the chosen people of a divinely calibrated history" (Martin, *In the Spirit of the Earth*, 102). See Mitchell's study of nineteenth-century America, *Witnesses to a Vanishing America*, which discusses the pervasiveness of the "ambivalence [which was] felt among even those who participated in the nation's triumphant conquest of the wilderness" (xiv).

24. Ringe has a series of articles that explore the connections between the various writers and artists who shared this aesthetic philosophy: see "Kindred Spirits," "Painting as Poem," and "James Fenimore Cooper and Thomas Cole." Ringe's *The Pictorial Mode* offers a booklength treatment of James Fenimore Cooper, Washington Irving, and William Cullen Bryant in relation to the Hudson River School. James Fenimore Cooper described Cole's monumental, five-part series *The Course of Empire* (1836) as "a great epic poem," anointing it "the work of the highest genius this country has ever produced" (Beard, *Letters and* Journals V:397 and 398; also quoted in Powell, *Thomas Cole*, 70). Also see Peck, "Unlikely Kindred Spirits," for the relationship between Asher B. Durand and Henry David Thoreau. Conron's ambitious study *American Picturesque* discusses the pervasiveness of the American picturesque in American culture generally (see especially 195–230).

25. I cite Bryant's "The Prairies" as it appears in *The Poems of William Cullen Bryant*.

26. Fisher, *Hard Facts*, 36. Many scholars have pointed to the ways in which Cooper's Leatherstocking Tales reflect the tensions in nineteenth-century America between nature

and civilization, sacrifice and progress, and despoliation and development. These dichotomies are articulated by Mitchell, *Witnesses to a Vanishing America*, 45. See also Fisher, *Hard Facts*; Greenfield, *Narrating Discovery* (especially 203); Karcher, Introduction; and Slotkin, *Regeneration through Violence*.

27. James Fenimore Cooper, *Last of the Mohicans*, 350; emphasis mine. In his Leatherstocking Tales, Cooper participates in a story of the landscape explained by Philip Fisher: during the 1840s especially, "the historical consciousness" as expressed in American letters is "fixed" on this "moment just before [the] beginning"—on the period just prior to America's founding and settlement by Europeans (*Hard Facts*, 26). Yet most authors, Fisher goes on to argue, use the trope of the vanishing wilderness in order to signal "the collapse of pre-history" (26). As authors represent this moment just before the nation's beginnings, they depict the natural world as a wilderness scene about to give way to civilization. In Fisher's words, "The wilderness is always understood as vanishing or threatened" (18). This is the case because writers most often treat the wilderness from the perspective of one removed from it in time and accepting of its changes. The image of the vanishing wilderness allows nostalgia for wilderness that assumes the inevitably, celebrated, continued progress of civilization. The loss of wilderness is not, then, loss at all. Writers invoke prehistory in order to "train resignation" or depict "forces as beyond control"—to signal, in other words, the manifest destiny of Euro-American civilization (18). James Fenimore Cooper's works perpetuate this vision. His Leatherstocking Tales are "based on a single dark premise—that American culture is a successor culture that founds itself by extinguishing the culture already in place" (30).

28. Maddox, *Removals*, 49; Cooper, introduction to *Last of the Mohicans*, 7.

29. Angela Miller convincingly argues that Cole was actually "misread" by artists seeking to emulate his aesthetics, and that he, in fact, disagreed with the "nationalism that was such a key element in the landscape art" that purportedly grew under his influence (*Empire of the Eye*, 5 and 4; see also 22–64, in which Miller explains this "misreading.")

30. Cole, "Essay," 102; Ibid., 109 (my emphasis).

31. Angela Miller also discusses Cole's skepticism concerning American exceptionalism and nationalism (see *Empire of the Eye*, especially 22–64). Boime points out that nineteenth-century painters "participated in the very system they condemned and projected it symbolically in their work" (*Magisterial Gaze*, 5).

32. Quoted in Powell, *Thomas Cole*, 64.

33. Perry Miller, *Nature's Nation*, 305; Powell, *Thomas Cole*, 67. On Cole's *Course* as a pointed critique of Jacksonian America, see Stansell and Wilentz, "Cole's America: An Introduction" (especially 19) and Wallach, "Thomas Cole," 92–94.

34. Powell, *Thomas Cole*, 64.

35. Cole, Letter to Robert Gilmor Jr., 74.

36. Quoted in Novak, *American Painting*, 69. Wallach discusses responses to Cole's *Course* that assumed the United States would be exempt from this typical "course of empire" due to its grounding in democracy ("Thomas Cole," 90 and 95). See also Angela Miller, *Empire of the Eye*, 33–34. Lassiter notes that "The extravagance that Cole had depicted in 'The Consummation of Empire' was symbolic of New York in 1836. Reckless expansion and luxurious living had turned the city into a harbor of bad taste and flaunted wealth" (*American Wilderness*, 43–44).

37. Hoppin, "Depicting Mount Holyoke," offers a discussion of the popularity of the particular vista that Cole depicts in *The Oxbow*. See McCoubrey, *American Tradition in Painting*, on the American public's preference for realistic art (especially 22).

38. Angela Miller also interprets *The Oxbow* as "collapsing the sequential narrative of *The Course of Empire* into a single image, transforming temporal into spatial terms" (*Empire of the Eye*, 44).

39. Many critics have discussed the import of Cole's divided canvas. For instance, Wallach suggests that the two distinct but "related vistas" in *The Oxbow* "are compressed or jammed against each other so that a viewer scanning the landscape experiences both a feeling of panoramic breadth and a sense of imminent split or breakdown" ("Thomas Cole," 76). Angela Miller similarly claims that Cole's "dichotomous compositions," such as *The Oxbow*, "convey a radical ambivalence toward the course of American history" (*Empire of the Eye*, 5). Cronon argues that, through its juxtaposition of the dark wilderness scene with the clear, cultivated valley, *The Oxbow* shows Cole's "fears for a future in which the pastoral valley will swallow up the sublime mountainside and then be swallowed in turn by the urban-industrial empire to follow" ("Telling Tales" 43). Conron discusses the prevalence of the "divided landscape" in the American picturesque more generally (129).

40. I am grateful to Garth Claassen for his instruction regarding this aspect of Cole's work. Angela Miller recently suggests that this figure in Cole's painting is Cole himself, who "turns and looks at us, making us complicit with his act of representation and, by extension, moral witnesses to the changes in the land" ("The Fate of Wilderness," 101).

41. Hoppin, "Depicting Mount Holyoke," discusses specific alterations that Cole made to the scene (33). See Boime, *Magisterial Gaze*, on the "association of Cole's landscape with the dispossession of hereditary Indian land" (51–52); also see Clark, Halloran, and Woodford, "Thomas Cole's Vision," 278, on the ways in which Cole's landscape paintings silence other ways in which the landscape had been altered by American progress and industry—in particular the tanning industry's impact on the Catskill Mountains, which are frequently featured in his works. Hoppin and Clark, Halloran, and Woodford, argue that the tradition of depictions of the American landscape initiated by Cole continues to appeal to audiences today. I want to distinguish my use of the terms "real" and "ideal" in reference to Cole's art from Barbara Novak's use in *American Painting*; as she discusses audiences' bland responses to *The Course of Empire*, she refers to Cole as "an idealist in a world that demanded a more discreet blend of the real with the ideal" (63). Novak's use of these terms is meant to distinguish Cole's more realistic landscape paintings (the real) from his more allegorical ones (the ideal). While my use of the terms differs from hers, I am nonetheless indebted to her recognition of this tension in Cole's works.

42. Danly, "Mount Holyoke," recounts the history of the development of Mount Holyoke.

43. Hoppin, "Depiciting Mount Holyoke," 35.

44. Angela Miller, *Empire of the Eye*, 48 (emphasis in original).

45. Cooper, *Rural Hours*, 68, 69.

46. Ibid., 69.

47. The June 27 entry runs from pages 88 to 93 in Cooper's *Rural Hours*.

48. Cooper, *Rural Hours*, 88–89.

49. Ibid., 89.

50. Ibid.

51. Ibid.

52. Ibid., 91, 91–92.

53. Contemporary geographer D. W. Meinig offers an important discussion of different perceptual frameworks that people can bring to their views of landscapes in "The Beholding Eye." In the passage from *Rural Hours* that I discuss here, Cooper adheres to Meinig's criteria for one who sees "landscape as history": "To such a viewer all that lies before his eyes is a complex cumulative record of the work of nature and man in this particular place" (43). In other passages, Cooper can be seen to adhere to other perceptual modes that Meinig delineates. His categories usefully illuminate various ways of "beholding" scenes.

54. See Deakin, Introduction.

55. Cooper, "A Dissolving View," 3; Boime, *Magisterial Gaze*, 96; Cooper, "A Dissolving View," 5. Find Cooper's *Rural Hours* discussion of autumn on pages 202–13 and 215–16.

56. Cooper, "A Dissolving View," 5 and 6.

57. Ibid., 7.

58. Ibid., 11 and 12.

59. Ibid., 12 and 12–13. One example Cooper gives is "the grand Palace of Glass" in London which, she rightly points out, could be razed in just a few hours. Cooper likely refers here to the Crystal Palace, which was built for the Great Exhibition of 1851 in London, a world-publicized event organized by Queen Victoria in celebration of England's leadership in the industrial revolution. Relocated to a park in the southern part of London following the Great Exhibition, the Palace was destroyed by fire on November 30, 1936 (12).

60. Cooper, "A Dissolving View," 13.

61. Ibid., 13, 13–14.

62. Ibid., 14.

63. Ibid., 14, 15.

64. Ibid., 15, 16, 15.

65. Faherty, "The Borderers of Civilization," 126n31; Cooper, "A Dissolving View," 16.

66. Ibid., 11, 15.

67. Martin, *In the Spirit of the Earth*, 62. I am grateful to Allan Axelrad for his insights into the importance of the Old World's preoccupation with ruins to James Fenimore Cooper. Some scholars have read Susan Fenimore Cooper's "A Dissolving View" as a statement of her similar devotion to a landscape with ruins. Buell, for instance, suggests that Cooper "flash[es] forward in time to an epoch when the comparatively unstylized landscape might effuse a certain antique old world charm" (*Environmental Imagination*, 410). However, this reading seems to fall short in light of the care that Cooper gives earlier in the essay to distinguishing the European storied lands from those of the New World. Taking into account more fully the essay's concerns with Cooper's nation's tendencies toward "novelty," Gianquitto reads this "game of architectural consequences" quite differently, suggesting that it serves as Cooper's "stern reprimand to her own culture, which she sees

as determined to 'pull down' its historical markers in its quest for 'novelty'" ("The Noble Designs of Nature," 184). Faherty, in "The Borderers of Civilization," similarly argues that "A Dissolving View" is best understood alongside *Rural Hours*, and that the essay further articulates Cooper's belief that, due to the nation's youth and distinct political heritage, the American landscape would look different from Old World landscapes (109).

68. Cooper, "A Dissolving View," 7.

69. Abrams, *Landscape and Ideology*, 6.

70. Fisher, *Hard Facts*, 87. See Mitchell, *Witnesses to a Vanishing America*, and Lucy Maddox, *Removals*.

71. Cooper, *Rural Hours*, 117.

72. See James Fenimore Cooper, Letter to Richard Bentley, August 6, 1851; Susan Fenimore Cooper, Letter to G. P. Putnam, August 27, 1851; and G. P. Putnam, Letter to Susan Fenimore Cooper, December 2, 1851. Also see Stephen Germic's discussion of Cooper's complex representations of Native Americans in "Land Claims, Natives, and Nativism." When Cooper published *Rural Hours*, she did so with her father's generous assistance: he negotiated the terms of her contracts with both her American and British publishers, and he served as Susan's consultant as she performed the final proofreading of her work. Cooper's dedication of *Rural Hours* to her father demonstrates her true appreciation, as does her reference there to *The Deerslayer*, one of the Leatherstocking Tales most rooted in their shared home landscape and most devoted to describing the lives of the fictionalized Natives with whom James Fenimore Cooper peopled the woods surrounding Cooperstown. On James Fenimore Cooper's role in assisting with the publication of *Rural Hours*, see Johnson and Patterson, Introduction to *Rural Hours*, xi–xiv.

73. For Cooper's discussions of the topics mentioned here, see *Rural Hours*, 39, 10, 36, 146, 188, 191, 314, and 115.

74. Cooper, *Rural Hours*, 112.

75. Ibid., 108.

76. Ibid., 56, 57.

77. Ibid., 57.

78. Ibid.

79. Ibid., 58.

80. Ibid., 303.

81. Ibid., 303–4.

82. Ibid., 120.

83. Powell, *Thomas Cole*, 9.

84. Abrams, *Landscape and Ideology*, 8; Angela Miller, *Empire of the Eye*, 12. As Mitchell notes, most of the expressions of grief over the predicament of Native Americans "hardly cut very deep" (*Witnesses to a Vanishing America*, 29).

85. Cronon, "The Riddle," 38. I first came across Feldman's term in Cronon's "The Riddle," although other environmentally inclined writers also use it to refer to the process of reintroducing habitat corridors and native flora and fauna in hopes of making landscapes more ecologically resilient.

86. Philippon, "Thoreau's Notes," 111, 114.

87. Cooper, introduction to John Leonard Knapp's *Country Rambles in England*, 22.

1. Cooper, "Village Improvement Societies," 67. Gronim, *Everyday Nature*, offers a discussion of some ways in which nature was associated with refinement in colonial America (106–17).

2. "Family Album," 160.

3. Burns, *Pastoral Inventions*, 7.

4. I borrow Bushman's phrasing from the title of his study of nineteenth-century culture, *The Refinement of America*.

5. Cooper, "The Talent of Reading Wisely," 18; Cooper, "Village Improvement Societies," 77.

6. Thornton, *Cultivating Gentlemen*, 164. Thornton also explores the relationship between horticultural pursuits and moral improvement in her "Cultivating the American Character." For a discussion of Emerson's interest in horticulture, see Richardson, *Emerson*, 433–34.

7. Bushman, *The Refinement of America*, xiii. Thornton similarly refers to a "repertoire of rural pursuits" that "constituted a style of living rich with cultural associations" that ensured one's status as a member of Boston's elite: these activities included "gentleman farming," "building an elegant house in a fashionable landscape, studying the classics, belonging to learned societies," and being a member of an agricultural society (*Cultivating Gentlemen*, 56). For a more general treatment of the elevating properties of nature, see Roderick Nash, who argues that the "capacity to appreciate wilderness" was "deemed one of the qualities of a gentleman" and perceived as "a function of gentility" (*Wilderness and the American Mind*, 60).

8. While I offer a discussion in the pages that follow of Alison's influence on Downing, interested readers will want also to consult Judith K. Major's *To Live in the New World* for a detailed, informed overview of Downing's gardening philosophy and Alison's influence on it.

9. See Cooper's discussions of architecture in *Rural Hours*, 237–40. Scholars who consider Cooper's gentility include Baym ("English Nature"), Lucy Maddox ("Susan Fenimore Cooper"), and Vera Norwood (*Made from This Earth*).

10. While significant studies of both American country life and developments in environmental literary history have scrutinized the nineteenth-century middle- and upper-class interest in rural life, in none of these studies does *Rural Hours* receive sustained discussion: see, for example, Burns, *Pastoral Inventions*; chap. 11 in Bushman, *The Refinement of America*; chaps. 3, 4, and 5 in Huth, *Nature and the American*; chap. 4 in Nash, *Wilderness and the American Mind*; Stilgoe, *Common Landscape of America* and *Borderland*; and Thornton, *Cultivating Gentlemen*.

11. "Editor's Table," 187; Ringe, *The Pictorial Mode*, 3. Scholars have explored Alison's influence on several aspects of nineteenth-century American culture. Bozeman, in *Protestantism in an Age of Science*, explains the presence of Scottish common sense philosophy generally on nineteenth-century religious thought. Camfield, in "The Moral Aesthetics of Sentimentality," and Dillon, in "Sentimental Aesthetics," treat the relevance of Alisonian theory to sentimental literature. Streeter, in "Association Psychology," offers an

analysis of the prominence of Alison's rhetoric in the *North American Review* in the years 1815 to 1825, arguing that we can see there the role of Alison's theory of taste in inculcating a nationalistic literature based on association. See Cahill, "Federalist Criticism," for a discussion of the intersections and divergences in understandings of taste and genius in the period.

12. In addition to the more general studies above, scholars have explored the influence of Alison's philosophy on several prominent nineteenth-century Americans relevant to this study. Ralph N. Miller ("Thomas Cole") offers an early explanation of Alison's influence on Thomas Cole; and Powell (*Thomas Cole*) offers a consideration of Cole's adherence to associationist doctrine (especially 39), as do Merritt ("A Wild Scene"; see especially 14–17) and Ringe (see "Painting as Poem," "Kindred Spirits," "Horatio Greenough," and *The Pictorial Mode*, especially 3–8). With regard to literature, Hudson ("Archibald Alison") explores Bryant's early encounters with Alison's text; Peck discusses association as it relates to the works of James Fenimore Cooper (see *A World by Itself*, especially 5–6); and Liebman ("The Origins of Emerson's Early Poetics") focuses on Emerson's encounters with Alison's work. Fenner ("Aesthetic Experience and Aesthetic Analysis") argues persuasively that Alison's philosophy continues to inform our aesthetic understandings. With regard to Alison's influence on conceptions of nature, specifically, Walls offers a brief exploration (*Seeing New Worlds*, 19–20).

13. Alison, *Essays*, iii. Alison distinguished the "sublime" from the "beautiful," but as his distinction does not affect my reading of his work, I omit a discussion of it here.

14. Alison, *Essays*, 23.

15. Ibid., iv.

16. Ibid.

17. Ibid., 17.

18. Ibid., 25 and iii.

19. Ibid., vii.

20. Camfield, "The Moral Aesthetics of Sentimentality," 332.

21. Alison, *Essays*, 418; "The Study of Natural History," 292; Alison, *Essays*, 418 and 24.

22. Alison, *Essays*, v and vii.

23. Ibid., 27.

24. Ibid., viii.

25. As Merritt states in his discussion of Alison, "matter is not beautiful in itself but derives its beauty from the expression of 'Mind' which, through organized and complex trains of associations (whether universal, national or individual), can give it aesthetic significance" ("A Wild Scene," 15).

26. Alison, *Essays*, viii.

27. Camfield, "The Moral Aesthetics of Sentimentality," 331. Camfield explains that Alison adopted this idea of a "moral sense" from the Earl of Shaftesbury (324).

28. Dillon, "Sentimental Aesthetics," 498; Alison, *Essays*, 24. The regulatory aspect of Alison's theory has led Dillon to claim that his version of taste serves as "a political and cultural practice" (497).

29. Camfield, "The Moral Aesthetics of Sentimentality," 337. It is this aspect of Alison's theory that has led Camfield to state: "Thus, while Alison professes a mimetic aesthetic,

it is a purified mimesis, closer in fact to what we would term allegory than to what we would now term realism" (337).

30. "View near Coldspring," 43; Alison, *Essays*, 37–38 and 38.

31. Willis, *American Scenery*, i (my emphasis).

32. Dillon, "Sentimental Aesthetics," 507; T. B. F., "Education of Public Taste," 369 and 370.

33. Tuckerman, "Flowers," 13.

34. Cooke, "Floral Lessons in Morals," 197 and 198. The moral value of flowers was well accepted in the middle decades of the nineteenth century. Beverly Seaton explores one manifestation of this belief in her study of the "flower language books" that gained popularity throughout the century. These books provided explanations for the emotional (or moral) meaning of specific flowers. As Seaton explains, however, the movement toward mastering the language of the flowers had little to do with nature study. The floral language was a "symbolic language," one that assigned a specific sentiment to a specific flower and allowed a person to arrange a bouquet, for example, that bore a particular coded meaning (1–2). The language of flowers was therefore quite removed from a scientific understanding of flowers. Thus, even while nineteenth-century America seemed to be increasingly celebrating its landscape in popular forms, most conceptions of the landscape, and hence of the natural world, relied on quite general and largely metaphoric understandings—or, to borrow Alisonian terminology, associations. Lawson's "An Inexhaustible Abundance" similarly notes the "broad-based appreciation of American nature" that, although "a crucial inspiration of cultural independence" (305), suggests that most Americans had only a superficial knowledge of their natural surroundings.

35. Alison, *Essays*, 24.

36. Ella, "Autumnal Reflections," 217; Ide, "November," 228; W. T. B., "The Coming," 145; Corolla, "Autumn Musings," 211.

37. Cooper, *Rural Hours*, 83.

38. Ibid., 212, 210, and 208.

39. Alison, *Essays*, 46; Cooper, *Rural Hours*, 166.

40. Cooper, *Rural Hours*, 167; Alison 24–25; Cooper, *Rural Hours*, 167.

41. As historian John Hingham notes, "a sense of intimacy with [nature] was dissolving" during this period, which perhaps led people to be satisfied with symbolic rather than literal interactions with their physical environment (*From Boundlessness to Consolidation*, 4). Cooper's response to Alisonian theory endorses this assessment.

42. See Alison, *Essays*, 79–82.

43. The phrase "apostle of taste" is Downing's own: see his "On the Improvement of Country Villages," 545. The phrase is also used as the title of one of the most recent critical studies of Downing's life and career: Schuyler's *Apostle of Taste*, which offers a thorough overview of his philosophy and career. For Downing's influence on American literature, see Sweeting, *Reading Houses and Building Books*, which explores "the intersections of literary and architectural tastes" following Downing's work (1). For other treatments of Downing's prominence, his influence on taste, and his concern with improving morality, see the essays in Tatum and MacDougall, *Prophet with Honor*. As evidence of America's interest in rural life and rural style generally, see Davis, *Rural Residences* (1837), a book recommending certain architectural styles; Wheeler, *Rural Homes* (1851); Allen, *Rural*

Architecture (1852); and Wetmore, *Rural Life in America* (1856; originally published as *Hermit's Dell* [1854]). The interest in rural matters also surfaces, in a different form, in the development of the picturesque aesthetic in American art and letters, evident in landscape painting of the day discussed in chapter 2 and, as I discuss above, in volumes featuring illustrations of rural life.

44. Downing, *Treatise on the Theory and Practice of Landscape Gardening*, 18 and 20.

45. Sweeting, *Reading Houses and Building Books*, 120; Downing, *Treatise*, ix. It is important to note that Downing's campaign to envision the cultivation of rural American landscapes as the cultivation of American refinement had a presence in American culture when he began his successful work. As early as 1835, for example, we find this assumed relationship between land and mind in the slogan of a farming magazine called *The Cultivator*: "To improve the soil and the mind." Indeed, agriculture had long been assumed to be an ennobling pursuit—the "most noble human employment," as the *New York Farmer, and American Gardener's Magazine* would put it in 1835 (Blydenburgh, "Address," 52). When Downing focused on home landscapes as evidence of refinement, he built on long held associations: "the improvement of horticulture" as a "minister" to "man's moral nature" had been noted much earlier in his century (C. C., "The Influence of Flowers," 359).

46. Schuyler, *Apostle of Taste*, 1; T. B. F., "The Education of Public Taste," 358.

47. Alison, *Essays*, 20.

48. Downing, [Editorial], 9; Downing, *Treatise*, v.

49. T. B. F., "The Education of Public Taste," 359.

50. Downing, *Treatise*, vi; Alison, *Essays*, 20.

51. As just one of many examples, see "Rural Architecture—Hope Cottage," the lead article in the *Cultivator*, which reproduces one of Downing's drawings and quotes from him as well; Downing, [Editorial], 10.

52. Downing, [Editorial], 11, 12, 11–12, and 14.

53. Thornton, *Cultivating Gentlemen*, 145.

54. Downing, *Treatise*, 18 and 26; Schuyler, 26 and 42; Downing, [Editorial], 9 (emphasis in original); Downing, *Treatise*, 18. As Sweeting states, "As a garden designer [Downing] had a professional interest in America's love affair with nature, yet that same interest demanded that he manipulate and control the unadorned landscape for peaceful domestic purposes" (*Reading Houses and Building Books*, 10).

55. Schuyler, *Apostle of Taste*, 105.

56. Meinig, "Environmental Appreciation," 1.

57. Downing, "Influence of Horticulture," 11; Cooper, *Rural Hours*, 76 (my emphasis); Downing, "Influence of Horticulture," 11.

58. Cooper, *Rural Hours*, 132 and 52.

59. For Cooper's comments on grouse, see *Rural Hours*, 190.

60. Ibid., 29.

61. Ibid., 53–54 (my emphasis) and 75.

62. Susman, "Gothic Revival Domestic Architecture," 54. Susman offers a detailed discussion of Cooper's home, which was called "Byberry Cottage" (or, "Riverside Cottage") and of its adherence to Downing's drawings (see especially 49–56). See also Vivienne Dawn Maddox's assessment of the cottage ("Seven Styles," 50–58). Cooper's remarks about her father are found in *Pages and Pictures* (14) and "A Glance" (202).

63. Dillon, "Sentimental Aesthetics," 507; Cooper, *Rural Hours*, 330n33. As I discuss in chapter 2, Cooper valued the picturesque aesthetic even while she saw its limitations in representing nature. Although Cooper employs techniques associated with the picturesque in *Rural Hours*, perhaps her most obvious position as a proponent of that aesthetic was through her contribution of an essay ("A Dissolving View") to the lavishly illustrated anthology, *The Home Book of the Picturesque*. While he does not mention Cooper, see Ringe, *The Pictorial Mode*, for a discussion of *The Home Book of the Picturesque* as a powerful illustration of the prevalence of Alisonian theory in the United States (see especially 8–11).

64. Downing, "On Feminine Taste," 45, 52, and 51–52. Elsewhere, Downing had made his commitments to American domesticity unmistakably clear: "[W]e believe, above all things under heaven, in the power and virtue of the *individual home*. We devote our life and humble efforts to raising its condition" ("Our Country Villages," 541). It is not surprising, then, that, in "On Feminine Taste in Rural Affairs," Downing recommends that women tend to "the garden" and "the lawn"—places closely associated with the home and with domesticity, and thus more closely aligned with the concerns of that womanly domain: the "private sphere." When he advises women "to live . . . not only the in-door but the out-of-door life," he suggests merely that they take a few steps beyond their parlors.

65. Downing, Review of *Rural Hours*, 230 and 231. For the *Horticulturist*'s excerpt of Cooper's *Rural Hours*, see Cooper, "A Plea for American Trees."

66. Downing, Review of *Rural Hours*, 231; Bremer, "To the Friends of A. J. Downing," lxix.

CHAPTER 4. THE METAPHOR OF REASON

1. Cooper, introduction to *The Rhyme and Reason of Country Life*, 40, 42, 40.

2. Emerson, *Nature*, 9. As Emerson himself said to his congregation in 1830, attention to nature, especially through the study of natural history, "may have the effect to supplant in some degree the absorbing passion for wealth by supplying new measures of happiness & simpler and more spiritual pleasures" (quoted in Robinson, "Fields of Investigation," 94.) Teichgraeber's *Sublime Thoughts/Penny Wisdom* discusses the various ways in which Emerson sought to challenge the "American market"—or, in other words, the popular, capitalistic society of the mid-nineteenth century. See also Gura, who argues that in *Nature*, "Emerson was asking his readers just how fulfilled a nation could be if it defined as the highest uses to which nature could be put such economic enterprises as the Erie Canal or the development of hundreds of miles of iron-railed roads" (*The Wisdom of Words*, 92). As far as we know, Emerson did not read *Rural Hours*.

Henry David Thoreau's *Walden*, which I discuss in a later chapter, is certainly the best known (and most cranky) mid-nineteenth-century expression of the need for busy Americans to attend to their physical environments. As I discussed in the previous chapter, the rise of landscape design was also connected to this desire to bring Americans closer to nature for the purposes of moral improvement. See Perry Miller, *Nature's Nation*, on the mid-nineteenth-century concerns about rising industry (especially 199). In a related fashion, Brown, *The Emerson Museum*, offers a discussion of scientific thinkers who advocated "the healthful effects of scientific study" as a means to social improvement (132).

3. Emerson, *Nature*, 26. Walls, *Emerson's Life in Science*, offers an important discussion of how the concept of a "culture of truth" informed Emerson's sense of his work and intellectual community (203–26).

4. Here I borrow Baym's subtitle to *American Women of Letters and the Nineteenth-Century Sciences: Styles of Affiliation*, which offers a chapter on Cooper. Other scholars have discussed Cooper's or Emerson's relationships to the science of their day: on Cooper and science, see Gianquitto, *"Good Observers of Nature"*; on Emerson, see Walls's entire *Emerson's Life in Science*, and especially 55–67. Also on Emerson, see Rossi's "Emerson, Nature, and Natural Science"; Robinson's "Emerson's Natural Theology" and "Fields of Investigation"; and Branch's "Ralph Waldo Emerson."

5. Fresonke, *West of Emerson*, 2–3. As Fresonke explains, the argument from design has its origins in Greek philosophy (see pp. 2–4). Rossi provides a helpful discussion of design, suggesting that natural theology "seeks to establish a knowledge of God accessible to all rational human beings without recourse to supernatural revelation. As promoted in the modern era by seventeenth-century deists, a theology based on nature could ground the existence of God through evidence of the lawlike regularity of the natural world (the argument from design), thereby rendering belief both rational and universal and thus avoiding sectarian dispute" ("Emerson, Nature, and Natural Science," 104). Regarding Emerson's introduction to design through Paley, see Richardson, *Emerson*, 7–8. Also see Walls, *Emerson's Life in Science*, on the theory of design as it developed in America and in Emerson's understanding, in particular (pp. 42–48 and 63–67). Rossi discusses the fact that the discourse of natural theology was ubiquitous in both America and Britain: people would have encountered its teachings and assumptions "from orthodox pulpits, in periodicals and in other print media, on the lyceum circuit, and in debates" in scientific circles ("Emerson, Nature, and Natural Science," 105 and 108).

6. Walls, *Emerson's Life in Science*, 48 and 49. Walls also discusses the varieties of the doctrine of correspondence in the romantic imagination (48–49).

7. The phrase is from Chai, *The Romantic Foundations*, 64. Chai offers a thorough study of "the assimilation and transformation of the cultural legacy of European romanticism from roughly 1780 to 1830" by mid-nineteenth-century American authors (xi). See also Keane, *Emerson, Romanticism, and Intuitive Reason*, on Emerson's relationship to British romanticism. In addition, Richardson's biography of Emerson discusses the many romantic influences on Emersonian philosophy. See Wolf, *Romantic Re-vision*, for an interpretation of romanticism as "engaged in a dialectic of consciousness with itself" (xvi).

8. Here I echo the title of William Ellery Channing's 1828 sermon, "Likeness to God," which claimed: "In ourselves are the elements of divinity" (9).

9. Chai, *The Romantic Foundations*, 64; Fresonke, *West of Emerson*, 4; Chai, *The Romantic Foundations*, 67. As Richardson notes of Emerson, "He does not reject the argument from design; indeed he welcomes it, but that argument is not what matters most. Emerson is much more interested in the relationship between the natural world and the human mind than he is the natural world as proof of a designing deity" (*Emerson*, 142).

10. Fresonke, *West of Emerson*, 4. Brown, *The Emerson Museum*, suggests that Emerson spearheaded a specifically American form of romanticism, 42.

11. Several scholars treat the changing role of natural history. Especially useful to this discussion are the following: Jardine, "*Naturphilosophie* and the Kingdoms of Nature," discusses the difficulties inherent in describing the precise relationship between romanticism and the changing culture of natural history in the nineteenth century; also see Brown, *The Emerson Museum*, on the complexity of these relationships. Rehbock, *The Philosophical Naturalists*, offers insight into the development of the field of biology out of the more general field of natural history, arguing, "It was precisely this search for laws or generalizations that, in the course of the nineteenth century, transformed the study of natural history into the science of biology" (40). For helpful overviews of the changing nature of science in the nineteenth century, see Rehbock, *The Philosophical Naturalists*; and Walls, *Emerson's Life in Science* and *Seeing New Worlds*. See Robinson, "Fields of Investigation," for a treatment of the relationship between natural history and religion.

12. Emerson, *Nature*, 18.

13. Ibid., 8 and 7.

14. Ibid., 23 and 8.

15. Ibid., 7; Richardson, *Emerson*, 226; Emerson, *Nature*, 8. This belief in a theory of all life is known as "holism." Emerson's interest in holism took many forms and was influenced by several thinkers. On the presence of Swedenborg's doctrine of correspondences in Emersonian thought, see Richardson, *Emerson*, 198–99.

16. Emerson, *Nature*, 7. Emerson's ideas here suggest his religious skepticism, which especially shows itself in his decision to resign the pulpit and leave the church over the issue of communion. See Richardson's *Emerson* (125–26) on this particular episode in his life.

17. Emerson, *Nature*, 8 and 17. As Brown states, "Anyone who reads Emerson must come to terms with the depth of his insistence on the paradigm of visual perception" (*The Emerson Museum*, 44). See especially 43–58 of Brown's book for a consideration of vision and the trope of "transparency" in Emerson's work.

18. Richardson states that Emerson might as well have named the "Discipline" section "Education" (*Emerson*, 231). On "Language" as key to understanding Emerson's philosophy, see Branch, "Ralph Waldo Emerson," 294.

19. Emerson, *Nature*, 11, 12, 11, and 12.

20. Ibid., 12, 13, 15, and 16.

21. Ibid., 16.

22. Ibid., 17 and 18.

23. Ibid., 18. See Gura, *The Wisdom of Words*, for an analysis of this "fully developed symbolist theory of language" in the context of "attempts to discredit the varied interpretations of biblical language that had contributed to the rise of denominationalism" (6). Gura's study also explores more generally "how the study of language created a climate in which the possibility of symbolic discourse was entertained and ambiguity was regarded as a viable mode for discerning truth" (11).

24. Emerson, *Nature*, 18, 19, and 18.

25. Ibid., 21, 29, and 21.

26. Ibid., 23.

27. Williams, *Keywords* (in the entry on "Idealism"), 125; Emerson, *Nature*, 29. Also see Richardson and Walls on Emerson's particular relation to philosophical idealism

(Richardson, *Emerson*, 231–34; Walls, *Seeing New Worlds*, 21–23.). We find in the "Spirit" section that Emerson is quite drawn to the Ideal Theory, as it explains "the total disparity between the evidence of our own being and the evidence of the world's being" (Emerson, *Nature*, 41–42).

28. Emerson, *Nature*, 37. As Walls notes, Emerson also suggests in "Spirit" that the natural world must be real insofar as it serves as an enabler of any actual experience whatsoever (*Emerson's Life in Science*, 103–4).

29. Emerson, *Nature*, 29, 42, 43, and 45.

30. Jardine, *Naturphilosophie*, 245 (or, as Elisa New phrases it, Emerson is "confusing his will with the universe's" ["The Line's Eye," 1]); Walls, *Emerson's Life in Science*, 221; New, "The Line's Eye," 2.

31. Emerson, *Nature*, 9, 8, 25, and 23.

32. Ibid., 21 and 23.

33. For the paragraphs of *Nature* devoted to natural phenomena and the January sunset, see especially 13–14. As John Gatta remarks, "critics have rarely focused directly on [Emerson's] response to the biotic environment" (*Making Nature Sacred*, 89). See, however, Brown, *The Emerson Museum*; Robinson, "Emerson's Natural Theology," and Rossi, "Emerson, Nature, and Natural Science," 113, on Emerson's now-famous and shaping moment at the Muséum d'Historie Naturelle in Paris. Branch reminds us that Emerson's early works (his sermons, journals, and early lectures) "document his passionate attraction to natural history" ("Ralph Waldo Emerson," 302). On Emerson's interest in spending time in nature, see Richardson, *Emerson*, especially 282, 283, 430, and 465–66. Included here are discussions of Emerson's frequent walks and close observations of natural phenomena, as well as his one-time desire to build a hut and live, as Thoreau did, along the shores of Walden Pond.

34. Emerson, *Nature*, 9, 8, and 9.

35. Ibid., 10, 9, 10, and 9.

36. Ibid., 10.

37. Ibid., 10.

38. Ibid., 19, 26, 11, 12, 11, 16, 17, 18, 25, 25, and 26.

39. Ibid., 25. See Branch, "Ralph Waldo Emerson," for a discussion of how Emerson's "critical reputation has not always fared well among scholars of American nature writing" because of this emphasis in his work on anthropocentrism (302). Branch makes a powerful argument, however, concerning the ecologically redeeming qualities of Emerson's vision.

40. Emerson, "The Poet," 9; Emerson, *Nature*, 25; Walls, *Emerson's Life in Science*, 28.

41. Cooper, introduction to *The Rhyme and Reason*, 40.

42. Ibid., 40.

43. Cooper, *Rural Hours*, 268–69, 295–96, 25–27, 179, and 13–17. For Baym's views, see "English Nature."

44. Cooper, *Rural Hours*, 330n33.

45. Cooper, introduction to *The Rhyme and Reason*, 32, 38, and 39; Cooper, "A Dissolving View," 6.

46. Cooper, *Rural Hours*, 3. Cooper likely encountered the quotation and Hooker's treatise in its 1845 edition (arranged by John Keble), which included the quotation in

a biographical sketch of Hooker by Izaac Walton, himself a noted naturalist in Britain whom Cooper had read (see her references to him in *The Rhyme and Reason of Country Life*, 103–4 and 164–68). Cooper was also a fan of Keble; she refers to him as "a distinguished living poet of England" and includes his endorsement of rural poetry in her introduction to *The Rhyme and Reason* (39), and she also includes several of his poems in that volume (see 224–25, 255–56, 287; 296–98). Hooker's theological writings convey an attitude toward nature that some scholars have deemed protoecological. Booty claims that Hooker "provides the basis for a theology that is ecologically attuned" ("Richard Hooker," 22); in a similar vein, Dowden emphasizes Hooker's conception of a universe "as a vast harmonious system" (*Puritan and Anglican*, 88). My thanks to Ginny Johnson for helping me locate Hooker's work.

47. The characterization of White is from Buell, *The Environmental Imagination*, 209. For Cooper's remark on White and Knapp standing "side by side," see her introduction to John Leonard Knapp's *Country Rambles in England*, 17. Additional evidence that Cooper hoped her book would contribute to this literary history of natural history comes from Richard Bentley, Cooper's London publisher, who advertised *Rural Hours* in his press's promotional literature by characterizing it in reference to only to two other books: Gilbert White's *Natural History of Selborne* and Audubon's *Ornithological Biography*—very significant texts in English and American natural history writing, respectively. I should add that Bentley recognized that *Rural Hours* was not solely a work of natural history: "Not alone as a record of the natural history of America is the publication highly interesting, but as a picture of its rural manners" (Bentley, "Books for the Country," 341). Also see the discussion of Cooper's sense of herself as a nature writer as gleaned from her introduction to *Rhyme and Reason* in the introduction to Johnson and Patterson, *Susan Fenimore Cooper*, xvi–xix.

48. Robinson, "Fields of Investigation," 95; Cooper, *Rural Hours*, 208.

49. Cooper, *Rural Hours*, 49.

50. Cooper, introduction to John Leonard Knapp's *Country Rambles*, 2, 20.

51. Ibid., 22.

52. Cooper's special fascination with ornithology is also clear through her series of essays called "Otsego Leaves," which, among other discussions of bird life, chronicles the declining bird populations in her area. Her late essay "A Lament for the Birds" is also relevant in this regard.

53. Cooper, *Rural Hours*, 299, 303, 299, and 303. Emerson also regretted that the United States "must wear the name of a thief . . . Amerigo Vespucci" (quoted in Richardson, *Emerson*, 521).

54. Cooper, *Rural Hours*, 305. Cooper's remarks here are especially interesting given the name of her particular locale: "Cooperstown." She does forgive the practice to some degree, however, when she states that "in extraordinary cases growing out of peculiar circumstances," it may be appropriate (305). Nonetheless, she clearly prefers naming places based on some natural feature.

55. Cooper, *Rural Hours*, 83, 84. Also see Richardson, *Emerson*, on the "artificial" nature of Linnean taxonomy, 140.

56. Cooper, *Rural Hours*, 87.

57. Ibid., 212–13, my emphases.

58. Ibid. 330n33 and 134.

59. Ibid., 134–35, my emphases.

60. I use "transcend" here in the sense of "moving beyond." As Walls helpfully notes, Emerson's notion of transcendence *is* rooted in the real earth, but then leads away from it: "Transcendence was located not above the Earth but everywhere around us, in the human power to remake nature in the image of our desire" (*Emerson's Life in Science*, 225). Also important to note here is that Emerson's later work, starting with his 1844 "Experience," reveals a philosopher not nearly so sure of himself or nature's—and humanity's—ultimate meanings. For a general introduction to the changes in Emerson's thinking later in his career, see Rossi, "Emerson, Nature, and Natural Science." A fuller treatment of the later Emerson appears in Robinson, *Emerson and the Conduct of Life*. My thanks go to Laura Dassow Walls for reminding me of this intriguing change in Emerson's tone.

61. Emerson, "The American Scholar," 54; Emerson, "The Poet," 24; Cooper, "A Dissolving View," 6; Cooper, introduction to *The Rhyme and Reason*, 27. As John Gatta notes, "From the standpoint of present-day environmentalism, Emerson's obvious defect as a nature writer is the dearth of concrete particulars—of named organisms and objects—invoked in his writing" (*Making Nature Sacred*, 89). Gatta goes so far with his argument as to suggest that "the worldview represented in *Nature* is more radically anthropocentric than the Christian orthodoxy it sought to displace" (89). However, Gatta's ultimate argument about Emerson's famous text is that it can be read as an early contribution toward an environmental theology, in that Emerson insists on nature's sacrality rather than on its being used in a solely utilitarian way (90). Also see Branch's "Ralph Waldo Emerson" for a consideration of Emerson's particularly valuable contributions to modern-day ecological thinking (especially 302).

62. De Man, *The Resistance to Theory*, 11.

63. Walls, *Emerson's Life in Science*, 104, 105, and 104–5. (Page 225 is also relevant).

64. Cooper, introduction to *The Rhyme and Reason*, 41.

CHAPTER 5. PASSION FOR NATURE BEYOND METAPHOR

1. Thoreau, *Journal* 2:176 and 178–79 (August 23, 1845); my emphasis. As is customary in citing Thoreau's journals, I cite the Princeton edition of Thoreau's journals by indicating the volume number in Arabic numbers, and I indicate the volumes of the older Torrey and Allen edition through Roman numerals.

2. My discussion builds on a well-established tradition of explorations of Thoreau and language. Beginning with Cavell, scholars have long been fascinated by Thoreau's use of language to convey nature. Peck's "Thoreau's Lakes of Light" offers a helpful overview of the last several decades of scholarship in this vein.

3. Thoreau, *Journal* 2:178–79 (August 23, 1845).

4. Thoreau, *Walden*, 111; emphasis mine.

5. Ibid., 28.

6. Other scholars have examined Thoreau's interests in history/American progress, landscape painting, and landscape design. On Thoreau's interest in history, see Burbick, *Thoreau's Alternative History*; on Thoreau and American exceptionalism, see Fresonke,

West of Emerson, and Schneider, "Wildness and Geographic Determinism." Also see Greenfield, who offers a reading of Thoreau's "Ktaadn" as a confrontation with American history (*Narrating Discovery*, especially 190). On Thoreau and nineteenth-century landscape painters, see Richardson's *Henry Thoreau* (especially 260–62) and Smithson's "Thoreau, Thomas Cole, and Asher Durand," as well as Peck's "Unlikely Kindred Spirits." Masteller and Masteller, "Rural Architecture," and Sweeting, *Reading Houses and Building Books* (185), discuss Thoreau's interest in Andrew Jackson Downing's philosophies and work; Baym argues that Thoreau rejects aspects of Downing's philosophy ("English Nature," 177–80).

7. Newman, *Our Common Dwelling*, xiii. Jane Tompkins offers a helpful analysis of the phenomena of canonization in *Sensational Designs*.

8. Foucault, *Archeology of Knowledge*, 209; Tompkins, *Sensational Designs*, xvi.

9. Emerson, "The Poet," 9.

10. For the phrase "the 'end' of nature," see McKibben, *The End of Nature*. For a historian's account of nineteenth-century changes to the land, see Merchant's *The Death of Nature*; McPhee's *The Control of Nature* is also relevant, as is Cronon's *Nature's Metropolis* and Nash's *Wilderness and the American Mind* (especially chaps. 3 and 4).

11. Foucault uses the term "common articulation," *Archeology*, 209; Myers, "On the Cultural Construction," 59.

12. Emerson, *Nature*, 25 and 19.

13. Thoreau, *Journal* 2:178.

14. Thoreau, *Journal* 2:357 (after December 2, 1846). Walls also provides an illuminating discussion of Thoreau's attempts "to braid together the physical facts of the natural world and the truths of transcendental higher law" ("Romancing the Real," 124), as does Dean, "Natural History, Romanticism, and Thoreau."

15. Emerson, *Nature*, 40 and 20. Several writers have explored Emerson and Thoreau's differing views. Perry Miller discusses Thoreau in the context of "one of the major problems of the Romantic movement," namely, "striking and maintaining the delicate balance between object and reflection, of fact and truth, of minute observation and generalized concept" (*Nature's Nation*, 177). West, *Transcendental Wordplay*, analyzes the relation between names and things in terms of the philosophy of John Locke (especially 27–67). Cafaro, *Thoreau's Living Ethics*, notes Thoreau's movement away from Emerson's anthropocentrism (13). See also Robinson, however, who argues that Thoreau found in Emerson's *Nature* "a theory that gave facts significance because of their interrelations" ("Thoreau and Idealism," 33; the discussion appears in revised form in *Natural Life*).

16. See *Faith in a Seed* and *Wild Fruits* for Thoreau's most recently published natural history projects, of which Walls offers a compelling reading (*Seeing New Worlds*, 179–99), suggesting that Thoreau "literalizes metaphor" in his late work (194). Here I want to qualify my statement that Thoreau moves away from metaphor in his journal. As Cameron notes, Thoreau of course employs metaphor throughout his life as a writer. However, as she argues, "The point of metaphor . . . [is increasingly] not to compare natural and human worlds, but rather to expand the domain of the former, to insist on nature's infinite self-referentiality" (*Writing Nature*, 13). While Thoreau continues to use metaphor, then, after the publication of *Walden* his writing grants nature more authenticity, using metaphor in ways that help him understand nature in and of itself, rather than as a means

to his self-cultivation. With regard to Thoreau's changing approach to his journal and to nature after 1850, see Walls "Romancing the Real" and *Seeing New Worlds*; McGregor, *A Wider View*, 3; and Hodder, *Thoreau's Ecstatic Witness*, 165, 275, where he argues on behalf of seeing this development in Thoreau's thought in "spiritual" terms. The precise date of this change in Thoreau's emphasis remains open to debate: Howarth points to 1852 as the time when the journal shifts (*The Book of Concord*, 80); more recently, Bradley P. Dean suggests that Thoreau's "dramatic reorientation" occurred in the period between the fall of 1849 and the fall of 1850 (Dean, "Natural History, Romanticism, and Thoreau," 82). Lance Newman, *Our Common Dwelling*, offers a compelling account of this development in Thoreau's career and its significance in terms of his political vision, which Newman argues grew more radical alongside Thoreau's increasing materialist vision (162–70).

17. Emerson, *Nature*, 40; Thoreau, *Walden*, 111.

18. McGregor, *A Wider View*, 120. Howarth also suggested seeing *Walden* not as the climax of Thoreau's career but as one of the early steps of his "continuous ascent" as a writer (*The Book of Concord*, xvii). The best biographies of Thoreau, which inevitably include discussion of his life in nature, remain Harding's *The Days of Henry Thoreau* and Richardson's *Henry Thoreau*. Critical studies of Thoreau's life in nature are abundant, and this discussion is particularly indebted to several. First, some writers have analyzed what James McIntosh calls Thoreau's "shifting stance" toward nature (*Thoreau as Romantic Naturalist*): see, in addition to McIntosh, Buell, *The Environmental Imagination* (especially 549); Robinson, *Natural Life*; Richardson, *Henry Thoreau*; and Simmons, "Speaking for Nature." Burbick, *Thoreau's Alternative History*; Hildebidle, *Thoreau*; and McGregor, *A Wider View*, focus on Thoreau as a naturalist. Walls's *Seeing New Worlds* is especially useful; she documents Thoreau's turn away from the "metaphorical dualisms" of *Walden* and toward the "murmur of multiple voices and actions" of the natural world (13). Other scholars have taken up the more philosophical question of what Hodder terms Thoreau's "encounter [with] consciousness and objective reality" (*Thoreau's Ecstatic Witness*, 293). For such explorations of Thoreau's relationship to language, phenomena, and noumena, see (in addition to Hodder) Cafaro, *Thoreau's Living Ethics*; Cavell, *The Senses of Walden*; Peck, *Thoreau's Morning Work* (some of the thinking of which Peck revises in "Thoreau's Lakes of Light"); and Tauber, *Henry David Thoreau*. On the journal in particular, also see Peck's "Better Mythology."

19. Thoreau, *Walden*, 107, 108.

20. Ibid., 110; emphasis in original.

21. Ibid., 111.

22. Ibid., 115, 124, 126, 115–16, 125, and 111. Here I disagree with Friesen, who argues that "sounds are the language without metaphor" (258). Although I agree that Thoreau's chapter title suggests that sounds comprise this language, I do not believe that the complexities of the chapter allow us to accept this one meaning for "the language which all things and events speak without metaphor." West discusses the possibility that Thoreau had in mind Berkeley's philosophy of scientific language as limited in terms of conveying nature (*Transcendental Wordplay*, 30).

23. Ibid., 128.

24. Peck, *Thoreau's Morning Work*, 120.

25. Ibid., 120.

26. The first passage (from the fall of 1845) occurs in the *Journal* (2:213–14). With regard to the appearance of this passage in the first version of *Walden*, see Shanley, *The Making of Walden*, 193. For the October 8, 1852, passage, see the *Journal* (5:367–69).

27. Thoreau, *Walden*, 233, 161, 233, 234, 235.

28. Ibid., 233, 234, 236, 234, 236.

29. Quinn, "The Cultural Basis of Metaphor," 135; Mills, "Metaphorical Vision," 237. Robert E. Abrams, in explaining what he calls the "deconstructive vehemence of Thoreau's writing" ("Image, Object, and Perception," 257), claims that we find this failed representation of perception commonly in Thoreau's prose: "perception encounters a permanent gap or 'interval' that cannot be closed—a depth . . . between the observer and what he cannot fix definitively in his sights" (255). In his analysis of Thoreau's "wild rhetoric," Henry Golemba somewhat similarly argues that Thoreau, throughout his career, "refined his special rhetorical ability to achieve the effect of meaning's perpetual immanence . . . to create a style that includes gaps, dissolves, and contradictions" (*Thoreau's Wild Rhetoric*, 5–6). Golemba argues that Thoreau's "language of desire" purposefully and "constantly affirmed the remoteness of meaning" (231).

30. Thoreau, *Walden*, 236.

31. Buell, *Environmental Imagination*, 266.

32. Peck, "Thoreau's Lakes of Light," 90, 91, and 95; Newman, *Our Common Dwelling*, 135 and 145; Thoreau, *Journal* 2:178 (August 23, 1845). In a slightly different context, Peck has called Thoreau's extensive use of symbolism his "extravagant metaphor" ("Thoreau's Lakes of Light," 95).

33. Newman, *Our Common Dwelling*, xii; Dean, "Natural History, Romanticism, and Thoreau," 77. See Cameron's *Writing Nature*, Robinson's *Natural Life*, and Walls's *Seeing New Worlds* for discussions of misperceptions of Thoreau as an isolated hermit. Newman's study argues that "the reality to which our most canonical authors [of romanticism] were responding most directly was class division" (xiii) and offers a compelling account of the social changes that gave rise to romanticism's views of "the restorative discipline of nature" and of transcendentalism as a social movement (43; see especially 25–43).

34. Thoreau, *Journal* VII:79 (December 6, 1854).

35. Thoreau, *Journal* 4:296 (January 27, 1852).

36. Thoreau, *Walden*, 324; emphasis in original.

37. Thoreau, *Journal* 5:250–51 (July 26, 1852).

38. Thoreau, *Journal* 5:261 (July 27, 1852).

39. Thoreau, *Journal* 5:164 (June 30, 1852); Newman, *Our Common Dwelling*, 175; Richardson, *Henry Thoreau*, 380.

40. Thoreau, "Walking," 208 and 209.

41. Dean, "Natural History, Romanticism, and Thoreau," 83.

42. Thoreau, *Journal* 3:305 (July 14 1851).

43. Thoreau, *Journal* 5:245 (July 25, 1852); Walls, "Romancing the Real," 134.

44. Thoreau, *Journal* 4:296 (January 27 and 28, 1852).

45. Walls explains, "The kind of writerly technology Thoreau developed and deployed through the 1850s is usually associated with science, for it demanded conscientious and

repeated observation, careful measurement, and painstaking identification of natural objects and phenomena by their scientific names" ("Romancing the Real," 141). For a thorough description of Thoreau's techniques as a naturalist, see Walls, *Seeing New Worlds*, 134–40.

46. Richardson's *Henry Thoreau*, 380; on Howarth's term, see his *Book of Concord*; Dean, "Natural History, Romanticism, and Thoreau," 86. Richardson also offers a helpful description of Thoreau's later works in his introduction to *Faith in a Seed*, 5–6; see also McGregor, *A Wider View*, 187. McGregor describes Thoreau's journal as I have: as "at once a faithful record of natural phenomena and a presentation framed in prose poetry—science and art" (177). As several writers have shown, Thoreau's Kalendar project suggests his interest in a more objective, "scientific" description, one preserving to a much greater degree his observations of natural phenomena and relying much less on his traditional tools of prose, lesson making, and figurative language. Young, "Two Blue Herons," offers an insightful close reading of two short passages from Thoreau's journal, illustrating Thoreau's shift from being a writer concerned with the "myths" associated with natural phenomena to a writer who has an "appreciation" for natural phenomena in and of themselves. On Thoreau as scientist, see Baym's early "Thoreau's View of Science," some of the conclusions of which have been challenged by Walls (*Seeing New Worlds*). See also Richardson's "Thoreau and Science" and his *Henry Thoreau*, as well as the essays in the "Thoreau as Scientist" section of Schofield and Baron, *Thoreau's World and Ours: A Natural Legacy*. Tauber, *Henry David Thoreau*, provides an overview of these and other writings on Thoreau and science (104–5).

47. Peck, "Thoreau's Lakes of Light," explores Thoreau's interest in these philosophical issues as they emerge in "The Ponds" chapter of *Walden*. Cameron observes that Thoreau's journal suggests "that nature is a subject in its own right; that nature is the whole subject; that what is monotonous about nature—its predictable repetitiveness—is what is moving about nature" (*Writing Nature*, 105). Similarly, McGregor argues that for Thoreau, "Nature was not symbol, not allegory, but the essence of existence itself" (*A Wider View*, 86). Cafaro also comments on Thoreau's insistence "that nature has value in its own right" (*Thoreau's Living Ethics*, 13); however, Cafaro concentrates his analysis on *Walden*, arguing that it is a nonanthropocentric text (139) due to its suggestion that "knowledge of nature furthers personal expression" (156). Cafaro argues that Thoreau's *Walden* serves the natural world by demonstrating its value, but, as Cafaro himself shows, Thoreau does so by indicating nature's value for the individual human being. Such a view of nature's value is ultimately anthropocentric precisely because it serves human beings.

48. Emerson, "The Poet," 23. The definition of "exponent" is from the American Heritage Dictionary. My use of the word "relinquish" in the final sentence of this paragraph echoes Buell's use of that term: in chapter 5 of his *Environmental Imagination*, he develops a lengthy and compelling discussion of an "aesthetics of relinquishment" in American nature writing (see 143–79).

49. Richardson, *Henry Thoreau*, 381. See Bradley P. Dean's description of the manuscript materials comprising *Wild Fruits* and of their treatment over the years in his introduction and notes to Thoreau's *Wild Fruits*, ix–xvii and 289.

50. Thoreau, *Wild Fruits*, 60, 62–63, and 63–64.

51. Thoreau, *Wild Fruits*, 116; Cooper, *Rural Hours*, 13–17; Thoreau, *Wild Fruits*, 102–7, 92; Cooper, *Rural Hours*, 54, 75; Thoreau, *Wild Fruits*, 5, 58; for examples of their calls for the preservation of trees, see Cooper, *Rural Hours*, 128, and Thoreau, *Wild Fruits*, 235–36.

52. Cooper, *Rural Hours*, 133; Thoreau, *Wild Fruits*, 168; Cooper, introduction to John Leonard Knapp's *Country Rambles*, 22; Thoreau, *Wild Fruits*, 3; Thoreau, "Autumnal Tints," 256.

53. Thoreau, *Journal* 4:418–20 (April 2, 1852); Robinson, *Natural Life*, 8.

54. Thoreau, *Journal* 5:368; Cramer's remark occurs in his edition of Thoreau's *Walden* (225n62).

55. Newman, *Our Common Dwelling*, 182. Newman demonstrates that this work reflects Thoreau's desire to forge a connection between his deep concerns about the corrosive aspects of capitalistic America and his deep love for nature—the same concerns that occupy him as early as *Walden*.

56. Thoreau, *Journal* 1:104 (January 1840); Tuan, *Space and Place*, 203. As Peck notes, "for Thoreau, the world and its structures had an undeniable reality apart from their relation to the human mind" (*Thoreau's Morning Work*, 67).

57. Emerson, *Nature*, 19; Thoreau, *Journal* 4:296; Emerson, "Thoreau," 575, 577, 581, 585, and 582. Thoreau died from tuberculosis at age 44.

58. Botkin, *No Man's Garden*, xvi; Newman, *Our Common Dwelling*, 24, 164; Thoreau, "Natural History of Massachusetts," 27; Robinson, *Natural Life*, 15. Peck takes a slightly different view of the evolution of Thoreau's thinking, suggesting that "Thoreau remained committed to a symbolic understanding of nature's truths, but . . . the method of his journal led him implicitly to challenge the philosophical idealism that underlay such symbolism" ("Unlikely Kindred Spirits," 691). Similarly, Howarth, while acknowledging Thoreau's developing interest in natural facts, argues that he maintained throughout his life his "metaphorical vision" (*The Book of Concord*, xvii). However, the metaphor that Howarth identifies as unifying Thoreau's later works is that of "concord" itself: "His studies of Concord's natural history were moving toward a grand conclusion, that concord—harmony, integration—is the principle attribute of organic life" (182). Given the fact that I am arguing that Thoreau moves toward an understanding of nature's truth as residing in its physicality, my conclusions don't seem that different from Howarth's. McGregor, *A Wider View*, shares the view that Thoreau increasingly found meaning in natural facts themselves, as does Newman, who argues that Thoreau's "life was a journey from the orthodox extravagance of idealist speculation toward an increasingly open and careful engagement with the reality of nature in its own right" (*Our Common Dwelling*, 187).

CONCLUSION

1. Lopez, *Rediscovery*, 57. Several writers address these potential causes of the environmental crisis, but interested readers might begin with these titles: on economics, Barry Commoner's *The Closing Circle*, Tom Wessels's *The Myth of Progress*, and Herman Daly's *Beyond Growth* and *Steady-State Economics*; on Judeo-Christianity, Lynn White's historic essay, "The Historical Roots of Our Ecologic Crisis"; on science and positivism, C. P.

Snow's *The Two Cultures* and Carolyn Merchant's *The Death of Nature* and *Ecological Revolutions*.

2. See Oerlemans, *Romanticism and the Materiality of Nature.*

3. Lakoff and Johnson, *Metaphors We Live By*, 3, 247, 3, and 145; see Deborah E. and Frank J. Popper, "The Buffalo Commons."

4. Peck, *Thoreau's Morning Work*, 67.

5. Morton, *Ecology without Nature*, 78 and 67; Myers, "On the Cultural Construction of Landscape Experience," 59; Morton, *Ecology without Nature*, 67.

6. See Diamond, *Collapse: How Societies Choose to Fail or Succeed.*

7. Evernden, *The Social Creation of Nature*, 129–30.

8. On cell phone towers in national parks, see Bass and Beamish, "Development Poses Threats."

9. Price, *Flight Maps*, 254; Berry, *In the Presence of Fear*, 40.

10. Plumwood, *Environmental Culture*, 238; Hargrove, *Foundations of Environmental Ethics*, 175.

11. I am not immune to the irony that the present study also could be said to participate in this tradition (although it does so self-consciously). Arguably, it is this prevalence of inquiry into symbolism that makes Thoreau's *Walden* so attractive to us today. *Walden* lends itself well to such interpretive strategies, as the romantic vision contained therein centers on nature's ability to illuminate the human condition. In much of *Walden*, one can interpret the natural world as a means of developing one's individual mythology. For decades, scholars have celebrated such literary uses of nature, and *Walden* is especially amenable to such readings. This is the argument that Tauber makes: "The power of Thoreau's message consists, at least in part, in the persistent attraction of the Romantic sensibility in our own postmodern era, where the questions he posed remain ours, because the construction of the Romantic self in search of itself still prevails" (*Henry David Thoreau*, 214). In his study, Tauber offers a thorough argument that the romantic emphasis on the self and its issues are still with us (see especially 212–21).

12. Buell, *The Environmental Imagination*, 11. Buell's book exemplifies the recent scholarly interest in exploring the ways in which literature leads us back to the physical world. Cameron's recent study of Henry David Thoreau's journal and Walls's exploration of Thoreau's writings in the context of nineteenth-century natural science also make this move and argue on behalf of finding artistic value in Thoreau's "scientific" writings (see Cameron's *Writing Nature* and Walls's *Seeing New Worlds*). Several scholars are considering previously underexamined, environmentally related texts; developing courses in nature writing, ecopoetry, and environmental studies in general; and exploring voices throughout American history that cautioned against environmental degradation. See, as examples, Branch's *Reading the Roots*, Glotfelty and Fromm's *The Ecocriticism Reader*, and Kroeber's *Ecological Literary Criticism*. Most are interested in developing what Louise Westling has called an "ecological humanism," a mode of inquiry that "would restore appropriate humility, absorbing the lessons of quantum physics and emphasizing cooperative participation within the community of planetary life" (Contribution, 1104). Ursula Heise suggests "ecocriticism" as a mode for examining "how concepts of the natural are constructed in different cultures and expressed through a variety of literary practices"; as such, ecocriticism "analyzes the ways in which literature represents the human relation

to nature at particular moments of history, what values are assigned to nature and why, and how perceptions of the natural shape literary tropes and genres. In turn, it examines how such literary figures contribute to shaping social and cultural attitudes toward the environment" (Contribution, 1097).

13. Uhl, *Developing Ecological Consciousness*, 231.

14. See, for example, Berry, *In the Presence of Fear*.

15. Bush's speech is available online at http://www.whitehouse.gov/news/releases/2005/09/20050915–8.html.

16. Carson, quoted in Sanders, "A Few Earthy Words," 54.

17. Eagleton, *Literary Theory*, 5.

18. Tuan, *Escapism*, 6.

19. Apter, "The Aesthetics of Critical Habitats," 21. See the July 17, 2006, issue of *Newsweek*.

20. The following Web sites describe these projects: *Journal of Natural History*, http://www.naturalhistorynetwork.org/; Project BudBurst, http://www.windows.ucar.edu/citizen_science/budburst/.

21. See Finch and Williams, "Landscape, People, and Place," 43; see Nabhan and Zwinger, "Field Notes," 71; Sanders, "A Few Earthy Words," 54–55.

22. Philippon, *Conserving Words*, 15.

23. Thoreau, *Walden*, 324 and 28.

WORKS CITED

Abrams, Robert E. "Image, Object, and Perception in Thoreau's Landscapes: The Development of Anti-Geography." *Nineteenth-Century Literature* 46 (1991): 245–62.

———. *Landscape and Ideology in American Renaissance Literature.* New York: Cambridge University Press, 2004.

Alison, Archibald. *Essays on the Nature and Principles of Taste.* 1790. Reprint, Boston: Cummings and Hilliard, 1812.

Allen, Lewis F. *Rural Architecture.* New York: C. M. Saxton, 1852.

Allibone, S. Austin. *A Critical Dictionary of English Literature and British and American Authors . . .* Philadelphia: J. B. Lippincott Co., 1897.

"American Rural Life." *Literary World* 7, no. 184 (August 10, 1850): 107–8.

Apter, Emily. "The Aesthetics of Critical Habitats." *October* 99 (Winter 2002): 21–44.

Bass, Frank, and Rita Beamish. "Development Poses Threats in and around National Parks." *Idaho Statesman,* June 19, 2006, Main 11+.

Baym, Nina. *American Women of Letters and the Nineteenth-Century Sciences: Styles of Affiliation.* New Brunswick, N.J.: Rutgers University Press, 2001.

———. "English Nature, New York Nature, and *Walden*'s New England Nature." In *Transient and Permanent: The Transcendentalist Movement and its Contexts,* edited by Charles Capper and Conrad Edick Wright, 168–86. Boston: Massachusetts Historical Society/Northeastern University Press, 1999.

———. "Thoreau's View of Science." *Journal of the History of Ideas* 26, no. 2 (April–June 1965): 221–34.

Beard, James Franklin, ed. *The Letters and Journals of James Fenimore Cooper.* 6 vols. Cambridge, Mass.: Harvard University Press, 1960.

Bedell, Rebecca. *The Anatomy of Nature: Geology and American Landscape Painting, 1825–1875.* Princeton, N.J.: Princeton University Press, 2001.

Bentley, Richard. "Books for the Country." *Bentley's Miscellany* 28 (1850): 341.

Berry, Wendell. *In the Presence of Fear: Three Essays for a Changed World.* Great Barrington, Mass.: Orion, 2001.

Blydenburgh, S. "Address to the Annual Meeting of the Rensselaer County Agricultural Society, October 7, 1834." Reprinted in *New York Farmer, and American Gardener's Magazine* 8, no. 2 (February 1835): 51–53.

Boime, Albert. *The Magisterial Gaze: Manifest Destiny and American Landscape Painting c. 1830–1865.* Washington, D.C.: Smithsonian Institution Press, 1991.

Bonaparte, Charles Lucien. *American Ornithology; or, The Natural History of Birds Inhabiting the United States, Not Given by Wilson: With Figures Drawn, Engraved, and Coloured, From Nature.* 4 vols. Philadelphia: Carey, Lea, & Carey, 1828.

Booty, John. "Richard Hooker." In *The Spirit of Anglicanism: Hooker, Maurice, Temple,* edited by William J. Woolf, 1–45. Wilton, Conn.: Morehouse-Barlow, 1979.

Botkin, Daniel B. *No Man's Garden: Thoreau and a New Vision for Civilization and Nature.* Washington, D.C.: Island Press, 2001.

Bozeman, Theodore Dwight. *Protestantism in an Age of Science: The Baconian Ideal and Antebellum American Religious Thought.* Chapel Hill: University of North Carolina Press, 1977.

Branch, Michael P. "Ecocriticism: The Nature of Nature in Literary Theory and Practice." *Weber Studies* 11, no. 1 (Winter 1994): 41–55.

———. "Ralph Waldo Emerson." In *American Nature Writers,* Vol. 1, edited by John Elder, 287–307. New York: Scribner, 1996.

———, ed. *Reading the Roots: American Nature Writing before Walden.* Athens: University of Georgia Press, 2004.

Bremer, Frederika. "To the Friends of A. J. Downing." *Rural Essays,* by A. J. Downing, edited by Georgia William Curtis, lxi–lxxi. New York: Putnam, 1853.

Brown, Lee Rust. *The Emerson Museum: Practical Romanticism and the Pursuit of the Whole.* Cambridge, Mass.: Harvard University Press, 1997.

Bruce, Robert V. *The Launching of Modern American Science, 1846–1876.* Ithaca, N.Y.: Cornell University Press, 1987.

Bryant, William Cullen. "The Prairies." In *The Poems of William Cullen Bryant,* edited by Louis Untermeyer, 100–103. New York: Heritage Press, 1947.

Buell, Lawrence. *The Environmental Imagination: Thoreau, Nature Writing, and the Formation of American Culture.* Cambridge, Mass.: Harvard University Press, 1995.

———. "Henry Thoreau Enters the American Canon." In *New Essays on Walden,* edited by Robert F. Sayre, 23–52. New York: Cambridge University Press, 1992.

———. "The Thoreauvian Pilgrimage: The Structure of an American Cult." *American Literature* 61, no. 2 (May 1989): 175–99.

Burbick, Joan. *Thoreau's Alternative History: Changing Perspectives on Nature, Culture, and Language.* Philadelphia: University of Pennsylvania Press, 1987.

Burns, Sarah. *Pastoral Inventions: Rural Life in Nineteenth-Century American Art and Culture.* Philadelphia: Temple University Press, 1989.

Bush, George. Presidential speech. Jackson Square, New Orleans, Louisiana. September 15, 2005. Available on-line at: http://www.whitehouse.gov/news/releases/2005/09/20050915-8.html.

Bushman, Richard L. *The Refinement of America: Persons, Houses and Cities.* New York: Knopf, 1992.

C. C. "The Influence of Flowers." *New York Farmer, and Gardener's Magazine* 8, no. 12 (December 1835): 359.

Cafaro, Philip. *Thoreau's Living Ethics: Walden and the Pursuit of Virtue.* Athens: University of Georgia Press, 2004.

Cahill, Edward. "Federalist Criticism and the Fate of Genius." *American Literature* 76, no. 4 (December 2004): 687–717.

Cameron, Sharon. *Writing Nature: Henry Thoreau's "Journal."* Chicago: University of Chicago Press, 1985.

Camfield, Gregg. "The Moral Aesthetics of Sentimentality: A Missing Key to *Uncle Tom's Cabin*." *Nineteenth-Century Literature* 43, no. 3 (December 1988): 319–45.

Cavell, Stanley. *The Senses of Walden: An Expanded Edition*. 1972. Reprint, Chicago: University of Chicago Press, 1992.

Chai, Leon. *The Romantic Foundations of the American Renaissance*. Ithaca, N.Y.: Cornell University Press, 1987.

Channing, William Ellery. "Likeness to God." 1828. In *Transcendentalism: A Reader*, edited by Joel Myerson, 3–20. New York: Oxford University Press, 2000.

Clark, Gregory, S. Michael Halloran, and Allison Woodford. "Thomas Cole's Vision of 'Nature' and the Conquest Theme in American Culture." In *Green Culture: Environmental Rhetoric in Contemporary America*, edited by Carl G. Herndl and Stuart Brown, 261–80. Madison: University of Wisconsin Press, 1996.

Coates, Peter. *American Perceptions of Immigrant and Invasive Species*. Berkeley: University of California Press, 2006.

Cole, Thomas. "Essay on American Scenery." 1835. In *American Art, 1700–1960*, edited by John W. McCoubrey, 98–110. Englewood Cliffs, N.J.: Prentice-Hall, 1965.

———. Letter to Robert Gilmor Jr. January 29, 1832. In *Studies on Thomas Cole, An American Romanticist*, "Appendix I: Correspondence between Thomas Cole and Robert Gilmor, Jr.," edited by Howard S. Merritt, 72–74. Baltimore: Baltimore Museum of Art, 1967.

Commoner, Barry. *The Closing Circle: Nature, Man, and Technology*. New York: Bantam Books, 1971.

Conron, John. *American Picturesque*. University Park: Pennsylvania State University Press, 2000.

Conway, Jill Ker, Kenneth Keniston, and Leo Marx. "The New Environmentalism." In *Earth, Air, Water, Fire: Humanistic Studies of the Environment*, edited by Jill Ker Conway, Kenneth Keniston, and Leo Marx, 1–29. Amherst: University of Massachusetts Press, 1999.

Cooke, Margaret. "Floral Lessons in Morals." *Godey's Lady's Book* 26 (April 1843): 197–98.

Cooper, James Fenimore. *The Last of the Mohicans. The Writings of James Fenimore Cooper*, edited by James Franklin Beard, E. N. Feltskog, and James A. Sappenfield. Albany: State University of New York Press, 1983.

———. Letter to Richard Bentley, August 6, 1851. Beinecke Rare Book and Manuscript Library, Yale University, New Haven, Conn.

Cooper, James Fenimore (1858–1938). *Reminiscences of Mid-Victorian Cooperstown and a Sketch of William Cooper*. Cooperstown: Otsego County Historical Society, 1936.

Cooper, Susan Fenimore, ed. *Appleton's Illustrated Almanac for 1870*. New York: D. Appleton and Co., 1869.

———. "A Dissolving View." In *The Home Book of the Picturesque: Or American Scenery, Art, and Literature*, 79–94. New York: Putnam, 1852. Reprint, Gainesville, Fla.: Scholars' Facsimiles and Reprints, 1967. "A Dissolving View" is reprinted in *Susan*

Fenimore Cooper: Essays on Nature and Landscape, edited by Rochelle Johnson and Daniel Patterson, 3–16. Athens: University of Georgia Press, 2002.

———. *Elinor Wyllys; or, The Young Folk of Longbridge.* Philadelphia: Carey and Hart, 1846.

———. "A Glance Backward." *Atlantic Monthly* 59 (February 1887): 199–206.

———. Introduction. In *Country Rambles in England; Or Journal of a Naturalist; With Notes and Additions, by the Author of "Rural Hours," by John Leonard Knapp*, 11–20. Buffalo, New York: Phinney, 1853.

———. Introduction. In *The Rhyme and Reason of Country Life: or, Selections from Fields Old and New*, edited by Susan Fenimore Cooper, 13–34. New York: Putnam, 1855. Reprinted in *Susan Fenimore Cooper: Essays on Nature and Landscape*, eds. Rochelle Johnson and Daniel Patterson, 24–44. Athens: University of Georgia Press, 2002.

———. "A Lament for the Birds." *Harper's New Monthly Magazine* 87 (August 1893): 472–74. Reprinted in *Susan Fenimore Cooper: Essays on Nature and Landscape*, edited by Rochelle Johnson and Daniel Patterson, 110–14. Athens: University of Georgia Press, 2002.

———. Letter to George Putnam, August 27, 1851. George Palmer Putnam Papers, Manuscripts and Archives Division, New York Public Library, Astor, Lenox, and Tilden Foundations.

———. "Missions to the Oneidas." *Living Church*, February 20, 1886, 709–10; February 27, 1996, 720–21; March 6, 1886, 736–37; Match 13, 1886, 753; March 20, 1886, 768–69; March 27, 1886, 784; April 10, 1886, 28; April 24, 1886, 60–61; May 1, 1886, 75–76; May 15, 1886, 107–08; May 22, 1886, 123–24; May 29, 1886, 139; June 5, 1886, 155.

———. "Otsego Leaves I, II, and III." 1878. Reprinted in *Susan Fenimore Cooper: Essays on Nature and Landscape*, edited by Rochelle Johnson and Daniel Patterson, 78–109. Athens: University of Georgia Press, 2002.

———. *Pages and Pictures, from the Writings of James Fenimore Cooper, with Notes by Susan Fenimore Cooper.* New York: W. A. Townsend, 1861.

———. "A Plea for American Trees: From Miss Cooper's 'Rural Hours,'" edited by Andrew Jackson Downing. *The Horticulturist, and Journal of Rural Art and Rural Taste* 5, no. 3 (September 1850): 136–39.

———, ed. *The Rhyme and Reason of Country Life.* New York: G. P. Putnam, 1854.

———. *Rural Hours.* 1850. Critical Edition, edited by Rochelle Johnson and Daniel Patterson. Athens: University of Georgia Press, 1998.

———. "Small Family Memories." *Correspondence of James Fenimore Cooper*, edited by James Fenimore Cooper, vol. 1, 7–72. New Haven: Yale University Press, 1922.

———. "The Talent of Reading Wisely." *The Ladies' Home Journal* 9, no.3 (February 1892): 18.

———. "Village Improvement Societies." *Putman's Magazine* 4 (September 1869): 359–66. Reprinted in *Susan Fenimore Cooper: Essays on Nature and Landscape*, edited by Rochelle Johnson and Daniel Patterson, 64–77. Athens: University of Georgia Press, 2002.

Corolla. "Autumn Musings." *Godey's Lady's Book* 37 (October 1848): 211.

Cott, Nancy. *The Bonds of Womanhood: "Woman's Sphere" in New England, 1780–1835.* New Haven, Conn.: Yale University Press, 1977.

Cox, George W. *Alien Species in North America and Hawaii: Impacts on Natural Ecosystems.* Washington D.C.: Island Press, 1999.

Cramer, Jeffrey S. *"Walden," by Henry David Thoreau: A Fully Annotated Edition.* New Haven, Conn.: Yale University Press, 2004.

Cronon, William. *Changes in the Land: Indians, Colonists, and the Ecology of New England.* New York: Hill and Wang, 1983.

———. Foreword. *Mountain Gloom and Mountain Glory: The Development of the Aesthetics of the Infinite*, by Marjorie Hope Nicholson. 1959. Reprint, Seattle: University of Washington Press, 1997, vii–xii.

———. *Nature's Metropolis: Chicago and the Great West.* New York: W. W. Norton, 1991.

———. "The Riddle of the Apostle Islands." *Orion* (May/June 2003): 36–42.

———. "Telling Tales on Canvas: Landscapes of Frontier Change." In *Discovered Lands, Invented Pasts: Transforming Visions of the American West*, edited by Jules David Prown, Nancy K. Anderson, William Cronon, Brian W. Dippie, Martha A. Sandweiss, Susan Pendergast Schoelwer, and Howard R. Lamar, 37–87. New Haven, Conn.: Yale University Press, 1992.

———. "The Trouble with Wilderness; or, Getting Back to the Wrong Nature." In *Uncommon Ground: Rethinking the Human Place in Nature*, edited by William Cronon, 69–90. New York: W. W. Norton, 1995.

Crosby, Alfred W. *Ecological Imperialism: The Biological Expansion of Europe, 900–1900.* Cambridge: Cambridge University Press, 1986.

Daly, Herman E. *Beyond Growth: The Economics of Sustainable Development.* Boston: Beacon Press, 1996.

———. *Steady-State Economics: The Economics of Biophysical Equilibrium and Moral Growth.* San Francisco: W. H. Freeman, 1977.

Danly, Susan. "Mount Holyoke: 'The Grandest Cultivated View in the World'." In *Changing Prospects: The View from Mount Holyoke*, edited by Marianne Doezema, 13–28. Ithaca, N.Y.: Cornell University Press, 2002.

Davis, Alexander Jackson. *Rural Residences.* New York: New York University Press, 1837.

Deakin, Motley F. Introduction. In *The Home Book of the Picturesque: Or, American Scenery, Art, and Literature.* Gainesville, Florida: Scholars' Facsimiles & Reprints, 1976.

Dean, Bradley, and Gary Scharnhorst. "The Contemporary Reception of *Walden*." *Studies in the American Renaissance* (1990): 293–328.

Dean, Bradley P. "Natural History, Romanticism, and Thoreau." In *American Wilderness: A New History*, edited by Michael Lewis, 73–89. New York: Oxford University Press, 2007.

de Man, Paul. *The Resistance to Theory.* Minneapolis: University of Minnesota Press, 1986.

Desmond, Ray. *Great Natural History Books and Their Creators.* New Castle, Del.: Oak Knoll Press, 2003.

de Tocqueville, Alexis. *Democracy in America.* 1835 and 1840. Edited and translated by Harvey C. Mansfield and Delba Winthrop. Chicago: University of Chicago Press, 2000.

Diamond, Jared. *Collapse: How Societies Choose to Fail or Succeed.* New York: Penguin Books, 2005.

Dillon, Elizabeth Maddock. "Sentimental Aesthetics." *American Literature* 76, no. 3 (September 2004): 495–523.

Dowden, Edward. *Puritan and Anglican: Studies in Literature.* 1901. Essay Index Reprint Series. Freeport, N.Y.: Books for Libraries Press, 1967.

Downing, Andrew Jackson. *The Architecture of Country Houses; Including Designs for Cottages, Farm-Houses, and Villas.* New York: D. Appleton and Co., 1850.

———. *Cottage Residences; or, A Series of Designs for Rural Cottages and Cottage-Villas, and Their Gardens and Grounds.* New York: Wiley and Putnam, 1842.

———. [Editorial.] *The Horticulturist and Journal of Rural Art and Rural Taste* 3, no. 1 (July 1848): 9–14.

———. "Influence of Horticulture." *The Horticulturist and Journal of Rural Art and Rural Taste* 2, no. 1 (July 1847): 9–11.

———. "On Feminine Taste in Rural Affairs." *The Horticulturist and Journal of Rural Art and Rural Taste* 7 (April 1849): 449–55. Reprinted in *Rural Essays*, edited by George William Curtis, 44–54. New York: Putnam, 1853.

———. "On the Improvement of Country Villages." *The Horticulturist and Journal of Rural Art and Rural Taste* 3 (June 1849): 545–49.

———. "Our Country Villages." *The Horticulturist and Journal of Rural Art and Rural Taste* 4, no. 12 (June 1850): 537–41.

———. Review of *Rural Hours*, by Susan Fenimore Cooper. *The Horticulturist and Journal of Rural Art and Rural Taste* 5, no. 5 (November 1850): 230–32.

———. *A Treatise on the Theory and Practice of Landscape Gardening, Adapted to North America . . .* 1841. 4th ed., enlarged, revised, and newly illustrated. New York: George Putnam, 1850.

Driscoll, John. *"All that is Glorious around us:" Paintings from the Hudson River School.* Ithaca, N.Y.: Cornell University Press, 1997.

Eagleton, Terry. *Literary Theory.* Minneapolis: University of Minnesota Press, 1983.

"Editor's Table." *The Knickerbocker* 25, no. 2 (February 1845): 187–88.

Ella. "Autumnal Reflections." *American Agriculturist* 1, no. 7 (October 1842): 217–18.

Emerson, Ralph Waldo. "The American Scholar." In *The Collected Works of Ralph Waldo Emerson*, Vol. 1, edited by Alfred R. Ferguson, 52–70. Cambridge, Mass.: Harvard University Press, 1971.

———. *Nature.* In *The Collected Works of Ralph Waldo Emerson*, Vol. 1, edited by Alfred R. Ferguson, 7–45. Cambridge, Mass.: Harvard University Press, 1971.

———. "The Poet." In *The Collected Works of Ralph Waldo Emerson*, Vol. 3, edited by Alfred R. Ferguson and Jean Ferguson Carr, 3–24. Cambridge, Mass.: Harvard University Press, 1983.

———. "Thoreau." In *The Portable Emerson*, edited by Carl Bode, 573–93. New York: Penguin Books, 1981.

"The Enjoyment of Reading." *New-York Farmer, and American Gardener's Magazine* 7 (May 1834): 156.

Epstein, Barbara. *The Politics of Domesticity: Women, Evangelism, and Temperance in Nineteenth-Century America.* Middletown, Conn.: Wesleyan University Press, 1981.

Evernden, Neil. *The Social Creation of Nature.* Baltimore: Johns Hopkins University Press, 1992.

Faherty, Duncan. "The Borderers of Civilization: Susan Fenimore Cooper's View of American Development." In *Susan Fenimore Cooper: New Essays on "Rural Hours" and Other Works*, edited by Rochelle Johnson and Daniel Patterson, 109–26. Athens: University of Georgia Press, 2001.

"Family Album." *New-York Farmer, and American Gardener's Magazine* 7 (May 1834): 160.

"Female Authors." *The North American Review* 72, no. 150 (January 1851): 151–77.

Fenner, David E. W. "Aesthetic Experience and Aesthetic Analysis." *Journal of Aesthetic Education* 37, no. 1 (Spring 2003): 40–53.

Finch, Robert, and Terry Tempest Williams. "Landscape, People, and Place." In *Writing Natural History: Dialogues with Authors*, edited by Edward Lueders, 37–65. Salt Lake City: University of Utah Press, 1989.

Fisher, Philip. *Hard Facts: Setting and Form in the American Novel*. New York: Oxford University Press, 1987.

Foucault, Michel. *The Archaeology of Knowledge and The Discourse on Language*. Translated By A. M. Sheridan Smith. New York: Pantheon, 1972.

———. *The Order of Things: An Archeology of the Human Sciences*. New York: Vintage, 1970.

Fresonke, Kris. *West of Emerson: The Design of Manifest Destiny*. Berkeley: University of California Press, 2003.

Friedman, Benjamin M. *The Moral Consequences of Economic Growth*. New York: Alfred A. Knopf, 2005.

Friesen, Victor Carl. "A Tonic of Wilderness: Sensuousness in Henry David Thoreau." In *Empire of the Senses: The Sensual Culture Reader*, edited by David Howes, 251–64. Oxford: Berg, 2005.

Gatta, John. *Making Nature Sacred: Literature, Religion, and Environment in America from the Puritans to the Present*. New York: Oxford University Press, 2004.

Germic, Stephen. "Land Claims, Natives, and Nativism: Susan Fenimore Cooper's Fealty to Place." *American Literature* 79, no. 3 (September 2007): 475–500.

Gianquitto, Tina. *"Good Observers of Nature": American Women and the Scientific Study of the Natural World, 1820–1885*. Athens: University of Georgia Press, 2007.

———. "The Noble Designs of Nature: God, Science, and the Picturesque in Susan Fenimore Cooper's *Rural Hours*." In *Susan Fenimore Cooper: New Essays on Rural Hours and Other Works*, edited by Rochelle Johnson and Daniel Patterson, 169–90. Athens: University of Georgia Press, 2001.

Glotfelty, Cheryll, and Harold Fromm, eds. *The Ecocriticism Reader: Landmarks in Literary Ecology*. Athens: University of Georgia Press, 1996.

Golemba, Henry. *Thoreau's Wild Rhetoric*. New York: New York University Press, 1990.

Greenfield, Bruce Robert. *Narrating Discovery: The Romantic Explorer in American Literature, 1790–1855*. New York: Columbia University Press, 1992.

Gronim, Sara S. *Everyday Nature: Knowledge of the Natural World in Colonial New York*. New Brunswick, N.J.: Rutgers University Press, 2007.

Gura, Philip F. *The Wisdom of Words: Language, Theology, and Literature in the New England Renaissance*. Middletown, Conn.: Wesleyan University Press, 1981.

Harding, Walter. *The Days of Henry Thoreau*. Rev. ed. New York: Dover: 1982.

Hargrove, Eugene C. *Foundations of Environmental Ethics*. Englewood Cliffs, N.J.: Prentice Hall, 1989.

Hart, John S. *The Female Prose Writers of America. With Portraits Biographical notices, and Specimens of Their Writings*. 2d ed. Philadelphia: E. H. Butler, 1855.

Heise, Ursula K. Contribution to "Forum on Literatures of the Environment." *PMLA* 114, no. 5 (October 1999): 1096–97.

———. "The Hitchhiker's Guide to Ecocriticism." *PMLA* 121, no. 2 (March 2006): 503–16.

Hildebidle, John. *Thoreau: A Naturalist's Liberty*. Cambridge, Mass.: Harvard University Press, 1983.

Hingham, John. *From Boundlessness to Consolidation: The Transformation of American Culture, 1848–1860*. Ann Arbor, Mich.: William L. Clements Library, 1969.

Hodder, Alan D. *Thoreau's Ecstatic Witness*. New Haven, Conn.: Yale University Press, 2001.

Hoppin, Martha. "Depicting Mount Holyoke: A Dialogue with the Past." In *Changing Prospects: The View from Mount Holyoke*, edited by Marianne Doezema, 31–61. Ithaca, N.Y.: Cornell University Press, 2002.

Howarth, William. *The Book of Concord: Thoreau's Life as a Writer*. New York: Viking, 1982.

Hudson, William Palmer. "Archibald Alison and William Cullen Bryant." *American Literature* 12, no. 1 (1940): 59–68.

Huth, Hans. *Nature and the American: Three Centuries of Changing Attitudes*. Berkeley: University of California Press, 1957.

Ide, A. M., Jr. "November." *The Knickerbocker* 30, no. 3 (March 1845): 227–28.

Jackson, John Brinckerhoff. *American Space: The Centennial Years, 1865–1876*. New York: W. W. Norton, 1972.

Jardine, Nicholas. "*Naturphilosophie* and the Kingdoms of Nature." In *Cultures of Natural History*, edited by N. Jardine, J. A. Secord, and E. C. Spary, 230–45. Cambridge: Cambridge University Press, 1996.

Jehlen, Myra. *American Incarnation: The Individual, the Nation, and the Continent*. Cambridge, Mass.: Harvard University Press, 1986.

Jenkins, Alan C. *The Naturalists: Pioneers of Natural History*. New York: Mayflower, 1978.

Johnson, Rochelle. "Placing *Rural Hours*." In *Reading under the Sign of Nature*, edited by John Tallmadge and Henry Harrington, 64–84. Salt Lake City: University of Utah Press, 2000.

Johnson, Rochelle, and Daniel Patterson. Introduction. In *Rural Hours* (1850), by Susan Fenimore Cooper, edited by Rochelle Johnson and Daniel Patterson. ix–xxii. Athens: University of Georgia Press, 1998.

———, eds. *Susan Fenimore Cooper: New Essays on Rural Hours and Other Works*. Athens: University of Georgia Press, 2001.

Judd, Richard W. *Common Lands, Common People: The Origins of Conservation in Northern New England*. Cambridge, Mass.: Harvard University Press, 1997.

Karcher, Carolyn. Introduction. In *Hobomok and Other Writings by Lydia Maria Child*, edited by Carolyn Karcher, ix–xxxviii. New Brunswick, N.J.: Rutgers University Press, 1986.

Keane, Patrick J. *Emerson, Romanticism, and Intuitive Reason: The Transatlantic "Light of All Our Day."* Columbia, Mo.: University of Missouri Press, 2005.

Keeney, Elizabeth. *The Botanizers: Amateur Scientists in Nineteenth-Century America.* Chapel Hill: University of North Carolina Press, 1992.

Kellert, Stephen R. *The Value of Life: Biological Diversity and Human Society.* Washington D.C.: Island Press, 1996.

Kelley, Mary. *Private Woman, Public Stage: Literary Domesticity in Nineteenth-Century America.* New York: Oxford University Press, 1984.

Kilcup, Karen L. "'I Like These Plants That You Call Weeds': Historicizing American Women's Nature Writing." *Nineteenth-Century Literature* 58, no. 1 (June 2003): 42–74.

Kirwan, James. "Vicarious Edification: Radcliffe and the Sublime." In *The Greening of Literary Scholarship: Literature, Theory, and the Environment*, edited by Steven Rosendale, 224–45. Iowa City: University of Iowa Press, 2002.

Knight, David M. *Natural Science Books in English, 1600–1900.* New York: Praeger, 1972.

Kohlstedt, Sally Gregory. "In from the Periphery: American Women in Science, 1830–1880." *Signs* 4, no. 1 (Autumn 1978): 81–96.

———. "The Nineteenth-Century Amateur Tradition: The Case of the Boston Society of Natural History." In *Science and its Public: The Changing Relationship*, edited by Gerald Holton and William A. Blanfield, 173–90. Boston: D. Reidel, 1976.

———. "Parlors, Primers, and Public Schooling: Education for Science in Nineteenth-Century America." *Isis* 81, no. 3 (Sept. 1990): 424–45.

Kolodny, Annette. *The Lay of the Land: Metaphor as Experience and History in American Life and Letters.* Chapel Hill: University of North Carolina Press, 1975.

Kroeber, Karl. *Ecological Literary Criticism: Romantic Imagining and the Biology of Mind.* New York: Columbia University Press, 1994.

Lakoff, George, and Mark Johnson. *Metaphors We Live By.* 1980. Chicago: University of Chicago Press, 2003.

Larson, James L. *Interpreting Nature: The Science of Living Form from Linnaeus to Kant.* Baltimore: Johns Hopkins University Press, 1994.

Lassiter, Barbara Babcock. *American Wilderness: The Hudson River School of Painting.* Garden City, N.Y.: Doubleday, 1978.

Lawson, Karol Ann Peard. "An Inexhaustible Abundance: The National Landscape Depicted in American Magazines, 1780–1820." *Journal of the Early Republic* 12 (Fall 1992): 303–30.

Lears, T. J. Jackson. "The Concept of Cultural Hegemony: Problems and Possibilities." *American Historical Review* 90, no. 3 (June 1985): 567–93.

Levine, Lawrence W. *Highbrow/Lowbrow: The Emergence of Cultural Hierarchy in America.* Cambridge, Mass.: Harvard University Press, 1988.

Lewis, Michael, ed. *American Wilderness: A New History.* New York: Oxford University Press, 2007.

Liebman, Sheldon W. "The Origins of Emerson's Early Poetics: His Reading in the Scottish Common Sense Critics." *American Literature* 45, no. 1 (March 1973): 23–33.

Lopez, Barry. *The Rediscovery of North America.* New York: Vintage, 1992.

Louv, Richard. *Last Child in the Woods: Saving Our Children from Nature-Deficit Disorder.* Chapel Hill, N.C.: Algonquin Books of Chapel Hill, 2005.

Maddox, Lucy. *Removals: Nineteenth-Century American Literature and the Politics of Indian Affairs.* New York: Oxford University Press, 1991.

———. "Susan Fenimore Cooper and the Plain Daughters of America." *American Quarterly* 40, no. 2 (1988): 131–46.

Maddox, Vivienne Dawn. "Seven Styles of Nineteenth-Century Residential Architecture in Cooperstown, New York." M.A. Thesis. State University of New York College at Oneonta, 1970.

Major, Judith K. *To Live in the New World: A.J. Downing and American Landscape Gardening.* Cambridge, Mass.: MIT Press, 1997.

Martin, Calvin Luther. *In the Spirit of the Earth: Rethinking History and Time.* Baltimore: Johns Hopkins University Press, 1992.

Marx, Leo. *The Machine in the Garden: Technology and the Pastoral Ideal in America.* New York: Oxford University Press, 1964.

Masteller, Richard N., and Jean Carwile Masteller. "Rural Architecture in Andrew Jackson Downing and Henry David Thoreau: Pattern Book Parody in Walden." *The New England Quarterly* 57, no. 4 (December 1984): 483–510.

Mayr, Ernst. *The Growth of Biological Thought: Diversity, Evolution, and Inheritance.* Cambridge, Mass.: Harvard University Press, 1982.

McCoubrey, John. *American Tradition in Painting.* 2nd ed. Philadelphia: University of Pennsylvania Press, 2000.

McGregor, Robert Kuhn. *A Wider View of the Universe: Henry Thoreau's Study of Nature.* Urbana: University of Illinois Press, 1997.

McIntosh, James. *Thoreau as Romantic Naturalist: His Shifting Stance Toward Nature.* Ithaca, N.Y.: Cornell University Press, 1974.

McKibben, Bill. *The End of Nature.* New York: Random House, 1989.

McPhee, John. *The Control of Nature.* New York: Farrar, Straus and Giroux, 1989.

Meinig, D. W. "The Beholding Eye: Ten Versions of the Same Scene." In *The Interpretation of Ordinary Landscapes: Geographical Essays*, edited by D. W. Meinig, 33–48. New York: Oxford University Press, 1979.

———. "Environmental Appreciation: Localities as a Humane Art." *Western Humanities Review* 25 (1971): 1–11.

Merchant, Carolyn. *The Death of Nature: Women, Ecology, and the Scientific Revolution.* New York: Harper Collins, 1980.

———. *Ecological Revolutions: Nature, Gender, and Science in New England.* Chapel Hill: University of North Carolina Press, 1989.

Merritt, Howard S. "A Wild Scene, Genesis of a Painting." In *Baltimore Museum Annual 2: Studies on Thomas Cole, An American Romanticist*, 7–40. Baltimore: Baltimore Museum of Art, 1967.

Meyer, Michael. *Several More Lives to Live: Thoreau's Political Reputation in America.* Westport, Conn.: Greenwood, 1977.

Miller, Angela. *The Empire of the Eye: Landscape Representation and American Cultural Politics, 1825–1875.* Ithaca, N.Y.: Cornell University Press, 1993.

————. "The Fate of Wilderness in American Landscape Art: The Dilemmas of 'Nature's Nation'." In *American Wilderness: A New History*, edited by Michael Lewis, 91–112. New York: Oxford University Press, 2007.

Miller, Perry. *Nature's Nation*. Cambridge, Mass.: Harvard University Press, 1967.

Miller, Ralph N. "Thomas Cole and Alison's Essays on Taste." *New York History* 37 (1956): 281–99.

Mills, William J. "Metaphorical Vision: Changes in Western Attitudes to the Environment." *Annals of the Association of American Geographers* 72 (1982): 237–53.

Mitchell, Lee Clark. *Witnesses to a Vanishing America: The Nineteenth-Century Response*. Princeton, N.J.: Princeton University Press, 1981.

Morton, Timothy. *Ecology without Nature: Rethinking Environmental Aesthetics*. Cambridge, Mass.: Harvard University Press, 2007.

Myers, Kenneth John. "On the Cultural Construction of Landscape Experience: Contact to 1830." In *American Iconology: New Approaches to Nineteenth-Century Art and Literature*, edited by David C. Miller, 58–79. New Haven, Conn.: Yale University Press, 1993.

Nabhan, Gary Paul, and Ann Zwinger. "Field Notes and the Literary Process." In *Writing Natural History: Dialogues with Authors*, edited by Edward Lueders, 67–90. Salt Lake City: University of Utah Press, 1989.

Nash, Roderick Frazier. *Wilderness and the American Mind*. 1967. 4th ed. New Haven, Conn.: Yale University Press, 2001.

New, Elisa. *The Line's Eye: Poetic Experience, American Sight*. Cambridge, Mass.: Harvard University Press, 1998.

Newman, Lance. *Our Common Dwelling: Henry Thoreau, Transcendentalism, and the Class Politics of Nature*. New York: Palgrave Macmillan, 2005.

Nicholson, Marjorie Hope. *Mountain Gloom and Mountain Glory: The Development of the Aesthetics of the Infinite*. Ithaca, N.Y.: Cornell University Press, 1959. Reprint, Seattle: University of Washington Press, 1997.

Norwood, Vera. *Made from This Earth: American Women and Nature*. Chapel Hill: University of North Carolina Press, 1993.

Novak, Barbara. *American Painting of the Nineteenth Century*. 2nd ed. New York: Harper & Row, 1979.

Odum, Eugene P., and Gary W. Barrett. *Fundamentals of Ecology*. 5th ed. Belmont, Calif.: Thomson Brooks/Cole, 2005.

Oerlemans, Onno. *Romanticism and the Materiality of Nature*. Toronto: University of Toronto Press, 2002.

Outram, Dorinda. "New Spaces in Natural History." In *Cultures of Natural History*, edited by Nicholas Jardine, James A. Secord, and E. C. Spary, 249–65. Cambridge: Cambridge University Press, 1996.

Oxford Dictionary of Ecology. 3rd ed. Edited by Michael Allaby. New York: Oxford University Press, 2005.

Parrish, Susan Scott. *American Curiosity: Cultures of Natural History in the Colonial British Atlantic World*. Chapel Hill: University of North Carolina Press, 2006.

Peck, H. Daniel. *A World by Itself: The Pastoral Moment in Cooper's Fiction*. New Haven, Conn.: Yale University Press, 1977.

———. "Better Mythology: Perception and Emergence in Thoreau's Journal." *North Dakota Quarterly* (Spring 1991): 33–44.

———. "Thoreau's Lakes of Light: Modes of Representation and the Enactment of Philosophy in *Walden*." *Midwest Studies in Philosophy* 28 (2004): 85–101.

———. *Thoreau's Morning Work: Memory and Perception in "A Week on the Concord and Merrimack Rivers," the "Journal," and "Walden."* New Haven, Conn.: Yale University Press, 1990.

———. "Unlikely Kindred Spirits: A New Vision of Landscape in the Works of Henry David Thoreau and Asher B. Durand." *American Literary History* 17, no. 4 (Winter 2005): 687–713.

Philippon, Daniel J. *Conserving Words: How American Nature Writers Shaped the Environmental Movement*. Athens: University of Georgia Press, 2004.

———. "Thoreau's Notes on the *Journey West*: Nature Writing or Environmental History?" *ATQ* 18, no. 2 (June 2004): 105–17.

Plumwood, Val. *Environmental Culture: The Ecological Crisis of Reason*. New York: Routledge, 2002.

Popper, Deborah E., and Frank J. Popper. "The Buffalo Commons: Using Regional Metaphor to Envision the Future." *Wild Earth* 9, no. 4 (Winter 1999/2000): 30–37.

Porter, Charlotte M. *The Eagle's Nest: Natural History and American Ideas, 1812–1842*. Tuscaloosa: University of Alabama Press, 1986.

Powell, Earl A. *Thomas Cole*. New York: Harry N. Abrams, 1990.

Pre-publication notice for *Rural Hours*, by Susan Fenimore Cooper. *The Home Journal* 233 (July 27, 1850): [3].

Pre-publication notice for *Rural Hours*, by Susan Fenimore Cooper. *The Literary World* 174 (June 1, 1850): 533.

Pre-publication notice for *Rural Hours*, by Susan Fenimore Cooper. *The Literary World* 177 (June 22, 1850): 623.

Price, Jennifer. *Flight Maps: Adventures with Nature in Modern America*. New York: Basic Books, 1999.

Publication notice for *Rural Hours*, by Susan Fenimore Cooper. *Godey's Lady's Book* (October 1850): 252.

Putnam, G. P. Letter to Susan Fenimore Cooper, New York, December 2, 1851. Beinecke Rare Book and Manuscript Library, Yale University, New Haven, Conn.

Pyle, Robert Michael. *The Thunder Tree: Lessons from an Urban Wildland*. New York: Lyons Press, 1998.

Quinn, Naomi. "The Cultural Basis of Metaphor." In *Beyond Metaphor: The Theory of Tropes in Anthropology*, edited by James W. Fernandez, 56–93. Stanford, Calif.: Stanford University Press, 1991.

Rainey, Sue. *Creating Picturesque America: Monument to the Natural and Cultural Landscape*. Nashville: Vanderbilt University Press, 1994.

Ravage, Jessie. *A Region of Romance*. Cooperstown, N.Y.: Smithy≈Pioneer Gallery and Otsego 2000, 1997.

Regis, Pamela. *Describing Early America: Bartram, Jefferson, Crèvecoeur, and the Influence of Natural History*. Philadelphia: University of Pennsylvania Press, 1992.

Rehbock, Philip F. *The Philosophical Naturalists: Themes in Early Nineteenth-Century British Biology*. Madison: University of Wisconsin Press, 1983.

Review of *Rural Hours*, by Susan Fenimore Cooper. *Graham's Magazine* 37, no. 5 (November 1850): 324.

Review of *Rural Hours*, by Susan Fenimore Cooper. *Harper's New Monthly Magazine* 1, no. 5 (October 1850): 713.

Review of *Rural Hours*, by Susan Fenimore Cooper. *International Weekly Miscellany* 1, no. 3 (July 1850): 72.

Review of *Rural Hours*, by Susan Fenimore Cooper. *The Knickerbocker* 36, no. 3 (September 1850): 278–79.

Review of *Rural Hours*, by Susan Fenimore Cooper. *Littell's Living Age* 26, no. 328 (August 1850): 414–15.

Review of *Rural Hours*, by Susan Fenimore Cooper. *New Englander* 8, no. 32 (November 1850): 653.

Review of *Rural Hours*, by Susan Fenimore Cooper. *Southern Quarterly Review* 2, no. 4 (November 1850): 539.

Richardson, Robert D., Jr. *Emerson: The Mind on Fire*. Berkeley: University of California Press, 1995.

———. Introduction. In *Faith in a Seed: The Dispersion of Seeds and Other Late Natural History Writings*, by Henry D. Thoreau, edited by Bradley Dean, 3–17. Washington, D.C.: Island Press, 1993.

———. *Henry Thoreau: A Life of the Mind*. Berkeley: University of California Press, 1986.

———. "Thoreau and Science." In *American Literature and Science*, edited by Robert J. Scholnick, 110–27. Lexington: University of Kentucky Press, 1992.

Ringe, Donald A. "Horatio Greenough, Archibald Alison, and the Functionalist Theory of Art." *College Art Journal* 19, no. 4 (Summer 1960): 314–21.

———. "James Fenimore Cooper and Thomas Cole: An Analogous Technique." *American Literature* 30, no. 1 (March 1958): 26–36.

———. "Kindred Spirits: Bryant and Cole." *American Quarterly* 6, no. 3 (Autumn 1954): 233–44.

———. "Painting as Poem in the Hudson River Aesthetic." *American Quarterly* 12, no. 1 (Spring 1960): 71–83.

———. *The Pictorial Mode: Space and Time in the Art of Bryant, Irving, and Cooper*. Lexington: University of Kentucky Press, 1971.

Robinson, David. *Emerson and the Conduct of Life: Pragmatism and Ethical Purpose in the Later Work*. Cambridge: Cambridge University Press, 1993.

———. "Emerson's Natural Theology and the Paris Naturalists: Toward a Theory of Animated Nature." *Journal of the History of Ideas* 41, no. 1 (January–March 1980): 69–88.

———. "Fields of Investigation: Emerson and Natural History." In *American Literature and Science*, edited by Robert J. Scholnick, 94–109. Lexington: University of Kentucky Press, 1992.

———. *Natural Life: Thoreau's Worldly Transcendentalism*. Ithaca, N.Y.: Cornell University Press, 2004.

―――. "Thoreau and Idealism: 'Face to Face to a Fact'." *Nineteenth-Century Prose* 31, no. 2 (Fall 2004): 30–50.

Rogers, Pattiann. "This Nature." In *Dream of a Marsh Wren: Writing as Reciprocal Creation*, 37–41. Minneapolis: Milkweed, 1999.

Roque, Oswaldo Rodriguez. "The Exaltation of American Landscape Painting." In *American Paradise: The World of the Hudson River School*, 21–48. New York: Metropolitan Museum of Art, 1987.

Rosenthal, Bernard. *City of Nature: Journeys to Nature in the Age of American Romanticism*. Newark, Del.: University of Delaware Press, 1980.

Rossi, William. "Emerson, Nature, and Natural Science." In *A Historical Guide to Ralph Waldo Emerson*, edited by Joel Ports, 101–50. New York: Oxford University Press, 2000.

Ruland, Richard. *The Rediscovery of American Literature: Premises of Critical Taste, 1900–1940*. Cambridge, Mass.: Harvard University Press, 1967.

"Rural Architecture-Hope Cottage." *The Cultivator* 5, no. 1 (January 1848): 1–2.

Sanders, Scott Russell. "A Few Earthy Words." In *The Story Handbook: Language and Storytelling for Land Conservationists*, edited by Helen Whybrow, 54–67. San Francisco: Trust for Public Land, 2002.

―――. *Writing from the Center*. Bloomington: Indiana University Press, 1995.

Schneider, Richard J. "Wildness and Geographic Determinism in Thoreau's 'Walking'." In *Thoreau's Sense of Place: Essays in American Environmental Writing*, edited by Richard J. Schneider, 44–60. Iowa City: University of Iowa Press, 2000.

Schofield, Edmund A., and Robert C. Baron, eds. *Thoreau's World and Ours: A Natural Legacy*. Golden, Co.: North American Press, 1993.

Schuyler, David. *Apostle of Taste: Andrew Jackson Downing, 1815–1852*. Baltimore: Johns Hopkins University Press, 1996.

Seaton, Beverly. "The Flower Language Books of the Nineteenth Century." *The Morton Arboretum Quarterly* 16 (1980): 1–11.

Shanley, J. Lyndon. *The Making of "Walden."* Chicago: University of Chicago Press, 1957.

Shepard, Paul, Jr. "Paintings of the New England Landscape: A Scientist Looks at Their Geomorphology." *College Art Journal* 17, no. 1 (Autumn 1957): 30–43.

Shi, David E. *The Simple Life: Plain Living and High Thinking in American Culture*. New York: Oxford University Press, 1985.

Simmons, Nancy Craig. "Speaking for Nature: Thoreau and the 'Problem' of 'Nature Writing.'" In *Thoreau's Sense of Place: Essays in American Environmental Writing*, edited by Richard J. Schneider, 223–34. Iowa City: University of Iowa Press, 2000.

Slotkin, Richard. *Regeneration through Violence: The Mythology of the American Frontier, 1600–1860*. Middletown, Conn.: Wesleyan University Press, 1973.

Slovic, Scott. Foreword. In *The Greening of Literary Scholarship: Literature, Theory, and the Environment*, edited by Steven Rosendale, vii–xi. Iowa City: University of Iowa Press, 2002.

Smith, Henry Nash. *Virgin Land: The American West as Symbol and Myth*. New York: Vintage, 1950.

Smith, Jonathan. *Fact and Feeling: Baconian Science and the Nineteenth-Century Literary Imagination*. Madison: University of Wisconsin Press, 1994.

Smithson, Isaiah. "Thoreau, Thomas Cole, and Asher Durand: Composing the American Landscape." In *Thoreau's Sense of Place: Essays in American Environmental Writing*, edited by Richard J. Schneider, 93–114. Iowa City: University of Iowa Press, 2000.

Snow, C[harles]. P. *The Two Cultures and the Scientific Revolution* .1959. Reprinted, New York: Cambridge University Press, 1962.

Spencer, Benjamin T. *The Quest for Nationality: An American Literary Campaign*. Syracuse, N.Y.: Syracuse University Press, 1957.

Stansell, Christine, and Sean Wilentz. "Cole's America: An Introduction." In *Thomas Cole: Landscape into History*, edited by William H. Truettner and Alan Wallach, 3–21. New Haven, Conn.: Yale University Press, 1994.

Stewart, Frank. *A Natural History of Nature Writing*. Washington, D.C.: Island Press/ Shearwater Books, 1995.

Stilgoe, John R. *Borderland: Origins of the American Suburb, 1820–1939*. New Haven, Conn.: Yale University Press, 1988.

———. *Common Landscape of America, 1580–1845*. New Haven, Conn.: Yale University Press, 1982.

Streeter, Robert E. "Association Psychology and Literary Nationalism in the North American Review, 1815–1825." *American Literature* 17, no. 3 (November 1945): 243–54.

"The Study of Natural History as a School Classic." *The Knickerbocker* 25, no. 4 (April 1845): 283–96.

Susman, Katherine E. "Gothic Revival Domestic Architecture in Cooperstown, New York, 1834–1868: The Evolution of a Style." M.A. Thesis. State University of New York College at Oneonta, 1971.

Sweeting, Adam. *Reading Houses and Building Books: Andrew Jackson Downing and the Architecture of Popular Antebellum Literature, 1835–1855*. Hanover, N.H.: University Press of New England, 1996.

T. B. F. "The Education of Public Taste." *Christian Examiner* 53 (November 1852): 358–72.

Tatum, George B., and Elisabeth Blair MacDougall, eds. *Prophet with Honor: The Career of Andrew Jackson Downing 1815–1852*. Washington, D.C.: Dumbarton Oaks, 1989.

Tauber, Alfred I. *Henry David Thoreau and the Moral Agency of Knowing*. Berkeley: University of California Press, 2001.

Taylor, Alan. *William Cooper's Town: Power and Persuasion on the Frontier of the Early American Republic*. New York: Vintage, 1995.

Teichgraeber, Richard F., III. *Sublime Thoughts/Penny Wisdom: Situating Emerson and Thoreau in the American Market*. Baltimore: Johns Hopkins University Press, 1995.

Thomas, Keith. *Man and the Natural World: Changing Attitudes in England 1500–1800*. Oxford: Oxford University Press, 1983.

Thoreau, Henry David. "Autumnal Tints." 1862. Reprinted in *Excursions*, edited by Joseph J. Moldenhauer, 223–59. Princeton, N.J.: Princeton University Press, 2007.

———. *Faith in a Seed: The Dispersion of Seeds and Other Late Natural History Writings*. Edited by Bradley Dean. Washington, D.C.: Island, 1993.

———. *The Journal of Henry D. Thoreau*. 14 Vols. Edited by Bradford Torrey and Francis H. Allen. Cambridge, Mass.: Houghton Mifflin, 1906.

———. "Natural History of Massachusetts." 1842. Reprinted in *Excursions*, edited by Joseph Moldenhauer, 3–28. Princeton, N.J.: Princeton University Press, 2007.

———. *Walden*. 1854. Edited by J. Lyndon Shanley. Princeton, N.J.: Princeton University Press, 1971.

———. "Walking." 1862. Reprinted in *Excursions*, edited by Joseph Moldenhauer, 185–222. Princeton, N.J.: Princeton University Press, 2007.

———. "Wild Apples." 1862. Reprinted in *Excusions*, edited by Joseph Moldenhauer, 261–89. Princeton, N.J.: Princeton University Press, 2007.

———. *Wild Fruits*. Edited by Bradley P. Dean. New York: W. W. Norton, 2000.

———. *The Writings of Henry David Thoreau: Journal*. 5 vols. to date. General Editor, Robert Sattelmeyer. Princeton, N.J.: Princeton University Press, 1981–1998.

Thornton, Tamara Plakins. "Cultivating the American Character: Horticulture as Moral Reform in the Antebellum Era." *Orion Nature Quarterly* 4 (Spring 1985): 10–19.

———. *Cultivating Gentlemen: The Meaning of Country Life among the Boston Elite, 1785–1860*. New Haven, Conn.: Yale University Press, 1989.

Tichi, Cecelia. *New World, New Earth: Environmental Reform in American Literature from the Puritans through Whitman*. New Haven, Conn.: Yale University Press, 1979.

Todd, Kim. *Tinkering with Eden: A Natural History of Exotics in America*. New York: W. W. Norton, 2001.

Tompkins, Jane. *Sensational Designs: The Cultural Work of American Fiction, 1790–1860*. New York: Oxford University Press, 1985.

Torrey, John. *A Flora of the State of New-York*. Albany, N.Y.: Carroll and Cook, 1843.

Tuan, Yi-Fu. *Escapism*. Baltimore: Johns Hopkins University Press, 1998.

———. *Space and Place: The Perspective of Experience*. 1977. Reprinted, Minneapolis: University of Minnesota Press, 2001.

Tuckerman, H. T. "Flowers." *Godey's Lady's Book* 40 (January 1850): 13–18.

Uhl, Christopher. *Developing Ecological Consciousness: Paths to a Sustainable Future*. Lanham, Md: Rowman & Littlefield, 2004.

"View near Coldspring." *The Columbian Lady's and Gentleman's Magazine* 1 (1844): 43.

W. T. B., "The Coming of Autumn." *The Knickerbocker* 26, no. 2 (August 1845): 145.

Wallach, Alan. "Making a Picture of the View from Mount Holyoke." In *American Iconology: New Approaches to Nineteenth-Century Art and Literature*, edited by David C. Miller, 80–91. New Haven: Yale University Press, 1993.

———. "Thomas Cole: Landscape and the Course of American Empire." In *Thomas Cole: Landscape into History*, edited by William H. Truettner and Alan Wallach, 23–111. New Haven, Conn.: Yale University Press, 1994.

Walls, Laura Dassow. *Emerson's Life in Science: The Culture of Truth*. Ithaca, N.Y.: Cornell University Press, 2003.

———. "Romancing the Real: Thoreau's Technology of Inscription." In *A Historical Guide to Henry David Thoreau*, edited by William E. Cain, 123–51. New York: Oxford University Press, 2000.

———. *Seeing New Worlds: Henry David Thoreau and Nineteenth-Century Natural Science*. Madison: University of Wisconsin Press, 1995.

Welch, Margaret. *The Book of Nature: Natural History in the United States, 1825–1875*. Boston: Northeastern University Press, 1998.

Welter, Barbara. *Dimity Convictions: The American Woman in the Nineteenth Century*. Athens: Ohio University Press, 1976.

Wessels, Tom. *The Myth of Progress: Toward a Sustainable Future.* Burlington: University of Vermont Press, 2006.

West, Michael. *Transcendental Wordplay: America's Romantic Punsters and the Search for the Language of Nature.* Athens: Ohio University Press, 2000.

Westling, Louise. Contribution to "Forum on Literatures of the Environment." *PMLA* 114, no. 5 (October 1999): 1103–04.

Wetmore, Henry Carmer. *Rural Life in America.* 1856. Reprint of *Hermit's Dell.* New York: J. C. Derby, 1854.

Wheeler, Gervase. *Rural Homes.* New York: C. Scribner, 1852.

White, Lynn, Jr. "The Historical Roots of Our Ecologic Crisis." *Science* 155 (March 10, 1967): 1203–07.

Williams, Raymond. *Keywords: A Vocabulary of Culture and Society.* New York: Oxford University Press, 1976.

Willis, N[athaniel] P[arker]. *American Scenery; or, Land, Lake, and River: Illustrations of Transatlantic Nature.* New York: R. Martin/London: George Virtue, 1840. Reprint, Barre, Massachusetts: Imprint Society, 1971.

Wolf, Bryan Jay. *Romantic Re-vision: Culture and Consciousness in Nineteenth-Century American Painting and Literature.* Chicago: University of Chicago Press, 1982.

Young, Malcolm C. "Two Blue Herons." *Thoreau Society Bulletin* 261 (Winter 2008): 5–6.

INDEX

References to sustained discussions of a subject appear below in italics.
References to illustrations appear with an *f* following the page number.

"Autumnal Tints" (Thoreau), 211, 213
Axelrad, Allan, 251n67

Baron, Robert C., 266n46
Bartlett, William, 88, 89f, 90
Bass, Frank, 268n8
Baym, Nina: 241n20, 242n17, 244n34, 246n67, 253n9; on Downing and Thoreau, 263n6; on *Rural Hours*, 168; on science, 148; on Thoreau as scientist, 266n46
Beamish, Rita, 268n8
Bedell, Rebecca, 248n16
Bentley, Richard, 252n72, 261n47
Berkeley, George, 160, 264n22
berries: cranberry, 212; honeysuckle, 33; strawberry, 133; whortleberry, 104
Berry, Wendell, xi, xiii, 226, 269n14
Bierstadt, Albert, 248n17
birds, 49, 61, 261n52; Baltimore oriole, 49; barn swallow, 34; black-poll warbler, 34; bluebird, 31, 34; bobolink (reed-bird), 194; chickadee, 34; chimney swallow, 31; crow, 27; dipper, 32, 33; flicker, 34; goldfinch, 34; goose, 47; harrier, northern, 80; hummingbird, 48; kingfisher, 34; loon, 30, 196–99; nightingale, 48; osprey, 194; partridge, 36; passenger (wild) pigeon, 36, 104, 194; phoebe, 31, 34; pinnated grouse, 36, 40; purple martin, 34, 104; quail, 36; robin, 31, 34; ruby-crowned kinglet, 34; ruffed grouse, 139; screech owl, 194; skylark, 48; song sparrow, 31; tree swallow, 34; whippoorwill, 194; wild turkey, 37; wood cock, 47; wood duck, 104; wood pewee, 34; yellow red-poll, 34
Blydenburgh, S., 256n45
Boime, Albert, 247nn10–11, 249n31, 250n41, 251n55
Bonaparte, Charles Lucien, 31, 32
Booty, John, 261n46
botany, 27, 44, 242n17; and association, 127; as moral refinement, 127–28; and nomenclature, 174–75. *See also* plants

Botkin, Daniel, 267n58
Bozeman, Theodore Dwight, 253n11
Branch, Michael P., xiii, 243n22; on Emerson, 258n4, 259n18, 260n33, 260n39, 262n61; on environmental literary scholarship, 268n12; on Thoreau, 239n2 (intro.)
Bremer, Frederika, 143–44
Brown, John, 201
Brown, Lee Rust, 257n2; on Emerson, 258n10, 259n17, 260n33; on romanticism, 259n11
Bruce, Robert, 244n34
Bryant, William Cullen, 9, 70, 83, 96; and Cooper, Susan Fenimore, 79; influence of, on writers and artists, 79; and Native Americans, 80, 103
—works of: *Letters of a Traveller*, 54; "The Prairies," 80–81, 100; "Water-fowl," 47
Buell, Lawrence: on canonization, 14–15; on Cooper, Susan Fenimore, 241n20, 245n43, 251n67; on environmental literary scholarship, 231; on relinquishment, 266n48; on Thoreau, 3, 199, 239n2, 241n18, 264n18; on White, Gilbert, 261n47
Burbick, Joan, 67, 262n6, 264n18
Burke, Edmund, 71
Burns, Robert, 175
Burns, Sarah, 114, 253n10
Bush, George W., 233
bushes. *See* shrubs
Bushman, Richard, 112, 114, 115, 253n10
Byberry Cottage. *See* Riverside Cottage

Cafaro, Philip, 263n15, 264n18, 266n47
Cahill, Edward, 254n11
Cameron, Sharon, 201; on Thoreau, 263n16, 265n33; on Thoreau's journal, 266n47, 268n12
Camfield, Gregg, 122, 124, 125, 253n11, 254n29
canalization: disturbances to, 236; of metaphor, 223–25; and truth, 224

and Thoreau, 248n24, 263n6; on
nature's materiality, 222; on Thoreau
265n32, 267n56, 267n58; on Thoreau's
journal, 264n18; on *Walden*, 196, 200,
262n2, 264n18, 266n47

Penfeather, Amabel, 60

Philippon, Daniel, 69, 111, 243n21, 243n23,
247n6; on discursive analysis, 12; on
knowing nature, 236

physical environment, usage of, defined,
xiii

picturesque (American): and abstraction,
71; and Alison, 127; ancient ruins
in, 72, 74, 75; and Cole, 71–78; and
Cooper, Susan Fenimore, 71, *90–102*,
141; and Downing, 141; formulaic
nature of, 72, 78; and literature, 79–82;
and progress, 70–71, 73–74, 76; and
Rural Hours, 90, 91–95

Pike, Zebulon, 4

plants: abstraction of, 212; asparagus,
133; grains, 211; grasses, 35, 227, 228;
and leafing, 31–32; skunk cabbage, 31;
succession of, 38–39; *See also* berries;
flowers; forests; shrubs; species; trees;
wildflowers

Plato, 160

"Plea for American Trees, A" (Susan
Fenimore Cooper), 257n65

Plumwood, Val, 229

"Poet, The" (Emerson), 165, 179, 209, 215,
263n9

Pope, Alexander, 58

population, nineteenth-century shifts in,
5–6

Porter, Charlotte M., 241n27, 244n34

Portland Courier, 113

Powell, Earl A., 110, 247n8, 247n15,
249n33, 254n12

Powell, John, 4

"Prairies, The" (Bryant), 80–81, 100

Price, Jennifer, xiii, 22, 226

progress: and Cole, 82, 86–87; and
Cooper, James Fenimore, 81–82;
ethic of, 67–69, 226; as history, 67;
as metaphor for nature, *66–111*, 221,
225–26, 232–33; and picturesque,
70–71, 73–74, 76. See also under *Rural
Hours*

Project Budburst, 235

Putnam, George P., 103, 252n72

Putnam's Monthly Magazine, 215

Pyle, Robert Michael, 39, 40, 243n22

Quinn, Naomi, 198

Rainey, Sue, 241n18

Ravage, Jessie, 246n71

reason: and Cooper, Susan Fenimore, 166–
67; and Emerson, 148, 151, 161–62, 163,
165; as metaphor for nature, *146–80*,
222, 229–31, 233; and romanticism, 150;
shifting understandings of, 150–51

Reed, Luman, 83

refinement: and Alison, 120; and
Cooper, Susan Fenimore, 114, 117;
and Downing, 115–16, 133, 137; and
landscape, 115–16; and lawns, 227–28;
as metaphor for nature, *112–45*, 221,
227–29

Regis, Pamela, 45, 46, 47, 244n32, 244n33,
244n35

Rehbock, Philip F., 259n11

Rhyme and Reason of Country Life, The
(Susan Fenimore Cooper, ed.), 54,
60, 167, 257n1, 260nn41–42, 260n45,
261n46, 262n61, 262n64

Richardson, Robert D.: on Emerson,
253n6, 258n7, 259nn15–16, 259n18,
260n33; on Emerson and design, 258n5,
258n9; on Emerson and idealism, 259–
60n27; on Emerson and Swedenborg,
259n15; on Linnean taxonomy, 261n55;
on Thoreau, 205, 264n18, 266n46;
on Thoreau and landscape painters,
263n6; on Thoreau's Kalendar, 208–9,
211; on *Wild Fruits*, 211

Ricoeur, Paul, 199

Ringe, Donald, 118, 248n16, 248n24,
254n12, 254n63

River in the Catskills (Cole), 73–74, 75, 76, 86

Riverside Cottage, 62, 142f, 256n62

Robinson, David: on Emerson, 257n2, 258n4, 260n33, 261n48, 262n60; on natural history, 259n11; on Thoreau, 201, 214, 217, 263n15, 264n18, 265n33

Rogers, Pattiann, 240n13

romanticism, American, 149–51

Roque, Oswaldo Rodriguez, 73, 247n8

Rosenthal, Bernard, 230

Rossi, William, 258n4, 258n5, 260n33, 262n60

Ruland, Richard, 241n18

Rural Hours (Susan Fenimore Cooper), 2, 15, 19, *23–65*, 26f; and abstraction, 59, 64–65; and Alison, 127–31; on autumn, 32, 58–59, 129–30, 176–77; and Christianity, 50, 51–52, 59; on deforestation, 37, 38, 41, 51, 62; description of, 2, 25, 27–28; on disappearing species, 35–42, 61, 144, 212; and Downing, 117, 137–40, 141, 143–45; Downing's review of, 54; educational purpose of, 25, 33, 35; as environmental history, 37, 43, 61; on exotic species, 38–39; and fish, 62; on forests, 41–42, 50–52, 94, 108–9, 144; and fungi, 1–2, 104; and gratitude, 175–77; on history, 29–42, 93–95, 102, 110; humility in, *48–52*, 53, 143; and ignorance (of nature), 129, 212–13; on invasive species, 35–40, 98; later editions of, 60–61; and literature, 31–32, 58; and loss, 103, 108, 109; metaphor in, 29, 59–60, 65, 91, 95, 117; as model relation to nature, 28; on naming, 40, 107, 151, 152–53, 173, 174–75, 213; nationalism in, 34–36; and Native Americans, 94–95, 102–8; on native species, 15, 30, 33–39, 66, 108; and natural history, 30, 31, 43, 46–47; nineteenth-century reviews of, 52–57, 143–44; observation in, *43–48*, 130, 131; on pastures, 94; persona in, 23, 48, 49; and picturesque, 90, 91–95; preface to, 23, 169–70; on progress, 51, 57–58, 59, 105, 108–9; and the "real," 25, 58–60, 65, 66, 78, 91, 190; and seasonal change, 30–31; and sight, 175, 176; and simplicity, 23, 25, 28, 46, 49, 55, 56; and "truth," 28, 59–60, 65, 130, 131, 168–72, 215; on weeds, 35–36, 38; and *Wild Fruits*, 211–13, 215. *See also* animals; birds; insects; plants

Sanders, Scott Russell, 16, 235–36

Saussure, Ferdinand de, 69

Scharnhorst, Gary, 241n18

Schneider, Richard J., 263n6

Schofield, Edmund A., 266n46

Schuyler, David, 136, 137, 241n18, 255n43, 256n46

sciences, 9–10, 44, 45

scientific revolution, 9, 10

Seaton, Beverly, 242n17, 255n34

sentimentalism, 124

Shakespeare, William, 31, 58

Shanley, J. Lyndon, 265n26

Shepard, Paul, Jr., 248n16

Shi, David E., 242n2

Shield, The (Susan Fenimore Cooper), 103

shrubs: azalea, 37; gooseberry, 211; honeysuckle, varieties of, 33–34; Juneberry, 32, 171; rose (wild), 133, 140; sagebrush, 228; witch-hazel, 99

Simmons, Nancy Craig, 264n18

simplicity, 132. See also under *Rural Hours*

Slotkin, Richard, 230, 249n26

Slovic, Scott, 22

"Small Family Memories" (Susan Fenimore Cooper), 245n41

Smith, Henry Nash, 230

Smith, Jonathan, 240n11

Smithson, Isaiah, 263n6

Snow, C. P., 9–10, 267–68n1

Southern Quarterly Review, 57

species: disappearing, 35–42, 61, 144, 212; exotic, 38–39; invasive, 35–40, 98; native, 15, 33–39, 66, 108, 212

urbanization, 146–47; and demographic changes, 5–6

U.S. Census Bureau, 5, 6

Vespucci, Amerigo, 173, 261n53

View from Mount Holyoke, after a Thunderstorm—The Oxbow (Cole), *86–88*, 90, 96

"View near Coldspring" (Ormsby), 125, 126f

View on the Catskill—Early Autumn (Cole), 73, 75, 76, 86, 247n13

"Village Improvement Societies" (Susan Fenimore Cooper), 112, 114, 193

Walden (Thoreau), 27, *193–201*; "Brute Neighbors," 196–99; and description, 200–201; "Former Inhabitants," 106; and limits of language, 183–84, 203–4; and metaphor, 191, 192, 193–95, 196–99, 200–201, 216; nineteenth-century reception of, 9, 15; "Reading," 193; and the "real," 216; reputation of, 3–4, 10–11, 16, 257n2; and "Sounds," 193–95, 206; and symbolism, 268n11

Walden Pond, 181, 194, 197–201 passim

"Walking" (Thoreau), 205–6, 240n8

Wallach, Alan, 247n10, 248n16, 249n33, 249n36, 250n39

Walls, Laura Dassow, 201, 240n11, 241n25; on Alison, 254n12; on correspondence, 149; on design, 258n5; on Emerson and science, 258n4; on Emerson and "truth," 258n3; on Emerson's *Nature*, 161, 165, 180, 259–60n27, 260n28; on science, 259n11; on Thoreau and community, 265n33; on Thoreau and nature's value, 207; on Thoreau as naturalist, 263n14, 263–64n16, 264n18; on

Thoreau as scientist, 265–66n45, 266n46, 268n12

Walton, Isaac, 261n46

"Water-fowl" (Bryant), 47

weeds: Darwin on, 38; Gray on, 38; in *Rural Hours*, 35–36, 38

Welch, Margaret, 14, 43, 242n17, 244n34; on natural-history knowledge, 6; on popularity of natural history, 4, 5, 7

Welter, Barbara, 242n17

Wessels, Tom, 68, 267n1

West, Michael, 263n15, 264n22

Westling, Louise, 268n12

Wetmore, Henry Carmer, 256n43

Wheeler, Gervase, 255n43

White, Gilbert, 170, 261n47

White, Lynn, 267n1

Whitman, Walt, 220

"Wild Apples" (Thoreau), 211

wildflowers, 37, 38, 212; arum, 171; biscuitroot, 228; cahoshes, 94; carnation, 175; gyromia, 94; hare-bell, 175; moccasin-flower, 37; night-shade, 171; penstemon, 228; pitcher plant, 37; primrose, 174; sarsaparilla, 94, 211; spicy gilliflower, 174; trillium (moose-flowers), 48, 94, 171–72; wake-robin, 171

Wild Fruits (Thoreau), 211–13, 215, 263n16

Wilentz, Sean, 249n33

Williams, Raymond, 259n27

Williams, Terry Tempest, 235

Willis, Nathaniel P., 125; and *American Scenery*, 90, 127; and association, 127

Wilson, Alexander, 49

Wolf, Bryan Jay, 258n7

Woman's Record, 54

Woodford, Allison, 250n41

Wordsworth, William, 31, 149, 175

Young, Malcolm C., 266n46